PRODUCING GREAT SOUND

for Digital Video

Jay Rose

CMP books.

San Francisco

Dedication
To my cat

Published by CMP Books
An imprint of CMP Media, Inc.
600 Harrison Street, San Francisco, CA 94107

Distributed to the book trade in the U.S. and Canada by
Publishers Group West, 1700 Fourth Street, Berkeley, CA 94710

Interior Design: Brad Greene

Library of Congress Cataloging-in-Publication Data

Rose, Jay
      Providing great sound for digital video/by Jay Rose
            p. cm
      ISBN 0-87930-597-5 (alk. paper)
      1. Sound—Recording and reproducing—Digital techniques. 2 Television soundtracks.
      3. Motion picture soundtracks. I. Title.
TK7881.4.R67 1999
778.5'244—dc21   99-43323
                                                              CIP

Printed in the United States of America

   00 01 02 03 04   5 4 3 2

TABLE OF CONTENTS

Acknowledgments

A lot of people helped with this book. Matt Kelsey and Dorothy Cox of Miller Freeman Books, and Jim Feeley of *Digital Video* magazine, helped me bridge the tremendous gap between thinking about a book and actually publishing one. Jim also took the time to read through various versions of the original manuscript and to offer useful suggestions on content and style. I'm grateful for the working professionals who let me pick their brains about the techniques they use, including location sound expert and Cinema Audio Society member John Garret, *Videography* magazine's Bob Turner, and PBS narrators Wendie Sakakeeny and Don Wescott. Thanks also to Don Wescott and Omnimusic president Doug Wood for contributing some of the examples in this book.

Special thanks to Richard Pierce, principal software developer at broadcast manufacturer Orban, for the countless times he answered my phone calls about the finer points of acoustics and digital audio. And thanks to Dave Moulton, nationally-respected audio educator, researcher, and developer of the *Golden Ears* training course, for reviewing the manuscript and offering suggestions. Of course, anything I misinterpreted from either of these gentlemen is my own fault.

It's customary for authors to thank their families, but mine went far beyond the norm. My son, Dan—also a sound engineer—has a deeper academic background than me. He spotted and helped me clean up ambiguities in the technical chapters. And my wife, Carla, did much more than provide a spouse's usual patience and support: As author of more than 25 successful books on computers and digital graphics, she was able to teach me the practical realities of getting a manuscript out the door . . . and in the time it took me to write this book, she finished three others.

Introduction

There's a good chance you picked up this book because you're working on a project and are having trouble with one aspect of its sound. So the first thing we've included is a list of Frequently Asked Questions: a bunch of common audio problems, and either how to fix them or—if the fix is complicated—where in this book you'll find a complete solution.

Consult the FAQ if you have to put out fires in a hurry.

Read the rest of this book if you want tracks that are truly hot.

I'm going to try to guess some things about you. You may have taken a few film or video courses, but most of your production knowledge is self-taught. You improve your skills by watching the videos you've produced, seeing what you don't like, and changing it the next time. You look at still frames to analyze your lighting or composition, or compare your editing techniques with what's on television and the movies you rent. Since you're primarily an artist, your eyes are your guide. You can see what you've done wrong.

One other guess: you've discovered it's almost impossible to learn how to create a good soundtrack that way. There are too many variables. If the finished mix has dialog that's hard to understand, there's no intuitive way to guess whether it was because the boom was placed badly . . . or levels weren't set properly during digitization . . . or if it was mixed on the wrong kind of speakers. Often, trying to fix one sound problem makes other aspects of the track worse.

Even if you also play a musical instrument, your sense of aesthetics doesn't bail you out when the track isn't working. There's a reason for this:

Good soundtracks aren't just a question of art. You also have to understand the science.

In this book, we cover both.

It's Not Rocket Science

Don't be scared about the science part. The math is mainly stuff you learned in elementary school, and the physics is common sense.

Don't be scared of the art, either. This is not a book on the aesthetics of sound (there *are* books like that, filled with critical essays about classic film directors, and they're completely irrelevant to what we're trying to do here). I'm not going to try to change what you think is good.

And don't be scared of me. The "art" of this book is the tricks, shortcuts, and industry practices that have been developed over 75 years of talking pictures, and that I've been working with since the late 1960s. There's a lot to be shared after years of creating tracks for everything from corporate videos to national spots, working in every kind of facility from local stations to large post houses, contributing to the design of some of the industry's standard pieces of digital audio equipment, and seeing projects I've worked on win Clios, an Emmy, and hundreds of other awards.

How This Book is Organized

The first section of this book is an explanation of how sound works: the physics of sound in space and the technology of digital recording. I've put this material in front because it's important. I've also put it in plain English without jargon or complicated formulas, and with plenty of drawings and examples. It shouldn't take more than a couple of evenings to read.

Then we get to step-by-step advice—the bulk of these pages. First, preproduction: how to plan the track, figure the budget, and pick the location. Second, acquisition: using microphones on the location and in the studio, and working with the people and things that make sound. Finally, postproduction: editing voices, adding and editing music and effects, processing for the best possible sound, and mixing for various viewing situations.

There's also an accompanying CD with examples and tutorials. I made it an audio CD, playable on any standard stereo, rather than a CD-ROM because I wanted you to be able to hear it on the best speakers you own. There should be no problem importing the tutorials into your editing system.

Staying Up-to-Date

While styles change, the techniques behind good audio remain constant. The physics of sound aren't going to change without a major overhaul of the universe. You should be able to hang onto this book for a while.

I've stayed away from recommendations of specific brands or models, or instructions based on particular software. These things *do* change. Instead, we'll talk about generic software and controls that should show up on any decent processor. You'll be able to use this book with the best tools available when you're ready to buy.

For current information, consult a good monthly magazine like *DV/Digital Video*. They've got up-to-date reviews and recommendations, and there's a good chance I'm still writing a monthly audio tutorial column for them. (Back issues of the column are on the Internet at www.dv.com.) Or ask a friendly professional: we're not at all territorial and are usually willing to share ideas and information. You can reach me through my studio's Web site: www.dplay.com.

How to Create a Great Soundtrack (in a Quarter Page)

Here are the rules:

- Know what you're doing before you start.
- Plan the audio as carefully as you plan the video.
- Get good elements.
- Treat them with respect.
- Do as little processing as possible until the mix.
- Listen very carefully while you do mix.
- Follow the tips in this book.

    The rest is just details.

"Help! It doesn't sound right!"

If you're hearing a specific problem in your project and need to find out how to fix it in a hurry, this section of Frequently Asked Questions is for you.

As an engineer, I'd prefer you read the whole book. That way you'll learn how sound really works and be able to make choices that get you to the best possible track with the least amount of effort. But as a pragmatist—and someone who's lived with years of project deadlines—I understand this may not be possible right now.

So flip through this section until you find the problem that's bothering you. If it can be repaired easily, you'll find the instructions right here. If the fix is slightly more complicated, I'll point you to which chapter in this book has the answers. One or the other will probably be enough to get you back on track.

Then, when you get time, read the rest of the book. It'll save you from this kind of panic situation on your next job.

Problems with On-Camera Dialog

Don't feel bad; this happens all the time in Hollywood. Unfortunately, often the only way to fix a bad dialog track is to re-record in the actors in sync with their pictures. This is standard practice in feature films and TV movies. It's also time-consuming, annoys the actors, introduces problems of its own, and almost never works for the long talking-head sequences you find in most video productions.

You can avoid the need to replace dialog by listening carefully during the shoot, either on a good speaker in a separate control room or with high-quality headphones. Play back the first take as well, so you can catch equipment or tape troubles. Then follow the steps below to fix any problems you hear.

It's not easy to remember during the heat of production, but "wasting" five minutes on the set to move a microphone or hang a sound blanket over a window can save you hours in postproduction . . . and possibly save a day's shooting from ending up in the scrap heap.

If you've already got bad tracks and reshooting isn't an option, you may have to live with the problems. I'll give you what advice I can to clean them up, but don't expect miracles. The section on dialog replacement in sync with picture is in Chapter 8.

"It's Hard to Understand the Words!"

If the actors are mumbling, send them to acting school. If you can hear them clearly on the set but have to strain to hear them on the tape, here are some likely causes:

Too much room echo around their voices

This is the most common problem with dialog tracks. You need to either treat the room with *lots* of sound absorbing material (Chapter 5) or get the mic closer to their mouths (Chapter 7). Moving the mic is probably more practical.

A camera-mounted shotgun mic will almost always be too far away for effective dialog recording indoors. If you can place a shotgun on a boom, no more than a foot or so above the talent's head, you'll get the most realistic dialog. Where you put the mic and how you aim it is critical: it has to be close to the actors' mouths and pointed towards them, without getting close to or pointing towards reflective surfaces.

If you don't have the time or resources to use a boom mic effectively, a lavaliere or tie tack will do a better job. Get the mic as close as possible to the talent's mouth, hiding it in their clothing or hair if necessary. Remember: you can make a close mic sound distant by adding reverberation in postproduction. But the only way to make a distant mic sound close-up is to move it at the shoot.

Too much echo *and* more random room noises than seem appropriate

Your camera's automatic volume control is lowering the recording volume while the actors talk, and raising it whenever they pause. Turn it off.

If you can't defeat the automatic control, try lowering the microphone signal level with a simple attenuator or mixer. You may have to experiment to find a level that doesn't make the automatic control work so hard but still avoids electronic noise. Don't attempt to defeat the automatic volume control by moving the mic farther from the talent. That just increases room echo.

More echo on one actor than on another

If you're using a single mic, make sure it's aimed properly or someone is panning it between the actors. If that doesn't help, try adding some strategically placed absorption.

If you're using multiple body mics, there's a good chance Sue's microphone is picking up George's voice and vice versa. If this is the situation, you'll hear echoes when they're across the room from each other and a hollowness when they come close together. Set up a mixer and assign someone to turn each actor's mic down whenever they don't have a line. Or assign each mic to a separate track in your recorder, and sort them out in postproduction.

Too Many Background Noises

Too much machinery noise, traffic, footsteps . . .

Acoustic noise problems are similar to echo ones and almost always improved by moving the mic closer.

The most common acoustic noises in business videos are air conditioners and computer fans. If you can't turn a building air conditioner off, try removing its grill. The only cure for computer fans is isolation: move the tower, or throw a sound-absorbing blanket over it.

If actors' footsteps are a problem, throw a blanket down for them to walk on when their feet aren't in camera range. If prop-handling noises are a problem, block the scene so the noises occur during pauses in dialog. Put a piece of foam-core board or a foam place mat on a table to dampen the sound when a prop is put down.

If traffic noises are a problem in an interior, make sure all the windows are closed tightly. Then hang sound blankets over the windows. Low-frequency traffic rumbles can be controlled by a mic's low-end rolloff switch, and further filtered in post.

Noise in a radio mic

These things can be unpredictable, so always bring a wired alternative.

Before you give up on a radio mic, make sure you're using fresh batteries: it's not unusual to have to replace the batteries two or even three times during a long shoot day. Get the receiving antenna as close to the mic as possible while maintaining line-of-sight (large metal objects can disrupt the signal), and orient it in the same direction as the transmitter's antenna.

If the signal fades or distorts as talent walks around, it's probably bouncing unpredictably between metal elements in the building: get a diversity receiver (see Chapter 6).

Electronic hum during the recording

Hum can be introduced by the mic cable, particularly when you're using small digital cameras with mini-jack mic inputs. Get an XLR balancing adapter that uses transformers: the improvement, with a good mic, will amaze you.

Even with a balancing transformer, a microphone's tiny signal is easily polluted by electronic noise. Keep all mic cables away from AC power or video lines. If the cable must cross one of these noisy wires, do it at a right angle to minimize the area where pickup can occur.

If you're borrowing signals from a computer, PA system, or playback device, and things start to hum, you may have a voltage mismatch—these things should never be plugged into a mic input—but a ground loop is more likely. The best solution is an isolation transformer in the audio line. If one isn't available you might be able to get a clean signal by running the camera on a battery instead of AC supply. Disconnect the camera from monitors or anything else plugged into an AC outlet. Try to arrange things so that the only item plugged into the wall is the house sound system.

We often refer to ground loop noise as "60-cycle hum," but its effects extend throughout the audio band and are almost impossible to eliminate with filters.

Dialog Problems Introduced by the Recorder

Playback doesn't sound like the recording

Make sure the camera or recorder is properly adjusted. If you're using an analog recorder, the heads must be clean or you'll hear a muffled sound. If you're using a digital recorder, set it for the highest possible quality (16 bits rather than 12). Don't consider a shot "bought" until you've checked its audio playback.

Dialog seems uneven from shot to shot during editing

If you're using a lavaliere, this probably won't happen unless your actors are changing their projection on different shots. If you're using a boom that had to be pulled too far away for the long shot, try using audio from a close-up take . . . or at least do an L-cut (audio and video cut on different frames) to disguise the changes.

You may need to equalize or process the dialog track to smooth out these variations. Resist the temptation to do this during the editing process: it'll save time and be more effective to tweak the sound at the mix, where you'll have better monitors and be able to concentrate more on the track. Keep the mismatched camera angles' dialog on different audio tracks while editing, so you can apply global corrections during the mix instead of changing things clip by clip.

Background noises seem uneven from shot to shot during editing

If the noise level on the set changed during the shoot, fade in some background tone from the noisiest shots over the quieter ones. If noise levels stayed relatively constant during the shoot but are jumping around in the edited track, either the camera's automatic level control or some production assistant's fingers were too active. L-cuts and a little extra ambiance—either from the shoot or a library—will help you smooth over the changes.

Postproduction Audio Issues

If your system uses an analog audio connection into the editor, it's essential that you set digitizing levels properly. Don't trust an on-screen meter. Instead, calibrate your system using the tips in Chapter 9.

Lip-Sync Problems

If the track is largely in sync but you see errors on specific edits, it's probably an operator error. Some desktop systems are notoriously unintuitive for anything other than straight cuts. If this happens only once or twice in a project, it'll be faster to manually nudge the track rather than take an advanced software course.

Sync drift

If it's impossible to get stable sync—if you can get the first line to look right, but other lines in the scene are all over the place—it's probably a software problem. If the track stays in sync for the first five minutes or so, but then jumps wildly out and never comes back, you've most likely got hardware issues. Either way, contact the editing system manufacturer. There may be an update or workaround. You may have to reconfigure your computer, turn off some utilities, and restart. It's also possible you're using audio and video boards the manufacturer didn't qualify to work together.

If a track drifts out of sync at a constant rate, getting worse over time but never making any obvious jumps, you've probably got incompatible references. Is video sync or blackburst being distributed everywhere it's supposed to go? Do timecode or frame rate settings agree throughout your system? Manually sync the front and back of the video and measure how much it's drifted over time: this can help you or the manufacturer diagnose the problem (for example, an error of just under two frames per minute is almost always related to differences between 30 fps audio and 29.97 fps NTSC video). If nothing else, figuring the error as a percentage will let you apply a speed correction to the track and finish the job that way.

Separate audio and video

If you recorded double-system—using separate audio and video recorders—you may have to go back to original footage and use the slate to resync.

If you recorded without a slate, or used a totally nonsync medium like analog audio cassettes or DC-motorized film cameras, you're in for a nightmare of manual resyncing and trimming. A sound engineer with lip-sync experience and a good audio-for-video workstation may be able to save you time and money.

Hum and Noise

If a track gets noisy but the original footage is clean, it's best to redigitize. But first, check the connections between recorder and computer (Chapter 9). Make sure the computer is set for 16-bit or higher resolution. Even if your final goal is a low-resolution medium like the Internet, always record at the highest possible bit setting.

Background noises that couldn't be eliminated at the shoot

If you're willing to sacrifice realism for intelligibility, get a good filter and start with settings like this:

- Sharp rolloff (at least 12 dB/octave) below 200 Hz and above 8 kHz
- Consonant peak, 6 dB around one octave wide, at 1.75 kHz
- Optional warmth boost around 2 dB at 250 Hz

Fine-tune the settings with a good audio monitor, always listening for distortion. If you're not sure what things like dB and Hz are, check Chapter 1. If you're not sure how to use a filter, check Chapter 13. If you don't have good monitor speakers, don't do anything. You'll have to go to a sound studio for the final mix—it's impossible to do a good mix without accurate speakers—and you can put off the corrections until then.

Power-line hum is seldom just at power-line frequencies and can't be fixed with a standard filter. A comb filter, with mathematically related notches like the teeth of a comb, can help a lot (see Chapter 14).

Hum and hiss that don't obscure the dialog, but are annoying during pauses, can be eliminated with sliding filters and multiband noise gates. That's in Chapter 14 also.

Narration Problems

Radio and TV have conditioned us to expect voice-overs to be cleanly recorded, disembodied voices speaking directly to us from limbo (hey, I don't make the rules). You can't record them in the kind of real-world reverberant spaces that are appropriate for dramatic dialog. Read Chapter 8 for some tips on recording them properly.

Voice-over recording lacks clarity

If an analog tape recorded in a professional studio sounds dull or muffled, suspect your tape recorder's heads. Sometimes all that's needed is a good cleaning with a cotton swab and alcohol. Make sure the alcohol is wiped off with a clean swab before rethreading the tape. If that doesn't help, suspect head alignment: a tiny screw near the playback head can be adjusted to tilt the head for maximum high-frequency transfer. But if you're not familiar with the procedure and it's not covered in the recorder's manual, it's best to call a technician.

If an analog tape sounds very weak and muffled, check to make sure it hasn't been inadvertently flipped and you're trying to play through the back of the tape (I've seen this happen in major radio stations). The recording is on the smooth side with the eggshell semigloss surface. Depending on the tape, the back is either very glossy or very dull: this side should face away from the heads.

If an analog tape sounds squeezed, with breaths and mouth noises unnaturally emphasized or high frequencies that are very spitty, it may have been recorded with analog noise reduction encoding. Contact the studio for advice; they may be able to lend you a decoder or supply an unencoded version. On the other hand, it may have been recorded through inappropriate processing: this was a bad decision by the announcer, director, or recording engineer and can't be undone.

Voice-over sounds fine by itself but is weaker than other elements

A little processing is a good thing. See Chapter 14 for advice on using equalization and compression to make a voice punchier.

Computer Doesn't Play Audio Well

If you hear skipping, pops, or brief silences when you play from hard disk but not from the original track, suspect data flow problems. Don't assume that because you see relatively good video, the drive or CPU is capable of handling audio. The eye can forgive momentary lapses or uneven motion a lot more easily than the ear can.

Either the hard disk isn't accessing audio quickly enough, or the CPU is trying to do too many other things at the same time. Try defragmenting the hard disk or copying the audio file to a faster drive. Contact the editing system manufacturer: you may need to change your computer's startup configuration and reboot. As a last resort, lower the sample rate or use mono instead of stereo.

Periodic clicking in a file

This is almost always the result of digital audio being out of sync with itself. Check that your sound card and software settings match. If you copied the audio digitally from a DAT, stand-alone CD player, or DV recorder, make sure the sound card and the source shared the same sync reference: either both should be locked to a blackburst generator, or the card must be set to use its own input as the reference.

Random squeaks, whistles, or edginess mixed with the high-pitched sounds

This is aliasing distortion. The file was recorded at a sample rate that the sound card doesn't properly support (no matter what the manufacturer printed on its box). See Chapter 2.

Maybe you're lucky and the problem is in the card's playback filters. Try playing the file on a different computer. If it sounds okay, get a different brand of sound card.

But it's more likely the problem was created during the original recording, and the file can't be repaired. Try redigitizing at the highest sample rate your software will support. If that results in a cleaner file, you may then convert to a lower rate in software and avoid this problem. But the best solution is to get a card that was properly designed in the first place. Don't just let price be your guide: a thousand-dollar unit from a leading manufacturer of editing systems had this problem. (And this was their flagship Macintosh card well into the mid-1990s; fortunately, they've since corrected the problem.)

Editing Problems

Sound effects or dialog edits seem fine in previews, but are out of sync in the final movie

You can't edit sound at anything less than the full frame rate. A 15 fps preview or timeline set to larger than one-frame resolution will hide a lot of problems. Kick your software up a notch and try re-editing.

Some problems may be hardware or software related; see the discussion of lip sync at the start of this section.

Music edits don't sound smooth

Although there's an art to music editing (one you can learn easily; see Chapter 12), the problem may be mechanical. Although one-frame resolution may be fine for effects and dialog, a thirtieth of a second can be an eternity in music. If you can't set your video-editing software to mark in- and out-points with at least quarter-frame accuracy, export the music to an audio program before you cut it to length. (Professionals usually mark edits to single-sample accuracy, which is on the order of a thousandth of a frame.)

Mix Problems

If you don't have good monitor speakers in a well-designed environment, the ability to process sounds in real time, and a system that will let you independently adjust the level of many tracks at the same time, it might be worthwhile to hire a studio to mix critical projects. An experienced engineer with the right equipment can save you time, assure a good on-air sound, and fix audio problems that aren't repairable in a desktop video-editing system. Mixing on the wrong equipment, or trying to do a complex mix with a mouse and "rubber band" volume lines, is a sure-fire recipe for disaster.

Besides, it's how I make my living.

The mix sounded great on the desktop or mixing studio, but bad on the air or in the conference room

If the music disappears but dialog sounds okay, chances are you're using home hi-fi speakers optimized for pop music, or small multimedia speakers supplemented by subwoofers. The speakers emphasized the extreme highs and lows, so you turned down the music track to compensate. This problem can also result from too reverberant a mixing room: since reverb is more obvious on voice than on music, you may have turned down the music so it wouldn't interfere.

If the dialog disappears and the music sounds too loud, your speakers emphasized the midrange. This is common with midsized multimedia speakers and the cube speakers often placed on top of mixing consoles.

The solution for both problems is to remix using good speakers in a proper environment, but tweaking an equalizer during playback can provide a temporary fix. It can also generate distortion that fights intelligibility, so making an equalized dub of a bad mix isn't a good option.

The mix proportions were right, but it was too soft/loud/distorted on the air

Make sure the line-up tone at the head of your tape is accurate. Not only should it match the standard zero setting on your recorder; it also has to match the "average loud" level of your program. Most broadcasters and dub houses rely on the tone exclusively when setting levels and don't try to compensate if program audio doesn't match.

Broadcast audio on digital videotape is usually standardized with tone and average program level at -20 dBfs, and no peaks higher than -10 dBfs. "dBfs" (decibels related to full scale) is defined in Chapter 2.

Broadcast audio on analog videotape is usually standardized with tone and average level at the magnetic level represented by 0 VU on the recorder's meter, with peaks no higher than +6 VU. The average-to-peak difference appears smaller on analog meters than digital ones because analog meters can't respond to fast peaks as well.

If you're having trouble keeping the average level in the right place while peaks stay below the maximum, try moderate compression on individual elements in your track as well as peak limiting on the overall mix. Tips for using these processors appear in Chapter 14.

Some elements sound fine in stereo, but completely disappear when the tape is broadcast in mono

Something is out of phase. The signal on the left channel is pushing while the one on the right is pulling by exactly the same amount. (If that doesn't make sense to you, you'll either have to trust me or read Chapter 1.) When the two channels for that element are combined, they cancel each other out.

This most often happens because of a cable problem, where two wires in a balanced cable are reversed. It doesn't cause a problem when the cable is being used by itself for a mono signal, but shows up when stereo channels are combined. Some low-cost synthesizers and effects processors reverse the phase of one channel intentionally, to hype the "stereoness" of their output.

This can also happen when the monaural balanced output of a mixer appears on phone jacks, and a stereo-to-mono phone plug adapter is used to split its signal to two channels.

You need to go back to the original tracks and check individual stereo pairs by combining them to mono. When you hear the pair that disappears in mono, use the phase-invert function of your mixing console or software to invert just one channel. If you don't have that ability, redub the original source through a correctly wired cable. Then remix.

In a pinch, you may be able to broadcast in mono by using just one channel of your original stereo mix.

The entire mix sounds very wide in stereo, but disappears in mono

This is a variation of the above problem, but much easier to fix. It probably occurred when you dubbed the output of your editing system to a final videotape master because one of the two balanced cables was miswired. Redub, using two correctly wired cables. Or if you can tolerate the generation loss, make a submaster by copying the stereo tracks from the original master with one correctly wired cable and the miswired one. This will flip things back the way they should be. It doesn't matter which channel you reverse when making the submaster.

If the miswired cable was also feeding your monitor speakers during the mix, the result could have suppressed mono elements somewhat when the two speakers combined in the room. This could fool you into making the dialog and narration too loud, or—because the effect is more pronounced at low frequencies—equalizing those tracks badly. Remix.

Other Common Questions

Where can I find cheap talent/music/sound effects?

Voice-over casting advice is in Chapter 8. Music scoring is Chapter 12. You usually get what you pay for, but there are some strategies for stretching the budget.

Sound effects are free if you record them yourself or have a friend create them on a synthesizer. But even professionally recorded, fully licensed ones are cheap—often only a few dollars per minute—if you buy them individually over the Internet. Check www.sounddogs.com and www.sound-ideas.com.

Is it a copyright violation to use pop music recordings in an educational or nonprofit video? How about classical music?

Yes. It doesn't matter how noble the intended use is. And while most classical compositions are no longer protected by copyright, the recorded performances probably are.

Only an attorney can give legal advice, but as a general rule "fair use" applies only to private viewing at home or brief excerpts in a critical review of the music itself.

What software should I use? What brand of sound card? Mac or PC?

The science of sound and the technique of the sound track—what this book is really about—have taken most of a century to develop and are well understood. Digital recording hasn't been around as long, and radical developments in the technology take many years to make it from lab to common practice. So it's my expectation that you'll be able to use this book for a while.

On the other hand, new computer and digital video products are introduced every month. Rather than risk misleading you with outdated information, I've avoided specific brand and model recommendations in this book. If you want to keep up, read the monthly magazine *Digital Video:* it's remarkably free from hype and rehashed press releases. Besides, I'm a contributing editor. (*Digital Video* is available at most large newsstands and computer stores, and back issues are posted at www.dv.com.)

INTRODUCTION TO SECTION I

This is the technical stuff: how sound exists and is perceived by the brain, how it can be turned into computer data, and how it gets conducted over wires in a studio. This is the foundation everything else in this book is built on.

I've avoided formulas. You should be able to understand these concepts using no more than grade-school science or math, and your own common-sense understanding of how things work. A lot of it is based on visual analogies, on the assumption that videographers are pretty good at looking at the world.

But it *is* technical, and I don't want to trigger any deep-seated phobia. You can skip this material—if you must—and go directly to the practical tips and techniques that compose this book's other chapters. But I promise that if you *do* read it, the rest of the book will make a lot more sense. In fact, since you'll know how sound actually works, it'll be easier to get better tracks without worrying about the specifics.

And that will make it easier to concentrate on the fun stuff.

CHAPTER 1

How Sound Works

A Brief Note . . .

This is the most technical chapter of the book, but I've avoided complex formulas and theorems—the only math and science you'll need is the kind you learned in grade school. Instead, you'll use your visual imagination and common-sense knowledge of how the world works.

You can skip this chapter if you must. But if you read through it, you'll understand what sound really is, how it moves around a shooting stage or editing room, and how the words that describe it relate to reality. And once you have that knowledge, the rest of this book—the practical tips for making sound do what you want in a production—will be a piece of cake.

R O S E ' S   R U L E S

➪ Sound is messy stuff. It spreads out, bends around corners, and bounces off objects. The way it bounces can hurt your track

➪ As sound spreads out, it gets drastically weaker. If you know how this happens, you'll find it easier to control the bouncing.

Music-sicle?

"Architecture is frozen music." When Friedrich von Schelling wrote that, he was being poetic. The scientific truth is if there were such a thing as frozen music, it would be *pressure*. This is usually air pressure, but it can also be pressure in water, wood, or anything else that conducts sound. It's not precisely the kind of pressure you feel when deadlines approach, but the pressure that compresses molecules together.

Sound usually travels over air molecules, but the same principles hold when the molecules are of some other substance.

If the pressure keeps changing repeatedly within certain speed ranges, you've got sound. Something—a drum skin, human vocal cords, the cone of a loudspeaker, or anything else that makes noise—starts vibrating back and forth. As its surface moves towards us, it squeezes air molecules together. As it moves away from us, it creates a very slight vacuum that pulls the molecules apart.

If we *could* freeze sound and see the individual molecules, they'd look like Figure 1.

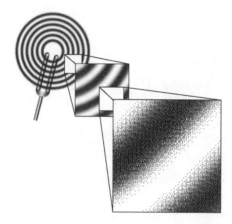

Figure 1: If we could see sound, it would look like this. Air molecules are squeezed together and pulled apart by the vibrations of the tuning fork.

Think of Figure 1 as a snapshot of a single moment in the life of a sound. Air molecules are represented as tiny black dots . . . and as we enlarge sections of the picture, we can see individual ones.

The Life of a Sound

The tuning fork vibrates back and forth. When its surface moves towards the air molecules next to it, it squeezes them together. Those compressed molecules push against the ones a little farther from the tuning fork, and that squeezes the farther molecules together. The farther molecules now push against ones even farther, and so on: as the squeezing spreads out to successive layers of molecules, the pressure spreads out.

Air molecules, like everything else in the physical universe, take time to move from one place to another. So even while the pressure is spreading outward, the tuning fork—which is vibrating back and forth—may start moving back in the other direction. The air molecules next to the fork rush back in to fill the space where it was, pulling them a little further apart than normal. This very slight vacuum—engineers call it *rarefaction*—pulls on the next layer of molecules a little farther from the tuning fork, spacing them apart. And the process repeats to successive layers.

Everybody Feels the Pressure

As you can imagine, pent-up molecules try to push away from what's squeezing them together. They don't necessarily push in a straight line from the sound source, so the sound spreads in all directions. Because of this basic principle:

> ➤ You can point a light, but you can't point a sound.
>
> ➤ You can aim a lens to avoid something out-of-frame, but you can't effectively aim a microphone to "miss" a distracting sound.

Eventually the waves of pressure and rarefaction reach our ears. The eardrum vibrates in response, and the vibration is carried across tiny bones to a canal filled with nerves. Different nerves are sensitive to vibrations at different speeds, so they tell the brain how fast the vibrations are occurring. Those nerve messages about the speed of the vibrations, how strong the vibrations are, and how their strength changes over time, are what we hear as sound.

It Matters how Frequently You Do It

Since sound is changes of pressure, its only characteristics are how much pressure exists at any moment and how often the pressure changes. Let's deal with the "how often" part first.

Think back to the imaginary world of Figure 1, where we could see individual molecules. If we stand in one place, we would see waves of pressure and rarefaction go past us. With an imaginary stopwatch, we could measure the time from the most intense pressure of one wave to the most intense pressure of the next. This timing reflects how quickly the tuning fork is vibrating, changing from pushing molecules in one direction to pulling them back in the other.

Figure 2 shows two peaks that are one second apart. If the vibration continues at this rate, we could say it's vibrating with a frequency of one cycle per second. That's a mouthful, so we use the term Hertz—named after a 19th century German physicist—or its abbreviation Hz instead.

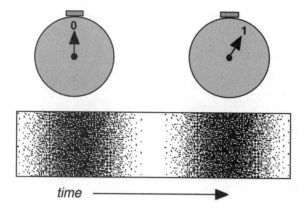

Figure 2: Timing from one pressure peak to the next

A Hertz is one complete cycle per second. That's too slow for us to hear as a sound. Another measurement—kiloHertz, or kHz—represents 1,000 cycles per second.

Fast Pressure Changes Are Heard as Sounds

It's generally accepted that humans can hear sounds in a range between 20 Hz and 20 kHz. This is a little like saying, "Humans can run a mile in four minutes." A few exceptional humans can hear this range, and even the best hearing deteriorates as you get older. Fortunately, very few useful sounds extend to these limits. If all you consider are basic vibrations:

- The highest note of a violin is about 3.5 kHz.

- The highest note on an oboe is around 1.8 kHz.

- In fact, of all the instruments in the orchestra, only the pipe organ can vibrate faster than 5 kHz.

Figure 3 shows the basic vibration of various instruments.

Harmonics

The fastest that a violin string or oboe reed can vibrate is considerably less than 5 kHz. But frequencies higher than that are still important. To see how, we need to refine how we look at the pressure waves.

A microphone converts sound pressure into electrical voltage. If we connect the microphone to an oscilloscope—a device that displays a graph of voltage changes over time (a video waveform monitor is one form of oscilloscope)—we can see the wave with considerable detail. Figure 4 shows how an ideal wave looks.

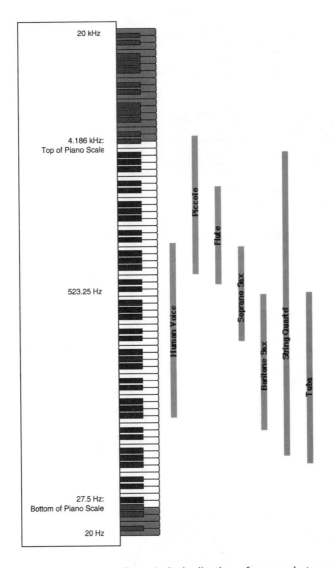

Figure 3: Basic vibrations of common instruments

Positive pressure generates a positive voltage, forming the peaks. Negative pressure generates negative voltage, forming the valleys. The two voltage peaks A and B represent the two pressure peaks in Figure 2.

But this is a pure wave, also known as a sine wave from its mathematical function (this may be the only time you'll see "mathematical function" in this book). I generated it electronically because pure sine waves almost never occur in nature. In

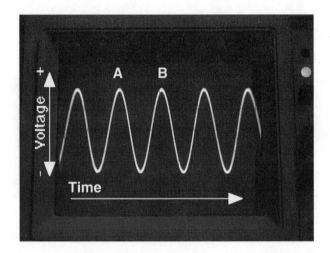

Figure 4: A pure wave on an oscilloscope.

the real world, most things that vibrate don't have this perfect, symmetrical back-and-forth movement.

The basic back-and-forth movement is called the *fundamental.* It carries most of the energy and is what we hear as the pitch of a sound.

But there also are imperfections in the movement, caused by how the mechanism vibrates. The imperfections take the form of softer higher-frequency waves, called *harmonics,* superimposed on the fundamental. The shape of the instrument and what it's made of determine how much of the harmonics we hear.

These higher harmonics make the difference between an oboe and a violin when they're playing the same note. (You can even see the difference, in Figures 5 and 6.)

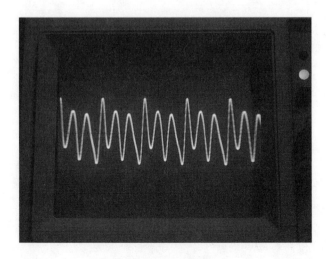

Figure 5: An oboe playing concert A . . .

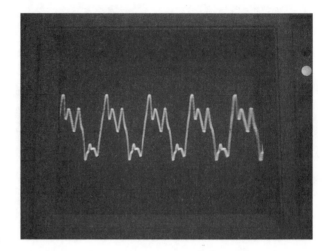

Figure 6: . . . and a violin playing the same note.

Notice how every third wave of the oboe is stronger than the others. This is the basic or fundamental vibrating frequency of its reed. The smaller peaks are a harmonic, three times as fast. The violin's strongest waves are exactly as far apart as the oboe's because they're both playing the same note. But it has a more complicated mixture of harmonics, ranging from two to eight times the fundamental. They combine to produce the complex pattern of the violin's wave, which is why you can tell an oboe from a fiddle when they're playing the same note.

Just for fun, here's the same note on a trumpet: the fundamental is much stronger than its very complex harmonic pattern (Figure 7).

You can hear harmonics at work. Track 1 of the CD that came with this book has the four waves you've just seen, played first at full fidelity, and then through a

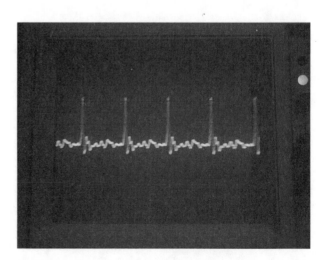

Figure 7: A trumpet's A shows a very different pattern.

sharp filter that eliminates frequencies above the fundamental. Listen to it on a good hi-fi system: you'll find it's easy to tell the instruments apart when you can hear the harmonics, but very difficult when you can't hear them. Then if you can, play the same track through a low-quality speaker—perhaps the one built into your computer's tower—and you'll find it's a lot harder to tell the difference between violin and oboe, even when the filter is turned off!

Say what?

Human speech has highly complex harmonic patterns. We control them by changing the shape of the mouth. Try singing "eee," "ooo," and "aah" on the same note. The fundamental pitch stays the same for each . . . but the harmonics change as you move your tongue back and forth.

Unpitched Sounds

Many sounds don't have regularly repeating waves at all. You can't pick a note for the sounds of an explosion or rustling leaves because they're caused by random movements. Instead of any particular pitch, each wave is a different length. The lengths can fall within certain limits: when we talk about a high-pitched noise (such as a hissing air) or a low-pitched one (like thunder), we're really describing its frequency limits.

Human speech is a combination of pitches with harmonics (the vowels), unpitched noises (about half of the consonants), and noises at the same time as pitches (the other consonants).

The Myths of Frequency Response

One of the ways to rate the quality of a sound system is to measure the highest frequency it can carry. For a system to be considered "high fidelity," we usually expect it to be able to handle harmonics up to 20 kHz. But in a lot of cases, this much range isn't necessary.

- Until HDTV becomes a strong force in the marketplace, the upper limit for television and FM radio broadcasting in the United States is 15 kHz. Frequencies higher than that cause problems with the transmission system.

- Most Hollywood films made before the 1970s—including all the great musicals—carried harmonics only up to about 12.5 kHz, and most theater sound systems weren't designed to handle much more than that.

- We don't need high frequencies to recognize people's voices or understand speech. Telephones don't carry anything above 3.5 kHz . . . but most people would describe a telephone as lacking bass notes, not high ones. National Public Radio often limits its FM network news and interview shows to 7.5 kHz, to save transmission costs.

- Even most high-fidelity systems aren't hi-fi. Although it's easy to build an amplifier with 20 kHz response, very few speakers can handle those high-frequency sounds accurately. Manufacturers regularly manipulate ratings, or use deliberately imprecise measurements, when describing their speakers.

Track 2 of this book's CD can help you tell how well your own systems handle high frequencies. It consists of musical selections that alternate between being played at full fidelity and through different filters that eliminate various high frequencies. If your speakers (and ears) are capable of handling the highest tones, you'll notice a distinct difference when the filters are switched on and off. But if those frequencies aren't making it through your system anyway, the filters won't have any effect.

Most people won't hear any difference between the unfiltered version and the version with an 18 kHz cutoff. Depending on their age, many won't even hear a significant loss with a 15 kHz cutoff.

Try playing this part of the CD at your editing station as well. You might be amazed how much you're missing through typical multimedia or personal monitoring speakers.

Somewhat Slower Pressure Changes Are Heard as Envelopes

We know that fast pressure changes—above 1/20th of a second or so—are heard as sounds. But if we compare the peak pressure from one wave to the next, we'll also see slower changes over time. This is the sound's *envelope,* how it varies between loud and soft over a period as short as a fraction of a second. Figure 8 shows the envelope of about a second and a half of dialog. This is too long a period to display on an oscilloscope, so I'm using a screen shot from an audio-editing program instead. But the display is exactly the same: the vertical axis is sound pressure translated into voltage, and the horizontal axis is time.

If you look closely you can see individual waves. But if you look at the larger picture—which I've traced with a heavy gray line—you can see the slower changes of volume that make up the envelope.

Speech envelopes are very seldom related to individual words, because people tend to elide words together: We. Don't. Talk. Like. This. The voice in Figure 8 is saying "Oh yeah, that's great . . . thank you," but it's difficult to correlate those

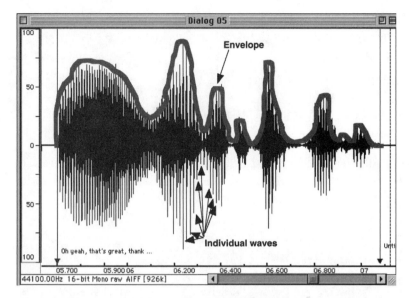

Figure 8: Envelope of a human voice

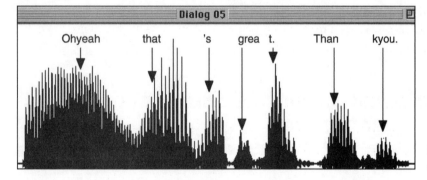

Figure 9: Words and their envelopes.

sounds with the peaks of the envelope unless you've had a lot of editing experience. I've done it for you in Figure 9: note how some peaks are shared by more than one word, while some words have more than one peak.

This suggests two rules:

> ➤ You don't edit words in a soundtrack. You edit envelopes.
> ➤ It's almost impossible to edit sound strictly by eye. You have to hear what you're doing.

Obviously, envelope plays a large part in how we understand speech. But it's also important in how we differentiate musical instruments. Compare the clarinet in Figure 10 with the trumpet in Figure 11: the clarinet starts its sound slowly, as the reed's vibrations get reinforced by the resonance of the tube. The trumpet starts with a burst that's characteristic of all brass instruments, as the musician's lips start vibrating from built-up air pressure (it's often called a *brass blip* by people who work with synthesizers).

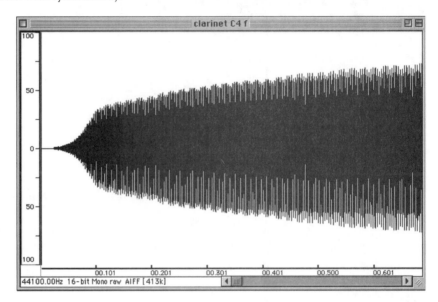

Figure 10: Clarinet
envelope

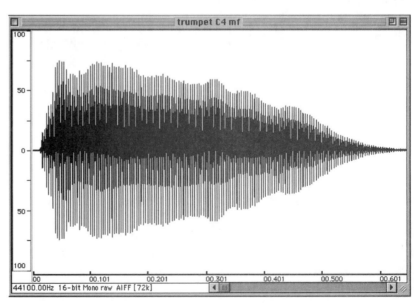

Figure 11: Trumpet
envelope

In Chapter 14, you'll see how devices like a compressor can manipulate the envelope to make a sound stronger . . . or to completely change its character.

When Envelopes and Frequencies Overlap

The time scale in the previous screenshots is calibrated in seconds. If you look closely at Figure 11, you can see that the "blip" takes about .03 second. But we've already learned that frequencies higher than 20 Hz—or .05 second per wave—are audible. So is the blip part of the envelope or a sound by itself?

In this case it's part of the envelope because the repeating wave is a lot faster: 0.0038 second (261 Hz), corresponding to C4 on the piano. But the issue becomes important when you're dealing with predominantly low-frequency sounds, including many male voices, because the equipment can't differentiate between envelopes and waves unless you adjust it carefully.

Slow Changes of Pressure Are Loudness

You can play that trumpet note through a pocket radio at its lowest volume, or blast it out of a giant stadium sound system, and still hear it as a trumpet. The range of overall sound levels we can hear is amazing. A jet plane landing is about ten trillion times more powerful than the quietest sound audiologists use to test your ears.

Our brains can handle such a wide range of pressure because they deal with volume changes as ratios rather than absolute amounts. A sound that would be absolutely jarring in a quiet setting is practically ignored in a noisy one. (A crying baby is a major distraction in a public library . . . but put that baby in a noisy factory, and you can't hear it at all.) The standard way to think about loudness ratios is to use decibels. Here's how they work.

Warning

The following dozen paragraphs contain some math. It's simple math, but it's numbers nonetheless.

If this scares you, just skip down to the box labeled "Bottom Line."

The Need for a Reference

Since our brains hear loudness as ratios, we can't describe how loud a sound is unless we relate it to some other sound. Scientists have agreed on a standardized "other" sound, nominally the softest thing an average healthy person can hear. It's often called the *threshold of hearing*. A quiet living room may have a sound pressure level about a thousand times the standard. The level at a busy city street is about five million times the standard.

Adjusting a sound's volume means multiplying its positive and negative pressure by a specific ratio. But its original volume was measured as a ratio to the threshold of hearing, so the new volume is the product of both ratios combined. You start with the ratio between the original sound and the standard, and then multiply it by another ratio that represents the change. These ratios are usually fairly complex, rather than something easy like the ratio of three to one, so the math can get messy. We use a shortcut—logarithms—to make life easier.

The Logarithm

"Help! I don't know a thing about logarithms!"

Just remember two rules:

➤ Any logarithm is a ratio expressed as a single number. The ratio "three to one" is the log ".477." (Nobody remembers all the logarithms; you look them up in tables or use a calculator when you need them.)

➤ If you have to multiply two ratios, you can just add their logs instead. If you have to divide two ratios, just subtract their logs. Complex problems involving multiple ratios become simple matters of addition or subtraction.

Here's an example of how logarithms save you time: A reasonable pressure level for an announcer's voice, standing one foot away, is 349,485 times the threshold of hearing, or a ratio expressed as log 5.8. Suppose we have to make that voice twice as loud. Loudness is influenced by a lot of subjective factors, but if we're considering just sound pressure, we'd want to multiply it by two. The ratio 2:1 is the logarithm 0.3010299957 (close enough to .3 for any practical purpose).

Sound pressure is the product of two factors, power and the area it occupies. To give something twice as much pressure, we either have to double both factors or double just the power *twice*.

So we have to multiply the ratio of the announcer's voice to the threshold of hearing, times two, times two. On a piece of paper it would look like

```
ratio of one to    349,485
                 ×       2
                 ×       2
                 _____
ratio of one to 1,397,940
```

Logs make the job a lot easier:

```
   5.8
+   .3
+   .3
-------
   6.4
```

So if we turn up an amplifier so that the voice is mathematically twice as loud as it was before, the result is log 6.4 times as loud as the threshold of hearing.

The Decibel

The engineering term for the logarithm of any two acoustic or electric power levels is the *Bel,* named for the fellow who invented telephones. A decibel is actually 1/10th of a Bel, which is why it's abbreviated dB. We use a tenth of a Bel because it multiplies the log by 10, making it easier to think about (trust me, that's how logs work). So the announcer's voice at one foot had a sound pressure level with a ratio of 58 dB to the standard reference, commonly written as 58 dB SPL.

Bottom line

The software and equipment you use to manipulate sounds works in terms of voltage, representing pressure. So to double an electrical volume, we turn its knob up 6 dB.

The Speed of Sound Matters to a Videographer

Sound pressure travels through the air, as one molecule bumps the one next to it. This takes time: roughly a thousandth of a second to go one foot. (In nonrough numbers, 1087 feet/second at 32° Fahrenheit, speeding up as things get warmer.)

A thousandth of a second doesn't seem like much when you're producing a video. But it adds up: when an object is 30 feet away, its sound takes about a frame to reach us. This can be critical if you're shooting distant events with a long lens and a camera-mounted mic, because the visual distance to the image won't match the timing to its sound. This is made worse by the conventions of the small screen: we expect to hear an effect exactly in sync with the picture, no matter how far away it's supposed to be. An explosion a hundred feet away, placed realistically, will strike most viewers as being three frames late.

Sync errors because of distance also affect how we hear sound in a large theater. An effect that's perfectly in sync for the front row can appear two or three frames late in the back of the hall. There's nothing film producers can do about this.

Echoes and Colorations

The speed of sound also determines how we (or our microphones) hear sounds in enclosed spaces. Sound bounces off hard surfaces—air molecules can't relieve their pressure by moving the wall or ceiling, so they spring back in the opposite direction—and the reflected waves mix with the original ones.

If we hear the reflection later than about a tenth of a second after the original sound, it's perceived as an echo. In some cases, the sound keeps bouncing between surfaces in the room: many echoes, randomly spaced, are heard as reverberation. If the sound can travel a distance between bounces, and the space has lots of different surfaces to bounce off, the reverb sounds richer. But almost any enclosed shooting space—not just cathedrals and courtrooms—will have some form of echoes. They can add realism to a scene, but they can also interfere with intelligibility, so we'll devote a lot of space to controlling them in later chapters.

Echoes in small rooms

We're usually not aware of how sound bounces in small spaces like offices or editing rooms, because the reflections arrive very quickly. But they can cause major problems if you want to record or critically listen in the room, because of how they combine with the original sound.

Think of the compression-rarefaction cycle of a sound wave like the phases of the moon. A moon goes through continuous cycles from dark to bright and back, just as a sound wave cycles between pressure and partial vacuum. In fact, the word *phase* refers to the timing of any repeating phenomenon: the moon, sound waves, or even rotating engine parts.

Now, if we had two moons in our sky and each was in its full phase at the same time, we'd have a very bright night. But if one moon was new while the other was full—if the phases didn't match—it wouldn't be as bright.

When two sound waves are in the same phase, they add together the same way. Figure 12A shows how this works with our familiar pressure-over-time graph. Where both waves are providing positive pressure, we have twice as much pressure; where both are in their vacuum phase, we have twice as much vacuum.

But Figure 12B shows what happens if one of the sounds is later in its cycle. Where the top sound has pressure, the bottom one is almost at its strongest vacuum and absorbs the pressure. Where the bottom one is pushing, the top one is pulling. The two forces cancel each other, leaving very little sound. Since both sounds are at the same frequency, this cancellation continues for each wave.

This is more than just an academic exercise. These cancellations happen all the time in the real world. In Figure 13, our listener hears both a direct sound from the

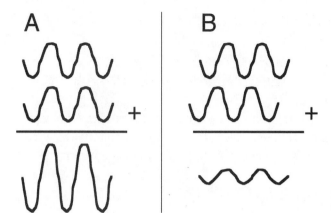

Figure 12: Sounds add differently depending on their phase.

tuning fork and a reflected one from a nearby wall. Unfortunately, since the reflected path is a different length than the direct one, the reflection takes longer to arrive and is at a different phase when it gets to the listener. The reflected sound is compressing while the direct sound is in rarefaction. The two paths cancel each other's sound.

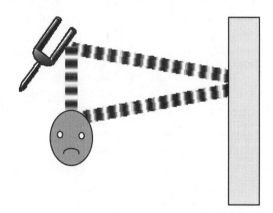

Figure 13: A reflection can arrive at a different phase from the original sound.

If you moved the listener's head in the drawing, the relationship between direct and reflected sound would be different. At some positions, the waves reinforce; at others, they'll cancel.

If you want to actually hear this happening, grab a small hard-surfaced object like a clipboard or a notebook. Then play track 3 of the CD: a steady high-frequency tone (7.5 kHz) recorded on one channel only. Set it so the sound comes out of one speaker at a moderately low volume, and get three or four feet away from the speaker. Move your head a foot or so in either direction, and you'll hear the sound get louder and softer. Hold your head steady with the hard-surfaced object parallel to your ear and about a foot away, and then move it farther and closer. You'll hear the sound change volume as you do.

The situation gets worse when you start dealing with complex sounds. Different frequencies will be at different phases, depending on how far they've traveled. So when the direct path's sound mixes with its reflection, some frequencies will cancel but others will reinforce. In Figure 14, a loudspeaker generating two tones replaces the tuning fork.

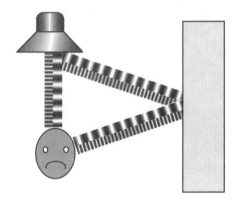

Figure 14: Different frequency sounds get canceled differently by their echoes.

Over the direct path, the high frequency (closely spaced waves) and the low frequency (waves are farther apart) both happen to be compressing when they reach the listener. When the reflected low frequency reaches the listener, it also happens to be compressing: the two paths reinforce each other. But when the reflected high frequency reaches the listener, it's in rarefaction. It cancels the direct path. As far as Figure 14's listener is concerned, the sound has a lot less treble.

Track 4 of the CD demonstrates this, with a 400 Hz low frequency added to the 7.5 kHz high one. Play it like you did track 3: get at least four feet from the speaker, and start moving your head around. Unless you're in a room with very few reflections, at some positions you'll hear the high frequency predominate. At others, the lower frequency will seem louder.

Real-world sounds have a lot more frequencies, and real rooms have lots of reflecting paths. Full and partial cancellations occur at random places throughout the spectrum. So what you hear at any given point in the room depends a lot on the size and shape of the room. (Ever notice how the inside of a phone booth sounds "boxy"? That's why.)

We get used to rooms very quickly (as soon as you're into the conversation, you forget how boxy the phone booth sounds) because we use our eyes and ears together to correlate the sound of a room with its shape.

But if we put a microphone in one room, and then listen to the playback somewhere else, the cancellations become more obvious. And if the characters are moving around as they talk, the cancellations are constantly changing . . . just as they did when you moved around the room while listening to track 4. The result is a distracting hollowness or boxiness, the most common reason why a soundtrack may sound less than fully professional.

The Inverse-Square Law

Fortunately, physics is on our side. As sound spreads out from a source, the pressure waves have to cover a larger area. But the total amount of power doesn't change, so the pressure at any one point is less. Light works the same way: as you get farther from a spotlight, the size of the beam increases but its brightness diminishes.

In fact, under ideal conditions (a nondirectional sound source and an echo-free listening environment) the intensity of a sound diminishes with the square of the distance. This is called the inverse-square law. Figure 15 puts it in graphic terms.

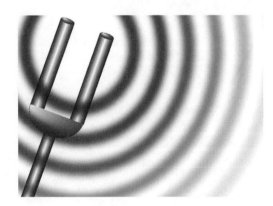

Figure 15: As you get farther away, the pressure gets less intense.

Since decibels compare the loudness of two sounds, and they use logarithms to make things like squares easier to compute, the inverse-square law can be very simply stated:

> Each time you double the distance from a sound source, its sound pressure becomes 6 dB less.

If a microphone hears an instrument as 58 dB SPL at one foot, it'll hear it as 52 dB SPL at two feet, or 46 dB SPL at four feet.

The inverse-square law applies to ideal conditions, with a nondirectional sound source and no hard surfaces to stop sound from spreading. Most sources are directional at some frequencies, and anywhere you shoot is going to have hard surfaces. But the law still holds up fairly well in the real world:

If you can get closer to a sound source—and farther from interfering sounds or reflective surfaces—you'll record it better.

If we take our bad-sounding setup in Figure 14, but increase the distance to the wall, the inverse-square law reduces the amount of cancellation. Figure 16 shows how this works.

Figure 16: When we get farther from a reflecting surface, there's much less cancellation.

Make the inverse-square law your friend:

➤ Try to place a microphone at least three times closer to the sound source than it is to any source of interference.

➤ If you want to listen to a playback in a less-than-perfect editing room, try to be at least three times closer to the speakers than to any reflecting walls.

The first rule explains why camera-mounted microphones rarely do a good job of rejecting interference or echoes. The camera is usually too far away from the sound source.

The second rule is the principle behind the "nearfield" speakers that sit on the console of just about every recording studio in the world.

"Soundproofing"

The wedge-shaped foam panels, special tiles, or tuned cavities you see in recording studios aren't there to stop sound from entering or leaving the room. They're there to reduce reflections by absorbing sound energy and turning it into mechanical motion. Sound studios also frequently have rigid curved or sculpted panels along one wall to diffuse the reflections so cancellations don't build up at a particular frequency.

Later in this book, we'll discuss specific ways to use absorption and diffusion for better sound when you're shooting, recording voice-overs, and mixing.

We'll also discuss the use (and limitations) of portable sound barriers and how to take advantage of existing building features to block sound. But true soundproofing—stopping outside noises from getting into a room, or keeping a loud mixing session from disturbing the neighbors—requires special construction techniques and belongs in a different book.

For the practical video producer, the best soundproofing is understanding:

Know how to avoid situations where reflected or incidental sounds will interfere with what you're trying to do.

Very Slow Changes of Pressure are Weather

Barometric pressure—the stuff reported in the evening weather forecast—is exactly the same kind of molecular pressure as sound, changing over hours and days instead of seconds and milliseconds. I include it here for the sake of completeness, to suggest there's a cosmic continuum that links all things, and because after this chapter you could use some comic relief.

CHAPTER 2

How Digital Audio Works

> ### R O S E ' S   R U L E S
>
> ⇨ Digital isn't necessarily better than analog. But it's a lot more practical for real-world production.
>
> ⇨ Analog isn't necessarily better than digital, no matter what some golden-eared audiophile says. A system's components and design are a lot more important to its sound than whether it uses analog voltages or digital numbers.
>
> ⇨ Modern techniques let you squeeze a lot of digital audio details through very small bandwidth. They're not foolproof . . . but they can do a good job if you know how they work.

Why Digital?

Audio, when it's vibrating through the air, is definitely not digital. Pressure varies smoothly between compression and rarefaction, rather than in steps that can be related to specific numbers. Or to put it another way, the tines of a tuning fork don't click back and forth like the one on the left in Figure 1; they vibrate continuously like the one on the right.

Figure 1: A digital tuning fork—if there were such a thing—could instantly click between two positions (left). But real ones (right) move smoothly through every possible position.

A microphone turns this changing sound pressure into continuously changing voltage. If we want, we can store these voltage changes for later playback:

- We can use them to wiggle a needle and cut grooves in a moving phono disk.

- We can use them to wiggle a shutter and cast shadows on a moving film track.

- We can send them through a coil and make patterns of varying magnetism on a moving tape with iron particles.

Then we can reverse the process, create a varying voltage from what we've stored, and send it to a speaker diaphragm that pushes or pulls the air . . . recreating a sound. What we've really stored is a mechanical, optical, or magnetic analogy of the sound. Analog recording is a century old, well refined, and works pretty well.

So why complicate matters by trying to turn the sound into a computer code?

We Don't Use Digital Audio Because It's Nonlinear; We Use It Because It's Robust

The nonlinear revolution primarily affected video production. Film and audio tape have always been nonlinear: you could open any scene or sequence, any time, and trim or add new material. Computerized sound editing may be faster or less messy than splicing tape (in some cases, it's slower), but that's not why the industry adopted digital sound.

Historically, media production is the process of copying images or sound from one place onto another. Pieces of movie film are copied onto others for special effects, composite masters, and release prints. Videotape can't be spliced, so it's edited by copying from one deck to another. Music originates on multitrack recorders, is copied to a master tape, and then dubbed again before being turned into a cassette or CD. A movie soundtrack may go through six or more copies between the shooting stage and the theater.

But analog doesn't copy well. When analog images are copied, grain builds up and subtle shadings are lost. A similar thing happens when you copy analog audio: noise builds up and high frequencies are lost. Each time you play an analog tape, it wears out a little and sounds a tiny bit worse.

Digital data doesn't slowly deteriorate. When you copy a number, you get exactly that number—never a little more or less. You can store digital data, play it countless times, manipulate various aspects of it, transmit it across great distances, and it'll always be the numbers you expect. Digits are ideal for the "copy-after-copy" style of media production.

Figure 2 shows a simple visual analogy. If we photocopy the cat, and then copy the copy, we start to lose details. After a few generations, we have nothing left but a blob with whiskers. But if we invent a digital code that spells the word CAT, we can make as many successive copies as we want.

Figure 2: A multigenerational cat, analog and digital

Digital Audio Hides Its Mistakes

If one of the analog pictures got scratched before its copy was made, we'd be stuck with the scratch forever . . . but we'd still recognize the cat. If that copy got scratched, *its* copy would be even worse.

Digital audio handles data loss differently:

- Small data errors are reconstructed perfectly. The system uses checking digits to find out what the missing data should have been, and recreates it.

- Medium data errors are hidden. The checking digits let the system know that *something* is missing, but it doesn't have enough data to make a perfect reproduction. Instead, the system guesses the missing data by interpolating from the numbers it knows are good. In almost every case, the repair is transparent.

- Large data errors are also detected because of the checking digits. But since there isn't enough known-good data, the whole signal deteriorates into noise or is turned off.

In an analog system, even slight problems cause noise or distortion. But large problems may still leave recognizable—if not attractive—signals. In digital you can't hear the small problems at all, and the big ones are catastrophic. Figure 3 charts this difference.

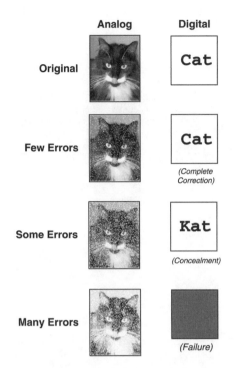

	Analog	Digital
Original		Cat
Few Errors		Cat *(Complete Correction)*
Some Errors		Kat *(Concealment)*
Many Errors		*(Failure)*

Figure 3: Analog and digital handle errors differently.

As with any other data, it's just common sense to back up anything you may ever want to keep:

- Make copies of all masters. If a digital audio tape gets damaged, it may not be recoverable.

- After a few years, it's a good idea to make copies of the *copies* on truly important projects.

The idea behind making periodic copies of important backups is to catch errors before they become too large to accurately correct. If a tape has deteriorated so much that error concealment is taking place, you might not hear there's a problem . . . but subsequent generations can make it a lot worse.

Turning Analog to Digital

Digital circuits are immune to gradual noise because they ignore ambiguity. A bit of information is either zero or one. If a signal falls between those two values, the circuit picks one and ignores the difference. But analog signals are always changing and seldom are precisely one value or another. To take advantage of the digital process, we have to change a smoothly varying voltage into unambiguous numbers.

We do this by taking a snapshot of the voltage at a particular moment, measuring and reporting the voltage, and then taking another snapshot.

- Each snapshot is called a *sample*.

- How often we take these snapshots is the *sample frequency*.

- How precisely we measure the voltage is the *sample depth*.

Those two qualities—sample depth and frequency—determine the limits of how accurately a digital stream can represent a sound.

Sample Depth

We used an oscilloscope in Chapter 1 to show sound waves. This analog gadget displays varying voltage along the vertical and ongoing time along the horizontal. Aside from being a vital piece of test equipment, it's handy for visualizing audio processes.

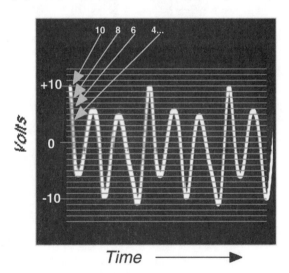

Figure 4: An oscilloscope displays voltage over time.

In Figure 4, I've drawn horizontal lines across the oscilloscope to represent voltage levels. (These lines are actually printed on the faces of most scopes, but don't show up well in the photo.) The numerical units I've assigned to them are completely arbitrary, but for the sake of simplicity we'll call them volts. The signal is an oboe, amplified so it's approximately +10 volts where the microphone picked up its highest compression and -10 volts where it picked up its lowest rarefaction.

The arrows in the upper left show how the waveform reaches different voltages at different times.

It's very easy to build an electrical comparator: a circuit that turns on when an input reaches a particular level, and off when the input falls below the level. If we had a bunch of comparators, each one set to turn on at a different voltage, we could change the analog signal into a digital one. The highest-voltage comparator that's turned on is the unambiguous digital value.

But if we zoom in on the waveform, we can see there might be problems.

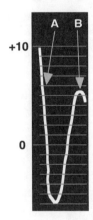

Figure 5: An ambiguous voltage at B

Figure 5 shows the same waveform, redrawn twice as large. The value at time A is six volts. But what about time B? Five and a half volts is an illegal value in a system that requires whole numbers. The comparators would say it's five volts, but they'd be wrong.

The solution is to use a *lot* of comparators, spaced very closely together. Computer designers combine bits together to represent high numbers, and each time they add another bit they double the number of possibilities.

Adding bits can make a big difference. Figure 6 shows our cat in both two- and three-bit versions. With two bits, there are four possible values: black, white, and two grays. But a three-bit photo has eight possible values: black, white, and *six* different grays. It makes a big difference to kitty.

The 16-bit solution

The minimum standard for professional digital audio is to use 16 bits, representing 65,536 possible different values for each sample. In terms of sound, that's a pressure change of about 0.00013 dB. Real audio circuits round up as well as down, so the worst error will occur when an analog signal falls precisely between two of those tiny slices: the digital value will be wrong by exactly half a slice, or less than 0.00007 dB.

Figure 6: Two-bit cat (upper left) has only black, white, and two grays. Three-bit cat (lower right) has four more grays, for more detail.

Trust me: an error that tiny doesn't matter in media production.

The error can get worse, however. Once you've digitized that signal, you'll probably want to do things to it: change the level, or equalize it, or do other mathematical processing. Each time you do, there's another chance for the result to fall between two sample levels. Professionals usually do their processing at 24 bits or higher, for a possible error of roughly 0.00000026 dB. (As far as I'm concerned, an error of a quarter-millionth of a dB is pretty accurate. But my digital audio workstation uses 32-bit precision for mixing . . . I can't print that in precise decibels, because my calculator doesn't handle logarithms that small.)

Bits as dynamic range

You can also look at bit depth another way. Each bit doubles the possible values for a sample. We know from the previous chapter that doubling a voltage means increasing it just about 6 dB. So each bit represents a 6 dB range between the lowest and highest level the system can handle. An 8-bit signal (common in early computers, and still used on the Internet) has a 48 dB range between its loudest sound and where the signal gets buried by ambiguous noise. This is similar to the range for AM radio or 16mm film.

A 16-bit signal has twice the range, or 96 dB (16 times 6 is 96). This is considerably better than FM radio, and close to the limits of human hearing. A 24-bit signal has 144 dB dynamic range, well beyond the limits of even the most golden-eared listener. Those extra bits provide a margin for calculation errors.

An Analog Myth:

"Analog audio is better than digital because digital is 'steppy': some voltages will fall between steps and get lost."

The logic is right, but the conclusion is wrong. While a 24-bit system has nearly 17 million possible voltage levels, the sound wave itself can have an infinite number of values. So, yes, some subtle variations will fall between possible digital levels and get lost: this is called a *quantizing error*. It doesn't happen in an analog system.

But analog systems have a random background noise that doesn't exist in digital. You can see, with an oscilloscope, how this noise can have the same effect as quantizing errors. Compare the smooth wave in Figure 7 with the quantized one in Figure 8.

I used a 7-bit digital signal, with 128 possible levels, to make the quantization error more obvious. Obviously, some detail is getting lost among the stair steps of the digital version. We know the original waveform falls *somewhere* between those steps, but for any given step we can't know whether the original was at the top, the bottom, or anywhere in between. (By the way, the steps are perfectly flat in the digital domain. Some of them look slanted in the figure because I photographed an analog oscilloscope.)

But remember, this particular digital signal is a pretty awful one: at 6 dB per bit, a 7-bit signal has only a 42 dB range between the loudest and the softest sound possible—less than an AM radio broadcast. It's unfair to compare this low-quality

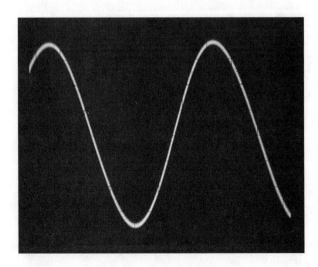

Figure 7: A smooth analog wave . . .

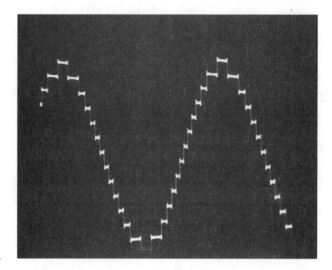

Figure 8: . . . and its 7-bit quantized version.

digital signal with what you could achieve with the finest analog system, so let's level the playing field.

An analog system's dynamic range is the distance between the loudest signal it can handle and the noise made by the system itself. If we raise the analog noise to −42 dB below the scope's maximum—matching the range of our 7-bit digital signal—it looks like Figure 9.

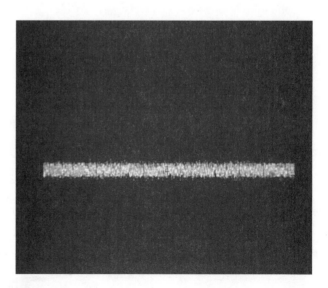

Figure 9: Analog noise at -42 dB, a quality equivalent to 7-bit digital audio

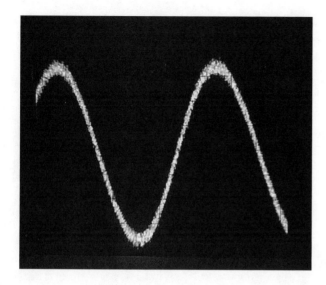

Figure 10: Analog signal with -42 dB noise

In analog systems, the noise mixes with the signal and appears to "ride on top of it," as in Figure 10.

This is a much broader scope trace than what we saw in Figure 7. It's ambiguous, because the analog noise obscures some of the wave's details. We know the original wave falls *somewhere* in that broad trace; but at any given moment we can't tell whether the original was at the top, the bottom, or anywhere in between.

Sound familiar? That's exactly the problem we had with the digital stair steps in Figure 8. Once you level the playing field—once you compare audio systems of identical quality—quantization errors aren't any more or less of a problem than analog noise.

By the way, the audio output of a complete digital circuit will never have the kind of steps as in our scope photo. A filter in the circuit smoothes the signal from the midpoint of one step to the midpoint of the next.

Dither: making the most of those bits

The analog myth-mongers are right about one thing: even with the best digital systems, you'll eventually encounter signal details at the tiny level represented by only one bit. The quantization error is small—it takes trained ears and excellent monitors to hear it in a 16-bit system—but it can be ugly. That's because it creates a distortion that follows the signal but isn't harmonically related.

The solution is to add the same stuff that causes so much trouble in analog circuits: noise. Digital designers add a tiny amount of analog noise, at a level about one-third what a single bit represents. When this random noise has a positive voltage, it pushes the signal details to where the comparator sees it as a 1. When it's negative, it pulls the details down to 0. Since this happens totally randomly, it adds distortion across the entire band . . . not following the desired signal.

This process—called *dithering*—not only reduces distortion at low levels; it even makes it possible to hear some details that are smaller than the lowest possible value! The ear is good at picking up specific sounds even when they're obscured by random noise, something you've probably noticed if you've ever tried to follow a conversation at a noisy cocktail party.

It's easy to understand dither with a visual analogy. Hold your hand in front of this page (as in Figure 11), and some of the words are obscured . . . just as if they'd fallen below the lowest level of a digital signal and were zeroed out.

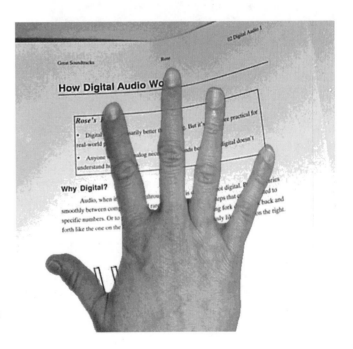

Figure 11: A steady hand obscures some of the page . . .

Now start waving your fingers rapidly side-to-side (Figure 12). The fingers don't go away—they still cover as much of the page at any one time—but your mind can pick the meaningful words out from the randomly obscuring fingers.

Dither is best used when going from a high-resolution medium to a lower one. Well-designed professional systems apply it during the initial quantization, and on the output of high-bitrate processes. Most desktop video editors never reach this kind of precision, and dither isn't available. Either way, you don't have to make decisions about its use.

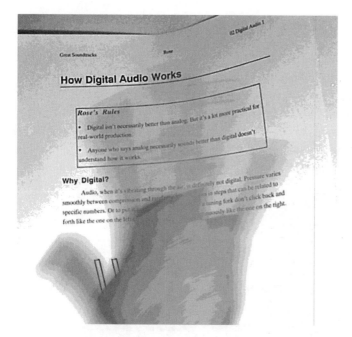

Figure 12: . . . but when the hand moves rapidly, you can "see behind it."

But if a program gives you the option of dither when converting 16-bit files to 8 bits for older multimedia systems, turn it on. As 20- and 24-bit digital audio equipment becomes more common in the video studio, you'll want to use dithering every time you move to a lower bit depth.

> ➤ Avoid low bit depths. The 12-bit recording supported by some digital video equipment *will* be noisy.
> ➤ You can't improve a low-bit signal by converting it to a higher depth, because the damage is already done. But changing to a higher bit depth will keep it from getting worse in subsequent processing.

Track 5 of this book's CD lets you hear the effect of different bit depths. The same recording was truncated to 7 bits, 8 bits, and 12 bits. It was then re-encoded at 16 bits so it could be included on a standard CD, but this process doesn't affect the damage done by the lower bit depths.

Sample Rate

Bit rate is only half the equation for digital audio. Since audio only exists as changes of pressure or voltage *over time*, you have to measure it repeatedly if you want to recreate the sound. The more often you measure, the more accurately you'll be able to reproduce the sound.

We'll start with another scope photo. In Figure 13, I've added eight vertical lines spaced evenly apart. The scope's electron beam sweeps horizontally across its face at a controlled speed, so each vertical line marks a different time in its sweep. For simplicity, we'll say the vertical lines are one millisecond apart.

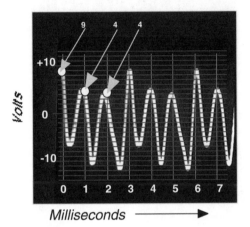

Figure 13: Sampling over time, at a low sample rate

At the start of this section of sound, the signal is nine volts. A millisecond later, it's four volts. And a millisecond after that, it's four volts again. These are the first three samples, and what a digital system would store at this sample rate. Since the samples are one millisecond apart, this system has a sample rate of a thousand times per second (usually written as 1 kHz s/r).

On playback, the system averages these values to produce an output like the gray line in Figure 14. This output doesn't look very much like the input, and it

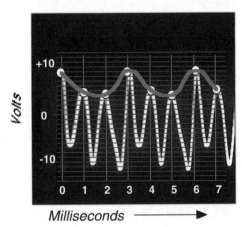

Figure 14: Badly recreated signal from a very low sample rate

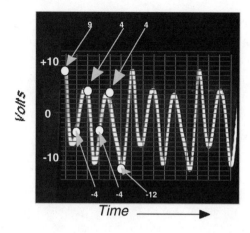

Figure 15: Doubling the sample rate gives us more data.

wouldn't sound like it either. Obviously this is a bad recording (1 kHz s/r is a ridiculously low rate for digital audio).

But suppose we check the voltage *twice* each millisecond. This raises the sample rate to 2 kHz, doubling the amount of data generated (Figure 15).

When we average these samples, we get a somewhat more accurate result (Figure 16). Still not perfect, but better.

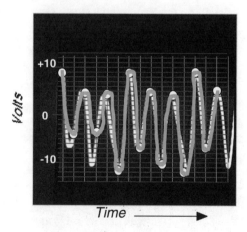

Figure 16: More samples give us a more faithful picture.

As you add more samples, you get a better representation of the sound. A typical multimedia computer system checks slightly more than 22 samples each millisecond, or a sample rate of 22.050 kHz. Compact discs double that, for a sample rate of 44.1 kHz. Professional digital broadcast formats operate at 48 kHz s/r, and DVD doubles that to 96 kHz. Many sound engineers doubt that a 96 kHz sample rate is necessary (except as marketing hype), but there's a definite relationship between sample rate and sound quality.

The Nyquist limit and aliasing

In the 1920s Harry Nyquist, an engineer at Bell Labs, proved mathematically that the highest frequency you can faithfully reproduce has to be less than one-half the sample rate. Since U.S. analog FM and TV don't carry audio higher than 15 kHz (to protect other parts of the broadcast signal), the Nyquist theorem suggests a broadcaster doesn't need a sample rate of more than 30 kHz. In fact, a lot of what you hear on the air has been sampled at 32 kHz.

Unfortunately, all Nyquist guarantees is that sounds *below* this limit will be reproduced accurately. A broadcaster's microphone could easily pick up a sound at 17 kHz. Above the Nyquist limit, digital recording does very strange things: it combines the signal with the sample frequency, implying additional signals that are totally unrelated to any harmonics. A simple sine wave will have two additional *aliases*—other waves that could fit the same data. A complex musical signal, with lots of harmonics, may have thousands of aliases. The playback system turns them all back into analog audio, creating a combination of squeaks and whistles accompanying the high frequencies. It isn't pretty, as you can hear from the example on track 6 of this book's CD.

The only solution is to use an *aliasing filter:* an equalizer that absolutely blocks any frequency higher than half the sample rate and doesn't affect any frequency below it. With no frequencies above the Nyquist limit, there can't be any aliases. The only problem is that a perfect filter like this can't exist.

You can't design a filter with infinite cutoff at one frequency and absolutely no effect on frequencies below it. Any real-world hi-cut filter will have two characteristics:

- A slope between what passes through and what's blocked. As the frequency rises, the volume is slowly turned down . . . not instantly turned off.

- Some degradation to signals below but close to the cutoff frequency. Even though those lower-frequency signals are passed, they get distorted.

Early digital devices were designed with a safety margin—usually around 10% of the sample rate—to allow for that first characteristic. The first compact disc recorders started their filters sloping slightly below 20 kHz, so they could achieve a good cutoff by the time they reached half the 44.1 kHz sample rate. Many computer sound cards are still designed the same way.

But there's no way to compensate for the second characteristic. The sharper a filter gets, the more it affects sounds below its nominal cutoff frequency. And affordable analog filter components lose their calibration as they get older, further compounding the problem. Depending on what compromises the designer made, early digital devices suffered from high-frequency distortion, aliasing, or both. They earned a reputation for having less-than-ideal sound.

Oversampling

Modern professional equipment solves this problem by using an initial sampling frequency many times higher than the nominal sample rate, as much as two million samples a second or more. This raises the Nyquist limit so that very gentle superhigh frequency filters can be used, which have no effect on desired audio. The high sample rate signal is then filtered using digital techniques, which are more accurate than analog ones, and down-converted to the desired rate.

Oversampling presents other advantages as well, in that digital artifacts can be spread across a much wider band and not affect the audio signal as much. But it's also more expensive to design and build circuits that use it, because the high data rates require very precise timing. So multimedia equipment seldom takes advantage of the technique.

If you're concerned with getting the best quality audio from analog sources in a desktop video-editing system, avoid the built-in inputs. Instead, use a professional external analog-to-digital converter with oversampling. Or have a sound studio do the conversions and provide you with data on CD-ROM or removable hard drive.

Working with sample rates

Broadcast digital videotape uses a sample rate of 48 kHz, so if you're going to be broadcasting your project digitally, it may make sense to keep your equipment at that setting. But a lot of projects are intended for analog videotape, CD-ROM, or Internet delivery; or will be broadcast in analog format from a digital tape. If that's the case, you should weigh the costs of a high sample rate against its advantages.

- Samples have to be processed. A high sample rate means the CPU will take longer to do data-intensive tasks such as non-real-time effects. Since many systems give priority to audio processing (jumpy sound is a lot more distressing than an occasional skipped video frame), it diverts resources that could be used to improve the video.

- Samples have to be stored. 48 kHz, 16-bit stereo eats more than 11 megabytes of storage space per minute. While hard drive space isn't very expensive, CD-ROM real estate can be.

- Samples have to be transmitted. Data bandwidth is a precious commodity, particularly on the Internet. While MPEG compression techniques (discussed below) can help, they don't work as well on signals with very high bitrates.

The best way to choose a sample rate is to consider the final audience. You've probably already used this book's CD and some of the tests in Chapter 1 to discover that your monitoring system isn't really as wide-range as the manufacturer may have claimed. (If you're over 30, you probably discovered that your ears aren't very wide-range either.) Unless you're sure of a high-quality listening environment, it's unlikely that your audience will ever be in the presence of anything above 17 kHz.

Analog broadcast television cuts off at 15 kHz: this is a limitation of the transmission medium, and even the best home-theater systems can't get around it. Most multimedia and kiosk systems aren't very accurate above 12 kHz, and presentations that are mostly spoken word don't have much going on above 10 kHz.

Once you've decided on the highest frequency your project will need to support, double it (to allow for the Nyquist limit), add a safety margin, and choose the closest sample rate. For analog broadcast, that's 32 kHz s/r. For multimedia, it can be as low as 22 kHz.

Most modern software does a good job of sample rate conversion. Even if your final output has to be at 48 kHz s/r for digital video, it can be worth the time and storage space advantages of working at a lower sample rate and not converting until after you've mixed.

➤ The high-frequency loss of a lower sample rate is not cumulative and doesn't get worse when you digitally dub or mix a track.

➤ Once a sound has been sampled at one rate, there's almost never any benefit to converting it to a higher rate except for transfer compatibility.

There is one exception to that second rule. *Harmonic enhancers* are processors that change the timbre of a sound, brightening it by creating artificial harmonics at frequencies an octave higher than the original recording. A very low sample rate recording can often be subjectively improved by converting it to a higher rate and then using an enhancer. But bear in mind that the equalizers provided with audio- and video-editing software are not enhancers and won't improve low-rate recordings.

Audio Data Reduction

If the goal is simply to reduce storage space or Internet bandwidth, there are better strategies than lowering the sample rate or bit depth. Audio data reduction or compression relies on statistical and psychoacoustic principles to squeeze a lot of sound into the smallest number of bits. While they do compromise the sound quality—and are often referred to as *lossy compression* by audio engineers—they don't damage it anywhere near the amount that an equivalent sample rate or depth reduction would. In fact, these techniques are considered so benign that they're part of the specification for digital television, multitrack digital film sound, and DVD.

> ➤ As good as data reduction techniques get, they're not perfect. And subsequent mixing, editing, and rereduction make the sound a lot worse. So if you're using them, be sure to keep an uncompressed version on a backup tape or disk.

Standard redundancy compression methods like PKZIP and Stuffit aren't much good for audio. They rely on finding repeating patterns in the data, and normal audio is just too random—in a numeric sense—to have these patterns. The best they can do with a typical track is only a few percent reduction.

Delta Encoding

Fortunately, most sounds do have one predictable element: from one sample to the next, the incremental change isn't very great. Figure 17 shows how this works, using a 16-bit recording of a piano.

From one extreme of this wave to the other, there's a difference of about 47,500 digital values. It would take a full 16-bit word to represent it accurately. But from one sample to the next, the biggest difference is never more than about 5,000

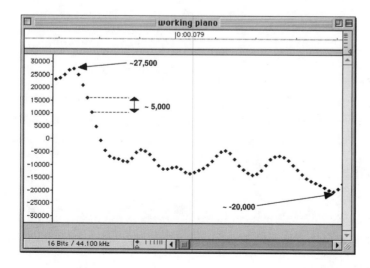

Figure 17: Individual sample data in a 16-bit recording of a piano

digital values. We need just 13 bits to record the jump from a single sample to the one after it.

This *delta encoding* is the basis of QuickTime IMA, one of the first popular multimedia compression methods and still found on many editing systems. It can cut files down to a quarter of their original size without seriously affecting the audio quality.

Delta coding has the advantage of easy math, can be played back on virtually any CPU, and doesn't add much distortion to most well-recorded speech or music. But it can't cope with very sudden changes: beeps, clicks, and sharp sound effects can be surrounded by noise. Track 7 of this book's CD shows examples of IMA encoded signals.

Perceptual Encoding and Masking

Psychoacoustic researchers have known for most of the past century that our ears aren't very good at the extremes of the audio band. We evolved with our most sensitive hearing in the midrange, probably because that's where we can best hear predators or the warnings of fellow tribe members. Figure 18 shows a typical threshold of hearing curve. Sounds that are louder than the curve at a particular frequency will be heard; those softer than the curve at their frequency—or within the hatched area—disappear for most listeners.

There are actually many threshold of hearing curves, because the relative sensitivity to different frequencies will change based on how loud a sound is. But in almost every case, your ears will be the most sensitive within the speech range of around 350 to 3,500 Hz. Most people can hear more than 16 bits' worth of detail at the top of that range.

A relatively soft sound at 1 kHz (the gray bar) is perfectly audible because it falls above the curve. But at other frequencies, the threshold rises, and equally soft

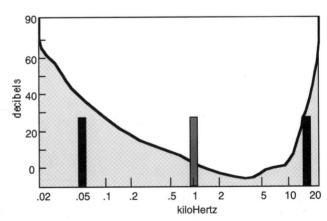

Figure 18: The threshold of hearing changes with frequency

sounds at 500 Hz and 15 kHz (the black bars) won't be heard by most listeners. At 50 Hz, many people hear only about six bits' worth of detail. At 18 kHz, two bits may be sufficient.

But Figure 18 shows a static threshold with sounds superimposed on it. Researchers have discovered that real-world thresholds are constantly shifting, based on what you're listening to at the time. A loud sound raises the threshold around it, as shown in Figure 19. The signal at 1 kHz (gray bar) stops you from hearing the slightly softer signals at 700 Hz and 1.5 kHz (black bars). The figure is slightly exaggerated to highlight the effect, but some degree of frequency masking exists in every listener depending on their individual hearing and how carefully they've trained their ears. As a practical example, consider the case of an orchestra playing a full chord: one instrument may be slightly out of tune, but it's unlikely that anyone other than the conductor (and a few music critics) will notice.

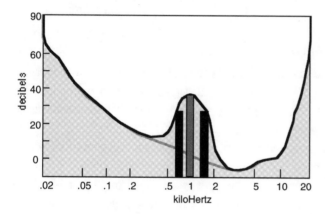

Figure 19: Louder sounds raise the threshold around them.

Layer 3

It takes sophisticated processing to predict how various threshold shifts will mask specific sounds. But once that's done, there's no reason you can't remove the sounds that are being hidden. One of the most popular algorithms was established by the International Standards Organization's Moving Pictures Expert Group in 1992. Its most complex implementation, ISO/MPEG Layer 3, uses 576 separate frequency bands to analyze the sound. Stereo tracks are further processed to find the details that are identical on both channels and encode them only once. The resulting sound stream not only uses fewer bits because masked or redundant sounds are eliminated; it's also more predictable, and redundancy coding can be used on it.

Layer 3 is scalable depending on how much detail you're willing to sacrifice. It's used in broadcasting and postproduction to carry high-quality audio in real time over ISDN, with data that's about 12% of its original size. But it's found the biggest application on the Internet, where it is known as the MP3 format, which became popular in the late 1990s. Well-encoded MP3 files can keep most musical values at 4% of their original size; voice tracks remain intelligible when as small as 0.5% of the original. Track 8 of this book's CD demonstrates different degrees of MP3 encoding, translated back to 16-bit noncompressed so you can play it on a standard system.

A less complex cousin, Layer 2, uses fewer bands and masks fewer details. It became popular because it could be implemented on simpler processors, and it is still preferred for high-bandwidth applications like satellites and hard-disk audio storage systems.

It takes the ear a few milliseconds to recover from loud sounds, so threshold shifts continue even after the masking sound has ended. Layer 3 takes some advantage of this as a side effect of its very sharp filters. The Advanced Audio Coding (AAC) algorithm exploits this further and even eliminates sounds that occur slightly *before* the masking signal. AAC streams can be some 30% smaller than Layer 3.

Other encoding standards

MPEG and AAC are open standards, supported by many manufacturers. Macromedia Shockwave and Microsoft ASF also use the MPEG Layer 3 algorithm, with some additional nonaudio data functions. You may also encounter older open standards such as mu-law encoding (the Internet .au format), developed for telephone calls. And there are proprietary schemes promoted by companies, including Dolby and APT, which may find their way into broadcast or Internet standards.

Perceptual encoding is probably the most volatile field in all of professional audio. The demands of quality, data bandwidth, and copyright protection are spurring institutional and private developers to try new schemes all the time. As a practical matter:

➤ Don't just assume that the encoding you use will be compatible with your viewers or clients. If you're not sure, do a test or revert to the most basic standards.

➤ If you want the smallest files or the fastest data transfers with the least effect on audio quality, check the World Wide Web. A new standard may have evolved while you were reading these page.

Audio on a Wire

At some time in the near future, audio and video content may exist only as non-real-time files. You'll pull a disk or chip out of a camera, stick it into an editor, and send the finished project to your client via e-mail.

But in the meantime we have to move audio around the studio and editing suite, as analog voltages or digital serial data streams over a copper wire. The trick is to do this without losing any signal quality.

Analog Wiring

When the phone company made up the rules for audio wiring, about a century ago, most devices' inputs were powered by the audio signal itself. Audio levels were measured in terms of their power, as decibels related to a standard wattage. Transferring this power efficiently meant you had to pay attention both to voltage and impedance, a measure of how a device draws current. This practice lasted through most of the century: until the mid-1970s, TV stations and large recording studios were wired using methods developed in the days of hand-cranked phones.

Modern analog audio equipment doesn't care very much about power transfer. Circuits use just a tiny amount of current from the input signal, and react to its voltage instead. This simplifies things a lot and lets you do things like splitting a signal to two or more different devices easily. If you pay attention to the basic voltage range, connecting equipment is about as complicated as hooking up Christmas tree lights.

However, current and impedance still matter for equipment that's powered by the audio signal itself. Speakers and headphones should be somewhat matched to the output they're connected to. You can often connect two speakers to a single amplifier output, but if you try to use more than two you run the risk of distorting the sound (and even damaging the output).

Microphones are a special case. While most mic inputs are voltage-based, the microphones produce so little power that large impedance mismatches can cause problems.

Setting the Standard

In 1940, the phone company and radio networks agreed on standard levels for long-distance broadcast and telephone lines: zero decibels would match 1/1000 watt (one milliwatt); any audio power from the tiniest microphone signal to the biggest amplifier output could be described as a ratio in dBm (decibels referred to that milliwatt). Wattage is a function of voltage and impedance, but telephone lines always had 600 ohms impedance, so 0 dBm on a phone line always equaled .775 volts. Broadcasters pushed a little more signal through their standard lines, eventually setting a standard of +4 dBm or 1.228 volts across 600 ohms.

➤ *Professional sound equipment is often rated "+4 dBm line level" and operates at a nominal signal level of roughly 1.25 volts.* Of course, +4 dBm can equal that voltage only at 600 ohms. Engineers realized the folly of using milliwatts to measure voltage, so two other standards evolved. In the United States, the National Association of Broadcasters took just the voltage part of the phone company standard and called it 0 dBu—the "u" stands for "unterminated," an open circuit with no impedance.

➤ *Modern pro gear may be specified as "+4 dBu" instead of "+4 dBm."* Unless you're dealing with transformers or very long transmission lines—both of which almost never appear in a modern video studio—the two units are equivalent.

➤ *Hi-fi, prosumer, and computer multimedia equipment is often rated "−10 dBV line level" and operates at a nominal signal level of roughly 0.3 volts.*

In Europe, the IEC said exactly 1 volt would be a more rational reference: they called it 0 dBV. It turned out that tubed hi-fi equipment worked best with an input voltage around 10 dB below this reference, or 0.316 volts. This is also sometimes called the IHF standard because it was adopted by the Institute of High Fidelity.

So we have two different standards—three if you have to consider impedance—to describe the nominal input voltage of a circuit. Since they're all based on the same rules of physics and math, they're easily related (Table 1).

TABLE 1: Voltage compared to dBV and dBu		
Level in dBV	Voltage	Level in dBu (or dBm across 600 ohms)
+6	2.0	+8.2
+4	1.6	+6.2
+1.78	1.228	+4 (Pro standard)
+0	1	+2.2
−2.2	0.775	0
−6	0.5	−3.8
−8.2	0.388	−6
−10 (Consumer standard)	0.316	−7.8
−20	0.1	−17.8

Nominal levels

Line levels are equivalent to "zero level," where the equipment's volume unit (VU) meter (Figure 1) reads zero near the top of its scale. In a broadcast station or magnetic recorder, zero level relates to a precise amount of transmitter modulation or magnetism on the tape. In other equipment, it's the operating voltage that results in the best compromise between noise and distortion.

Of course, analog audio is a constantly changing voltage, not a constant tone at a particular level. The dynamic range of any piece of equipment may extend from as much as 12 dB above the nominal zero to around 60 dB below it. Calling something "+4 dBu" or "−10 dBV" is just a convenient way to describe the normal operating voltage, so you can connect devices together with some hope of good sound.

Figure 1: A typical VU meter showing zero level

Level and dynamic range

Figure 1 might look like the equipment is set precisely to a standard, but inside any piece of gear this level is completely arbitrary.

Analog equipment has a continuum between the lowest levels, where signals have too much noise, to the highest levels, where there's too much distortion. Since "too much" is a completely subjective term, and there's no reason you can't record an analog signal louder than zero, you can redefine the standard level depending on how much noise or distortion you want to tolerate. Figure 2 shows how this could work: a rock music studio might record at a higher level, moving the signal farther away from the noise floor, because distortion is already part of the sound of many rock instruments. On the other hand, a broadcast studio may be more sensitive to distortion, and it may set its nominal level slightly lower. These decisions have to do with how a signal is handled internally, not how it connects to the outside world.

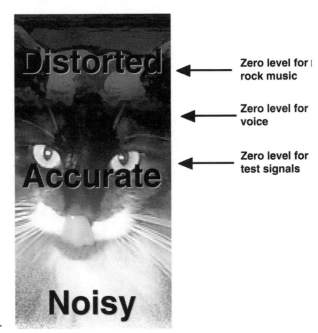

Zero level for rock music

Zero level for voice

Zero level for test signals

Figure 2: Zero can be an arbitrary level.

Analog equipment manufacturers often make similar choices, specifying a higher level if they want to brag about low noise, or a lower one so they can brag about low distortion.

> ➤ +4 dBu and −10 dBV are just voltages. There's no physical reason why one should sound any better than the other.
>
> ➤ However, higher-quality equipment is usually designed for the higher voltage standard. That's a marketing decision, not physics.

Cross-connecting −10 dBV and +4 dBu equipment

If you plug the output of a consumer-level mixer into a professional recorder, you may get a usable signal. As Table 1 indicates, the mixer's idea of zero is only about 12 dB lower than the recorder's. But since the signal will be that much closer to the recorder's noise floor, the tape will be about 12 dB (or four times) noisier. The best solution is to put a small amplifier in between the units, converting the mixer's −10 dBV output to +4 dBu.

If you plug the output of a professional-level mixer into a consumer recorder, you'll probably hear very bad distortion. Since this distortion occurs in the input stages of the recorder, lowering its volume control won't help. You need a network of resistors between the two units to lower the voltage.

Equipment with transformers in their output often need impedance matching. Connecting older equipment—or newer devices that use vacuum tubes—to modern studio gear may require a 680 ohm resistor across the output to prevent high-frequency problems.

Details about this kind of connection appear in Chapters 7 and 9.

Noise on the Line

While the idea of impedance matching has mostly been abandoned, another telephone company idea is still very much with us. Phone calls have to travel over hundreds or thousands of miles of low-quality wire, often near power lines and other interference sources, without picking up too much noise. The technique phone companies developed to cope with this, balanced wiring, is used today by professional broadcast and sound studios for the same reason.

If your editing setup is plagued by noise and low-frequency hum, chances are you don't have balanced wiring. Here's what's really happening inside your equipment:

People hum when they don't know the words. Circuits hum when they're not sure what silence should sound like. The sensitive circuits in audio amplifiers and processors need a reference they can be sure is zero volts. They compare the input signal to this reference, amplify and process as necessary, and generate an output signal that's also compared to the reference. Designers designate one point within a piece of equipment, usually connected to an external ground screw or the grounding pin of the power plug, and call it "ground": all voltages within the equipment are referenced to it.

That's fine for a single piece of equipment, but problems arise when you try to connect equipment together. Both pieces have to agree on a reference zero, but if you use a wire to connect one reference point to the other, it can act as an antenna, picking up stray electric fields being radiated by all the other wires in the vicinity. Since most of the wiring in a building is carrying high-current AC to wall outlets and lights, these fields tend to be at the power-line frequency of 50 Hz or 60 Hz. This interference mixes with the reference and is amplified along with the signal.

Also, the signal wire itself acts as an antenna to pick up interference. You can eliminate some of this by wrapping a shield around the signal wire, usually as a copper braid or metal foil. The shield is connected to ground and shorts out the interference before it can reach the signal wire. But now there are two ground paths—one through the shield, and one through the external ground connections or power plugs—forming an even more efficient loop antenna for the power-line interference. Figure 3 shows how this can happen. These ground "loops" are difficult to predict, since you don't know the internal details of all your equipment, and can appear even in very simple installations. In a practical video studio, the situation is apt to be far worse: between the ground connections of audio and video wiring, Ethernet, RS-232 and RS-422 control, MIDI, or even cable television, there can be many ground loops.

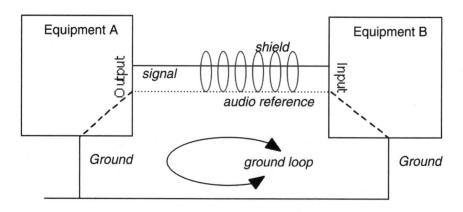

Figure 3: A ground loop

Balanced wiring

Professional equipment solves this problem by using two closely spaced conductors twisted together. The audio is balanced equally between these wires, flowing in a positive direction on one wire while in a negative direction on the other. Equipment looks at the voltage difference between them and never references ground at all. There might still be an antenna created between the cable's shield and ground, but since it isn't part of the audio path, nobody cares. Figure 4 shows the basic setup.

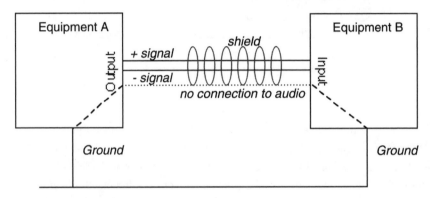

Figure 4: Balanced wiring eliminates ground loops.

The two conductors in a balanced wiring scheme are often labeled + and − for convenience, but they're not strictly positive and negative. Analog audio is an alternating current, with electrons flowing back and forth on the same wire depending on the original air pressure. Sometimes the current flow is positive on one wire; sometimes it's negative. Depending on the circuit design, audio current may also flow to ground . . . but this ground connection is ignored by the next device's input.

Balanced wires have another advantage in their ability to reject noise that isn't coming from a ground loop. The two wires are twisted closely together in a single cable, so any interference radiated into the cable will be transmitted to both wires. Since subsequent circuits look for differences between the wires, the noise is ignored.

Figure 5 shows this happening in a balanced circuit. In Figure 5a, the top wire carries one volt positive while the bottom one carries one volt negative. The difference between them is the audio signal of two volts. But in Figure 5b, one volt of noise is picked up by the cable. The top wire gets an additional volt and now carries two volts positive. The bottom wire also gets an additional volt, which adds to its negative signal for a total of zero volts. The difference between the wires is still exactly two volts.

Of course, both the signal and the noise are constantly switching polarity depending on the frequencies involved, but the effect remains the same: since noise is added equally to both legs of a balanced circuit, it cancels itself out.

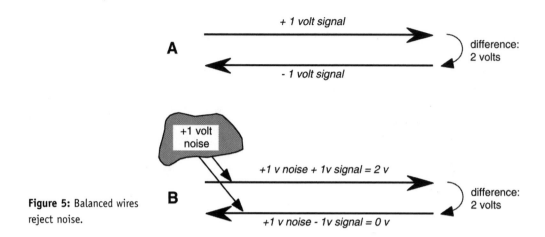

Figure 5: Balanced wires reject noise.

There are many different ways to build a balanced input or output circuit, and some are more successful than others at rejecting noise. But balancing will always add to cost and complexity, so it's often omitted in prosumer or music-industry audio equipment. This equipment is called *unbalanced*, or occasionally *single-ended*.

> ➤ In a simple studio setup, with only a few pieces of equipment and short cable lengths, noise pick-up may be so low that balanced wiring isn't necessary for line-level signals.
>
> ➤ If you do hear ground loops in a simple unbalanced setup, the easiest cure might be to break the loop. See Chapter 9.
>
> ➤ Microphone signals are much weaker than line level, and more prone to interference. Balanced wiring is almost always necessary for microphones.

You can't tell a wire by its connector

Balanced wiring is sometimes mistakenly called "XLR wiring" because it often uses three-pin connectors matching the Cannon XLR standard (Figure 6). It's dangerous to assume that an XLR plug or jack is balanced. Although most manufacturers reserve these connectors for balanced circuits, there are some exceptions. Check the spec sheet to be sure.

You can also get into trouble assuming that other kinds of connectors aren't balanced. Some manufacturers save money and space by putting balanced signals on three-conductor phone jacks. From the front panel, these jacks look identical to unbalanced two-conductor ones. But if you connect a three-conductor phone plug—also

Figure 6: XLR-style male connector

known as "tip-ring-sleeve" (TRS), and also used for stereo headphones (Figure 7)—
you can access the balanced circuit. Again, check the specs.

The worst thing you can do is split a single balanced phone-jack output by using a stereo Y cable and
send it to a stereo device. You'll hear a signal on each end of the Y, but the two signals will be of opposite polarity. If you then listen in mono, they'll cancel each other and the audio will disappear!

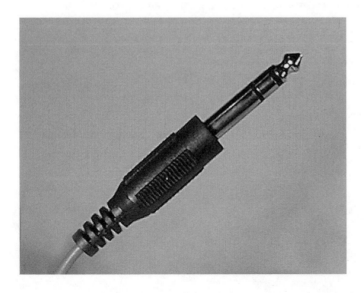

Figure 7: Three-conductor phone plug,
sometimes used for balanced signals

Cross-connecting balanced and unbalanced wiring

You can directly connect a balanced circuit to an unbalanced input or output without damaging the signal, but the entire connecting cable becomes unbalanced, and you lose its noise immunity. (If the wires are short or in a benign environment, this may be perfectly acceptable.)

To make this cross-connection work, you have to make sure that both devices see the signal path they've been designed for. The best way to do this depends on how the balanced circuit was designed. Tables 2 and 3 are intended just as a starting point for systems using modern video equipment and might not always yield the best noise performance. There are tips for debugging these connections in Chapter 9.

TABLE 2: Directly connecting unbalanced sources to balanced inputs			
Unbalanced Output	Balanced Input		
	Conductor	XLR	Phone
Signal	+	Pin 2	Tip
Ground	−	Pin 3	Ring
(no connection	Shield	Pin 1	Sleeve*

*Some balanced phone-plug inputs are designed so that you can plug an unbalanced two-conductor plug directly into them.

TABLE 3: Directly connecting balanced sources to unbalanced inputs			
Balanced Output			Unbalanced Input
XLR	Phone	Conductor	
Pin 2	Tip	+	Signal
Pin 3	Ring	−	(no connection)
Pin 1	Sleeve	Shield	Shield

The best way to hook balanced and unbalanced equipment together is not to attempt a direct connection, but to use a separate balancing transformer or electronic interface at the unbalanced end. Then, balanced wiring—with its inherent noise immunity—can be used. It can also provide a necessary voltage conversion as well, since unbalanced devices are usually designed for −10 dBV and balanced ones are usually +4 dBu.

Prosumer digital cameras often have unbalanced microphone inputs. Although unbalanced mic cables can be used for one or two feet, realistic distances between subject and camera are too long for this kind of wiring. A transformer adapter, described in Chapter 6, will let you use balanced connections. They're almost always necessary to get good sound with these cameras.

Fancy Wiring?

A lot has been written in audiophile magazines about the need for special "oxygen free" cables, sometimes with patented braided construction or solid-gold connectors. These allegedly add a unique audio transparency that golden-eared types can appreciate. They certainly add a unique price tag to the installation.

As of this writing, nobody has been able to show me scientific evidence that these cables make any measurable difference to the sound, compared to more reasonably priced wire with similar electrical specifications. There isn't even a body of repeatable studies showing audible differences that can't be measured.

You're welcome to spend money on the things. Personally, I'd rather invest in better equipment or more comprehensive music and effects libraries.

Digital Wiring

Since digital audio cables carry only ones and zeros, they're unlikely to be affected by noise and ground loops. However, digital audio uses very fast signals: the individual bits are sent serially, with both channels of a stereo pair interleaved in the same data stream. Clock rates for a 48 kHz s/r signal can be above 6 *mega*Hertz!

At these speeds, the wire itself and how a signal is reflected by connected devices become significant:

> ➤ Always use a cable matched to the impedance of the digital audio signal.
> ➤ Make sure cables are properly terminated.

Impedance matching is simply a matter of using cables rated for the particular kind of digital signal, rather than just grabbing something with the right kinds of connectors. Termination occurs automatically in digital equipment, but can be ruined if you try to route a digital signal using analog wiring techniques. Use patchbays, switchers, and splitters designed for the signal format.

Digital Audio Wiring Standards

Digital audio wiring almost always follows one of two standards. The data formats of these standards are virtually identical, with minor changes in such things as how it marks pre-emphasis (now obsolete), copy protection (ignored in professional equipment), or extra digital audio bits. There is absolutely no audio quality difference between them.

Standard digital audio formats carry both channels of a stereo pair as one data stream. Signals travel in one direction—the output of one device to the input of another—rather than as handshaked bidirectional computer data.

Audio levels are implicit in the connection—signals are referenced to zero decibels full-scale (dBfs), where every bit is turned on—rather than depending on particular voltages.

AES/EBU

This standard was set by the international Audio Engineering Society and the European Broadcast Union and is found on virtually all professional digital equipment. It uses 5-volt balanced signals with 110-ohm impedance, almost always terminating in XLR connectors. Although its cables often look like standard microphone extensions, they don't work the same way. Running AES/EBU audio over an analog cable can result in problems.

s/pdif

This standard was invented by consumer audio manufacturers (Sony/Philips Digital Interface Format) and adopted by electronic manufacturers' associations in Europe and Japan. It puts a half-volt signal on 75-ohm coaxial cable, terminating in either phono or BNC video connectors. Standard analog video cables are perfectly acceptable for s/pdif.

You may come across equipment that uses AES/EBU-formatted data on 75-ohm jacks, though you probably won't notice: in most applications (other than 20- or 24-bit audio) and with most equipment, the two bit streams are interchangeable.

Toslink

This optical standard is often found on consumer equipment. It puts similar-format data on a plastic fiber as visible light from an LED.

Firewire

This electrical standard, also known as IEEE Standard 1394, was designed to let computers transfer large amounts of data quickly. It was adopted by digital video camera manufacturers to send audio and video simultaneously to an editing system, but can also be used for AES/EBU-format audio transfers.

However, Firewire is much more complicated and expensive than is needed for simple audio cabling. As of this writing, it's supported by only a few isolated audio-only devices.

Multitrack formats

Small multitrack digital recorders often use proprietary data formats. Since two of these recorders have become de facto standards—the Alesis ADAT in music studios, and the Tascam DA-88 in film and video—you may have to deal with their connections. The safest thing to do is buy jumper cables from the equipment manufacturers, or adapters to convert their signals to standard AES/EBU or s/pdif.

Cross-Connecting Digital Formats

The most common cross-connection is between s/pdif and AES/EBU. Since the impedances, balancing, and voltages are different, you can't plug one into another with a simple audio adapter. Simple in-line transformer adapters, designed for digital audio, are available from pro audio and video dealers. Standard analog XLR-to-phono adapters from local electronics stores don't contain these transformers and may damage the equipment.

Most equipment is tolerant of the tiny data differences between professional and consumer digital audio streams. Once you get the wiring right, the signal should follow. However, some gear is very picky about what it sees in the bit stream. A transformer that works well in one situation might not work in another.

Other signal formats require powered adapters to sort and condition the data before it can be cross-connected.

Digital Audio Errors

If you don't treat digital audio properly, it may jump up and bite you. Some of the ways include

- Data errors, resulting in dropouts or loud, sporadic popping. Check the cables. Chances are an AES/EBU signal is running through a microphone cord, or an s/pdif signal through an analog phono cable.

- Timing errors, heard as periodic clicking in the sound or sometimes no sound at all. This can happen when a digital input isn't in sync with a device's internal clock, and usually can be fixed by changing the equipment's settings. Sound studios often distribute a separate digital audio sync signal, called Word Clock, to all their equipment. Every audio signal is then aligned to this clock.

- Many digital video recorders require that digital audio timing is related to the video frame rate. In most cases this means your key audio components will also have to accept blackburst, and you'll have to give them the same signal that locks your video equipment.

A third kind of digital audio error, jitter, can cause subtle problems with stereo imaging and compatibility. But almost all modern equipment treats the incoming signal to eliminate this problem.

INTRODUCTION TO SECTION II

When I was a kid, some friends and I decided to build a playhouse in one of our backyards. Since my father was an accomplished carpenter and had a successful business building new homes, I figured we'd have an easy time obtaining the necessary materials.

Dad asked what we'd need.

"Well, a couple of pieces of plywood and some two-by-fours, and maybe some shingles for the roof. Oh, and red paint. What do you think, Dad?"

"I think you forgot the paper and tape."

I wasn't figuring on any fancy flooring that would require rosin paper, fiber house-wrap hadn't been invented, and I *knew* nails were more appropriate than duct tape for holding buildings together. Then he handed me a tape measure and some graph paper.

"Plan first. Measure the area, and make scale drawings. Do up a bill of materials. Until you know what you're trying to accomplish, the details are just guesswork."

This from a guy who could stroll into a lumber yard, point at materials seemingly at random, and then throw together a complex bookcase or cabinet from a sketch on the back of a napkin.

* * *

Years later I realized that Dad really did work from elaborate plans, but that they were in his head. All the napkin sketch provided was a reminder.

After a while, you'll be able to produce video tracks the same way. Until then, rely on the next two chapters. Chapter 4 describes the various elements that can be used to make an effective soundtrack, and why they're appropriate—there are probably some options you haven't thought of. Chapter 5 tells you how much it'll cost in time and cash, and what to look for when scouting locations.

Planning for Sound

The Need for Sound

Many videographers approach their projects as a chance to shoot interesting pictures and string them together in an effective way. Sound is secondary: after all, you weren't hired to create an *audio* cassette.

But communication isn't necessarily a visual phenomenon. Psychologists estimate that more than two-thirds of everything a person knows was experienced through their ears. The other four senses contribute less than 30%. Except for a few rare cases like some technical animations, no video can be effective unless picture and track work together. Neither is secondary.

This hasn't always been true for our medium. Obviously, early motion pictures had no sound. But producers were quick to realize the benefit of adding music, often sending suggested scores—with sound effects—to be played on piano or organ while the film was projected . . . but it wasn't a soundtrack. Even some thirty years after sound films became popular, Warner Brothers still tested cartoons by showing them silently to preview audiences. If Bugs and Daffy could get a laugh as mimes, they knew they had a hit. The genius-level contributions of Mel Blanc and Carl Stalling only added to the hilarity.

That was then. Today, network television is almost entirely driven by dialog. Try to imagine any popular program without sound. The most immediate and often most compelling use of pictures, breaking news events, are accompanied by voice-over and surrounded by talking heads. There's even less visualization in most sitcoms, game shows, soaps, and, of course, late-night talk shows; most would be equally effective on radio. Even the visually rich documentaries on educational channels are primarily pictures illustrating a soundtrack. The only exceptions seem to be action/adventure shows . . . and most of their screen time is filled with dialog rather than fights or car chases.

That's what people are watching, folks. And if sound is that important to the big-time media, it deserves some careful planning in smaller projects.

The metaphors we choose tell us a lot.

Ask your clients which they'd prefer: "A lot of *flash*?" Or, "More *bang* for the buck?"

People Are Conditioned to Expect Good Sound

Maybe you think it's a corporate document or cable access essay, but your audience knows they're watching TV. They don't have your commitment to the message, and they haven't sat through the lengthy development and production. The only yardstick they have for your project is what they saw on the tube last night.

Even if all they saw was an infomercial, it used good production techniques. The set was lit properly, shots were in focus, the editing made sense, and the sound was clean and easy to understand. The people who make a living doing this work (myself included) know their crafts, and the production process is well-defined. You need a TV show? I can call a bunch of my colleagues in other disciplines, and we'll all put together a darned good one. Of course, you'll have to pay us.

That may not be an option with desktop or low-budget production. There just aren't the resources to hire specialists for every job. A producer often has to write the script, simultaneously direct and shoot, and serve as both editor and mixer. This high distraction level means that sound is often neglected: video is more demanding (and more interesting for producers with film or graphics training).

Wisely Invested Time Can Save a Lot of Money

Even if you don't have deep pockets, you can still have a good track. But you have to face the fact that you may not be able to pay much attention to sound during the shoot, and plan accordingly:

> ➤ Start prepping the track while you're still developing the script and budget. Know what it'll sound like, how you'll get the necessary elements, and what resources you won't be able to live without.
>
> ➤ Verify that the location and equipment will support the track you want.
>
> ➤ Make sure you have the skills you'll need. Know which buttons to push before you start production. Know which other buttons to push when things go wrong.
>
> ➤ Don't expect to point a microphone and get lucky, and don't expect that whatever you record will be fixable in post. The former never happens, and the latter can be expensive.

If you can hire someone to concentrate on audio during the shoot—even someone who isn't necessarily trained in the field—you've got a better chance of getting a good track. But you have to give them the opportunity to learn what they'll need before the shoot. Don't count on a production assistant magically knowing how to handle a boom or mix multiple mics. Even a music studio or radio broadcasting background doesn't necessarily guarantee that someone will have the right skills.

This isn't rocket science. If someone has average intelligence and a cooperative attitude, they can learn how to gather good sound. But you'll have to lend them a copy of this book or some other training resource and make sure they have adequate time to practice with the equipment they'll be using.

> Take your pick:
>
> You can plan properly and train the people you work with.
>
> You can hire professionals to worry about sound for you.
>
> Or you can have an echoey, muffled track that says, "This video isn't as important as the average infomercial."

How a Good Soundtrack Can Help
Good sound adds believability

We spend our lives hearing the sounds around us. We've learned what voices sound like in a conversation, how environments can affect the sound of a voice, and what kind of noises everyday objects make. But a microphone doesn't hear the world the same way, and careless sound is a constant, subtle reminder that what's on the screen isn't real. It makes it harder for a viewer to identify with the character or the message.

Sound often has to be more realistic than picture. Nobody looks at a TV and assumes they're seeing a window into another world. We're constantly aware of camera movement and editing, reminding us that a director has defined reality for us. It's what dramatists call the willing suspension of disbelief. But in a properly done soundtrack, the only unbelievable element is the music.

Or to put it another way: you can build a small set in a corner of a giant studio and shoot a scene that looks like an intimate bedroom. Even though we're intellectually aware there has to have been camera, lights, and a lot of people around, we agree to accept the actors' version of things and let ourselves get wrapped up in the story. However, if one of them murmurs, "I love you," and it sounds like they're in a gymnasium, the illusion is shattered.

I've seen videos like that. If you haven't, turn on your local cable access channel.

As technology gets better, maintaining the illusion becomes harder.

When TV was black and white, and the sound came out of a tinny speaker, it was easy to accept technical limitations. We knew that Lucy's hair and Ricky's skin weren't really gray, but we didn't care. Or we filled in the red and tan ourselves.

Color television made it harder to suspend our disbelief. Although gray hair was acceptable for Lucy, orange wasn't. Lighting and makeup became much more important

The same thing has happened to sound. The increased audio clarity of digital tape, better speakers and amplifiers in TV sets, and the prevalence of stereo conspire to let us hear more of the track. Since it's no longer obviously canned, it has to be *right*.

As budgets go down, spend proportionally *more* on sound

If you plan audio properly, it's much more cost-effective than video. You don't need sets or locations, the equipment costs less, and it takes less time to put it together. Good sound can add the professionalism you might not be able to afford with pictures.

- Voice-overs are cheaper to record than on-camera spokespersons are to shoot. The money saved here can buy you a more experienced (and convincing) actor.

- A small buyout score will cost as little as 10 or 15 dollars a minute. Even a full symphonic score, played by a world-class orchestra, can cost less than 50 dollars a minute from a needle-drop library. It's the cheapest special effect you can buy.

- Sound effects cost virtually nothing and can add realism to most video scenes. A few well-placed actors backed up by a crowd recording costs a lot less than shooting a room full of extras. The noise of an explosion, a flashing light, and a horrified on-camera reaction has *got* to be cheaper than blowing up a building.

Think About the Overall Track

A track is more than the sum of its sounds. If this idea sounds strange to you, you're not alone. Too many Hollywood features are nothing but continuous noise. The current idea of Sound Design is to create a track with nonstop gunshots, car crashes, explosions, and alien growls—it isn't interesting; it's just loud. After the initial adrenaline reaction to sound pressure wears off, it isn't even exciting.

A lot of sound effects isn't necessarily a lot of effective sound. On the other hand, well-chosen sounds—including pauses and quiet ambiences as well as hard effects—can almost become another character: it builds a world around your actors and helps the viewer believe the message.

Start with the Script

Many producers believe that sound happens in postproduction. *Good* sound begins when you first start writing the script. This doesn't mean you need to work in a lot of car crashes and laser zaps—most scripts have no place for them—but you need to think about the overall sound of the video while you're writing. A couple of techniques can help.

Listen to the words in your mind

Hear the script in your head while you're writing it. Don't just type

```
Sfx:    phone rings

Sue:    Hello? George! I've been waiting to hear
        from you...
```

and leave it at that. That's not what's going to happen on the screen.

Instead, hear the sequence. You'll realize that what actually happens is

```
Sfx:    phone starts to ring

Sue looks at phone, reaches toward it, picks it up

Sfx:    ring is interrupted
        handset pick-up sound

Sue holds handset, talks into it

Sue:    Hello?
```

```
Sue pauses, then reacts to voice

Sue:    George! I've been waiting to hear from you...
```

You don't have to type all that on the script, of course. But hearing it in your head makes you realize how much this simple action affects the pacing. The scene plays slower than you might have originally thought. (If you're writing a commercial, this can be critical.)

Working this way also lets you explore other sound options. Is there music under previous dialog or as a transition into the scene? Ending the music on the first ring will have a very different effect than waiting until Sue recognizes George's voice.

Are there background sounds? If Sue is watching TV when the phone rings, what happened to its speaker? Perhaps she was in her office. Just by maintaining the ambience and conversations, you can tell us Sue's busy life wasn't on hold. She wasn't *really* waiting to hear from George.

This is real Sound Design. At first, it'll take a little longer to write scripts this way. But you'll get used to the technique quickly, write more realistic dialog, and eventually find yourself writing better scripts—with fewer time-consuming revisions.

Be aware that sounds may need a reference

Often, sounds that make sense in the script become "widowed" in the track because they're hard for the viewer to identify. Many sounds aren't obvious unless there's a visual or verbal reference to them.

Imagine a film noir sequence in a cheap hotel room on a rainy night, with the sound of a neon sign flashing. A realistic recording of rain through a tightly closed window could easily be mistaken for static. The rhythmic bzzap of a neon sign only adds to that confusion. You can solve this sound problem with an establishing shot, perhaps a point of view looking out through the window to see rain splashing on the glass and part of the sign. If that's too expensive, you could have a character comment on the weather while rhythmically flashing a red light onto the set. Either way, the sound is established. After that, you're free to block the rest of the scene any way you want; viewers will remember that the noises mean rain and neon.

It takes a lot more experience to imagine a score in your head while also thinking dialog and effects, but now's the time to think about how the music will work. Don't just write "music fades up" on the script; specify what the music is trying to convey. If it's there to build an emotion, describe the emotion. If it's a bridge, describe it in terms of the attitude and style of the scene that's coming. Including details about music in the script can help you pace the actors when you're directing.

It'll also guide the composer in postproduction, or—if you're using library music—help you find appropriate pieces faster.

Make Room for Sound

Real people stop talking every now and then, and when they do, we hear the world around them. Try to avoid writing dialog over noisy actions (Sue shouldn't be talking to another character while she hangs up the phone); this complicates mic placement and makes a good mix more difficult.

Even if a sound effect will be added in post, leave room for it in the dialog. A character shouldn't start screaming at the same moment there's a car crash or explosion—that just detracts from both sounds. Let them scream in anticipation as the car careens towards the wall, or react after the crash occurs.

Since different sounds have different frequency ranges, consider how their brightness or deepness might conflict. The metallic crunch of car against wall has a similar timbre to an adult male shouting, so you won't hear both if they're happening at the same time. But substitute either breaking glass or a female scream and they'll coexist together.

This also affects how you specify the music. Good scoring composers are very aware of how instrumental timbres fit in the overall track. When John Williams orchestrated the rolling rock in *Raiders of the Lost Ark,* he relied almost exclusively on high, staccato strings. That way the rumbles of the rock itself could show through. The low notes of his theme for *Jaws* aren't just ominous; they also leave room for the ocean and seagull effects. Even if your budget is limited to library cuts, you can use the same kind of thinking. Solo brass and winds occupy the same range as the human voice, so avoid that lonely sax player in the window if there's simultaneous dialog.

Sound and picture also have to make room for each other. If you want viewers to follow complex visuals, lighten up on the track. Consider the classic recapitulation at the end of many mysteries: as the detective finally describes what really happened, we see a montage of flashbacks showing the murder . . . but the sound effects in that montage are almost always underplayed. We may hear a gunshot and body fall, but that's about it.

Provide Texture Changes

When people know what to expect, they stop paying attention. This even happens at the subtle level of room reverberation and background sounds.

Long dialog sequences with static actors get very boring acoustically, even if the words themselves are interesting. Let the characters move around the room, so we can hear differences as their voices bounce off different surfaces. Move some of the dialog into a hallway or another room with different acoustics. Or let them continue some of the conversation outdoors or in their car. If your budget is limited to a single setup, at least give the characters a chance to stop talking and react to an off-camera sound. Instead of just walking a new actor into the scene, let everyone else stop as we hear the off-camera sounds of a car stopping, a door slamming, and footsteps.

Music helps break up boring sequences but may become a cliché. A stab after a dramatic line can give a soap-opera feel to a scene . . . but it might be just what's needed to let us think about a dramatic point. If a sequence is light on dialog, try specifying an underscore instead of matched sound effects to fill the pauses. If your video has a lot of music, leave some scenes unscored to make them stand out.

Remember the Medium

Even if you've got the money to spend, a business video's track has to be more limited than a theatrical film's. That's because film sound designers have surround sound and much wider frequency and dynamic ranges to play with. Business videos have to play on a conference room TV. If you're relying on the slam-bang effects you saw in the latest adventure thriller, you'll be disappointed at the result.

Sound can be most ambitious in videos that will be shown only under controlled circumstances. If you know you'll be using high-quality digital or BetaSP playback in an auditorium with a good stereo system, you can rely on stereo and differences of loudness and texture to help carry your message. It's reasonable to think in terms of six or more sound layers: dialog, up-front effects, effects that aren't sharply on camera, ambiences, and music. The stereo field and high playback quality help the viewer sort things out.

Broadcast sound is a lot less flexible. Even though most stations transmit in stereo, many cable networks are squashed to mono by the local cable system. And even if a viewer has a stereo set, it's likely to be off to one side of the room. In most stereo sets, the speakers are too close together to project a realistic stereo field. The truth is, most stereo TV broadcasting isn't. Listen carefully to those high-priced network dramas: you'll find that most dialog is dead-center—even as the characters are moving around the room—and only music and effects are stereo.

Broadcasters also deliberately limit their dynamic range, so viewers can hear normal dialog without having to constantly compensate for screaming commercials. Don't count on more than three layers in a broadcast track, and pay careful attention to avoid dialog and foreground effects from conflicting.

The most limiting medium is Internet or CD-ROM audio. Expect many viewers' playback to be on tiny speakers, in noisy rooms. Internet compression techniques further muddy the sound. And don't try anything at all ambitious if the track may be played on a laptop: even voice and music will fight each other.

It's Not Just the Writer's Responsibility

If you're creating the script, you've got a great opportunity to write for sound. But if you're shooting someone else's script, you must still go through the process of hearing it in your head, marking sound cues, and possibly breaking things up to make room for audio. It's the best way to assure that the track will go together smoothly and predictably.

Planning and the Bottom Line

Planning a track long before production will save money you can spend elsewhere in the video.

- If you know what sounds you'll need, you can get them at the shoot. It's a lot cheaper to grab an off-camera line, crowd walla, or specific object sound while you've got the actors, extras, and props already there.

- If you know what you won't need, you don't have to waste time recording it.

- If you think about the final track while you're shooting, editing will be smoother because you won't be trying to fudge existing footage to make room for audio.

Elements of the Soundtrack

> ➤ There are a lot of different flavors that can go into your soundtrack. Mix 'em up! Too much of anything can be boring.

It's standard practice, after mixing a TV show, to give the producer a tape with separate tracks for voice, music, and effects. This simplifies the process of creating foreign-language versions and allows additional freedom when cutting promos or lifts.

But don't let that three-track tape fool you into thinking there are only three kinds of sound. Within the broad areas of voice, music, and effects are enough subcategories to satisfy the most ambitious sound designer. If you train yourself to think in terms of these subcategories, rather than just "we'll use a voice," you can create more interesting tracks and do a better job of engaging the viewer.

Spoken Words

Video is driven by the spoken word. It affects the visual editing rhythm and style as well as the choice of shots. But you've got a lot of freedom where those words will come from and how you'll control them.

On-Camera Dialog

This is the primary way to get words across in dramatic videos, many corporate pieces, and some commercials. Obviously, on-camera voices are recorded while you're shooting picture; in digital video production they're almost always recorded on the same tape. But that doesn't mean they have to stay together forever.

You can often improve a track by breaking the link between on-camera faces and the voices that were recorded at the same time. It's common practice in Hollywood to use voices from a close-up against pictures from a long shot, or even to re-record dialog after the shoot.

Modern audio workstations let you take the process even further: I'll frequently use words from a discarded take to fix sound problems in the take that was actually used, even if the shot is fairly tight on the actor's face. I'll also take individual phonemes to fix a word that might have been mispronounced or clipped by the video editor. It's more important that the dialog be understandable than that every frame be in perfect lip sync. It takes a few seconds before sync problems become obvious, so you can have one or two words that are slightly out in an otherwise synchronized take, and nobody will be the wiser.

If your editing skills aren't up to replacing individual words against picture (you'll get plenty of practice in Chapter 11), there's still lots of freedom to edit the on-camera voice during cutaways. Any time we're not seeing the characters' lips,

---

Editing tip:

The easiest way to mess with words during a cutaway without risking sync errors during on-camera segments is to split the voice onto two separate tracks in your editor. Keep on-camera segments on a track that's linked to picture, and use a temporary work track for the highly edited stuff. After you're sure it all works together, move the edited version back to the main track and discard the temporary one.

you can make their voices do anything you want. Feel free to grab a better reading from an alternate take, or to edit out long breaths. Use time compression to pick up the pace slightly so there's room to hear other sounds. Or use time expansion to stretch individual words for emphasis. The only limit is that you be back in sync within a few frames of cutting back to the actor's face.

On-camera dialog and on-camera narration have different sounds

We usually think in terms of characters talking to each other on screen, because that's what we see most often in movies and episodic TV. But in corporate and commercial projects, the actor frequently talks directly to camera. This affects the texture of the sound as well as the writing and performance.

Dialog in a dramatic scene requires a sound that matches the environment where we see the actors. If they're in a normal room, they'll usually be boomed from slightly above their heads, so the mic also picks up some room reverb. If it's a long shot in a very big room where booming is impossible, they're probably wearing radio mics only a few inches from their mouths. Very little of the room is picked up when the mic is this close, so artificial reverb is added to match the shot. The idea in both cases is that we're eavesdropping on the conversation these people are having, so the room they're in is a natural part of the sound.

But if a spokesperson is in a normal room and talking directly to camera, we—the viewers—are a presumed part of the conversation. The real room where we're sitting is as much a part of that conversation's environment as the shooting stage. In that case it's appropriate to reduce the reverb, or move the boom much closer to the actor, so the set's acoustics don't completely overpower the viewing room's.

If a spokesperson is in front of a drape or in limbo, there isn't any "room" at all. Any reverb would sound unnatural. This also applies to highly staged settings that aren't trying to be real-world rooms, such as a typical news set with desk, station logo, and monitor wall or chroma key. We're perfectly comfortable with the close lavaliere sound of the evening newscast because the anchors are talking directly to us.

Vérité audio

Documentaries and some commercials often depend on ad-lib comments, directed to an interviewer who's very close to the camera lens. The texture of these voices can be very different from a trained actor or spokesperson, lending additional interest to the track. Because these people aren't polished performers, their voices are often weaker and need to be miked with a very close boom or a lavaliere that rejects most of the room sound. This is entirely appropriate, since the presumption is they're talking to camera and to us: the environment works like it would for a spokeperson.

By the way, it's almost always a mistake to ask a vérité subject to deliver a spokesperson's scripted selling line. Nothing destroys a commercial faster than having an allegedly real customer shout into the camera, "I love the variety and selection!" That's not how humans talk.

Remember the room

Staying aware of the presumed acoustic environment of on-camera dialog can help you avoid conflicts where sounds don't match their apparent location, or where insert shots don't match the master.

In his seminal book on sound design, *The Responsive Chord*, Tony Schwartz pointed out how early versions of Johnny Carson's *Tonight Show* used a close desk mic for Johnny. An overhead boom picked up the guests, plus quite a bit of the studio's natural reverb. For this reason, the host always sounded more intimate and closer to the viewer. Later incarnations of the show kept the desk mic as a non-working prop, but put lavalieres on everybody.

But even modern, technically sophisticated shows can have similar problems. Just a month before writing this, I encountered one while mixing network promos for *Sesame Street*. One of the Muppet characters had to interact with a child. The puppeteer stood beneath a counter where the child was seated, holding his hands overhead to work the puppet. A head-mounted mic picked up his voice from an inch away. But the child was picked up by an overhead boom, at least a foot above his head. The obvious difference in room sounds hurt the illusion that Muppet and child were sharing a moment. I had to split out the Muppet's voice to another track and add artificial reverb to put them in the same room again.

Historic audio

Documentary producers can take advantage of almost a century of historic audio available from archives, stock footage sources, and the Library of Congress. Some of it has accompanying video or film. If you're planning to use historic sound with sync pictures, plan for a few still photos of crowd reactions as cutaways. This kind of sound almost always needs a lot of editing, both to correct technical problems and to pick its pace up to modern expectations.

Crowd Voices

If dialog takes place in a setting where there's a crowd, it's almost universal practice for the extras playing the crowd to mime their conversations, moving their lips but not making any noise. This is the only way to get a clean, editable recording of the principal dialog.

Appropriate crowd sounds or *walla* is then added in postproduction. Walla can be recorded at the shoot, after the scene is shot but before the extras go home, but this is seldom necessary or economical. Sound effects libraries have multiple discs of crowd backgrounds and reactions in every possible setting; if you don't have such a library, you can sneak an audio recorder into a crowded restaurant or building lobby and grab what you need. If the crowd has to have unique reactions or say particular key phrases, you can simulate a large crowd with four or five people ad-libbing conversations in different voices. Record this small group in a quiet studio, so you can run two or three separate ad-lib takes simultaneously without noise buildup. Then mix the result with prerecorded walla from a library.

Voice-over Narration

In most commercials, corporate and educational videos, and documentaries we never see who's doing most of the talking. A voice-over, by definition, exists in limbo; there shouldn't be any background ambience or room reverb around it. With nothing to suggest any distance between us and the narrator, it can become the most intimate part of the track and interpret the rest of the video for us.

Narrations should almost always be recorded in a sound studio designed for voices, or in an isolated space with plenty of absorption (see Chapter 6).

> There's a temptation, if you know a scene will be accompanied by narration, to shoot it without sound. This would be a mistake. Even if there's no dialog, point a mic at the scene. It doesn't cost any extra to record sound with video, and the ambience and action noises you pick up can add another texture to the mix . . . or at least provide a guide track if you later want to add cleanly recorded effects.
>
> This is one of the few times when a camera-mounted mic can be useful in dramatic production.

The idea of an intimate announcer is a relatively modern concept, which seems to have grown out of the one-on-one style of pioneer television talk hosts like Jack Paar. Voice-over announcers in films prior to the mid-1950s usually had formal "speaking to the masses" deliveries and were often mixed with reverb. You may want to experiment with this style of narration as yet another texture, one that evokes a nostalgic or historic feel.

Music

It may seem obvious, after watching the latest Hollywood blockbuster with a wall-to-wall orchestral score, that music can play an important part in a production. But many video producers don't do anything with music until the end of the editing process, and then simply add an opening and closing theme.

Music can be an important element throughout a production. Aside from the obvious title and end credit theme, it can be used to explain settings, tie scenes together, emphasize emotions, call attention to important plot or visual elements, or even be an additional character with an attitude of its own. In a video, music can be everywhere.

Source Music

The most obvious place to consider music is when it's a sound effect—something we can see happening on the screen. If the characters are at a parade, we must hear a marching band. If we see someone put a cassette into a player, we should hear music come out of the speakers.

Other kinds of scenes imply music even though we can't see the source. A school dance should have rock and roll, sounding either live or canned depending on the school's budget. But don't forget all the other places where canned music will make a scene more realistic: a restaurant scene can use pop, ethnic, or classical selections to establish its atmosphere quickly. And there probably isn't a large supermarket in the United States that doesn't have some kind of instrumental background at all times.

Source music—sometimes called *diegetic music* by film theorists—is an excellent way to build another layer into your soundtrack, since it occupies a place between the up-front dialog and any background scoring. The trick is that it has to sound like it's really there. You can't shoot the scene with the music playing because that would make voice pickup difficult and editing impossible. So a separate music track has to be heavily processed with echoes and equalization to put it in the same environment as the dialog. If the characters are hearing the music from a loud-speaker, remember that the viewer is hearing *the entire scene* from a loudspeaker: the music has to be extra processed, so it sounds even more canned than the dialog.

Source music also has to be chosen for musical and production values that match the scene. Background music in a supermarket has to be appropriately insipid. If the characters are listening to a pop radio station or jukebox, the music should be an authentic pop style and probably a vocal. This becomes most critical in cases like the school dance with a live band: a five-piece garage group will have a thinner sound and more inept playing than anything you're likely to find in a studio record-ing. Chapter 12 has some tips for getting source music.

Scoring

The kind of continuous underscoring found in theatrical films is too expensive for most video projects, but it still helps to think about music the way they do in

Hollywood. Once you know exactly what the music is trying to accomplish, it's easier to find what you want in a library or hire a composer to create a few short affordable cues.

Aside from the title and end credit sequences, there are three major ways scoring can be used in your project.

Music as an emotional statement

There's no question that sad, anxious, or romantic music riding under the dialog affects how we perceive a dramatic scene. But music can convey emotions even when there is no dialog. The pounding score under a car chase or fight scene, and the whimsical ditty under a comic montage, are both filling the same purpose: to help shape the viewer's reaction to what's on the screen. By extension, a montage of widget manufacture in a corporate video can use music the same way. Rather than settle for a background track, think about what the scene is supposed to convey: is Widgetronics including this sequence to show off their precision, or their efficiency, or their power, or the human way they care about every widget that comes off the line?

The classic film scores of the past were composed as miniature symphonies. They developed along musical lines while still being tightly timed to important moments in the scene. These days, it's more common to match every action to an appropriate chord or shimmer and then fill in the notes between (any musical development is an afterthought), or to use a piece of music that wasn't necessarily written for the scene and add occasional punctuations in sync with the picture. While these two conventions may represent a decline in the art of Hollywood scoring, they're a blessing for video producers: the matched-chord-and-shimmer approach can be executed economically on electronic keyboards, and even if you can't afford any original music, library cuts can be edited seamlessly to fit this occasional-punctuation style.

In its sparsest incarnation, this kind of scoring can punctuate dialog with just a few notes. A quick broken piano chord might be all you need to highlight a conflict; a string stab can call our attention to a dramatic foreshadowing. Even a few whimsical notes under some vaguely humorous action can help add texture to an otherwise static scene. The important thing when using music this way is to plan for it, leaving appropriate pauses during the shoot or creating them in the edit.

Music to identify a character or plot development

John Williams used motifs in the score for *Star Wars*: every major character had a unique theme, and these themes would interact and develop as the characters played out the plot. But he also used motifs in the score for *Superman*, linked to plot developments instead of characters. Whenever Superman went to fight villains, the score was based on the march music from the main title. But when he and Lois had a romantic moment, we'd hear a snippet of their love song.

You can do the same sort of thing when scoring a video. Recurring themes—even ones chosen from a library—can be used whenever a particular kind of plot development takes place. Using music this way isn't limited to dramatic videos: for a History Channel documentary about a major construction project, I used timpani-heavy variations of an orchestral theme under the heavy-equipment sequences, an electronic piece reminiscent of the theme when we were seeing the high-tech control rooms that controlled them, and classical instrumentations of the main theme during history and archeology scenes. And it all came from library cuts.

Music to set a scene

There is no faster way to establish an ethnic or nostalgic setting than to use appropriate music. Any good music library will have plenty of cuts designed for this purpose, and most composers welcome the challenge of working their music into a different style.

But scene-setting music doesn't have to be a caricature. You can use more mainstream styles to mark the passage of time, or a jump from one locale to another. You can also join two pieces of music that are related in key and texture, but different in tempo or dynamic, and use this new cue to show an abrupt change in mood.

The Pitfalls of Popular Music

It's common practice in mainstream films to introduce a number of pop songs either as source music or underscoring montage. These songs might be newly created for the film, be classic recordings, or be new covers of pop standards; no matter where they came from, they're sure to receive lots of radio airplay and be highlighted in the film's promotion.

It's possible there's a tiny bit of artistic justification for using these songs. But the incentive is more likely a financial one: a best-selling "soundtrack" album can contribute to the producers' income stream. (I put "soundtrack" in quotes because these albums seldom have much to do with the film's track: they often include songs heard only peripherally in the film, and covers by big-name artists that weren't part of the track at all. It's a certainty that very little of the actual underscore will be included.)

This Hollywood practice may tempt you to use popular songs in your video the same way. If so, remember two things:

- Unless you have permission from both the copyright owner and the performer, you're running the risk of major lawsuits. The fact that a video may be nonprofit, educational, or nobly intended is absolutely not a defense.

- Even if you have permission to use an existing song, your viewers have already linked it to events and feelings that have nothing to do with your video. Once you start playing *their* music, you don't control the experience any more. While there may be emotional justification for hearing "Lady in Red" when George first discovers how he feels about Sue at the company party, do you really want to remind a viewer about her own breakup with an ex-boyfriend who liked that music?

Pop music soundalikes are available from bigger music libraries, can be fully licensed to avoid lawsuits, and carry less emotional baggage.

Sound Effects

There's a rule in Hollywood: if you see it, you should probably hear it. While it's true that anything that moves air molecules quickly enough will make a noise, features and episodic television have taken this to extremes. I'm sorry, folks: no matter how good the action hero is at karate, his hands don't go "woosh" when they fly through the air. And the *Enterprise* doesn't even have air molecules to move as it swoops past us in the vacuum of space.

Video producers often err in the other direction. Both documentary and dramatic videos can suffer from a silence that never occurs in the real world. (Take a listen while you're reading this . . . there's probably a symphony of muted traffic noises, distant conversation, and small machines like clocks or computer fans. Even in the quietest library reading room, you'll hear footsteps and pages turning.)

Use sound effects to add richness and believability to your track.

Sound Effects Categories

As you're thinking about sounds in your video, you can break them into three categories.

Hard effects

The most common film definition of a hard effect is any noise that's linked to an on-screen action and must stay in sync with it. This includes the tiniest footsteps as well as gunshots and car crashes. In video production, many of the smaller sounds don't need to be in perfect synchronization. The smaller screen forgives some lack of precision, and budget realities force us to paint with a broader brush. So I prefer to use "hard effects" to refer to sync effects that are big, obvious, and usually help the plot;

of course this includes the car crashes and gunshots, but also Sue's telephone or the crunch of a briefcase hitting the desk.

Natural sounds

This is a subcategory of what a Hollywood sound editor would consider hard effects. Feature films usually add them in foley sessions where specialists walk, move props around, and fake fist fights to mimic the on-screen actions.

In video production, I prefer to use this term to denote the smaller sounds that add realism to the scene. They may be foleys, but they're more likely to be lifted from the production tracks or edited in from an effects library. Many times they're created by making small edits in an existing background or ambience track so that loud sounds happen around the same time as on-screen actions. These natural sounds might be in sync, but—as in the case of most clothing rustles, footsteps, or automobile passbys—they only have to *appear* to be in sync.

By the way, TV editors often refer to anything that isn't narration or music as "Nat Sound," including hard effects and even on-camera interviews. Their Nat Sound tracks can be an excellent source for natural sound in a scene.

Backgrounds and ambiences

Traffic, crowds, or random interior and exterior noises may be recorded at the shoot, but are more often lifted from a sound effects library or specially recorded by the sound editor.

Backgrounds usually aren't added until just before the mix, because one of the purposes of these tracks is to smooth over dialog edits with continuous sound. Fading in the background a few frames earlier than a scene starts, and holding it a few frames after the scene's end, can also help smooth over visual transitions.

Special Effects and Processing

Don't forget that creative editing and technical manipulations can create additional types of elements for your soundtrack. Ideas like these might be too avant-garde for the average video, but certainly are appropriate in an art piece:

*   Repetitive sound effects can be slowed down to a small fraction of their original speed and serve as the bass line of a piece of music.

*   Musical elements can be used as sound effects. Try placing a cymbal crash or drum hit on the same frame as a hard effect to thicken the sound. If the score uses similar cymbals or drums, it'll tie the music and action together—even if the action is nowhere near a musical beat.

- Tightly edited off-camera voices can serve as a rhythmic element that complements or replaces music. Tony Schwartz's track for the Academy Award–winning animated short *Frank Film* used a montage of individual words in the animator's voice to provide a driving rhythm under the animator's own voice-over.

- Processed off-camera voices can serve as an additional layer in the track. Ken Nordine pioneered the idea of running his own voice through a telephone filter, and mixing in the result as parenthetical comments in commercials he created; this is now common practice in radio station promos. I haven't heard or used the technique in a video project, so you might be breaking new ground.

The Layers of a Track

There's a definite order of importance of the various elements in a video track. Understanding this can help you plan the track better; assembling the track in this order can be the most efficient way to work.

- Dialog and narration come first. They have to be edited smoothly and stay in the foreground of the mix.

- Hard effects, if any, come second. They advance the plot and lend realism.

- Music comes third! This is contrary to the way feature films are often built, but in the world of video production resources are often more limited. A well-chosen and edited piece of music can eliminate the need for backgrounds and natural sounds.

- Backgrounds should be chosen and placed before worrying too much about natural sounds. Often, random noises in a prerecorded background will appear to be in sync and can serve the same purpose.

- Natural sounds should be finally added to scenes that don't have music or much of a background, or where an action definitely appears to be missing audio.

CHAPTER 5

Budgeting, Scheduling, and Preproduction

R O S E ' S   R U L E S

⇨ While sound is a lot faster and cheaper than video, it's not instantaneous and it's not free. Allow a few resources to do it right, or it'll pull down the perceived quality of your entire project.

⇨ When you're scouting locations, think about the track as well as the picture.

Digital camcorders and desktop video systems have become enormously capable, but they're not magic. If you want good pictures, you have to do more than simply point the camera and hope for the best. If you want a good track, you have to do more than simply point the camera-mounted microphone.

A proper soundtrack requires a commitment of time and money—nowhere near as much as for good visuals, but a commitment nonetheless. In many cases, you can trade these resources and spend a few dollars more for the sake of convenience, or work a little harder to save money.

There are only a few basic tools you'll need to do sound properly, and they're available for rent or purchase in production cities around the world. The more important decisions are whether you want to work with the sound yourself—meaning you have to learn how to do it right—or hire professionals who already know how to do the job. These decisions can be made on a task-by-task basis: it might make sense to get a professional sound operator for the shoot, but plan to edit the music track yourself.

To make these decisions efficiently, you have to know how much time or money each aspect of the track will cost. Remember: the golden triangle of production

(Figure 1) applies to sound, just as it does to every other aspect of our business. You can have it fast, cheap, or good: choose any two. You can't have all three.

Figure 1: The golden triangle: pick any two.

Budgeting for Sound

I'm assuming that, as a digital video producer, you already have a video-editing system and know how to work it. So we won't include any costs for basic sound editing. Using the tips later in this book, you should be able to do that with no trouble.

But unless you've got a fully equipped crew at your disposal, expect to spend a few dollars on audio at the shoot. Depending on your voice-over needs, you might also have to spend money for a recording studio. Many producers rely on outside scoring, sweetening, and mixing services because desktop video-editing systems simply aren't designed to be efficient at these tasks.

Here are some of the personnel and equipment costs you can expect. They were accurate when I wrote this book (late-1999) and had been stable for years. Barring major technology or economic changes, they should be accurate for a long time to come . . . or if we have rampant inflation, you'll at least be able to use them as a guideline.

The prices are based on nonunion corporate or documentary video productions in major production centers. Smaller towns are apt to have personnel with less experience or who split their time between audio and other gigs; they usually charge less. Union rates are similar but based on a fixed-length day, so overtime can get expensive. Commercial shoots are often more demanding, and personnel expect to be paid more for them.

Production Costs

Audio mixer/recordist

Experienced operators who bring their own equipment for miking and mixing the shoot may be the best investment you can make. They'll let you concentrate on getting good pictures and performances and guard against the acoustic problems that plague so many amateur productions and absolutely can't be fixed in post.

Plan on a preproduction meeting where you can fully describe the project and the location. For most video productions, there's no need to have the sound recordist actually make a sound recording on separate equipment; it's more likely they'll provide you with a clean audio feed to record in your own camera. What's important is that you can rely on their skills to take care of mic placement, acoustic concerns, boom and level control, and the setup of electronics and wireless mics. During the prepro, make sure they're familiar with the camera or recorder you'll be using and its audio specifications; a short compatibility test before the shoot might be a good idea.

Depending on the experience and equipment they bring, figure $250–$400/day.

Boom operator

If only one mic boom is needed and it won't be actively mixed with radio or other mics, the sound recordist will usually handle it. But if the recordist has to be constantly balancing multiple mics, or you need more than one boom, get an additional experienced operator. Figure $150–$300/day.

Don't assume that a boom operator is merely someone tall enough to hold a pole with a mic at the end. Aside from the physical endurance required, there's a lot of skill involved in pointing a mic accurately and quickly enough to cover back-and-forth dialog, while aiming the mic to avoid noise sources and changing its distance to compensate for the actors' delivery.

Equipment packages

The recordist may supply an equipment package as part of their basic fee or charge a nominal amount for its use. But if you're doing the sound yourself, you'll probably need to rent equipment. Professional gear is rented on a daily basis; many rental companies price their weekly rentals at three or four times the daily rate, and allow extra time for shipping to out-of-town customers.

All of this equipment is described in the next two chapters, along with directions on how to use it.

- Lavaliere mics (nonwireless): $10–$15/day

- Lavaliere mic systems (wireless), nondiversity: $45–$60/day

- Lavaliere mic systems (wireless), diversity: $75–$100/day

- Shotgun mics: $25–$50/day

- Microphone booms: $10–$15/day

- Microphone mixers: $25–$50/day

- XLR transformer adapters for DV cameras: $2–$5/day

- High-quality headphones: $5–$10/day

Of that list, the last item is the most important. You can't count on good sound unless you're absolutely sure of what you're recording. Walkman-style phones aren't appropriate: you need a set that will isolate you from the outside world, so you can hear how room acoustics are being recorded and if there's any noise on the track. If you're using a boom mic, the boom operator should also have a set of headphones and—depending on your camera setup—may also need a separate headphone amplifier ($10–$15/day).

Rental equipment usually comes with adequate cables for basic hookups; additional cables are available at trivial cost. I've left separate tape recorders off this list because they're seldom necessary in DV production: choosing a high-quality audio setting and turning off any automatic level control should give you good recordings with any well-adjusted DV recorder or camcorder. The limiting factor is how you use the microphone, not what you record it into.

If you're doing a multicamera shoot that relies on timecode and double-system sound or plan to use multitrack tape to catch ad-libs on multiple wireless mics, hire a pro. There are too many ways an inexperienced operator can ruin this kind of shoot.

Expendables

Most wireless mics use a standard 9-volt alkaline battery but burn through them quickly: to be safe, allow three battery changes per mic per day. Wireless receivers use one to three batteries each; change them once a day. While 9-volt batteries are available almost everywhere, it's important to use fresh ones. Batteries from an electronics store are usually better because they haven't sat on the shelf as long as those from a supermarket or drug store.

Most of the wired mics used in video production also require power, but don't consume it very quickly: one battery every day or two should be sufficient. It may be possible to skip the batteries and power wired mics from the mixer. Ask the rental house about "phantom powering."

Other things a sound operator should have handy are nonallergenic paper surgical tape (for mics and wires that have to be hidden on an actor's body), safety pins and gaffer tape (for the ones that are hidden within clothing), alcohol prep pads (for cleaning skin before and after mounting mics), a couple of rubber bands of various sizes (strain relief for wireless mic antennas and XLR assemblies), cheesecloth (emergency wind screens), and antistatic spray (for carpets and clothing). You may also want a couple of condoms: they're the preferred protection for mics that are going to be subjected to moisture or perspiration.

Since you'll be recording audio directly to videotape, separate audio stock isn't an issue.

Voice-over Recording

The acoustics of the room become very important when recording narration, so unless you have a space specifically built for this purpose, it's best to hire a studio. Look for a studio that does a lot of spoken word; the acoustics and techniques used for music recording are different.

In large cities, a good studio with an experienced engineer will cost between $150–$200/hour, plus stock. The amount of time a session takes depends on the talent's experience, how much jargon is in the script, and your own directing style; if you're efficient, you should be able to record 20 minutes' worth of material in an hour.

Most studios will normally record to DAT. However, if you don't have a DAT player or it's not connected digitally to your editing system, this introduces a needless analog conversion and another place to get the levels wrong or introduce noise. If your editor can import audio CDs digitally from a CD-ROM drive, ask if the studio can supply the session in that format for the same price.

If the studio will be editing selected takes together for you, it may be faster for them to hand you finished edits as AIFF or WAVE files on removable media or CD-ROM. Be aware that standard industry practice is for the studio to mark up all blank media: a DAT tape that costs $6 from an electronics supplier may appear on the invoice for as much as $25. Check the studio's pricing policy, and ask if you can bring your own stock (some facilities don't allow it).

Dial-up ISDN lets you walk into a local studio and record an announcer from a distant city, hearing them with perfect fidelity and even playing voice or music reference cues to them. The sound is carried real-time in compressed format (see Chapter 2) and recorded locally. Aside from a slight delay introduced by the encoding system, it's exactly as if they were in the next room.

Depending on the compression system used and the studio's policies, this service will add between $75–$300/hour to the local studio's charge. Internationally standardized MPEG Layer 2 or Layer 3 connections are on the lower end of the price scale; proprietary connections don't offer any significant advantage for voice recording but are more expensive. The distant studio will of course add their own charges.

They may also ask if you want them to record a backup tape, but this is seldom necessary (if there's a problem in the ISDN connection, you'll hear it immediately and can re-record).

You may be able to get the studio for free. Many professional narrators now have their own studios with good acoustics, professional equipment matched to their voices, and ISDN terminals. Most of them will throw in the studio services as part of their talent fee. If you're not using ISDN to a local studio, you can direct them via telephone from your desk, and have them courier or e-mail the finished tracks to you.

Voice-over talent costs are described in Chapter 8, along with how to pay voices without getting into trouble with the talent unions.

Postproduction Costs

Digitizing help

If you've got a lot of nonsync elements such as narration and music, there might be both a cost and quality advantage to having a local studio convert the tapes and CDs into files your editing system can read directly. This means you don't have to tie up your editing station for digitizing, don't have to rent a DAT player, and won't worry about proper digitizing levels and analog connections. Figure about $100/hour, plus media costs.

Music

Now we get to some real variability. Here are some guidelines for a corporate video shown to an internal audience. Music for commercials, broadcast programs, and videos for sale or public exhibition are more expensive: see Chapter 12 for a full breakdown.

Stock music: $15–$100 per selection, between $75–$350 for unlimited scoring in a 10-minute video. The lower end covers buyout music, typically basic arrangements on electronic keyboards. The higher end covers needle-drop libraries that use top film composers and arrangers and record using top session players, vocalists, and full orchestras when appropriate.

Original music will cost between $200–$1,000 per screen minute, depending on how good the composer is and how quickly you want it. At the higher end, it usually includes a mix of live instruments and high-quality samplers and can sound excellent.

While music prices have remained stable over the years, technical advances in the music industry keep raising the quality standards for both library and custom music. Shop around: you may find some incredible music for the money.

Sound effects

If you gather them yourself, or use some of the tricks in this book, sound effects are free. You can also download high-quality ones from the Internet for license fees of a few dollars per minute. Most audio post facilities have immense stock sound libraries with computerized catalogs; depending on studio policy, the cost may range from nothing (if you're mixing there) to $15 per effect. Or you can buy libraries of professionally recorded effects with license to use them in all your productions for $50–$75 per CD.

All of this is covered in Chapter 13.

Postproduction audio studio

A good studio that specializes in corporate or broadcast video sound, fully equipped and with a large stock library, will cost between $150–$250/hour in major production centers. Studios that specialize in advertising sound are somewhat more expensive because of the more intense client services and glitziness expected.

Depending on your project's complexity, they should be able to do multiple dialog fixes, add all the necessary sound effects and music, process tracks to improve their cleanliness and punchiness, and completely mix a 20-minute video in about a day. The time varies depending on what shape your tracks are in when you show up at the studio; see Chapter 15 for some tips. Any professional studio won't charge to walk through your project with you, estimate exactly what will be required, and show you ways to save money on transfers and file interchanges.

Allow Time for Sound

Again, I'm assuming you're already familiar with your editing equipment. Otherwise, all bets are off: you can waste hours rendering or processing sequences only to discover that the sound is damaged or out of sync because of a simple mis-set switch or a system conflict. Problems that are specific to particular brands or versions of editing systems are beyond the scope of this book.

Preproduction Time

It won't take more than an hour to go through all the planning and location audio considerations in this chapter. Now is also the time to line up a location sound crew if needed, and also start thinking about postproduction audio resources: sources for music, voice-over studios, and—if you're going to use one—a mixing facility.

If you're using an experienced sound operator at the shoot, spend at least a quarter hour on the phone with them describing the location and setup. If it's a complex production, it's a good idea to schedule a full prepro meeting with the videographer or director of photography, set designer, sound mixer, wardrobe supervisor, and any other craftsperson who will have a major role at the shoot. The best preproduction meetings also include postproduction specialists, who can suggest things to do at the shoot that'll save time or money later on.

Have your meetings with the people who will actually be providing technical services, not just an agent or booking manager. The former are involved in day-to-day problem solving; the latter just want to book as many days as possible.

Training time is an important resource

If you're running sound yourself, or assigning the job to a production assistant, allow enough time to get used to the equipment. I'd suggest a quarter to half a day, doing actual recordings in similar circumstances. You may need to enlist a colleague to serve as temporary talent during practice sessions with a mic boom.

A half day practicing with a boom mic or mixer?

Yes. Production sound is critical to the success of any dialog-driven project. The person responsible for sound has to know how to record a voice cleanly while compensating for room acoustics. This book explains the procedures, but hands-on—and ears-on—experience is essential.

If you can't afford the time to learn how to do this correctly, hire a professional. While almost any other kind of audio problem can be repaired (or resurrected) in postproduction, badly done production sound will haunt your video forever.

Time Requirements at the Shoot

If you have a separate audio operator who knows what they're doing, sound shouldn't take up much extra time during the shoot; most of the setup will take place while other people are worrying about sets, lights, and camera. Concealing a wireless mic on the talent can take a few minutes and should be coordinated with wardrobe and makeup. Make sure you have enough time to check bought takes to verify that both audio and video were running properly.

If you're using a boom mic with an inexperienced operator, allow for extra takes because the microphone or its shadow has gotten into the scene.

If you don't have a separate audio operator and are using a simple setup with one or two wired lavaliere mics, allow an extra quarter hour to get things right. If you're using wireless mics in a steel-framed building or a location you haven't tested, make it at least a half an hour. Count on a few extra takes when you notice, on playback, that a wireless battery was running down.

If you're renting sound equipment, allow enough time before the shoot to test it thoroughly.

Postproduction Time

Capture

If you recorded audio on the videotape and are transferring digitally, sync sound won't take any extra time at all. If you're transferring sync dialog as analog audio, allow 15 or 20 minutes to calibrate your system using the steps in Chapter 9. If you've never tried sync sound with your specific editing system, allow enough time to capture a few scenes, edit them, and render them as a moderately long sync test before attempting the entire project. There are some black holes of sync incompatibility that can take days to diagnose.

Capturing wild audio takes place in real time, plus a little extra for file management.

Editorial

Basic layout and trimming of scenes affect audio and video simultaneously, and the additional time to render or preview unfiltered audio is insignificant compared to video.

If dialog needs to be repaired (changing words or joining takes in the middle of a sentence, as opposed to trying to clean up bad recordings), the time required depends a lot on the skill of the editor and how flexible the editing system is. Replacing a single word of on-camera dialog may take a video editor 10 or 15 minutes in a frame-based desktop system. The same edit could take less than a minute for an experienced sound editor using an audio workstation. The tips in Chapter 11 will show you how to edit voices efficiently, but if you've got a lot of dialog to repair, you might want to export it to a more flexible audio program . . . or farm the whole job out to a specialist.

Sound effects placement is easier to predict. Adding one or two hard effects and a couple of backgrounds to a 5-minute video sequence shouldn't require more than 15 minutes of editing, assuming you already have a source for the effects. Finding the effects will only take a couple of minutes in a well-indexed library. But don't expect to achieve the deeply layered richness of a feature film in that amount of time: Hollywood sound cutters allow a week per 10-minute reel.

Finding stock music is a major variable. If you have only a few CDs to look through, the job will go quickly, but you're not likely to be thrilled with the choice.

If you have a large library available, and use the tips in Chapter 12, plan on spending 5 or 10 minutes per cue; main title or theme music may take longer. Picking music for a one-hour broadcast documentary should take about a third of a day.

Using the music also takes time. Figure around three times the running length of the music to capture a cut, place it against picture, and check the result. Fine-tuning stock music to match the length of a sequence depends on your skill as an editor (also in Chapter 12) but shouldn't take more than 10 or 15 minutes per scene. If you find it taking longer, try the alternatives recommended for dialog editing: export the music to an audio-only program that isn't restricted to frame boundaries—some of them will even automatically assemble the music to a predetermined length, though it's doubtful their internal edits will match your picture's cue points—or let a music editor handle the job.

Audio mixing

The time this takes depends both on your expectations and your level of equipment. If you're mixing within a basic desktop video-editing setup, you'll probably be using "rubber band" lines to indicate audio fades. Drawing and previewing them for a 5-minute video won't take more than a few minutes.

If you want to add basic compression or equalization using plug-ins, expect a minute or so to fine-tune each separate process. Chapter 14 will give you some starting points. Adding a lot of effects on multiple tracks can slow down audio rendering time by many hundred percent, but whether you'll notice this at all depends on how many video effects you're using—they take longer.

On the other hand, if you're mixing on hardware or a dedicated audio workstation with hands-on controls, there won't be any rendering at all. Simple mixes can be as fast as real time. But chances are you'll be more sensitive to the way level changes and effects interact when you can hear them in context, so you'll spend longer polishing them and get a better mix than you would with rubber bands. Mixing a 20-minute piece may take an hour before it sounds perfect.

Transferring individual tracks from a desktop editor to a dedicated audio workstation can be instantaneous, or take up to twice real time, depending on the file systems involved.

Checking Locations

If you're producing an action feature for theatrical release, you can choose locations based on how they look. If they're also good for sound, that's great; if not, you'll replace the dialog later. (And if replacing the dialog means a more stilted performance, who cares? It's an action feature.)

But if you're producing on videotape instead of film, you're probably paying tighter attention to budgets. Dialog replacement is usually too expensive an option. The location has to sound as good as it looks . . . which means you have to scout with your ears as well as your eyes.

Knowing in advance how a location will affect sound means you can prepare efficiently for the shoot and be ready to fix problems as they occur. If a location is just too beautiful to pass up but has insurmountable sound problems, try rewriting the script to eliminate or reduce dialog there.

Potential Problems

There are only three basic areas of concern when choosing a location for sound:

- Is it quiet enough for dialog?

- Does it have the right acoustic properties?

- Will you be able to use equipment without interference?

Other location issues—access, 'electrical power, legal clearance, and the like— are common to both audio and video, so you'll probably be checking them anyway.

Noise in exteriors

The microphone is a lot less selective than the lens. A city park may look as bucolic as a medieval pasture, if you avoid shooting past the trees and into the tall buildings. But you can't avoid the sounds of traffic and crowds; once they're on your track, you can't get rid of them without starting from scratch.

But while nobody would try to shoot *Robin Hood* in Central Park, other conflicts aren't as obvious. You have to visit the location, stand where the talent will, and listen. Whatever you hear will be part of your track. Here are some ways to avoid unpleasant surprises with exteriors:

- Scout at the same time of day you're planning to shoot. A suburban park that's quiet at four o'clock may be very noisy when school's in session. Traffic and crowd patterns change depending on the time of day, and major streets have been known to attract radio station helicopters during rush hour.

- Try moving 10 or 15 feet in various directions while listening to the background noise. Some mid- or high-pitched sounds, like automobiles passing by, get reflected and focused by large buildings. One side of an open field might be a lot noisier than another, without any visually obvious reason. On the other hand, low-frequency sounds generally aren't directional: if there are a lot of trucks on a nearby highway, their sound will infect the whole location.

- Be aware of airline flight patterns. Some times of day have more flights than others, and runways change from one day to the next. Ask neighbors what their experience has been.

Noise in interiors

Interior locations have fewer variables, but you still have to go to them and listen at the same time of day you'll be shooting. While scouting interiors, pay careful attention to windows: do they overlook a potential noise source, such as a loading dock or trash compactor? Can you get these operations shut down while you're shooting?

If a window lets a small amount of traffic noise through even when it's tightly shut, you can often control the sound by hanging sound dampening blankets over it. If the window is part of the shot and can't be covered, you can cut down its transmission by sealing a piece of thick Lexan or Plexiglas to the frame. If all else fails, plan a point-of-view shot through the window showing traffic on the other side. Include it early in the edited sequence so the viewer at least has a reference for the sound.

Check every opening into the room. Unless a door is specially constructed, it won't stop most sound. If there's a potentially noisy work area or hallway on the other side of the door, make arrangements to keep it quiet while you're actually shooting. Pay attention to media walls and built-in cabinets as well: these often are openings to another potentially noisy room.

Air-conditioning systems can be particularly troublesome at interior locations. Listen carefully for any sounds they make; the microphone will hear them a lot louder than you do. Try removing the ventilation grill from an air duct: turbulence over the vanes that direct air around the room are a major source of noise, and air in the duct itself may be relatively quiet. The high-frequency hiss from air ducts is particularly localized; you may find that the other side of the room is quiet enough to shoot.

The best solution is to have control over the system, and turn it off while you're rolling sound. The worst situation is a system that turns on and off automatically and can't be manually controlled: if some shots have air noise and others don't, it will be distracting when you cut between them. Plan to record some additional room tone with the air conditioner running, and cut it under the quieter shots.

Air-conditioning ducts are also sound paths to other parts of the building. You might not notice it when the air is on and blowing past the grill, but once things are quieter, conversations and footsteps will be able to waft through the ductwork.

A common shortcut in office building construction is to build partial walls that reach a suspended ceiling but don't extend above it. The area above the ceiling grid is an open plenum—sometimes extending completely across a building—where ducts and cables can be run. It's also an open path for any sounds, which pass up through the ceiling tiles in one room and then back down through the tiles where you're shooting. The only solution is to lay fiberglass blankets across the ceiling in both the noisy room and the one you want to keep quiet.

Acoustic problems

Even if you've found an incredibly quiet interior location, you still have to deal with room acoustics. Microphones pick up more reverberation than you notice when you're in the room and having a conversation. Once recorded, it can't be removed from the track.

The solution is usually a combination of added absorption, often provided by sound blankets and wrapped fiberglass panels, and close miking. Counterintuitively, larger spaces can be less of an echo problem because you can place the action in the middle of the room, where the reflecting walls are much farther from the microphone than the actors are. Specific tips for working with reverberant rooms are in the next chapter.

Reverberation is seldom a problem in exterior shooting, unless there's a large building nearby to reflect sound. If there is, it'll probably be in the shot, and viewers will expect to hear some slap from it.

Electronic interference

Wireless mics are subject to interference from television stations, police radios, video monitors, neon lights, bug zappers, electronic flea collars, and virtually anything else that relies on sparks or electronic circuits. It's not that the technology is particularly fragile; the problem is that a transmitter tiny enough to hide in somebody's sock or the small of their back isn't going to be very powerful. Their signals will also be reflected by reflections from a building's steel framework, nearby cars, or even large lights, causing the same kind of cancellations that affect sound in hard-walled rooms.

Getting the receiver as close to the transmitter as possible helps control these problems. Special receiving antennas, dual diversity receivers that pick the best signal from two separated antennas, and of course higher-quality transmitters and receivers can all help. But if you're planning to use wireless at any location, plan for a test before the shoot, or consult with the sound recordist about your concerns. And bring a wired backup, or adapters to use the wireless mic's pickup element with ordinary cables.

Some locations will even cause problems for wired mics. High-voltage transmission lines, power distribution transformers, medical equipment, and even lamp dimmers can radiate interference that's distributed by the building wiring and picked up by the mic. If you're at a location where this may be a problem, try a test first. Balanced wiring (Chapter 3) and a transformer adapter at the camera help a lot.

Location Considerations for Special Situations

Voice-overs

If a character or spokesperson is seen on camera and then intercut as a voice-over, the reverberation should match, or the edit will be distracting. The location also has to be quieter for voice-over than for on-camera dialog, since noises that might be excusable when we can see the source—such as nearby traffic at an exterior—are more objectionable when they're not identified. For compatibility, plan to record these voice-overs using the same microphone as the character's on-camera dialog.

If there's a lot of material to record this way and it can't be scheduled during down-time at the location, you may want to postpone the recording so you won't have an expensive crew standing idle. Returning to the original location (at the same time of day) will help the sounds match; but if that's impossible and you need to record in a studio, choose one with excellent acoustics and a reverb that can simulate the location. A studio is essential for this kind of matching: every location has its own unique sound, and trying to match a real-world shooting location with a randomly chosen room near your office—even if it's roughly the same dimensions—is seldom successful.

The studio engineer will need to know the microphone was set up at the location and should have a sample location track as a guide for processing. Hearing a location track will also help the talent match the original speaking style.

The reverse can also sometimes happen: you need just a couple of lines recorded without any room reverb, possibly for special effects or to narrate a promo that'll accompany the video. This is ideally done in a studio, but with only a few lines it might not be worth the time or expense to go to one. Folding portable sound booths, consisting of padded rigid panels that snap into a frame, are available as an on-location substitute. They don't provide any isolation—the area will have to be kept quiet—but they do control reverberation the same way as a good voice studio. In a pinch, you can build this kind of booth by creating a frame with light stands and hanging sound blankets around its perimeter and across the top.

Industrial locations and other noisy places

If you have to interview the manager at a construction site or inside a busy office, intelligibility is more important than looks. Get the mic as close as possible—even if it's in the shot—and hope for the best. If you have to shoot dramatic dialog at the same site, a close mic will probably be intrusive. You'll have to find a way to shut down most of the operations while shooting, or expect a dialog replacement session.

Very long shots

Since there's no place to put a boom, you have to use lavalieres. Since wireless mics work best when they're close to the receiver, a long shot may present its own problems. If possible, run mic cables down the characters' pants legs. If those would show, try hiding the wireless receiver behind some object in the shot. If that's not possible, you may have to rent small recorders that can be concealed in the characters' costumes.

Fortunately, lip sync is less of an issue when the shot is so long that you can't see a character's mouth distinctly.

On-set playback

Some sequences, particularly musical ones, require that talent work with a previously recorded track. If you don't intend to record dialog or effects during these sequences, the audio setup is simple: all you need is a stable playback medium such as DAT or Minidisk (the speed of analog audio cassettes drifts too much to be useful for playback), speakers close enough to the talent that they won't be confused by room echoes, and a feed from the playback device to your recorder for sync reference.

But these sequences can be more effective if you're also recording natural sounds, dialog, or the characters singing. This kind of shot requires preproduction planning, and you'll need an experienced production sound recordist to help you sort out the options:

- *Foldback.* This is the simplest kind of playback. Small speakers are used with just enough volume for the talent to hear the cues. Mic placement is critical to minimize pickup from these speakers, or else there'll be delay problems when the mic is mixed with the original recording.

- *IFB.* Small radio receivers, with tiny earpieces, are hidden on the talent. The cueing signal is transmitted to them. Mic placement is less critical, but the individual receivers can get expensive if you have to equip a large cast. The earpiece may show in very tight shots, and active movement—such as dancing—can shake the whole thing loose.

- *Thumper.* The lowest rhythmic notes of a piece of music are played through special speakers and conducted through the floor. Dancers literally "feel the beat." Miking is very flexible: any thumps that make it to the soundtrack can be filtered in postproduction.

Shoot Now, Record Later

Some locations have too many problems to allow successful dialog recording, and a dialog replacement session may be the only way to get an acceptable soundtrack. ADR (automatic dialog replacement, but it isn't really automatic at all), also known as looping, is an accepted part of Hollywood filmmaking. So are budgets that reach a hundred million dollars.

ADR is expensive, exacting, annoys the actors, and seldom gives you a wonderful soundtrack. It should only be considered as a last resort in video production; often, compromising slightly on the choice of location will yield a better overall project. If you must use ADR, it helps to plan ahead:

- Long shots are easier to loop than close-ups, because lip-sync errors aren't as obvious.

- Quick cuts with lots of cutaways are easier than longer takes, for the same reason.

- Short phrases are easier to loop than long speeches.

- Every word counts. The less dialog in a scene, the faster you'll be able to fix it.

The decision to use ADR doesn't absolve you of the responsibility to record sound in the field. Your actors will need a guide track to work efficiently, and some of the original dialog or effects may be salvageable.

The actual techniques for ADR are discussed in Chapter 8.

INTRODUCTION TO SECTION III

Enough theory and planning. Here's where we get down to practical realities.

This section is about production:

- Chapter 6 discusses how to choose and use various kinds of microphones. It's slightly technical, but it's not at all theoretical: the things in this chapter are as real as pointing a light or focusing a lens.

- Chapter 7 tells you what to do at the shoot. If you don't have an experienced professional sound recordist standing by, you'll need this chapter to learn everything from the best way to hold a boom mic to how to hide a lavaliere.

- Chapter 8 explains how to record additional voices and effects after the shoot is over . . . the techniques are totally different from those in Chapter 7. I've also included sections on how to record sync dialog to existing picture, and proven successful ways to direct a voice-over performer.

Let's make a video.

Microphones and Room Acoustics

We listen to the world through rose-colored ears. Within a few minutes of entering a room, most people learn to ignore its acoustics. The hum of machinery and computer fans that normally surrounds us seems to disappear as soon as we start paying attention to something else. It's no problem to pick out your child's voice in a crowded schoolyard, or your friend's conversation at a noisy cocktail party.

The real world doesn't sound like our perception of it. That's why, if you record a scene and then play it back without the spatial and visual cues to help focus our ears, all the noise and reverb come crashing back. The only way to avoid it is to take special care in how you set up the room and the mic.

About Microphones

A camera's lens defines a precise rectangle. Point it in the right direction, and you can frame a shot that includes only what you want the viewer to see (Figure 1). Everything else is out of camera range.

Unfortunately, the microphone hears sound from every direction; when we talk about a pickup pattern, we're merely indicating in which direction the mic is slightly more sensitive. There is no such thing as "just out of microphone range," and even the best shotgun microphone actually hears sounds from all around the room (Figure 2).

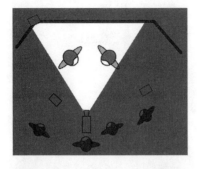

Figure 1: The lens defines a precise image . . .

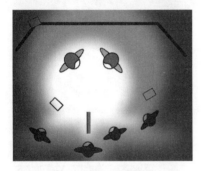

Figure 2: . . . but the mic hears almost everything in the room.

Types of Microphones

A microphone is just a pickup element to convert sound pressure into electrical voltages, mounted in a box. The construction of the pickup element determines how it translates pressure into electricity, but only a couple of methods—dynamic and condenser—are appropriate for video production. We'll cover those in a few pages.

Far more important is how the construction of the box determines how the microphone picks up pressure from different directions. Understanding this is the key to getting good sound.

Microphone Directionality

Omnidirectional

The most basic form of microphone has a solid box around the element's side and back, with a tiny hole to equalize barometric pressure (Figure 3). Air pressure waves strike the front of the element and generate a signal. The air inside the box acts as a resilient spring to push the diaphragm out when the sound wave is in rarefaction. Since the whole assembly is small compared to the wavelength of most sounds, it doesn't get in its own shadow. Any sound waves coming from the back refract around the mic and hit the element. (The size of the mic can get significant at high frequencies, but manufacturers compensate for this in other ways.)

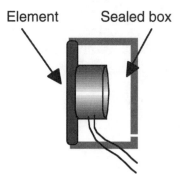

Figure 3: Omnidirectional mic

Since most of an omnidirectional mic is a sealed box, it's less sensitive to wind noise than other designs. Lavaliere microphones are often omnis, because this design can be made very small. Since they're close to the actor's mouth, they can rely on the inverse-square law to pick up lots of voice with very little reverb or noise. This kind of mic is also sometimes called a *pressure mic* because it reacts to any changes in sound pressure, anywhere around it.

Full-size omnis are often used in studio recording and as handheld stage performance mics, but their major use in video is as handheld close-up interview mics in very windy exteriors. They can also be used for recording background ambiences, when you want to pick up a diffuse impression of a space without any particular details.

For reference, an omni's pickup pattern looks like Figure 4. I've emphasized the shape of the pickup in all of these drawings to make them more understandable. In reality, there's a smooth and gradual falloff of sensitivity around the shape, more like Figure 2. In other words, all four of the dark gray crew members around the bottom of the picture will be recorded at about the same sensitivity as the two actors at the

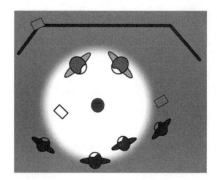

Figure 4: Omni pickup pattern

top. It doesn't make any difference whether they're precisely inside or outside the white circle.

The boundary mic is a variation on omnidirectional mic design, and it lends itself to video production. It was originally developed by Crown International as the Pressure-Zone Microphone, and boundary mics are still referred to as PZMs. A very small omni element is mounted a fraction of an inch above a large rigid plate (Figure 5), which is then taped to a wall or other flat surface. Sound waves can reach it from only one direction, so there's less of the interference caused by reflections coming from multiple paths. Because of their low profile, boundary mics can be concealed on the walls or floor of a set (placing a mousepad between the mic's plate and the floor will help isolate it from footsteps). They're also useful when you have to record in a reverberant space and can't get close enough to the source. The reverb is still there, but it doesn't color the sound as much. Some lavalieres come with mounting adapters to use them as boundary mics.

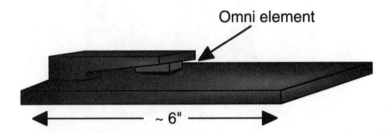

Figure 5: A boundary mic (PZM)

Cardioid

This kind of microphone, also known as a unidirectional, is like an elongated omni with a few large holes in the sides of the box (Figure 6).

When a sound comes from the rear (shown as the top path in the drawing), it enters the hole and strikes the back of the element. It can also refract around the

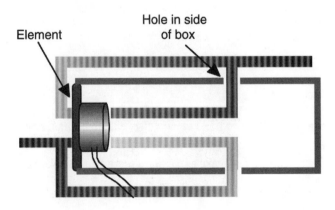

Figure 6: Cardioid microphone with sound coming from two directions

mic and strike the front of the element. Since these paths are about the same length, the front and back versions are the same strength and cancel each other out.

A sound coming from in front of the mic (bottom path) can also reach the back of the element. But in order to do so, it has to travel the length of the mic to the hole, and then back again to the element. By that time, it's considerably weaker than it is at the front of the mic and doesn't cancel itself.

The actual pickup pattern is mostly circular for three-quarters of the way around the mic and tucks in at the back. Viewed from above, it's sort of heart-shaped (Figure 7) . . . hence the name.

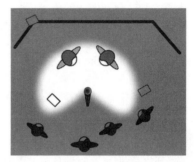

Figure 7: Cardioid pickup pattern

This directionality makes cardioids more useful on the video set. They can be aimed so their front is pointing to the actor, while the rear is pointing to a noise source or reverberating surface. The difference between front and back sensitivity decreases as the frequency goes down, and at very low frequencies the design is almost omnidirectional.

The holes in the sides of a directional mic are a critical part of its design. If you block them by grabbing the mic around its middle or gaffer-taping it to a support, you can seriously hurt the sound. It's counterintuitive, but cupping your hands around the end of most microphones—the way you'd cup them around your ear to concentrate on a sound—makes them *less* directional.

Shotgun

If you make the mic longer and add more holes of carefully calibrated dimensions, and possibly mount some tubes inside so that sounds coming in certain holes have to travel an even longer distance, you can make a mic that's more directional across more frequencies (Figure 8).

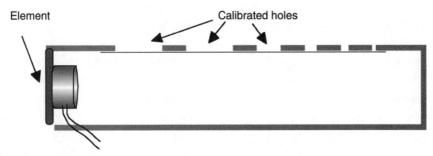

Figure 8: Shotgun mic

Shotgun mics are typically used on booms fairly close to the actors' heads, so they can reject a lot of the room noise and reverberation. They can also be handheld, just out of camera range, for interviews. Their pickup pattern may surprise you: while these mics are directional toward the front, depending on the design they will also have narrow areas of high sensitivity to the side, and of moderate sensitivity directly behind them or at a slight angle from the rear (Figure 9).

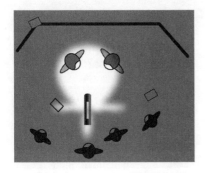

Figure 9: Shotgun pickup. The narrow, sensitive areas to the side and rear will vary with different mics, but some side and rear pickup will always exist.

Shotguns come in varying lengths, with shorter ones having wider pickup angles. A variation on the design, the hypercardioid mic, combines multiple elements for more rejection from the rear. Hypercardioids are used a lot in feature films for interiors, but good ones can be very expensive.

Real-world patterns

If you study the pattern drawings, you'll notice that the directional mics don't extend any farther into the set than the omni does. The difference is in how they reduce pickup from the sides or back. Because this tends to lower noise and reverb, we can choose to amplify the directional mic's signal more without hearing problems. But the extra "reach" is provided by the amplifier, not by the mic. When film sound mixers talk about the reach of a shotgun mic, they're really referring to how sensitive it is in all directions and how little electronic noise it contributes.

The best directional mics reject off-axis sounds by about 30 dB at mid and high frequencies. This is a significant amount, but certainly nothing like total rejection.

The only exception is a mic used with a parabolic reflector, which gathers sound pressure from a large area and focuses it in towards a small mic. Parabolics sacrifice frequency range for sensitivity, so they don't sound good for dialog recording. However, they're sometimes used in nature recording and surveillance.

By this point, I hope you've gotten the message:

➤ There is no such thing as a telephoto mic.

➤ All microphones are wide angle and have to be brought close to the subject.

➤ Some mics have wider angles than others.

Problems with directional mics

With nothing but patterns of holes and hollow tubes to work with, it's amazing that microphone designers can make their products as good as they are. But even the best of them are subject to physical limitations:

- *Off-axis response.* The holes and tubes cause cancellations and reinforcements depending on frequency . . . just as the walls of a room do (Chapter 1). This means that a directional mic can be accurate only for sounds coming in from its primary pickup area. Sounds from the rear and side will have their timbre affected. The more directional a mic is, the more pronounced this effect. Sounds coming from directly behind any directional mic, and those from the side of a shotgun, can be fairly muddy. Cut 9 of this book's CD lets you hear on- and off-axis response for different kinds of mics.

  This means shotguns have to be pointed precisely. If a single mic is used to cover dialog with two actors who aren't next to each other, it must be moved on each line. That's why boom operation takes some practice.

- *Proximity effect.* Directional mics emphasize bass notes as you get closer to them. Radio announcers frequently take advantage of this, working close to the mic to make their voices appear deeper. This also means that directional mics are more sensitive to "popped Ps": an overload caused by the sudden blast of air from a plosive vowel spoken too closely to the mic. At normal operating distances the proximity effect shouldn't be a problem.

- *Lack of low frequencies.* It's difficult to make a very directional mic directional for bass notes, so manufacturers often limit a shotgun mic's low-frequency response. The frequencies involved are too low to be of much concern for dialog, but you should be aware of this if using a shotgun for music or deep sound effects.

Types of Pickup

So far, we've spoken about a microphone's pickup element just as something that converts air movement to voltage. Here's how they work.

Dynamic mics

The simplest pickup element has a coil of wire attached to a plastic or foil diaphragm, suspended in a strong magnetic field. Air pressure waves make the diaphragm vibrate, and as the coil vibrates along with it, the magnetism creates an electric current (Figure 10). This is the same principle as an electric generator, only the ones in a power plant use turbines to continually rotate the coil instead of letting it just vibrate. In both cases, they turn physical movement into electricity.

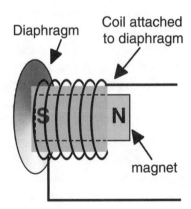

Figure 10: Dynamic microphone

Since a dynamic mic's voltage is directly generated by sound pressure, it takes a relatively large amount of pressure to get a usable output. Dynamic mics are not as sensitive as condenser mics, particularly in high frequencies. On the other hand, the simplicity of design makes them very rugged, and the lack of electronics in the mic itself means it can handle louder sounds than a condenser. The magnet in these mics can be fairly strong, so be careful with them around floppy disks.

Condenser mics

A condenser mic doesn't turn sound directly into output volts. A metalized plastic diaphragm is mounted close to a rigid plate, and an electric charge is applied to it. As sound pressure waves move the diaphragm closer or farther from the plate, a tiny but varying stream of electrons can jump across. This stream is too weak to send to a recorder—even a few feet of extra cable can damage the signal—so a preamplifier is mounted near the rigid plate (Figure 11). It uses an external voltage from a battery or the mixer to boost the signal to usable levels.

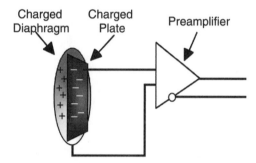

Figure 11: Condenser microphone

Traditional condenser mics charge the diaphragm with a constant high voltage (45–200 volts) that they derive from the incoming power. They can be extremely sensitive and are the full-sized mics used for most studio recordings and film production. Electret condenser mics are permanently charged at the factory, using electrochemical methods. While the best of them are almost as good as traditional ones, they can't be as sensitive, so their internal amplifiers generate comparatively more noise. However, the lack of a high-voltage supply means they can be smaller and less expensive.

Electret condensers are virtually the only type of pickup used in video production. The ones costing between fifty and a few hundred dollars, depending on their construction and pickup patterns, are more than adequate for this kind of work. Their size means that electrets are always preferred for lavalieres—even those used in major features.

Very cheap electrets—costing less than a dollar each—are found in toys, telephones, and multimedia computers. Don't expect the mic that came with your computer or sound card to be any more than a toy.

All condenser mics require some form of power supply:

- Very cheap electrets are usually powered directly from the circuits they're built into.

- Full-sized electrets used in production are powered either by a small battery in their bodies or via phantom powering (see below). Most traditional condenser mics use phantom power. Traditional condensers using tubes instead of transistors for their preamplifiers require dedicated power supplies with multiconductor cables.

- Tiny electrets used as lavalieres are powered by batteries in their plugs or phantom powering. If they're part of a wireless mic system, they'll get power from the transmitter's battery.

When power is first applied to a traditional condenser microphone, it may produce a loud "thunk" as the plate charges. Electrets may make clicking or popping noises when they're powered. As a general rule, leave a condenser mic's volume turned down when you change the battery or plug it into a phantom supply.

Dynamic or condenser?

Choose a condenser mic when you can for video work: the extra sensitivity translates into a better sounding track.

If the mic is going to be subject to humidity or physical abuse, or if you're planning to record very loud sounds, choose a dynamic mic.

Other microphone types

You may encounter a ribbon mic when you record the voice-over. Ribbons use the same generating principle as dynamics, but without a diaphragm: a delicate foil strip is suspended in a very strong magnetic field and is vibrated directly by the sound waves. Some announcers prefer the smoothness this adds to the sound. Ribbons are almost never found on a shooting set: they're too heavy to use on a boom, and not particularly sensitive. They're also fragile: a strong wind can knock the ribbon out of position.

Piezoelectric mics attach a crystal or ceramic element to the diaphragm, which generates electricity as it's flexed. Carbon mics rely on the principle that grains of carbon conduct electricity better when they're squeezed together. Both types of element are low fidelity, noisy, and have been largely replaced by cheap electrets.

Phantom Power

Balanced wiring, discussed in Chapter 3, uses a positive audio signal on one wire of a two-conductor cable while there's a negative signal on the other. This way it can reject noises that are picked up equally on both wires. A metallic shield is usually provided for additional noise protection. This scheme is used by all professional microphones that have to drive long cables.

When transistorized condenser microphones became popular for production, engineers realized the balanced microphone cables could also carry power for the diaphragm and preamplifier, without worrying about it contaminating the audio signal. A positive current (usually at 48 volts, but many mics will work at lower voltages) is applied to *both* wires of a balanced cable, with the current's negative side returning through the cable shield. Since this causes no voltage difference between the two signal wires, the audio circuitry totally ignores it.

In most equipment, phantom power is applied with a pair of precision resistors so the voltage is equal on both wires. A pair of capacitors keep the voltage from affecting the audio circuits, since capacitors block DC voltages (Figure 12). Some equipment uses a transformer to apply the voltage, in a circuit that's almost identical to the microphone's (Figure 13).

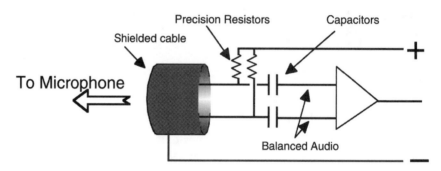

Figure 12: Phantom power in an input circuit

At the microphone end, a center-tapped transformer winding gathers DC voltage from both wires. DC can't jump from one winding of a transformer to the other, so it doesn't affect the mic's audio output. Transformers can be sensitive to AC hum in the vicinity, so some microphones use capacitors instead to block the phantom power from affecting the preamplifier output.

The voltage is called "phantom" because if a mic doesn't look for it, it disappears. The coil of a dynamic mic (Figure 10) is never connected to the cable shield. If a phantom voltage is fed equally to both of that mic's signal wires, it won't create any current flow through the microphone coil itself. As far as the mic is concerned, there never was any powering voltage coming from the mixer.

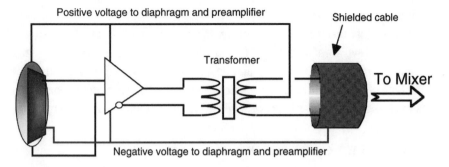

Figure 13: Balanced microphone

Beware the Phantom!

Phantom power works well in most professional applications. However, using it improperly can damage the microphone or mixer:

- If an unbalanced microphone is connected to a phantom supply, voltage will be applied across its element.

- If a cable or connector is damaged so that either conductor touches the shield, the phantom supply will be shorted out. Most plug-in XLR-to-phone-plug adapters will short out a phantom voltage this way.

- If a balanced line-level signal is applied to a microphone input that has phantom power, the voltage can damage the signal source.

On the other hand, phantom power lets you run wired condenser mics all day without worrying about changing batteries. If you're sure your microphones and cables are in good shape and need the voltage, leave it on. Otherwise, turn phantom power off.

T or Simplex Powering

Before phantom power became a standard, some condenser microphones used on film shoots were powered with a positive voltage on one wire and a negative voltage on the other. This is now obsolete, but some mics in rental inventories may still be wired this way. It's not compatible with any video production equipment.

Wireless mics

Although wireless mic kits generally include an omnidirectional lavaliere, any mic can be used with a wireless transmitter. So we'll deal with the radio link specifically, one of the most fragile aspects of sound production. So many things can contribute to its unreliability that wireless is often considered more voodoo than science.

There are two ways to measurably improve a wireless link: raise the frequency to where interference isn't as likely, and improve the way the receiver captures the signal. Both of these add to the cost and are often ignored in video production. There are also some techniques to improve wireless results that won't cost you anything.

Throwing Money at the Problem *Can* Help

Wireless is one of the areas where there's a direct relationship between how much you spend and how reliable the system will be. The high frequencies involved require precision design and components, and that doesn't come cheap. Budget systems, costing two to three hundred dollars, might be adequate for your production. But if you're unhappy with the results, know that professional systems—at three to four times the price—really are significantly better at getting a signal from one place to another. At least, all of this equipment is available from rental houses so you can try before committing.

The frequency a wireless system uses is controlled by precision crystals, and the system has to be carefully tuned for them. Many systems have to be set at the factory, and their operating channel can't be adjusted in the field. But while the ability to change channels adds to the cost, it may be the only way to avoid unexpected interference sources. If you're going to be using a wireless at a lot of different locations, look for a "frequency agile" system.

VHF vs UHF

VHF (Very High Frequency) wireless shares spectrum space with the upper part of the standard television band, under approximately 200 mHz. There's a lot of competition in this area, and you may find that particular frequencies aren't usable.

UHF (Ultra High Frequency) wireless operates around 800 mHz, where there's less going on and there are more frequencies available for multiple mics and to avoid interference. UHF can also transmit with three times more power than VHF in the United States, which can translate to a more reliable connection. UHF adds about a hundred dollars to a budget system; virtually all high-end systems already operate in that band.

Diversity reception

If the talent is moving around while wearing a wireless mic, you might encounter dead spots—places where reflections off metallic elements on the set (or in the building structure) cause radio cancellation, just as acoustic echoes can cause sound cancellation. The signal dies out or is replaced by bursts of noise.

Diversity receivers, available on both frequency ranges, can cure this. These are actually two separate receivers with antennas spaced far enough apart that they won't be in the same cancellation pattern. A circuit constantly compares the signals at each, switching to whichever is stronger. Diversity reception does not add much to the cost of a wireless system.

Better antennas

Special antenna systems are available that can be aimed away from sources of radio interference. Radio frequency filters can also be a small amount of help. These items aren't usually used in field recording but are available for rental or permanent installations.

Working Smarter

The biggest cause of wireless mic problems is weak batteries. These things eat current. Don't expect them to operate more than three or four hours on a single set.

Wireless mics are very sensitive to distance, and the signal can be disrupted by virtually anything—light stands, sets, or even production personnel. The best place to put the receiver will always be in line-of-sight with the transmitter, just out of camera range. This may mean hiding it behind a prop that's on camera. Sometimes it's best to have a production assistant carry the receiver around the set if the talent is moving around a lot.

If a proper receiver location means you'll need extra long cable to reach the recorder, so be it; a lot more can happen to damage a signal in the air than on a wire. If you have to separate the antenna from the receiver, use special low-loss 50-ohm cable and keep the wire as short as possible.

A wireless transmitter's antenna should be kept in a straight line and oriented in the same direction as the receiver. This means the free end of the antenna will usually have to be secured to clothing with a safety pin. Tying a rubber band between antenna wire and safety pin will provide some strain relief. Avoid placing the antenna directly against the body if there'll be a lot of perspiration, since moisture can dissipate the signal.

The wire from microphone to body pack can absorb some of a wireless mic's signal. Keep the wire as far from the antenna as possible, and never let it cross the antenna. Metallic objects on the actor—such as keys, coins, and jewelry—can also interfere. If the signal drops out while the actor is moving, have them empty their pockets or move the transmitter.

Wireless transmitters work best when they're adjusted for the mic and for the actor's delivery. Many systems include an LED on the transmitter, near a screwdriver adjustment for setting audio level. The LED should just start to blink on the loudest expected sound.

Watch out for anything that can generate interference on the set—neon lights, electronic dimmers, generators, even coils of powered cable. Video cameras, recorders, and monitors can also generate local interference that can be reduced by moving away from them.

And always bring a backup wired connection, whether it's another mic or an adapter to use the wireless rig's mic with a standard cable. Sometimes the voodoo doesn't work.

Connecting Microphone to Camera

(Okay, you're actually connecting the microphone to a *recorder*. But in video production, the recorder is almost always integrated with the camera.)

Professional cameras will have one or two balanced mic inputs, with separate level controls and switchable limiters. Using them with a professional microphone is simply a matter of plug-and-play.

Prosumer cameras usually have mini-plug unbalanced inputs. Because they're unbalanced, they can't be used with more than a couple of feet of cable without being subject to hum or noise. The mini-plug often also has a DC voltage applied to it to power the preamplifier of an electret mic. It's not phantom power, and if a professional mic is connected to it, the result can be additional noise.

The only proper cure is a balancing adapter. This is a small metal box that fits between the camera's baseplate and tripod, containing transformers to balance each mic channel and often also providing volume controls and an attenuator so the input can be used with line-level signals. The adapter lets you use balanced cables and microphones, which are virtually immune to wiring noise (Chapter 3). It costs a couple of hundred dollars.

Lower-priced XLR-to-mini cables, designed for use with prosumer cameras, are also available from video supply houses. These contain capacitors to block the DC voltage, but don't provide any balancing. They're usable if the mic cable will be kept very short, or if you're feeding the camera from a mixer near the camera. If the latter, you'll also need an attenuator to lower the mixer's line output to microphone level.

You can also get metal XLR-to-mini adapters for a couple of dollars at electronics chain stores. These don't block the DC voltage, don't provide balancing, and shouldn't be used.

Mini-plugs are physically and electrically fragile. If there's a strain on the cable—even from the weight of an XLR connector—they'll unplug. If they're plugged and unplugged too many times, their springs weaken and the contact becomes noisy. I have no idea why any manufacturer would think them appropriate in a four-thousand-dollar camera, but you may have to live with the little devils:

- Secure the plug with a rubber band wrapped around the plug and camera, or with a piece of gaffer tape.

- Provide strain relief for the weight of a cord-mounted XLR connector by taping it to the camera or tripod.

- If you're using a balancing adapter box, keep the box mounted to the camera and plugged in.

- If you anticipate plugging and unplugging a lot, get a short extension cable and leave it plugged in. Wear out the jack on the extension cable instead of the camera.

Automatic level controls

Prosumer cameras have automatic circuits that adjust their audio sensitivity to get the best recording on tape. These circuits aren't very smart. If the dialog pauses for a while, they'll look for something else to record; as they raise the input sensitivity, any acoustic or electronic noise is emphasized. As soon as the dialog resumes, they lower the sensitivity. When you play back the tape, you'll hear noise rushing up during every pause. When you cut two shots together, there will probably be a jump in the noise level.

These circuits should be turned off for any professional shooting. Some cameras turn automatic level control back on whenever you power up or change the tape or battery, so keep checking to make sure they've stayed turned off.

If the circuit can't be defeated, at least make sure you're sending the camera an appropriate level and that the signal path is very clean. These circuits also look at the average level on both input channels. If you're shooting with only one microphone, route it to both inputs through a mixer or else they'll set the record level too high.

Mixing Microphones

If you have only two microphones on the set, the easiest thing is to route each to a separate channel in the recorder and sort them out in post. Since you haven't committed to a mix at the shoot, this also gives you the option of using just one mic, processing the mics separately, or mixing them in any proportion.

If you're using more than two microphones and don't have enough isolated tracks in the recorder, you have to mix in the field. By and large, any active mixer you choose—one with its own battery or AC power supply—will do a good job. Most provide phantom power; many have limiters or wind-noise filters; some include slate mics and tone generators. Connect the output of the mixer to the line-level input of the camera or XLR balancing adapter. All of these mixers also have headphone outputs, which may be handy during setup or to feed the boom operator. But during actual shooting, it's better to plug your headphone into the camera; that way, you'll hear if there are any sound problems introduced at that stage.

There are also passive mixers available that combine the microphone signals but don't have a power supply and don't amplify the signals to line level. These are potential noisemakers and should be avoided.

Problems Introduced by Multiple Mics

When one sound source is picked up by two microphones at different distances, which are then mixed together, there's a good chance of cancellations coloring the sound or adding hollowness. This is exactly the same problem as the multiple sound paths described in Chapter 1; only the different-length paths are mixed electronically instead of acoustically at your ears.

Imagine two characters, each with their wireless hidden on them. George's is right under his shirt, so it picks him up much more strongly than it does Sue—when she's across the room.

But then she crosses to him. George and Sue are now only a foot apart, and his microphone hears almost as much of her as it does of him . . . but slightly delayed, since she's not as close to it. Similarly, Sue's hair mic hears almost as much of George as it does of her . . . but with a similar delay. If either one of them talks while both mics are being mixed, the sound will be hollow or metallic because of the cancellations. Worse, if either one of them moves while this is going on, the cancellations will shift frequencies as the distance between them changes.

In a case like this, you have to ride the volume controls on the mixer. Turn George's mic down when Sue speaks and vice versa. When they come together for the clinch, kill George's mic completely; Sue's hair mic should work fine for both of them.

Whenever multiple mics are being mixed on the set, someone has to actively monitor and control the mix. If you can't spare an experienced person to do this job, don't use a mixer.

Phase Errors

You can get into worse trouble if one or more of the mics is miswired to reverse the phase. Normally, microphones are built so they create a positive voltage on pin 2 of the XLR connector when there's positive air pressure. If pins 2 and 3 are reversed at the mic plug or in the extension cable, positive pressure will create a negative voltage. When this mic is mixed with a normal one, the positive and negative voltage will cancel each other out. Depending on how close the mics are together, this can happen just to bass notes or to most of the spectrum.

To test whether two mics are wired the same way, hold them close together and turn only one of them up. Then start speaking while you raise the volume on the second microphone. If all is well, the mixed microphone signal will get louder and louder. If there's cancellation, the mixed volume will start to go down as you bring in the second mic.

Mono Compatibility and MS Recording

If your stereo video is going to broadcast, multimedia, or Internet, there's a chance at least some viewers will hear it in mono. This can create the same problem as mixing microphones together on a set, only you don't have control of the relative intensity.

Production dialog is almost always mono in episodic television, even in programs that are broadcast as stereo. You should do the same: while it may be acoustically interesting to have a character's voice move from left to right as he crosses the set, this creates far more problems than it's worth.

On the other hand, some shoots—such as of musical performances—cry out for stereo. You can assure compatibility by using the mid-side (MS) mic technique. You'll need two microphones that are closely matched for sound quality, one with an omni or cardioid pickup and the other with a bidirectional (Figure 8) pickup. Bidirectional mics are so rare in video production that most catalogs don't list them. You'll have to get them from a music studio supplier. Many multipattern mics (also not used in video) have a bidirectional setting. A few manufacturers also make stereo microphones with matched omni and bidirectional elements in the same housing.

Place the microphones as close together as possible, with the omni or cardioid facing the performers. The bidirectional mic should be aligned sideways, so that its front is facing the left side and its back is facing the right (Figure 14). Since the mics are close together, the time delay between them is very slight.

Since the cardioid (light gray in the drawing) is facing the performers, it picks up the right and left side of the stage equally. The bidirectional (dark gray) is facing the left, so sounds from the left side of the stage reach the front of its element, with

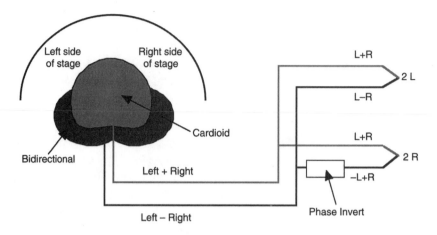

Figure 14: Mid-side miking to preserve mono compatibility

positive pressures producing a positive voltage. Sounds from the right side of the stage reach the back of its element, so positive pressures from that side produce a negative voltage. Its signal consists of +Left combined with –Right, or Left – Right.

If the two mic signals are then mixed, the positive and negative rights cancel out . . . and you get the left side of the stage only. But if the bidirectional's signal is inverted before they're mixed, easily done with an electronic circuit (or miswired connector), it consists of –Left and +Right. Mixing the two mics together now means the positive and negative lefts will cancel . . . and you get the right side of the stage only.

This may seem like a lot of work—it's really not—but it pays off when somebody listens in mono: when you combine the derived left and right outputs, the bidirectional mic completely cancels itself out! You're left with nothing but the cardioid's signal, and absolutely no coloration caused by time delay.

As a matter of fact, this same scheme is at the heart of analog stereo FM and TV. Using electronic inversions rather than a bidirectional mic, the left and right channels are combined into a main mono signal. This is what's broadcast in the usual band, and mono listeners hear it with no trouble. The "side" signal is broadcast in a slightly higher band that stereo receivers can get. The receiver then performs a similar translation, recreating left and right.

Mid-Side Tricks

Mid-side techniques can be used to create a stereo "zoom mic" for sound effects recordings. Set up the same way, only provide a volume control in the output of the bidirectional mic. When that mic is turned up, the stereo effect will be wide. As its level is reduced, the recording gets narrower and narrower. When it's all the way off, the recording is mono. You can use this to match the perceived width of an effect to its image, without sacrificing mono compatibility.

A variation of the technique doesn't require a bidirectional mic and doesn't create true stereo, but it can provide a spaciousness to scenes for stereo viewers. It's particularly helpful in areas where a good stereo recording would be hard to set up, such as a factory interior. Put a lavaliere on the actor or point a shotgun at the dialog, and call that the Left + Right channel. Then put an omni somewhere else—a boundary mic on the floor, in front of the action, works well for this. Call this the Left – Right channel, and mix them as if it were MS. It won't be true stereo, but it'll give you a lot of control during the final mix without any of the hollowness of trying to mix a typically spaced stereo pair. Check the results in mono, to make sure you haven't accidentally reversed the channels.

Rooms and Recording

I have an actress friend who used to dub the, uh, dialog in Swedish sex films. But when she told me about it, I topped her: I've done *my* job under blankets in a hotel room, in the back of a limousine, and with a professor inside a world map. The search for good sound on a location can make you do strange things, but the right technique will make a big difference in your finished tape.

The foam tiles on a sound studio's walls aren't part of the soundproofing—foam doesn't have much mass, and it has too many holes to stop airborne noise. Their purpose is to absorb reflections, since sound bouncing around a room can make a voice sound tubby or hollow (see Chapter 1).

Testing the Space

It's not practical to put up foam tiles when you're shooting in a conference room or factory floor, but you can still use a piece of foam to find out if there are going to be echoes. Before you decide where the camera will be, stand at the talent's position. Hold a square of foam—or a folded towel, couch cushion, or anything else absorbent—about two feet in front of your face and sing "ahh" at a fairly loud volume. Then take the absorber away and keep singing. If you hear any difference in the sound of your own voice, it's caused by reflections that can interfere with the sound.

Studios often have nonparallel walls to control reflections, so that sounds don't keep echoing between them to cause hollowness by reinforcing individual frequencies. If the sound can bounce at an angle, the reflections follow different paths each time, and the hollowness gets smoothed out. You can't push the walls away where you're shooting, but you can do the next best thing by keeping the talent at an angle to any reflective surfaces.

Both the distance and the angle between talent and wall are important. Walk around the room while you're doing the sing-into-the-foam test. If light or props mean that you have to place the talent in a less-than-ideal position, try rotating the setup a few degrees so that the voice strikes reflective surfaces at an angle. Figure 15 shows how changing the talent's position can make a big difference in a finished track.

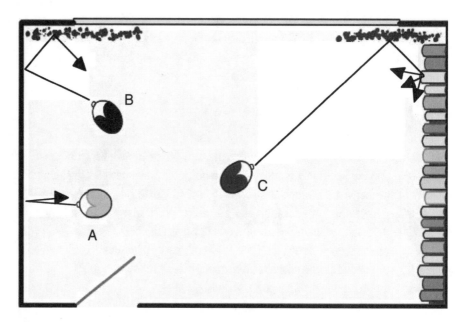

Figure 15: Where the talent stands in a room can make a difference.

The drawing shows a typical conference room with drapes and a bookshelf. Actor A is in the worst position, facing a wall (and close to any noise from the hallway). Actor B is better because, the angle gives echoes a longer path, and the drape absorbs some of the sound. Actor C is in the best position, taking advantage of distance, absorption, angles, and the way an uneven surface like a bookshelf breaks up the reflections.

Cutting Down Reflections

The reflections that really matter are the ones the talent is facing into—usually from the wall behind the camera. This means you've got some options for cutting them down, without worrying about how they'll look. The handiest is to carry a stack of sound blankets—heavy, padded cloths about six feet square, available from film and video supply houses. Hang them from the offending wall, at about the same height as the talent's mouth. Hanging a few on the sides of the room can also cut down the parallel-wall problem. If you don't want to attach them directly to walls, hang them from a light stand.

Sound blankets can be folded up and stored when they're not in use. A less flexible alternative (literally) but with better absorption is Owens-Corning type 703 fiberglass. This is a specially compressed version of the fibers used for house insulation, designed specifically for sound. It comes in lightweight panels, an inch thick by several feet square, and can be found at acoustical-ceiling supply companies and bigger home improvement centers. Wrap the panels in an old bedsheet or something similar to keep the fibers from irritating your skin. The panels are rigid enough to be leaned against a wall, and light enough that they can be hung from standard picture hooks.

You can soften a reflective surface by closing drapes, moving a sofa, or even lining up a row of heavily dressed production assistants against it. But there's another technique—diffusion—that can also conquer some of the offending echoes. That's because the biggest problem with a hard wall is that it reflects all the sound back in the same direction. If you can break up the surface so some of the reflections go elsewhere, there'll be less noticeable echo. If you don't have a bookshelf handy, try stacking up some road cases and equipment boxes at random angles. The round tubes used to ship tripods or light stands—or any large rounded objects—are particularly helpful, since they diffuse sound in all directions.

Be Flexible

Keep trying different placements and angles within a room—and other recording spaces—until you get a sense of how walls affect sound. That's how I got into some of the weird places referred to at the start of this section. The limo was parked in a dealer's showroom . . . but the room itself had gigantic glass windows and an opening to their machine shop, so we moved an interview into the car to gain isolation and absorption. The map was the kind with large sheets of heavy paper hanging from an easel; we were recording voice-over inserts in an echoey classroom, so we held some of the pages out to improvise a tent, and I put the professor inside of it.

CHAPTER 7

Recording Dialog

R O S E ' S   R U L E S

⇨ You can fake almost anything else, and undo or change it if you're not happy with the result. But a bad dialog recording is forever.

⇨ You can write, direct, shoot, edit, create graphics, and mix the whole project all by yourself, all in your own sweet time. But if you won't be able to give proper attention to sound *at the shoot*, have someone else help you.

No area of the production process seems more misunderstood by videographers than how to record sound while they're shooting. This is a shame, considering the process has been refined for close to three-quarters of a century in Hollywood. The folks who do sound for a living know how to do it right, and the information is freely available. It's not rocket science. In fact, once you know some basics about handling a boom or mounting a lavaliere, the rest is just common sense.

The main difference between boom and lav (other than size and how they're mounted) is how they tend to sound when used properly:

- Boom mics pick up the natural ambience of a scene. They help create the illusion we're overhearing something that's really happening. That's why they're the usual choice for dramatic dialog.

- Lavalieres concentrate on the performer's voice and help create the illusion that the person on camera is talking directly to us. They're the best choice for a spokesperson or demonstrator.

Of course, your own artistic sensibilities should outweigh any hard-and-fast rules. However, in dramatized feature films there's a definite hierarchy to miking methods. In order of preference:

1. Use a shotgun on a boom, over the actor's head and just out of camera range. If that's not possible . . .

2. Use a shotgun and boom, but from underneath and pointing up to the actor. If you can't use a boom . . .

3. Plant a cardioid or shotgun on the set, where it'll cover dialog. If there's nowhere to hide a full-size mic . . .

4. Plant a lavaliere on the set. They're small and easily hidden. If you absolutely can't plant a mic . . .

5. Put a lav on the actor, and run the cable down their pants leg. If their leg will be in the shot . . .

6. Use a wireless lav, and hope that radio problems don't ruin the take.

Of course, you can also use traditional handheld or stand-mounted mics if you don't mind them being in the shot. This is common in news reporting, and the technique is simply to get the mic as close to the subject as possible. But I've never seen it done in nonnews situations, except for tapes of club singers or standup comics—and they already know how to use their mics.

Using Boom Mics

You can't use a boom mic unless you're sure where to point it. Just aiming it vaguely toward the actor doesn't work; the more directional a microphone is, the worse things will sound if not coming from exactly the right direction. There's a world of difference between what you'll hear with a mic pointed at the mouth, and one pointed at the chest or forehead, even though the voice will be almost the same level in each.

To run a boom properly, you'll need two things:

- A headphone feed. Small monitor amplifiers are available as belt-packs that let the mic signal pass through unaffected. These can be handy for a single boom operator. If other mics are being mixed on the set, though, it's better to monitor the entire mix.

- An alert attitude. Pay attention during the rehearsal and the take. You have to know how the actors will exchange lines or move around the set, so that your mic is in the right place before a line begins. Starting a line off-mic and then moving it on-mic is as distracting as having the entire line badly miked. Pay attention to the actors' body language as well, so you can anticipate their movements.

Boom Placement

The best place to boom from is above and slightly in front of the actor's head, as low as possible without getting in the shot, with the mic pointed at an angle toward the mouth. If two characters are close together, you can often position the mic between them and just rotate it slightly as they exchange lines.

Overhead booming provides the most natural sound for dramatic dialog. Since the mouth is closest to the mic, voices are emphasized—a good thing— while the downward angle also picks up prop noises and footsteps.

If you're booming from above in a room with a low ceiling, remember that highly directional mics change the timbre of sounds coming from the back and sides. If the ceiling is too close to the mic, echoes from it may color the dialog. Check your headphones during the rehearsal, and if this happens choose a less directional mic or boom from below.

If there's no ceiling height or the shot requires a lot of headroom, booming from below is often an alternative. But it requires more cooperation on the set. Prop noises and footsteps will be louder, so lines have to be delivered without too much movement. If you can, persuade the director to stage the shot with characters sitting down: their mouths will be closer to the mic. There's a tendency to tilt the camera down as a shot gets wider, so the videographer will have to warn you before zooming out.

Booming from directly in front, with microphone parallel to the floor, is seldom a good idea. Echoes and noises from behind the actor will be picked up almost as loud as the voice. Mouth noises and sibilance are generally projected forward, so a close frontal mic will pick up more of them.

How to stay out of the shot

The boom operator wants the mic as close as possible. The videographer wants total freedom composing the shot. A reality check is always necessary, and—unless you have a video monitor available—you'll have to count on the camera operator to tell you during setup how close you can get.

You could start with the mic high and gradually lower it until someone says, "any lower and you'll be in the shot." But that almost always results in too much safety margin and more mic distance than is necessary.

It's better to start with the mic *in* the shot and gradually raise it until it can't be seen any more.

Some boom operators put a piece of white camera tape on the end of their windscreen, so it'll be immediately obvious in the viewfinder if the mic dips too low during a take.

Controlling Perspective

As a shot gets wider, you'll have to move the boom out so it won't be seen. This changes the ratio of direct to reflected sound, so the mic will pick up relatively more room reverberation. A small amount of this is not only acceptable, but appropriate: wide shots make the actor appear farther from us, and in real life we expect to hear more echo from a distant voice than a close one (even across a small room). The converse is also true: as the shot closes in, you have to move the mic in to pick up less echo.

If a shot is framed very wide but without much headroom, you might want to deliberately pick up more echo. Raise the mic slightly higher than usual, or point it more toward the floor.

Three tricks will help you keep mic perspective in, uh, perspective:

- The effect must be subtle. Once we're aware of changes in reverb, they become distracting. Early talking pictures changed the mic perspective with each edit: the effect was horrible, and sound operators quickly learned to leave their mics relatively stable.

- Each character's volume should stay constant during a scene. Since moving a mic farther away means less of the voice is picked up, you have to compensate by raising the recording level.

- Leave difficult decisions for postproduction. If you're not sure, stay close. It's easy to add reverb in the mix, but impossible to take it away.

Operating the Boom

It's no problem to work a mic boom (assuming you have enough stamina to hold your arms over your head for long periods of time), but it's not necessarily intuitive.

Extension

After you extend each boom section as far as it'll go, collapse the joint slightly so the pieces overlap a couple of inches. This will make it sturdier and less likely to creak at the joints. Figure 1 shows the wrong (top) and right (bottom) way to extend. It's better to extend three sections partway than two sections all the way.

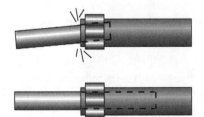

Figure 1: If a boom section is extended all the way (top), it won't be as strong as if it overlaps (bottom).

The clutch that locks the sections of a boom when they're extended can wear out and become difficult to use. A layer of plumber's Teflon tape around the threads usually fixes things.

Sometimes sections of a collapsed fiber boom can get stuck together, particularly if it was moist when stored. Gentle heating can usually get things moving again.

Overhead booming

Hold the boom with your arms straight up in an H position (Figure 2), rather than out like a Y (Figure 3). This way the weight is being supported by the bones in your arm, not by your muscles.

Figure 2: It's easier to hold the boom with your arms straight up . . .

Figure 3: . . . not out to the sides.

It may be tempting to hold the boom like a flagpole (Figure 4), but this gives you less control over how the mic is aimed. Since the boom itself will be at an angle, it's likely that it'll cross into a corner of the shot.

If you can, hold the pole a foot or so in toward the middle rather than at the very end. This way part of the boom can act as a counterweight, and you won't be stressing your wrists as much.

Figure 4: Don't hold the boom like a flagpole.

Cable management

The mic cable can make noise as you move the boom, by banging around inside the boom pole. This gets conducted up the cable and into the mic.

Isolate the microphone end by making a small loop in the cable and securing it with a piece of tape. The loop should be just big enough to keep from slipping into the boom.

Then, loop the mic cable around your finger where you're holding the boom, and pull slightly to keep the cable taut.

If you're using a boom where the cable has to run outside, tape the microphone end of the cable tightly to the boom. Wrap the cable around the boom a few times on its way down, and grab the cable along with the boom.

As the boom is swung around, a loose XLR connector may rattle and create electrical or mechanical noise. To be safe, secure the connector to the mic by wrapping it with tape.

Using Lavalieres

A lav works by being close to the source of sound—the actor's mouth—so that the inverse-square law (Chapter 1) assures a clean pickup with very little room reverb or natural noises. For dramatic dialog, this may end up being *too* clean. Don't try to compensate by moving the mic farther down the actor's body; all you'll gain is extra clothing noise. Instead, use a second mic for room ambience. Point a shotgun away from the actor, or put a boundary mic on the floor near a wall. If you can, record it to a separate channel, and mix them in post; otherwise, just mix a tiny bit of the room mic in with the lav.

Types of Lavs

The first lavalieres, in the early days of television, used dynamic elements and were so big and heavy they actually had to be worn on a lanyard around the neck—hence the name. (Louise de La Vallière, a girlfriend of Louis XIV, liked to suspend pendants from a gold chain around her neck. Never thought you'd find that in a book about digital sound, did you?)

Today, lavs almost always use electret condenser elements (Chapter 6), and they range in size from about a third of an inch diameter by half an inch long, to literally smaller than the head of a match. While the smallest mics are easier to conceal, as the element gets smaller it intercepts fewer moving air molecules. This generates less voltage, and electronic noise from the mic's preamplifier becomes more signifi-cant. As a general rule, smaller mics generate more self-noise, but today's mic man-ufacturers have learned how to make even tiny mics quiet enough for video tracks.

The preamps are powered by a small battery in the XLR connector or phantom voltage on the audio line. The batteries are usually good for at least a day's worth of shooting; when they get weak, you'll start to hear distortion. Some mics are made specifically to be used with wireless transmitters and are powered by them. Of course, batteries in a wireless transmitter don't last more than a few hours.

Lavs are sometimes described as having "reach," with some being better than others for distance miking. Actually, the main difference between them is how much noise their preamps make—quieter ones can be amplified more, so you record more details of the scene—and how evenly they pick up different frequencies. A mic with more bass is often considered a close-up mic and can be appropriate on a spokesper-son or demonstrator who's talking directly to camera. Mics with less bass are better matched to the sound of boom mics and can be intercut more easily in dramatic scenes. Some lavs have a "presence" peak around 3 kHz to pick out the voice bet-ter when an actor turns slightly away. A few deliberately boost all the high fre-quencies to compensate for the muffling effect of clothing. While either of these characteristics can be desirable on their own, they make matching with other mics more difficult.

Almost all lavs are designed as omnidirectional, but when you place them on an actor or on a wall of the set, one side of them is blocked. Some lavs have their ele-ment pointing toward the top of a cylindrical case, while others point toward the side. This makes no difference in the pickup pattern, though it does influence the shape and thickness of the mic. All lavs have a pattern of holes or a grill either on the top or side where the sound enters; be careful not to block it when mounting the mic.

A few directional lavalieres are available. They're difficult to hide in clothing, because they have to be precisely pointed, and because the tape used to mount a hidden mic blocks the holes that make them directional. However, they can be handy as planted mics.

Mounting Lavalieres

Decide whether the mic can be visible in the shot. A lot of times there's no need to hide a mic, either because the talent is obviously a spokesperson or because a shot is wide enough that a tiny dot on the lapel won't be noticeable. It's always easier, and always sounds better, to have the mic outside the clothing. Sometimes, all you need to do is wrap some paper tape around the mic and clip, and color it with a felt-tip pen to match wardrobe.

The smallest lavs are about an eighth of an inch in diameter and come in various tans, black, white, and neutral gray. (Don't believe someone can make a good-sounding mic that small? See Figure 5.) They're so small that they can be poked through a buttonhole or between the weave of a loose sweater and secured from the back with tape. If you choose a color that's close to brightness level of the wardrobe or skin, the normal color bleed of a video camera will blur over the microphone. It will be invisible in all but the tightest shots . . . and extreme close-ups concentrate on the face, not on the lapel.

Figure 5: Not a trick photo, just a very small lavaliere (courtesy Countryman Associates, Inc.)

Clip-on lavs

Lavs come with a variety of mounting clips and tie tacks to make the sound operator's job easier. Choose an appropriate one for the clothing, and you're almost all set.

The mic should be as close to the mouth as possible. A shirt collar or high up on a jacket lapel is always preferable to the middle of a necktie. If talent's head will be turning during the shot, choose the side that'll be favored—usually the side facing the interviewer or camera.

If the mic comes with a foam windscreen, you may want to use it to prevent popped Ps. You'll seldom need to use the wire mesh windscreen except in windy exteriors.

Don't let the wire dangle from the lavaliere. It's important to provide strain relief, both to prevent accidents and to isolate the mic from cable-borne noises. If you're using a clip, loop the wire up through the clip and into the clothing (Figure 6). Then grab it from behind with the clip's teeth (Figure 7) to hold the loop in place.

Figure 6: Loop a lav's cable up through the clip . . .

Figure 7: . . . then grab it with the clip's teeth.

If you're using a tie tack, make a loop of wire as a strain relief and hold it in place with tape. It will be similar to the strain relief shown in Figure 8.

Hidden mics

Lavs are commonly hidden between layers of clothing high up on the chest or under a collar. The preferred method of mounting is to take two pieces of one-inch tape and fold them into triangles, like folding a flag, with the sticky sides out. Put these half-inch sticky triangles on both sides of the mic, and stick the mic in place with the bottom one. Loop the cable below the mic as a strain relief, with a piece of tape or thread to hold the loop loosely enough so that there's some play if you tug on the wire. Tape the cable down below the loop. Figure 8 shows the completed assembly.

Then press the top layer of clothing onto the top sticky triangle. The top triangle holds the clothing in place so it can't rub against the mic.

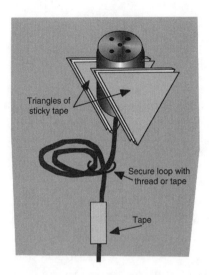

Triangles of sticky tape

Secure loop with thread or tape

Tape

Figure 8: Taping a concealed mic in place

If talent is wearing only one layer of clothing and you have to mount the mic directly to skin, use nonallergenic surgical paper tape. Wipe the skin with an alcohol prep pad first to remove grease and perspiration. The tape and pads are available at drugstores.

You can use similar mounting methods to hide a mic under long hair, the bill of a hat, or even, with a very small mic, on an eyeglass frame. One favorite trick is to hollow out a fountain pen and cut a hole in the top, then place the mic inside. A shirt pocket can be a reasonable place for a lav, and you don't have to worry about clothing noises. You'll have to make a small hole in the pocket for the wire, but presumably your video has some budget to repair wardrobe.

Cable termination

If talent is wearing a wireless transmitter, hide the transmitter somewhere on their body and you're done. Observe the precautions about wireless antennas from the previous chapter.

A wired connection is more reliable, so cable is usually run down a pants leg. Don't let the mic's XLR connector dangle! This puts extra strain on the thin mic cable, and if the character has to move around during a shot, the connector will make noise hitting the floor. Instead, loop the excess cable and secure the connector inside the pants. You can use a rubber band and safety pin to attach it to the inside cuff, or an ace bandage or ankle warmer to wrap it to the talent's leg.

If the character will be seated, you can run the wire out the back of their shirt or under their jacket. Stuff the XLR connector into a back pocket and secure it with a rubber band and safety pin.

Between takes, all the talent will have to do is reach up and unplug. Then they'll be free to roam around without you having to unrig them.

Avoiding Noise in Lavalieres

All other things being equal, a lav is electrically noisier than a shotgun. This is a function of the smaller element, and there's nothing you can do about it. If you turn its mixer channel all the way up, you may hear some hissing. Fortunately, a lav is almost always closer to the sound source than a shotgun; it picks up more sound pressure, so you don't need to raise its volume control so high.

Mechanical noise is a bigger problem, but easier to control. If you've mounted the mic properly, there shouldn't be any clothing rubbing directly against it. Clothing can also rub against the mic's cable, and the noise will be transmitted up the wire. If this happens, tape the wire someplace else to where it'll be protected. Some mics have special fiber inserts in their cables so they don't transmit as much noise.

Clothing can also rub against itself, and the mic will pick up the rustling sound. It may take some detective work to isolate the source. Once you do, use triangles of tape to hold the clothing in position. The antistatic solution sold for home clothes dryers can soften noisy layers of clothing. If a shirt has been heavily starched, spray water on it near the microphone for some local destarching.

Coordinate clothing choices with the wardrobe department or talent. Cottons and woolens will always be quieter than synthetics or nylons. Corduroy should be avoided.

Planted Mics

Because they're so small, lavs are usually used as plant mics. But their higher self-noise means they have to be close to the sound source. If you can hide a full-size mic in the same place, you'll find it sounds better.

If you're planting a lav at a desk or table, hiding it in a pencil jar or flower pot may pick up echoes. Depending on how the talent sits while they're talking, their voices might be directed at the table surface and bounce back to the mic. If the mic is a third of the way between table and mouth, the reflections can be almost as loud as the direct sound. To avoid this, use a directional lav, or mount the mic to some surface that can block reflections (such as the hidden side of a telephone or a computer monitor).

Watch for hidden low-level noise sources when you're planting a mic. A computer monitor, for example, will radiate electronic hash while it's turned on. A potted fern can be a good place to "plant" a mic, but its leaves will get noisy if there's a breeze.

The best way to pick up dialog in a car is to clip the mic to a sun visor rather than use a body mic. This avoids clothing noise, picks up the characteristic acoustic of an automobile, and on quiet roads can cover all the occupants of the car.

Room Tone

Every acoustic space has its own sound. This isn't just a combination of air conditioners, distant traffic, and other machinery coming through the windows, but rather, how the size and shape of the room itself modify these sounds. We're almost never aware of this sound, but if it goes away—perhaps because a line of dialog has to be opened up to accommodate a cutaway—we can tell that it's missing.

It's common practice in features, after all the shooting at a location is done but before equipment is struck, to record a minute of "room tone"—just the sound of the room itself, with the same general mic placement and volume settings as were used for dialog. Then in post, if a production track has to be muted or replaced with a studio version, the room tone is mixed in for acoustic continuity.

The practice is often ignored in video production. Since video sound is edited less precisely than film, broadcast through noisy channels, and played back at low volumes in home systems, it's thought that room tone won't be missed. Obviously, I don't agree. If you're doing an intense dramatic video, record tone. You'll need it.

On the other hand, if you're doing a fast-paced dialog sequence or a commercial, it may be possible to skip recording any separate room tone. A good sound editor, using a modern workstation, can usually pull enough tone from between words or at the heads and tails of takes to satisfy any dialog fixes in this kind of video.

Controlling Microphones

Shooting a dialog track that will be edited requires consistency, from shot to shot and from scene to scene. Otherwise the edited video will be full of distracting acoustic jump cuts. These take a long time to correct at the mix.

A character's dialog level, as read on the record level meter, should stay consistent throughout a scene. Of course, the volume may change if they shout or whisper, or if they're walking away from the scene, but that's related to what the character does on camera. We shouldn't be aware of any changes in their volume when you move the boom, or switch from boom to lav, because without any visual reference the shift becomes distracting. Since the electrical output of a mic varies both with the element type and distance from the speaker, the bottom line is you have to adjust the recording level as miking changes. A camera's automatic volume control doesn't work for this purpose, because it increases noise during pauses.

(Not all characters have to be at the same volume level. Differences in personality, or in their intensity during a scene, may mean that one voice is louder than another. But they should be fairly close—within 4 or 5 dB—or else the scene will be difficult to mix.)

If you're using just one or two mics, it may seem easiest to route them directly to the camera and record onto separate tracks with constant level. But if one of the mics is a boom with varying distances, there'll be audio jumps when the scene is edited unless someone was adjusting levels during the shot. It can be inconvenient or even impossible to do this with the camera's volume controls; many provide such coarse adjustment that the tiniest movement of the knob will be too big a change in the sound. The best solution is a separate mixer, even if it's just being used as a remote volume control and not mixing anything together.

If you're using more than two mics and don't have a good multitrack recorder, you must use a mixer. (Some cameras can record four separate audio channels, but they seriously sacrifice the quality of each track—recording at 12 bits—when they do. It's best to forget that the manufacturer even provided this mode.)

The Mixer

Mixers for video production come in two forms:

- Small, battery-powered ENG mixers usually have three or four inputs, plus a slate mic and tone generator, and a low cut filter to reduce wind rumble. They can be worn over the shoulder. Although their size makes them portable, it also dictates small knobs that may be difficult to use smoothly during dramatic dialog.

- Tabletop mixers offer between 6 and 16 inputs and are small versions of recording consoles. (They're also often found in musicians' home recording studios.) While they're not very big—the smallest are slightly larger than this book—they have large volume knobs or slide controls that make it easy to make fine adjustments during a take. They also often have equalization controls, but read my warning below before you use them.

Both types provide phantom power, have headphone outputs and some sort of metering, and may have rotary panning controls to move a signal continuously from the left output to the right. Resist the temptation to use those pan knobs to match visual positions on the screen—this is much better left for post. Instead, split multiple mics so they go only to the left or to the right channel of the camera. If you're using a single mic, keeping it centered may provide a better recording.

ENG mixer outputs are usually switchable between mic and line level. If your camera can handle the voltage, a line-level signal will give you a better recording. But if your camera is designed only for mic-level signals, there's no advantage to using a separate line-level adapter. Use the mic-level output and keep the cable short. You might need a cable with internal capacitors to block DC voltage on the mic input; details are in the previous chapter.

Desktop mixer outputs are always line level. If your camera can't handle that directly, you'll need an adapter. The transformer ones discussed in the previous chapter offer the most flexibility. Don't try to reduce a desktop mixer's output to mic level by turning down its volume controls; this just adds unacceptable noise.

Aligning the mixer's meters

Whether the mixer has VU meters with moving needles or a row of LEDs to indicate output level, they'll be set up as analog meters. Your camera's meters may be set up as digital meters, or to emulate analog meters, or to no particular standard at all. Don't expect to plug mixer into camera and have the meters instantly agree.

The best procedure is to record some test dialog. First, adjust the mixer controls so that most of the peaks reach zero VU on the mixer's meter. This usually requires compromises between the individual mic controls and the master volume setting to get the best-quality sound, so read the specific mixer's instructions for advice.

Then turn the camera's automatic level control *on.* Note how the camera's meters respond to dialog: this is what the manufacturer calibrated the automatic controls to and is probably the best recording level for that camera. Once you've got a feel for how high the camera's meters reach with automatic levels on, turn them off again. Adjust the camera's manual controls to get a similar meter reading. Note that you haven't touched the external mixer's controls at all during this paragraph.

From this point on, you should be able to rely on the mixer's meters. But check the camera's meters during a take or on playback. A meter designed for music recording can miss quick changes in dialog levels.

> The above procedure is best done with actual dialog, while the actors are rehearsing or with a friend talking at a constant level, rather than with a lineup tone. The relative response of analog and digital meters to tone is different from the way they respond to voice.

Equalization

The best rule for equalization is to avoid it, unless you're sure of what you're doing; then use as little as possible on your primary mic. It's always better to leave equalization decisions for the calmer atmosphere, better monitors, and tighter controls of postproduction. A bad decision in the field may be impossible to correct.

Equalize consistently. You can have one sound for interiors and one for exteriors; but unless conditions are drastic, don't try to use the equalizer to correct every little problem from one interior to the next.

It's acceptable to turn down the bass a little to compensate for wind noise or traffic rumble, but the rotary controls on a desktop mixer are usually too broad to do much of this without hurting the voice. If a mixer or mic has a bass cut switch, use it instead; it's more precise and repeatable from shot to shot.

If you're switching between a boom and lav or plant mics, there will probably be some difference in their sound. Leave whichever mic is going to carry most of the dialog alone, but it's okay to use a little bit of equalization on the others—no more than 3 or 4 dB—to make them match. Of course, that's only if you know what you're doing. And if you've got very good headphones at the shoot.

Controlling Wind Noise

An electronic filter can reduce the rumbling noise of a very light wind—the kind that would hardly ruffle a flag—but anything else requires a mechanical solution as well.

Shotgun mics should always have a windscreen because the holes that make them directional also pick up wind noise. Even swinging back and forth on a boom can create enough wind to be a problem. Low-cost foam windscreens that cover the entire mic should be adequate for interiors and may be usable for closely miked handheld interviews outdoors.

If you're using a boom outdoors, you'll need more protection than a foam windscreen can provide. Hard windscreens, consisting of a wire or open plastic frame surrounded by fine mesh, work by creating a low-turbulence area around the mic and can be very effective. They're often called *zeppelins* because of their shape. For extra protection, a layer of furry cloth can be wrapped around the windscreen; it makes the assembly look like a small animal, but it does cut down on noise. If you're using a zeppelin, a foam windscreen on the mic itself may also help. However, there must be at least a half inch of airspace between the windscreen and the interior of the zeppelin for it to work properly.

The tiny foam windscreens that come with lavalieres can reduce popped Ps, but don't provide any protection against outdoor wind. A metal mesh windscreen designed for the mic can help, using the same principle as the zeppelin on larger mics. If you don't have one of them available, try using a combination of these sound recordists' tricks:

- Pull the foam tip off a video head-cleaning swab. It's often just the right size to fit over a lav.

- With the swab in place over the mic, wrap a couple of layers of cheesecloth around it.

- Snip the fingertip off a child's woolen glove (remove the child first), and fit it over the cheesecloth for extra protection. This also gives you the opportunity to choose a glove color that will match the talent's overcoat, so you can leave the mic outside their clothing without it being too obvious. Putting the mic under a heavy overcoat protects it from wind, but cuts the voice down too much.

If you're shooting in a howling windstorm, the noise *will* get into the mic. The most you can expect from a windscreen and filter here is to reduce low-frequency sounds that can interfere with the recording. Get the mic as close to the speaker's mouth as possible, or wait for calmer weather.

Nothing can control airplane noise.

If there's a plane flying overhead, some of its noise will be picked up. It might not be enough to obscure dialog *in that shot*, but when you edit to it from a different take, there'll be a distracting shift in the background sound.

If you're planning to edit what you shoot, wait until the plane passes.

Using a Separate Audio Recorder

Often, videographers consider getting a separate DAT recorder because they're unsatisfied with the sound from their camcorder. This can be a waste of money. A good microphone, balancing adapter, and perhaps a mixer will make more of an improvement—and be a lot less trouble—than a separate DAT deck. Double-system recording (where there are separate recorders for sound and picture) is appropriate for film, but even professional video shoots with experienced sound crews usually end up recording sound in the camera.

Before you invest in more recording gear, check the following:

- Are you using your camera's maximum sound quality setting? Many are switchable between 12- and 16-bit recording. While 12-bit sound can be awful, 16-bit sound is good enough for modern Hollywood blockbusters.

- Are you using the camera's built-in mic? If so, you haven't been paying attention to what I've written. Here's a better use for this book: take it in one hand and whack the mic off your camera. I don't care what kind of mic it is. Next to the lens is an awful place for any mic, too far from dialog and too close to camera (and videographer) noises. Save this configuration for breaking news where there's no time to set up a proper microphone.

- Are you using the camera's automatic level control? Turn it off . . . unless you're using the camera-mounted mic for breaking news where there's no chance to set levels.

- Have you connected the external mic or mixer properly? Tips are in the previous chapter.

Syncing an External Recorder

If you must use a separate recorder, synchronization becomes an issue. It's actually two separate issues: keeping the speed stable so the playback takes exactly as long as the recording, and matching sound to picture.

Analog cassette recorders don't have any kind of speed control. The motor speed is determined by random DC voltage from the battery, and there's no mechanism to tell if the tape has slipped or the flywheel is feeling the effects of momentum. Don't use them for dialog.

Modern digital recorders have reliable internal crystals that will keep the speed stable for 10 or 15 minutes at a time, and control tracks that compensate for mechanical variation or slippage. If your takes are longer than 15 minutes or so, you may need a recorder that can lock to blackburst or video reference from the camera. High-end DAT recorders lock to blackburst, record and chase timecode, are typically used in feature film production, and cost as much as a good digital camera.

If you're using a lower-cost digital recorder that doesn't have timecode, the easiest way to keep things in sync is to record identical reference tracks in the camera and slide the separate audio to match when you start editing. Sometimes it's not possible to feed identical audio to sound and video recorders because the distance is too great, or a recorder may be hidden on a performer. If that's the case, a traditional film slate—one of those hinged boards with diagonal lines that you clap together right before the director yells, "Action!"—will help a lot. Match the first frame where the slate is closed with the banging sound, and you should be able to hold sync for all but the longest takes.

Sound can be matched to picture without any reference, but it's not a job for the casual desktop editor.

Multitrack Recording

Robert Altman pioneered a shooting style where performers were free to ad-lib and step on each other's lines. Each principal wore a lav, but there was no attempt to mix them at the shoot. Instead, they were all recorded separately on multitrack tape. The director made decisions about which lines to concentrate on while he was editing.

If you want to try the same thing on a camcorder, make sure the unit doesn't sacrifice quality when switched to multitrack mode. If it does, or if your system can't handle multiple tracks, use an external recorder. A DAT recorder can give you two extra tracks (see the section on sync, above), and eight-track digital recorders are common in postproduction and music studios. The multitrack units are rack-mount devices but are small enough to carry to the shoot. They have line-level inputs, so you'll need separate mixer outputs or preamplifiers for each track.

If you're not using the same recorder for recording and digitizing, make sure the formats match. Tascam DA-88 (aka DTRS) is the standard format for film and video production. Alesis ADAT is more typically found in music studios. Their sound quality is equivalent, but the recording methods aren't compatible.

If your editing system can import only two tracks at a time, you'll need to synchronize them manually before you edit. You'll get maximum flexibility if you can then lock all the synchronized tracks to picture, but this might not be possible in a particular nonlinear editor.

As a simpler alternative, record multitrack in the field but use a mixer when you're digitizing. Choose just the tracks that are of interest, and split them to two channels. If you ever change your mind and want to hear what some other character said, it's no problem to go back to the original multitrack tape.

CHAPTER 8

Recording Voice-Overs, ADR, and Effects

R O S E ' S   R U L E S

⇨ Compared to sound at the shoot, the technology for a voice-only recording is a piece of cake.

⇨ It's much easier to get a good performance in a sound studio than at the shoot. But the skills that make you a good videographer won't help: you have to know how to ask for a good sound take.

⇨ There are no rules for recording sound effects, only suggestions. If a sound fits, use it.

The Voice-over

My wife, Carla, used to do a lot of voice-over work. Since she's good with dialects and part Swede, she was booked as the Scandinavian spokesperson in a radio commercial series for Howard Johnson Motels. But the session didn't go well: the director kept telling her to "sound more Swedish." She poured on the accent, and finally started substituting authentic Swedish words, but nothing satisfied the director.

The problem was her hair! While Carla is statuesque, she's not a blonde. The producer couldn't look at this tall brunette and hear a Swede. So the engineer (not me) moved her to a far corner of the studio, where the director wouldn't see her. Once he was able to concentrate on her voice, he bought the next take.

The point isn't that some directors are stupid, but that too many people in this business learn to listen with their eyes. The visual skills that make you a good videographer or editor aren't of any value in a voice-over session. With no cameras to worry about, the technique of miking a voice recording is totally different than miking dialog. And the things you say to make an actor appear convincing on a set are usually ineffective when all you have to work with is their voice—that's why Hollywood uses dialog coaches in addition to directors.

But there is a body of easily learned techniques, mostly developed in radio, that will help you do a better job of recording and directing a narrator. Start by thinking about the voice-over process as two different jobs: you can be the recording engineer, or you can be the director. You can even learn to do both at the same time, but only if you approach them separately.

Engineering a Voice Recording

Videographers often wear many hats (or headphones) in their work, and it's entirely possible that you'll have to function as both engineer and director. But even if you're working in a studio with a staff engineer, you owe it to your project to understand the technical side of things. Part of the reason for this is to keep an eye on the engineer: if they're trained in music recording, they might be approaching a voice recording entirely the wrong way.

If you're going to do the engineering yourself, brush up on your audio skills before the session. Do some practice recordings with a colleague, until the button-pushing part becomes second nature. That way you'll be able to concentrate on directing when the high-priced talent shows up.

I've organized this part of the chapter to help you do both jobs with a minimum of schizophrenia: even though you'll have to perform the tasks simultaneously, engineering topics are discussed first, and directorial issues later. If you're working with an experienced voice-over engineer—major production cities have studios that specialize in radio and TV recording—you can skip to the next section.

Session planning

There's a lot of preparation to making a good recording, and you should start long before inviting that colleague in for the practice session. You have to make sure the recording space is suitable for a voice-over; you have to verify you've got the right kind of equipment; and you have to provide the nontechnical accessories that make a session go smoother.

The best way to find out if a room will work for voice-over is to walk around in it and listen for noise and echoes. A voice-over exists in limbo. There should be no sense of a physical space between the narrator and the viewer. Any reverberation can destroy that illusion of intimacy. Even most quiet music studios are too reverberant for a voice-over.

As you walk, face a far wall and make a loud vocal sound that suddenly stops—I prefer to open my throat and go, "UCK!" like a seal barking—and then listen for how the sound is reflected back to you. If you don't hear much of anything, the room will work well. If you do hear an echo but it's short and has the same timbre as your test sound, you're probably still okay. But if the echo rings for a while, or sounds filtered or hollow, look for someplace else to record. Do this echo test with a vocal sound, rather than by clapping your hands, because it'll tell you more about how the room responds to voice frequencies. You should also turn around to bark in different directions. Some rooms sound bad when you face one wall, but a lot better if you face a different wall or a far corner.

Once you've determined that a room is basically suitable, keep walking around until you find the position in the room that sounds best. If you do hear some echoes in a room that's otherwise ideal, all is not lost. There are some suggestions for improving room acoustics in Chapter 6.

Once you find that ideal position, stand quietly and listen. If you hear traffic or other loud noises, the room obviously isn't going to be usable. But more subtle rumbles and hiss can also affect a recording. Low-frequency sounds can come from bad fluorescent fixtures—easily fixed by turning off the light—or be transmitted across the building's structure from air-conditioning or elevator machinery. Voice-over recording usually has more bass than dialog recording (boom mics aren't very sensitive to extreme lows), so a rumble that would be tolerable at a location shoot can be a problem for the voice-over.

The high-pass filter built into many professional microphones and mixers can help reduce these rumbles. If a low-frequency sound is extreme, try the double-microphone technique in Figure 1.

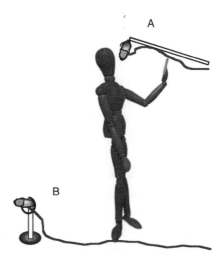

Figure 1: Using two mics to pick up room rumble

Microphone A picks up both the announcer and the rumble. Microphone B, facing away from the announcer, picks up mostly rumble. By inverting the phase of B, you can mix in a negative version of the rumble to cancel itself out. (The easiest way to invert the phase is an adapter that exchanges pins 2 and 3 of a balanced mic's XLR connector.) A couple of warnings: This technique only works on low frequencies, where the wavelength is long enough that both microphones hear the same part of the wave. And it can be tricky to balance the two microphones, so you might want to set this up long before the talent arrives. Adding a bass boost and a high-cut filter to mic B can help.

High-frequency hisses are usually the result of air vents or computer fans. You can quiet a vent by prying off its grill; most of the noise comes from turbulence around the vanes that direct air around the room. But if an equipment fan can't be turned off, you'll have to get as far away from it as possible. Fortunately, high-pitched sounds are easily controlled by sound blankets.

Make a sound check

It makes sense to gather and test all your equipment long before the session, so you can fix anything that's not up to snuff. If you're like most videographers, you might have to hunt for the right kind of microphone:

- The lavaliere mic that's so useful during a shoot is of little value for voice-overs. These mics are often omnidirectional and pick up more of the room's echoes than are desirable. If you absolutely have to use one, don't pin it to the announcer's chest. Suspend it a few inches above, and slightly to the side, of the announcer's mouth. And put in a fresh battery.

- Mid- or large cardioid (semidirectional) mics are usually the best choice in a studio. They can be aimed to avoid echoes bouncing off the control room glass or script stand—yes, that's a very real problem. But cardioids are more subject to popped Ps, so you may have to experiment to find the best position. A silk screen can be placed in front of the mic to reduce popping. It works both by slowing down the blast of air and by spiking the talent so they don't get too close to the mic.

- A short shotgun or hypercardioid mic can give you the most flexibility in a less-than-perfect studio. Place one 6 or 7 inches from the announcer's mouth, and it'll be far enough away to avoid popping but still manage to reject any residual room echoes.

- Condenser mics are almost always a better voice-over choice than dynamic ones. While radio engineers and stage performers love dynamics for their ruggedness, these mics lack the crispness and overall tonal balance that can make a voice-over track stand out.

You should also hunt for a microphone stand that's got the flexibility to let you place the mic in its best position. It's usually a bad idea to put the mic directly in front of the performer's mouth (example A in Figure 2); not only is this position more prone to popping and other mouth noises, it also gets in the way of reading the script. Above and slightly to the side (example B) is better, and moving the mic a few inches up or down from this position can help you avoid sibilance. A short shotgun (example C, shown without its windscreen) can be placed even higher. A mic stand with a short boom arm will give you the most flexibility.

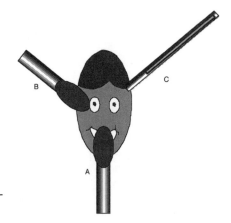

Figure 2: Three different voice-over mic positions. Avoid A.

The best recording equipment—particularly if you're trying to both direct and engineer at the same time—is whatever will let you put off decisions as long as possible. You want to be able to concentrate on the performance, not on a bunch of dials.

- Don't record directly into a nonlinear editor if you have a decent-quality tape medium available. Recording on a sound card is more exacting than using a tape recorder, and digitizing after the session gives you the chance to fine-tune things. Besides, tape is cheaper than hard disk space: recording to tape means you can save every take.

- Don't try to equalize or compress during the session. These processes are irreversible. If you've recorded to tape, you can experiment with settings and shape the sound when you digitize it into your editor. But it's best to put all these decisions off until the final mix, since music and dialog can affect how you process the voice-over.

The best recording chain for a professional announcer is a microphone, a simple preamplifier (perhaps with a bass rolloff switch), and a DAT recorder. The preamp doesn't have to be anything special; the multithousand dollar tubed units found in music studios are overkill. As a general rule, stay away from the preamplifiers built into low- or mid-price portable DAT recorders; they can be noisy.

You can also use your camcorder to record voice-overs. Make sure it's set to its highest-quality audio setting, and the automatic level control is turned off. If you're using a single mic, you may want to use an adapter that splits the signal to both of the camera channels; some units get noisy if there's no input connected to one channel. Don't use a built-in camera mic; they're seldom very good quality, and they pick up extra noise because they're so close to the camera. Besides, what announcer wants to have something as big as a camera a few inches from his head?

If the announcer is less than professional and doesn't control projection very well, a limiter can help rescue otherwise marginal takes. If a limiter seems to add noise or distortion, turn down the preamp's volume control. By the way, professional engineers regularly break this rule and apply all sorts of processing to the original recording. But unless you've had lots of experience with this kind of equipment, it's better to work with the safety net of an absolutely clean original tape. Or split the signal, and record absolutely clean to one channel and processed to the other. This only works if the recording medium doesn't combine the channels in an automatic level control.

A simpler recording chain will also help you make a cleaner recording, by avoiding extra circuitry that can contribute hum or noise. Enlist a colleague to help test your chain. Have them read a script and adjust the recording level for their voice, but then have them stop while you record about 30 seconds of silence at those settings. Play back, and when you get to the silent part, turn the monitors as loud as you can. If you hear hum or hiss, pause the tape. If the noise continues even when the tape stops, it's probably in the monitor. If the noise pauses with the tape, you've got problems in the recording equipment. These noises are almost impossible to remove and can make both editing and mixing more difficult. Get them fixed before you invest any money in a voice-over session.

You can monitor the recording via headphones, or with speakers in another room. Don't forget a monitor for the talent. Professional announcers need to hear themselves in high-quality headphones, so they can adjust their own performances. Closed-ear headphones are essential if they'll be working to music or other cues, to keep the cue sound from getting into their microphone. But these headphones tend to be big and heavy. If they don't need to hear cues, a pair of good-quality portable CD player headphones will be a lot more comfortable.

Don't be surprised if you see a performer take off one side of the headphones and cup their hand to an ear, just like old-time radio announcers did. Some very good contemporary narrators use the same trick, so they can catch tiny nuances that don't make it through the limited response of a headphone.

Those tiny IFB earpieces used by on-camera announcers and newscasters are also comfortable, but don't sound good enough to give an announcer useful feedback. If you're going to be monitoring through confidence heads, make sure the announcer has a nondelayed signal for their headphones. And provide a way to adjust their monitoring volume separately from your own. Electronics stores sell in-line volume controls for small headphones, and they can be a handy—if sometimes fragile—convenience.

You may need one other piece of equipment that's often overlooked in temporary recording situations: if you and the talent are going to be in separate rooms, make sure there's a way to communicate with them. Professional consoles often have a talkback system built in, but the simple mixers found in most video-editing suites don't. If nothing else is available, a cheap battery-operated intercom makes a good emergency talkback.

Nonelectronic essentials

Some other equipment can also make a big difference in the quality of a voice-over recording:

- A tall stool, if the script is more than a page or so. A good announcer will almost always prefer to stand—or at least, lean—while they work. If they're sitting in a low chair, they can't control breathing as well.

- A proper script stand. Typical music stands aren't tall enough for standing announcers, forcing them to look down as they read and constricting their throats. You need something tall enough to put the script at eye level. Also, you need a stand that won't echo. The talent's mouth, microphone, and stand are all very close together, and reflections from the stand can cause hollowness in the recorded sound. A partial solution is to put a piece of carpet over the stand. You can improvise a totally non-echo stand from a lighting flag and clothespins.

  One elegant solution appears in Figure 3. It consists of an ordinary mic stand, a gooseneck mic adapter, and a large clip from a stationery store. It's very easy for the talent to adjust for the best reading position. Make sure there's a solid table or counter nearby, so the talent can write down those inevitable script changes.

- Plenty of nonglare light. If you're using overhead lights, make sure the microphone (or talent's head) doesn't cast a shadow on the script. Some narrators prefer clip-on lights that can be attached directly to the script stand.

- For long sessions, some water. Bottled spring water at room temperature is usually best. Water is particularly important during periods of low humidity. As the

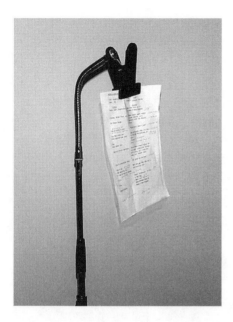

Figure 3: This versatile script stand is hardly there at all.

body loses moisture along with the breath, saliva in the mouth will thicken up and can cause snapping or crackling during consonants.

The Recording Session

If you've done the right preparation, engineering chores at the session itself are fairly simple, so you can concentrate on directing the performance. Before you begin working with the script, record about 30 seconds of the microphone or a test tone and then play it back. This not only verifies that the equipment is working, it also keeps you from losing something important to the kind of tape damage that's most likely at the head of the roll.

When the talent first walks up to the microphone, stay near them and ask them to read a little of the script. Every performer stands slightly differently while they're working, and this is the best time to fine-tune the microphone placement. Then go to your equipment and have them read a little more so you can adjust the recording level. Even if you've found the ideal level, you may want to keep one hand on the volume control during the first few takes. Inexperienced performers tend to read a little louder when they know it's for real.

Once you're ready to record, you have only a couple of ongoing responsibilities as engineer:

- Keep track of takes and take numbers, and write them down on the script. Even if you're using timecode or DAT index numbers, a verbal slate can save time during editing. This doesn't have to be any more complicated than "take three." If you don't have a slate mic in your setup, slate into the talkback system; the talent's mic will pick it up.

- Keep an ear open for problems that can build up during the session, and be ready to stop the session to fix them. As the narrator's mouth dries out, you might hear clicks and snaps in their voice; stop and give water. If they've moved too close to the microphone and are starting to pop, reposition the mic (or spike them by moving the script stand). If a mic battery starts getting weak and you hear distortion, replace it. It's difficult—if not impossible—to fix any of these problems during post.

- You may be asked to time the takes with a stopwatch. This is an art in itself: train yourself to start the watch immediately on the first syllable, and not to stop it until the final syllable is finished sounding. And for heavens' sake, don't use a watch that beeps near a live mic.

After the final take, play back a little bit to verify that the recorder is still working.

Recording Narration to Picture

Recording to picture makes things a lot more complicated, both for you and the performer. Since it's so easy to move voice tracks around in an NLE, it may make more sense to record to precise timings with a stopwatch instead of while watching picture. Or for scenes where the talent has to understand a visual rhythm or emotion, play it once and then let them perform. If you absolutely must record to picture:

- Give the talent a monitor that's near their script, so they don't have to keep refocusing. A monitor's glass will reflect the voice, so make sure it's on the dead side of the microphone. Listen carefully to make sure the monitor isn't adding a whistle or hum that's getting picked up by the mic.

- Give them some other form of cue along with the picture, such as a flashing light or series of beeps right before they're to start, or let them hear the dialog track immediately before their line. Very few performers can concentrate on both a written script and an on-screen image, and if they have to switch their concentration suddenly, they'll probably come in late.

- Don't obsess about timing. If a perfect take overlaps the next shot by a few seconds, you can probably fix it in the editing.

Timecode isn't as helpful as you might expect for this kind of recording. Unless you have an elaborate automatic logging system, you'll have to repeat the master video's timecode with each take. This confuses the edit controller or DAT recorder's chase circuitry, and the long preroll you'll need for each new timecode pass will just slow down the session.

The easiest way to synchronize multiple narration takes that have been recorded against picture is to start with some kind of reference audio—dialog, a scratch track, or a beep before the scene—on the videotape. With each take, dub the reference to one channel of your recorder and record the narrator on the other. After the recording is done, dub both the selected take and its reference back into your editor. Slide the stereo pair around in your editor until the two references match, and then you can delete the reference.

Dialog Replacement

If dialog recorded at the shoot isn't usable, you have to replace it. This is not an option to consider lightly. Even in Hollywood, where ADR (automated dialog replacement) or *looping* (from the original, nonautomated loops of picture and soundtrack that were used) is common, it's frequently done poorly and stands out in the film. On the other hand, Marlon Brando used to love looping as an opportunity to perfect his performance. Rumor has it that's why he mumbled so much in the original takes.

There are two engineering considerations for ADR. You have to match the sound of the original recording, and you have to cue the talent in a way they'll find helpful.

Matching the sound

To match the original recording, you'll need to use a microphone that's similar to the original principal mic, mounted at the same angle. This is the most critical aspect of making an ADR session work properly.

You'll also have to use some psychology: a voice-over studio shouldn't have any noticeable echo, but the natural room reverb at the original shoot helped the actors hear their own voices. When they get into the studio, if they don't hear at least some echo, they'll tend to push their voices harder to compensate. Even if they capture the mood perfectly, the voice won't match because the projection will be different.

On the other hand, if the studio has too much echo, you won't be able to match the original reverb at the location. Real rooms add unpredictable coloration to a sound, and it's unlikely that a studio's echo will be anything close to the reverb you picked up in the field. Technically, the best way to match is to record ADR with as little echo as possible, and then use a good digital reverberator to simulate the original room.

One solution is to build a voice-recording room that's highly absorbent along three walls, and slightly reflective in the front. Face the actor toward the front of the room, and position a cardioid or shotgun mic—whatever was used at the shoot—so its dead side is toward the reflective wall. Another is to record in a totally dead room, but mix a tiny amount of reverb along with the talent's voice in their headphones. Either of these solutions raises the ante for the recording facility: it must have a room built for this kind of recording, a console that can apply reverb to one set of headphones but not to the main monitor or recorder, and a reverb unit that can simulate small rooms (most music-studio reverbs have much too big a sound). But the process of ADR is so exacting that it's worthwhile hiring a professional studio; doing it yourself usually doesn't work.

Of course, you can also match the original room's acoustics by recording ADR lines in the original location. If the scene was shot at an in-house studio, this will be the easiest and cheapest solution.

ADR techniques

First, identify which lines need to be replaced and separate them by character. Actors' skills (and patience) for ADR vary; it might take one person a long time to do their lines, while someone else can breeze through theirs. There's no point to making one actor repeat a successful delivery while their partner blows take after take. So even if a scene has multiple characters, you'll be recording them in separate sessions.

The lines should be broken into short units, ideally no more than a few sentences at a time. It's a lot faster to match lip sync on two short speeches than a single long one.

If you're also the picture editor, you have some options that aren't available to us lowly sound people. If a scene needs massive dialog replacement, recut it to favor long shots where lip sync isn't as noticeable. ADR won't have to be as precise.

Or provide cutaways and reaction shots during longer speeches. This way there'll be some places to make tiny off-camera voice edits; these can restore sync to a line that "almost makes it."

There are two principal ways to record ADR, leading to occasional debates among sound recordists about which is best. If you've got the ability to use either one, leave the choice up to the actor.

The traditional method is to make picture dominant. Start a visual streamer right before the line starts. Originally, this was done by drawing or scribing diagonally across a few dozen frames of a copy of the film itself, creating a line that marched across the screen from left to right. These days, streamers are generated electronically and added to a video playback. The actor listens to a playback of the original line a few times to get comfortable with the delivery, then watches picture. As the streamer reaches the right side of the screen, the actor reads the line while watching mouth movements. Keep repeating until the sound seems to be in sync with picture. The advantages to this method are that the actor can feel freer to experiment with the delivery and doesn't have to wear headphones.

A modern alternative is to make sound dominant. Generate an audio streamer of three short beeps exactly one second apart. Put it on a separate track, exactly one second before the start of the line on a production dialog track. Set this audio track to play in a loop, and feed it to the headphones. The actor hears the rhythmic repetition of beeps and line, and within a few passes will be able to speak along with it. Keep repeating until actor and playback are in unison. The advantage to this method is that it can be faster with performers who aren't used to looping, and since it isn't necessary to concentrate on picture—video playback is optional—the actor can be looking at a script instead.

In both methods, it's important to establish a rhythm. Make sure that recueing the sound or picture is fast and always takes the same amount of time. If your system isn't equipped for loop play, make multiple copies of the streamer and original material on the timeline of an NLE or audio workstation.

As soon as you've got a successful take, mark it and move on to the next line. You can record the new version with the looped timecode from the original, or with new continuous timecode while you keep track of the offset, but the easiest way is to dub the original dialog on one track while you record the new performance on the other. After the session, take the last take of each line and slide it so the reference exactly matches the original uncut dialog. Then delete both the original track and the reference, leaving just the replacement.

The new track will sound drier than the original, since it doesn't have any room reverb (unless you recorded it at the original location). You can add temporary reverb to make the scene more realistic while you're editing, but don't commit to it until you've had a chance to compare original and new tracks on a good monitoring system.

Don't obsess over ADR. If many of the critical consonant movements are in sync, it's probably good enough. Modern audio workstations and multitrack audio editors give you a lot of flexibility to make tiny tweaks in the recording, or change the timing of individual words without affecting pitch.

Directing the Voice-over

I was watching TV with my son, many years ago when he was in the "What does daddy do at work?" stage. A commercial came on for a superhero action figure, with a voice-over suggesting:

```
Narr: Imagine you can make him fly.
```

"Daddy's job," I explained, "is to have him say those same words as

```
Narr: Imagine! You can make him fly!
```

While most professional narrators will deliver a credible reading on their own, you can't just settle for a pretty sound. You know the project's goals better than they do, you know what has to be conveyed, and you probably know a lot more about the subject. So be ready to add dramatic director or dialog coach to all the other hats you wear.

Casting and Talent Unions

It goes without saying that you can't direct a narration until you've hired someone to read your script. Otherwise, well . . . it goes without saying.

The right narrator can be as crucial to a project's success as the writing and visualizations. A lot of information—and subtle emotional information about your project and company—will be conveyed by this voice alone. Don't make casting a last-minute decision. Expect to spend some time, money, or both selecting an appropriate narrator. The golden triangle of production applies here, too: you can get a world-class narrator easily, if you're paying union rates; or you can look a little harder and find someone good who's less than scale; or you can save both time and money and get a voice that damages your project.

"The Union" is either AFTRA (American Federation of Television and Radio Artists) or SAG (Screen Actors' Guild), both operating in the United States only. Traditionally, AFTRA handled videotape and SAG confined itself to film. New technologies have blurred the lines, and SAG is trying to assert control over things like CD-ROMs.

Their contracts and rates are virtually identical for voice-overs, but their pension plans are slightly different, so I leave it up to the actors to decide which union they'd rather be paid through.

AFTRA is in New York at (212) 532-0800, SAG is in LA at (323) 954-1600, but don't call either until you've finished reading this section.

Defining the voice

First, ask yourself the basics: Why are you making this video? What's the primary message you're trying to convey, who's going to see it, and why are they paying attention? Then read through the script, aloud. You'll start to hear what kind of a voice you want, so you can make a list of appropriate adjectives like *light, serious, hip, warm, cultured.* (Even *neutral* can be appropriate, though it's more often a symptom of lazy casting.) Think also about whether you want a man or a woman—the answer shouldn't be automatic.

Now that you know who you're looking for, you can start the search:

- Call other producers. Most are willing to share their discoveries. If you hear a radio or TV spot you liked, ask the station which agency supplied it and call their casting director.

- If you're recording in a studio, ask for their recommendations. Many studios have cassettes or CDs with a selection of their favorite local performers and can send you a copy.

- If you're in a big city, call the talent agents. They have composite tapes also and will send them at no charge to any legitimate producer.

- If you're not in a big city but have a strong regional theater company, find out if they have any visiting players who do narration at home. Theater and voice-over skills are totally different, but many full-time actors are good at both.

- If you're paying scale and have signed a union contract, call the union and ask for their talent guide or directories. Bear in mind that the unions make absolutely no representation about the talents of their members, so you can find union turkeys as easily as nonunion ones. In many cities, union members have gotten together and produced composite CDs, so you can actually evaluate their voices and skills.

- Call the local producers' association, broadcast association, or ITVA, and ask for advice.

- Look on the Web. Some announcers have pages advertising their services, complete with downloadable demo reels. Set your favorite search engine for "narrator."

- As a last resort, call a casting company. While a few are good, a lot are visually oriented and don't understand voice-overs. They'll charge you to record a number of actors and models reading your material, but their choices and direction may be totally random.

Evaluating a demo

The only way to choose a voice is by listening to a demo cassette or CD. If an actor doesn't have one with excerpts from a lot of projects, he or she probably hasn't done enough work to be comfortable in the studio. When you first listen, make sure there's some variation between pieces. Every voice changes slightly from day to day, and every studio and director have a slightly different sound. If the different selections all sound the same, the actor probably threw it together in one long session—again, an indicator of inexperience.

It's a catch-22: actors won't get good until they've done a lot of work. They won't get a lot of work until they're good. If you're unsure of your own directing chops, go with the experienced actors—they'll help you a lot. But if you've got skill and patience, you might find a very talented novice who'll do a good job and work for less than the going rate.

Now consider four specific things:

- *Naturalness.* It takes both talent and experience to read a script and still be conversational. Even the most gifted beginner can tighten up when recording; under stress, throat muscles involuntarily constrict. That changes the sound, and while audiences won't know why, they'll feel uncomfortable in sympathy.

- *Technical chops.* Breath control is critical. Sentence endings should have as much support as beginnings, and emphasis should be done by pacing and pitch rather than volume. The energy must be consistent, so you can edit one take to the next. And there's certainly a craft to saying "magnetohydrodynamic" or "norepinephrine" the way your audience expects.

- *A professional attitude.* Professionals understand they've been hired to convey a message, not to display their beautiful voices. They know this video isn't about them.

- *Finally, the pipes.* Voice quality isn't as important as these other characteristics, and many of the best narrators just sound like ordinary people.

Union? Nonunion?

The talent unions do not control production. Nobody will bust your kneecaps if you hire a nonunion actor. Rather, they're associations of working professionals who've agreed to work only with producers who honor their contract. You're free to cast anyone you want, but actors may refuse to work for you if you're not on the union's list, or if the cast also includes nonunion performers. There has to be a "signatory producer of record" involved—it can be you, the recording studio or production company, or a casting agent. The signatory will have you sign a release guaranteeing contract provisions for this particular production, but this doesn't obligate you for any other production.

If your budget is really tight, you might be tempted to cast by asking colleagues to try a reading. Even if they'll work for free, it's a false economy. An amateur can waste money on studio and editing time, add a layer of cheesiness to your beautiful visuals, and make your audience wonder why you've wasted their time. College radio experience 10 years ago, weekend membership in a community theater, or even a bustling career as a stand-up comic doesn't equip someone to read a narration.

However, you can find good actors who'll work for less than scale. Many cities don't have a union local, and the narrators there charge whatever they want. Rates usually settle at about 75% of scale. Radio station production directors are usually underpaid, often moonlight, and may have the versatility to read your script without sounding like a disk jockey. The Internet, ISDN, and overnight couriers have eliminated the need to use local talent entirely. Many good performers have set up voice-over services out of their homes, with absolutely negotiable rates.

You'll find a large pool of nonunion talent in large production cities, but these are often the ones who can't compete with the pros. Some performers in midsized markets manage to play it both ways, working through the union for broadcast jobs but nonunion for corporate pieces. They tend to charge scale for their work, but don't require any of the union's extra payments (see below).

On the other hand, a union performer can be a real bargain. Actors like to work, and many voice-over stars with serious national credentials will do corporate projects or closed-audience videos for scale if they have the time.

Union rates

Scale for corporate voice-overs is based on two factors: how long the performer is in the studio, and whether the video will be kept in-house or shown to a larger audience (such as a trade show or point-of-purchase display). In 1999, base scale was $333 for a one-hour session of an in-house video. Rates typically increase just under 5% a year.

Union scale for commercials is based on a myriad of factors including the length of time on the air, the number of cities it'll be shown in, and even whether the airtime is being purchased from a regional network or all the individual stations in the region. (Networks are cheaper.) Minimum base scale is $360 for the recording . . . and then anywhere from a few dollars to thousands for the usage.

But that's just the base scale. Most performers are represented by agents, who tack on their 10% and may demand more than scale for busy performers doing commercials. Then there's the union itself: it insists that the performer become your employee for the duration of the session, making you responsible for payroll and unemployment taxes. And of course the union gets its own cut to support their health and pension funds. Figure another 28% for taxes and pension. And the total has to be received by the union within 12 working days of the session, or else serious penalties kick in.

Keeping all the math and procedures correct is no job for an amateur. Most producers who use union talent also employ paymasters who take care of the whole nasty mess, become the employer of record, and rent you the talent for a mere 10% more. This also lets the paymaster assume the liability for unemployment insurance, so your company's rates don't go up if you neglect to hire that actor the next week. Paymasters are franchised and regulated by the union. If you're using a studio or production company's contract to avoid becoming a signatory yourself, they'll probably charge you an additional 10% for the handling and prompt payment.

Fun, huh?

The only discount is when an actor has formed a separate "For Services Of" corporation for tax or liability reasons. You'll still need a paymaster, but the actors' F/S/O corporation assumes Social Security and other payroll taxes.

Planning Ahead

Successful directing starts long before the talent shows up. At least three days before the session, figure out how the reading should sound.

Sit at your desk and read the whole script, aloud and in full voice. Listen carefully to yourself. Do the sentences work for the ear? Is it obvious which words should be stressed, and is there a natural pattern that emphasizes them? Does it sound conversational? Make a note of any sentences that are hard to interpret, or don't make sense to your ear.

Then fix them. This can be as easy as adding a couple of extra commas or dashes to break the sentence up. Or it might require a change that has to be approved higher up, which is why you're doing this preparation long before the recording.

Deciding what to stress

There are two ways to decide what to emphasize in a sentence. You can say it a few different ways and see which sounds best, but that wastes time and can lead to monotony (the dreaded Ted Baxter syndrome). Or you can use some applied information theory.

Assume that the most important part of the sentence is that which conveys the most information. Information is directly related to unpredictability, so the most important words are the ones your audience hasn't heard before. Imagine a script:

```
Narr:   Joe Blow has served our district for nine-
        teen years. Joe Blow is honest, smart, and
        competent. Vote for Joe Blow!
```

It's certainly appropriate to stress the first mention of Joe's name. But if you stress the other two times, it'll just sound boring. You're throwing a lot of the commercial's information-carrying ability away.

In the second sentence, try stressing the adjectives instead. They're the newest information (though hardly unexpected in a political spot). In the third sentence, stress the verb—that's the command to action and the newest thought. Besides, by this time the viewers already know Joe's name. They won't remember it any better, or be more convinced to vote for the guy, just because you said his name stronger.

Don't make the radio announcer's mistake of stressing the conjunction. "Joe Blow is honest, smart, *and* competent" merely implies that the "and" part is unusual, and these three characteristics are seldom found in the same politician. This might be technically true, but that's a subject for a different book.

Stress enhancement techniques

Professionals use lots of different ways to emphasize a word in a sentence, and saying it louder is the worst of them. Changing the volume suddenly just makes things harder to record. Instead, they'll do the following:

- S-l-o-w the word down. This is particularly effective on client names, which may be more unfamiliar than other words. In fact, I'll often slow down the name with my workstation's time expansion feature if the talent hasn't done it for me.

- Raise the pitch slightly. Every sentence has an inflection pattern, but if you suddenly jump above the expected pitch, you'll call attention to the word. It's as effective as making the word louder, without the technical problems.

- Pause slightly before the word. It doesn't have to be a noticeable pause; just . . . break the rhythm slightly. I sometimes manually insert a one-frame or half-frame pause before important words.

Try these techniques aloud at your desk, and listen to the result. Your coworkers may think you're crazy, but you'll become a better director.

Prepare the announcer

As soon as you've got a final script, and ideally a couple of days before the session, note any technical words or jargon. Prepare a pronunciation guide, including which acronyms should be spelled out (such as *N. L. E.*) and which are pronounced as words (such as *Sim-Tee* timecode). Some narrators prefer the guide as a cassette tape; others as a page they can keep referring to. Print out a clean copy of the script, in at least 12-point double-spaced type and using upper- and lowercase. Send the guide and the script to the narrator. If you want to e-mail it, make absolutely sure they can handle the file format and any platform translations . . . or convert the script to ASCII text.

The announcer might not choose to mark up or even read the entire script, and most assuredly won't memorize it, but at least they'll have a chance to get prepared and familiarize themselves with any difficult terms. Most professionals are very good at glancing at a script and figuring out how to cope with the trouble spots.

If you're not going to have an approved script until the day of the session, send the talent a preliminary version and the pronunciation guide. But let them know how many changes to expect, or what areas are likely to be revised.

If you're using an outside studio, this is also a good time to get them prepared. Make sure the engineer knows how many people you'll be recording at a time and how many extra bodies to expect in the control room. If you're bringing reference audio- or videotapes, make sure the studio will have the equipment to play that format. Verify how you want the narration delivered—every take or just the approved ones; what kind of tape/disc/removable drive you prefer and whether it should be in a specific file format; and how you want any sync marks or timecode. If possible, talk to the engineer who'll be doing the job instead of the studio's traffic manager. Believe me, these messages can get mighty garbled on the way from office to studio.

With good preparation, everything will be ready at the appointed time. Actors charge the same per hour whether they're performing, waiting for you to figure out the meaning of a line, or waiting for a studio engineer to fetch a cassette deck or extra headset.

Script preparation

The day before the session, find the person who has ultimate approval over the project and make them initial a copy of the script. Remind them that changes will be expensive.

Then read through the final script and break it down, just as you would for a video shoot. Be sure you know where the logical breaks and emotional changes occur. This way, you can decide how the session should flow:

- Multiple takes of the full script might be appropriate for short narrations or when you need emotional continuity.

- Multiple takes of one- or two-page segments can help the actors develop their own characteristic interpretation.

- Recording straight through, stopping immediately for corrections and pickups, is most efficient for long narrations and anonymous narrators.

Besides, a script breakdown can save you hundreds of dollars in talent fees. If you can separate the characters and schedule them out of sequence, you won't be paying actors to sit around while you record other parts.

At the Session

Now you're ready to have some fun.

Radiate two things in the studio: a positive attitude about the project, and unambiguous directions.

I've seen sessions destroyed by a director complaining about the client, budget, or last-minute changes. It might make you feel good to vent those frustrations, but it also tells the talent you don't need their best work on this project. If you can't say anything nice, say something noncommittal that sounds good . . . but don't ever say nothing. The actors and engineer depend on you for specific instructions.

This should start before the tape rolls. Make sure everyone understands what you're looking for, and be ready for actors' questions about meaning or pronunciation. Listen carefully when the engineer is setting levels. If you need a different projection or energy level from the performer, this is the time to speak up. Pay attention to the technical aspects as well; if you don't like what you hear, fix it now before you commit to a setup. The wrong mic position, equalization, gating, or compression will be impossible to repair without re-recording.

As soon as everything's ready, start rolling. There's nothing to be gained from rehearsing an entire voice-over. If two actors will have to interact dramatically, something that almost never happens in a video voice-over, it may be worth rehearsing a couple of key sequences around a conference table so you can keep control over character and rhythm. But otherwise, send them into the studio and start the session.

Tape is cheap, and even the first take—with all its mispronunciations and bad timing—might yield some perfect phrases or a replacement syllable when you later discover a problem in the selected take. Record everything. Erase nothing. If you're so strapped that you absolutely must recycle tape stock, wait until after the project is mixed.

How to talk to an actor

There's a fine line between giving your performers sufficient feedback, and being a blabbermouth on the talkback. You have to let them know what to change, and it's always good to tell them what you liked. The key is keeping your directions meaningful. "That was real good, could you do another?" doesn't give the talent much to go on, no matter how many words you say it in.

Most actors will give a better performance if you tell them what you want fixed ("I need more of a sense of pride when you get to *serving our community*") and let them work out the details, rather than tell them exactly how to do it. But if you don't hear what you want on the next take, get more specific ("Slow down on those three words, and stress *community* a little"). If all else fails, give a line read: say it exactly the way you want to hear it, and let them mimic you.

Announcers, as opposed to actors, usually prefer line reads, but only if you as director can read the line properly. You might *think* you're delivering an Oscar-worthy performance, but if the announcer hears a string of monotonous syllables, that's what you'll get back. Improve your line reads by practicing some of the techniques in the section on stress patterns (above) and by getting feedback from colleagues.

While you should be decisive, you don't have to be a martinet. If you make a mistake, say so—and be prepared to accept the blame. The most effective direction I've ever heard is, "You did exactly what I asked for. But I guess it's not quite what I want." This also invites the performer to help you find a better solution. Directing isn't an adversarial process, and you don't win any points by making the person in the booth look bad.

Keep track of things

Slate every take verbally. If you're using a DAT recorder, you can save cueing time later by using the same numbers as both the verbal slate and tape ID. If you're recording to videotape, have someone note the timecode for each verbal take number.

Then take lots of notes. Once you hear a great reading for a particular line, write its take number on the script next to the line—even if the rest of the take wasn't very good. You're covered even if the talent never reads it that way again, and you'll save lots of time searching for those golden moments.

Notes on a voice-over session should be more comprehensive than a script log from a shoot. Don't just write down that a whole take was good or bad; give yourself enough details to know which phrases particularly impressed you. Then you'll be able to go to them immediately while editing, instead of having to play back the entire session again for evaluation. Figure 4 shows my notes as I made them during

The Narrators Speak

The best people to tell you how to direct are the performers themselves. So I spoke to two of PBS's busiest: Don Wescott has voiced more than 75 *Nova* episodes, as well as most of the promos for *Mystery*, *American Experience*, and *Masterpiece Theater*. Wendie Sakakeeny was *Nova's* first female voice and has done almost as many episodes as Don, along with narrations for *National Geographic* and many Fortune 500 companies. Even if you don't watch public television, you've heard both of them in thousands of commercials.

Don: The more you can tell me about the project, the better. It's great to know the audience and who you're trying to appeal to, as well as what's going on in the pictures.

Wendie: But don't waste our time with a whole lot of background information. It doesn't matter how many versions you've done before, or the history of each source in the video. Tell us the attitude and tone and who's going to see it, and then let us do our jobs. What we certainly don't need is for you to read the entire script, paragraph by paragraph.

Don: One guy gave me a 20-minute read . . . in a monotone. He read the entire script. That's crazy. If you have to do a line read, save it for the lines we've read wrong. But definitely give us constant feedback. I love to hear back, "I like this, I don't like that, speed up here, breathe here . . ." The more talkative a director, the better. You have to tell us what's good as well as what's bad.

Wendie: It's important to establish *how* you're going to give direction, and what you expect for retakes. If we make a mistake, let us finish the sentence but don't go on for several paragraphs. Catch us while we're still in the same frame of mind. Also, are you going to slate everything, or just pause? Do you want us to pick up whole paragraphs or just the previous sentence?

Don: There should be just one director. The fewer people in the control room, the better. The best sessions are just the performer, the producer, and the engineer.

Wendie: But make sure the producer is empowered to make changes if something doesn't work. The worst sessions are when the script is written by a committee, and nobody is available to answer questions about it.

Don: You want to be a good director? Come fully prepared and maintain an open flow of communications during the session. And know how to say it yourself.

a typical voice-over session. You can see how I've already marked which words will come from which takes. It's not very neat; but, boy, is it efficient.

Besides, once your script is covered with these numbers, you know you've gotten everything you need. Sign the actors' contracts and you're done.

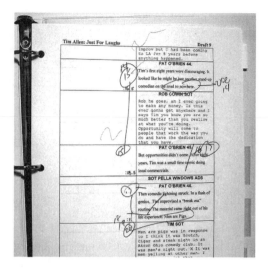

Figure 4: Script notes after a typical voice-over session

Directing children

Two factors conspire to add an element of unpredictability to sessions with young children, but if you're aware of them, you'll at least be able to maintain a small element of control:

- The child has to be cooperative.

- The parent—or whoever brought the child to the session—has to be relaxed and willing to let you do your job.

The biggest factor in the child's ability to cooperate is how alert and awake they are. Children have limited attention spans, so plan short sessions (under 10 minutes, if possible) with lots of interaction between you and the child. It often helps to break their part down to individual lines, do two or three takes of each with immediate verbal rewards and specific directions, and then move onto the next line. It also helps to be in the booth with the child, rather than directing via talkback.

One of my favorite props when working with the three- to seven-year-old set is a small stuffed tiger. When the child first shows up for the session, I ask—with complete seriousness—if they'll take care of my tiger for me. I hand them the toy and give the two a minute or so to get acquainted. Then I lead the child (who's still holding the tiger) into the booth and sit them on a chair.

A chair is essential. Otherwise the child will be all over the booth and a different distance from the mic for each line. A short shotgun is usually the best mic to use, since kids generally don't have much projection. The shotgun's lack of bass isn't a problem with young voices.

Figure 5: A tiger perched on a short shotgun, ready to record a child

When we're ready to record I put the tiger on the mic (Figure 5), giving the child a familiar face to talk to. This keeps their mouth focused in the right direction, without them having to sit rigidly (or even be aware this was the goal). Since the animal is soft, it doesn't cause reflections into the mic. Just be careful not to block the holes that give the mic directionality.

Kids are distracted by other kids. If you can, don't have more than one in the recording area at a time. Younger children will start paying attention to their compatriots. Older boys—10 years or so and up—start playing to each other and may turn into wise guys. Once one goes, the whole crowd is lost.

Parents should be told what to expect and be warned that it's unlikely they'll be in the room during the session. Ask them *not* to rehearse the lines; the whole reason you're using children is for their natural, spontaneous reads. (Don't even tell a parent what the lines will be like. They want their children to do an impressive job and may be tempted to do some rehearsing even though you've asked them not to.) Do ask the parents to make sure the child is fed and rested.

Also, tell parents that it's no problem for them to arrive a little late. Trying to get any kid somewhere unfamiliar at a precise time can produce anxiety for both parent and child. The alternative—arriving too early and then waiting in the car or building lobby—just builds suspense.

Recording Sound Effects

The best time to record prop noises may be during the shot itself. Throw an extra mic next to the noisy object, if necessary, and fade it up in time for the sound. The result will match the room's acoustics and be perfectly in sync.

A lot of times this may not be possible because the effect mic would be in the shot, because the sound takes place at a time that conflicts with dialog, or because the location is just too noisy. In the first two cases, simply record prop sounds right after the take. Everybody's eager to move on to the next setup, but a minute now can save you an hour in postproduction. Scream "room tone" (previous chapter) and everybody will stand still while you record 30 seconds of background sound. Then say "just a second, folks" and make the prop noises.

If you can't record prop noises at the shoot, you'll probably have to foley.

Foley

Today's sound libraries on CD and the Internet are remarkably comprehensive—there are collections full of footsteps, and others with nothing but solenoids and switches—and audio workstations let you adjust their sync at the touch of a button. We cover library effects in Chapter 13.

But it's often faster to create the little sounds in real time. Footsteps, clothing rustles, and pen-on-paper effects are prime candidates for what sound editors call *foley* sessions. The name honors Jack Foley, a Hollywood second-unit director and sound genius in the 1940s. The process is fairly simple: play back the picture, mimic what the actors do on screen, and record the result in sync. A good foley artist can watch a scene once, gather props, and record a fairly accurate imitation in a single take. But effective foley is more than just "going through the motions." Professionals have developed tricks over the years to make their foleys more effective, and many of them can be used in your productions.

Proper foley requires a setup similar to ADR, where recording is in sync with picture playback. You can also do what's sometimes called *digital foley*, recording the effects without picture, matching them later in an editing system or audio workstation.

Deciding what to ignore

It's a lot of fun to play with a bunch of noisemakers in the studio, but unless you've got a Hollywood budget and a full set of props, it's usually better to use prerecorded effects rather than foley. Business videos and local television don't need the kind of precision required for the big screen. Production dialog tracks may already have appropriate sounds that just need to be isolated and equalized.

It also helps to add the background sounds before recording foley. A lot of times you'll find a bang or a footstep in the background that can be slid to match the on-screen action. Not only does this save a lot of recording time; it saves tracks and makes mixing easier.

You might also save time by adding the music before a foley session. Hollywood sound editors like to give directors a lot of choices, so they'll create foleys for every little movement. Most never make it to the final mix. Productions with more limited budgets—including a lot of network shows—don't even worry about some foley while there's music playing.

Just the fx

Foley effects should be recorded as cleanly as possible, without any echoes or background noises. Echoes get in the way when you're editing and seldom fit the on-screen environment. Unless a studio is designed for voice recording, it's probably too reverberant to do a good job without lots of blankets or goboes.

Small effects are usually recorded best with a short shotgun mic, fairly close to the sound. Larger effects like footsteps need a bit more perspective, with a less directional mic, to keep a constant level. Roll off low frequencies below 90 Hz or so—many mics have a switch that does this—to eliminate the proximity bass boost and match the way the boom was used in production.

Usually foley is recorded in mono, since it'll be panned to the action when the show is mixed. Stereo just wastes tracks and invites phase errors. A lot of broadcast TV keeps foleys in mono during the mix to avoid playback incompatibility.

Record as loud as you can. Even small sounds like pencil taps should be recorded at a high volume. This makes it easier to add equalization at the mix and reduces system noise buildup.

Finding appropriate foley props

You'll want to gather a lot of toys—er, professional foley props—to do the job right. The most important is probably a suitcase full of old clothes and papers. Cotton, silk, and wool sound different, so have at least one item of each. A large jacket is usually the most versatile object of clothing, since you can put it on easily for a full sequence as well as rub or rustle it to simulate individual actions. Underwear is seldom necessary (as a sound prop).

Throw in stuff to write with. Newspaper, notepaper, cardboard, and fax paper all rattle differently. Pencil, ballpoint, and felt-tip pens have their own sound. Even the suitcase will be useful. You can creak the snaps, hinges, and leather flaps as everything from a briefcase to a pocketbook.

Stock your studio with a couple of different kinds of telephones. Old-fashioned black ones with mechanical bells have a distinctive resonance that you don't find in the modern plastic ones. And don't forget the phonebook: gaffer-tape a big city directory so the pages don't rattle, and throw it on the floor for an instant falling body. (Some people like to slam their arms against a table for falling bodies because it's easier to get the timing right. But it's just as easy to adjust the timing on a workstation. I prefer to reserve the use of my forearms as falling or jumping animals.)

Experiment with different ways to hold each prop. The same coffee cup can have three different sounds depending on whether you hold it by its handle, wrap your fingers around it, or grab it from the top. Even pens and pencils will have a different sound depending on how you hold them.

Foley footsteps

You'll also want pairs of hard- and soft-soled shoes. Unless the script calls for spike heels, the difference between men's and women's shoes is often just a question of equalization, gating, and walking style (see Chapter 14 for how to apply these effects).

Of course, you'll also need someplace to walk. Many Hollywood studios have *foley pits*—sections of studio floor equipped with sand, gravel, tile, and even waterproof pans for mud and puddles. Each surface has a unique sound. Chances are your building's management would object if you just throw this junk on the floor, but you can still have appropriate walking surfaces:

- If your studio is carpeted, try putting the microphone very close to the floor while you walk. With a little equalization, carpet can be a very convincing grass lawn.

- Of course, if your studio is carpeted, you won't be able to make convincing hardwood or concrete footsteps. It doesn't take much carpentry to build a walk board (see Figure 6) for carpeted studios. Take a piece of half-inch plywood, and glue or tack a few carpet strips on the bottom. The strips keep the wood from sliding around and make the floor sound more solid. Scatter some sand on the plywood, or change the equalization and echo, to get the sound of other surfaces.

- Use something more rigid, such as particle board or doubled plywood, for stairs. The airspace (Figure 7) adds an extra hollowness. To "walk" upstairs, use your full weight and scrape the front of your foot slightly against the top edge. For downstairs, eliminate the scraping and land heavily on your heels. If your studio has hardwood or linoleum floors, put some weather-stripping or old rubber tire along the bottom of the 2×6 so the stairs don't creep around.

- A slab of marble or slate from a home supply store can be everything from sidewalks to office lobbies.

- If you don't want to spread gravel around your studio floor, put it in a large canvas or burlap bag. Seal the bag, lay it flat, and go for a walk.

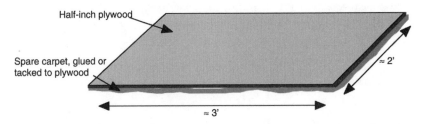

Figure 6: A walk board for carpeted studios

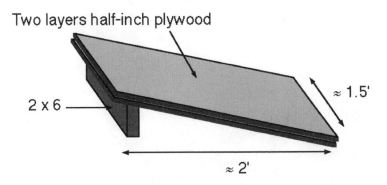

Figure 7: Stairs for your studio

Don't forget, you can also walk with your hands. Fill a large plastic dishpan with sand or gravel—or, to be kinder on your hands, use cornflakes or semisoft cat food—and punch your way across the scene. Close miking, equalization, and a little compression will make the sound bigger.

A supermarket of effects

You'll find a lot of sounds at your local grocery store. As you cruise the aisles, listen for the following:

- *Corn starch.* Look for the small rectangular box. Squeeze the front and back together for perfect footsteps in snow.

- *Dry cat food.* Its shape and consistency make it sound like gravel scraping.

- *Cookie sheets.* Some folks like to rattle them for a classic thunder effect, but I prefer the thunder in a good CD library. On the other hand, they're great for banging; depending on how you hold the sheets and damp their vibrations, they can be anything from the side of a submarine to the hood of a car.

- *Mason jars.* Remove the rubber ring, and you can scrape the glass top against the jar for anything from a mechanical scrape to an ancient stone tomb door. Legend has it that the Martian ships' hatches in Orson Welles's classic War of the Worlds broadcast were close-miked mayonnaise jars . . . but only when opened in the proper acoustic of the studio's tile bathroom.

- *Cabbage.* I like to make bodies fall by dropping phone books. But for a really gory fall, slam a head of cabbage against the table.

The art of manual effects owes much to the sound geniuses who brought radio dramas to life in the 1930s and '40s. Today we use digital libraries, workstations, and effects processors, but if you want to learn about the basics, read Robert Mott's classic *Radio Sound Effects* (1993, McFarland, ISBN 0-89950-747-6). And listen to everything.

Recording Ambiences

A continuous track of a separately recorded background, mixed under an entire scene, can smooth out individual edits and lend a sense of reality. Sometimes, it may be the only way to simulate reality. Consider a sequence that takes place in a restaurant or busy office. You'll want the extras to be as quiet as possible while you're shooting so you can concentrate on getting good (and editable) dialog tracks. Chances are, they'll mime their luncheon conversations or phone calls. But in the final mix, we have to hear the crowd's voices as well as the clatter of silverware or the office's telephones and printers. In fact, we should hear more than just the on-screen crowd; the assumption is there are other people just out of camera view, making the same kinds of noise.

Since we're hearing a lot more background sounds than we can see sources for on camera, sync becomes a nonissue. If prop sounds from the principal characters match up with their actions, the whole scene appears to be in sync. This means you don't have to worry about recording ambiences at the shoot. You can grab *any* similar restaurant, office, or whatever, and it'll sound right. In fact, using background sound is often the only way to achieve the effect of a large busy room with only a few extras and a small shooting stage.

Finding background locations

Look through the script and make a list of different locations that will need sound, including places where there should be active crowds, places with characteristic mechanical sounds (such as generating stations or airplane interiors), and exterior long shots where you're using lavs that won't pick up the natural environment.

You may find it's easiest to get some of the backgrounds from library CDs (Chapter 13). A $75 background CD can include clean recordings of all the environments you need, along with a license to use them in all of your productions. If you're planning to do the final mix at a sound studio, check with the studio's manager; most have large libraries they'll let you dip into for free or a nominal fee.

For backgrounds that won't come from a library, expand your list to include details about the sizes and shapes of the areas and what kind of activities take place in them. This is much better than just listing the areas by name and will keep you from making scouting mistakes. For example, something called "hotel lobby" can be busy or calm; vaulted or low-ceilinged; stark or with lots of furniture; or be next to a restaurant or swimming pool. When you're scouting places to record, look for the characteristics rather than just a building that matches the original name. Your local post office or library can make a better hotel lobby recording than the Holiday Inn down the street.

This can also help prevent you from getting stuck with ambiences that aren't usable. Supermarkets usually have music coming from their public address systems. Even if you can identify and license the cuts being played (background music services sometimes use production music libraries), you won't be able to edit it or change the mix. Find a retail operation that doesn't use music, such as a hardware or computer store. If you want to add music to it, use some of the tricks in Chapter 14 to give library cuts an authentic public-address texture that's still mixable and controllable.

Recording backgrounds

I've found that building managers usually won't care if you record backgrounds, so long as you're unobtrusive and the building or its occupants aren't identifiable. In most public spaces, the best strategy is to walk in with a small recorder and mic, make the recording you need, and get out. The only time I've ever been stopped was in a casino, where they have strict rules about recording game play; perhaps they don't want anyone actually tracking the odds.

Omnidirectional mics work nicely for mono recordings and are unobtrusive. Clip a lav to your jacket and carry a small DAT or Minidisk recorder in a shoulder bag. Even a high-quality cassette recorder will do a good job, since sync isn't an issue. Try to stay perfectly still while you record, so you don't pick up clothing noises. Record for at least a minute if there aren't many spoken voices. If there are voices, record a lot longer; you'll want to do some editing, and any looping to extend a background to fit a scene will become apparent as the voices repeat. If you're sure of your equipment, there's no need to monitor the recording (it's easy enough to go back and repeat a recording that didn't turn out well). But if you must monitor, use Walkman-type phones and pretend you're listening to music.

Since you're not worrying about picking up dialog or distinct sounds, you can use what you learned in Chapter 1 to change the acoustics around the mic and effectively modify the room where you're recording backgrounds. Is a luncheonette during a slow hour still too noisy to be the sophisticated restaurant you need? Hold the mic close to the bench where you're sitting; the back of the bench will mute sounds from that direction, and the padded cushions will absorb high frequencies from the other. Need an office lobby to be noisier and more echoey? Hold the mic close to the floor, near the building directory or some other area that attracts footsteps.

Stereo backgrounds are seldom necessary in video production, and any stereo field you record won't match what's on camera. It may be just as effective to record mono, but gather enough material that you can put different sections of it on separate tracks. Use two sections that were at least 30 seconds apart, panning one somewhat to the left and the other somewhat to the right. Add a little stereo echo to create a sense of environment. If you think stereo is necessary, be aware of possible mono compatibility issues. You can get a good stereo recording with a lav on each shoulder—your head provides separation—or by wearing a binaural mic (they look like headphones and use the shape of the head and ear to help define the sound field). But either of those techniques can sound hollow when summed to mono. For true stereo compatibility, you'll need to use some of the mid-side tricks described in Chapter 6 . . . but they aren't unobtrusive.

Vocal Sound Effects

Back in the pretape days, when radio commercials were recorded to vinyl in a single take, a New York sound effects artist was asked to bring some puppy barks to a pet food session. He played through his trunk full of 78s at the rehearsal, but nothing satisfied the producer. But when the big moment came, the bark was perfect. Afterward, the producer asked, "What did you do? Change the speed? Equalize? Play two barks at once?" The effects artist walked up to a nearby mic, screwed his mouth sideways, and went "wralf!"

Even with today's immense CD libraries, vocal sounds are used both for convenience and to create unique effects. Learning how to make and manipulate these silly noises can teach you a lot about the human voice and effects design in general . . . and besides, it's a fun topic to end a long chapter.

Vocal sounds are either voiced or unvoiced, depending on whether they're pure breath or if the vocal chords are used. (There's an exhaustive discussion of how vocal sounds are produced in Chapter 11.) Unvoiced noises are more useful as effects because it's easy to turn them into mechanical sounds. Voiced sounds are usually limited to organic things like monsters or insects.

If you work very closely to the microphone, you can also use high-pressure sounds like the plosive /p/ to generate distortion, which makes the sound richer. But you have to be very close, almost touching the mic with your lips. Electret condenser units tend to break up with an ugly crackling sound under these circumstances, so you might do better with a cheap dynamic.

A few things that can help:

- Use an omnidirectional mic, and put a handkerchief over it to protect from pops.

- Don't use a mic with a built-in windscreen, since you won't be able to get close enough to the diaphragm.

- Look for a mic with low sensitivity, so you can use more air pressure without overloading the preamplifier.

- Practice by listening to a playback, comparing yourself to sound effects recordings or live sounds. You can't do this with headphones in real time because bone conduction means you'll hear your voice differently than the mic does.

Mouth-sound processing

There's a lot more about editing and processing sound effects later in this book, but some processes apply specifically to vocal effects. Once you've got these sounds, you have to dehumanize them. The first step is to delete any mouth noises, breaths, and handling sounds. Leave some silence between sounds and at the end of the file, so there's someplace for an echo to go. Then listen through for additional cues that the sound came from a human mouth rather than something inhuman—sometimes you'll hear little clicks of saliva or errant voicings in an unvoiced sound—and edit those out. Now you're ready to play.

The first step is to change the pitch. For this purpose, it's better to use a program that doesn't try to preserve the timing, but instead works like varispeeding a tape. Once the sound gets more than an octave away from its original pitch, the resonances are changed enough so that it doesn't sound human any more. Try some radical shifts: at four octaves down, an /s/ sounds like a scraping rock. If your program supports it, play with pitch bending as well. An /s/ that rapidly drops from very high to very low makes a good laser gun.

Then play with the envelope. Mechanical sounds usually start abruptly, but human sounds build up over time. Delete the start of one of your noises to give it an abrupt beginning, or use your program's envelope control to simulate some of the natural envelopes in Chapter 1. Then play with the pitch again. A tiny slice from the middle of a /z/, at one-third normal pitch, becomes a frog's "ribbit."

To simulate a machine, collect a variety of short pitch-shifted unvoiced sounds. Edit them together, copy them all, and paste them as multiple loops. This rhythmic repetition can then be pitch-bent to make the machine start up or slow down. Add some flanging for a nice rotary motion.

Equalization helps turn a vocal sound into something less than human. Try dips around 1.75 kHz for unvoiced sounds, and around 300 Hz for the voiced ones, before you start playing with the ends of the band. Machine sounds frequently benefit from a few sharp peaks between 500 Hz and 1.5 kHz.

Many of the microphone techniques for creating vocal sound effects were developed by Wes Harrison, an entertainer who has built a career of mouth sounds and comedy as "Mr. Sound Effects." He started in the mid-1950s as many of the explosions in MGM's classic *Tom and Jerry* cartoons, and he was both the baby seal and the storm in Disney's *20,000 Leagues under the Sea*. As of this writing, he's still going strong, performing in nightclubs around the world. And he's still hilarious, with a comic style reminiscent of Red Skelton at his prime (but using noises instead of physical shtick). If you're lucky enough to catch his act, it'll be both professional education and entertainment. There's a short segment of his work, from his self-produced album, on this book's CD (track 38).

POSTPRODUCTION OVERVIEW AND TRICKS

There's a writer/producer I work with, who loves every part of the production except the very last step: saying the project is done. His preference would be to tweak projects endlessly in postproduction, in a search for creative perfection. Unfortunately, his clients and investors can't wait that long. He once told me, "A video is never finished. It's just taken away."

This last section of the book is about getting the best audio in the least amount of postproduction time, so you can use whatever's left—before they take the project away—for additional creative tweaking.

The whole idea of "postproduction" originated in the glory days of Hollywood, where tasks were broken up so studios could crank out dozens of films simultaneously. Films were shot—that's *production*—and then edited and mixed in *post*production, then they were released from the assembly line.

These days post is anything you do after you've struck the set and may include insert shots, new recording, computer-generated images, and a lot of other content creation. For some documentaries and commercials, the whole project is done with stock footage and computers; there's no production; only postpostproduction.

Linear and Nonlinear Editing

The world is linear. Noon always comes one minute after 11:59 AM. Productions are linear as well. Even interactive CDs and video discs are built out of essentially linear sequences. Humans can't handle nonlinear time, so the very idea of nonlinear editing is an oxymoron.

The terms "linear" and "nonlinear" actually refer to the timeline that a production is built on and how much control we have over it. It has nothing to do with whether a production is analog or digital.

But the decision to use linear or nonlinear editing can have important implications for how sound is handled.

Linear Editing

In linear editing, the timeline is inviolate. It starts at the head of the production, runs for the duration of the project, and then stops. You can copy things onto the timeline or erase things from it, but you can't change the timing of the line itself.

If you're editing video in a linear online session, the timeline is the master tape. Scenes are assembled by copying camera shots from a playback deck to the desired place on the master. Usually they're copied sequentially—shot 1, then shot 2—but there's no technical reason you can't copy them out of order, leave a hole for some shots to be put in later (Figure 1), or insert new video over an existing sequence. Dissolves and other effects are performed in real time and recorded on the master tape along with the images. Since the program is built onto the master tape, there's no rendering process; as soon as the last edit is complete, the job is done.

The problem is that once something is on a linear timeline, it can't be moved. You can erase or record over a scene, but you can't nudge it a couple of frames without re-recording it. If everything in a show is perfect except the third shot is four frames too long, you can't cut out just those frames. You have to re-record the next shot four frames earlier, and—unless you care to stretch something—you also have to re-record everything after it.

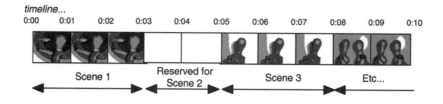

Figure 1: A linear edit timeline can be assembled out of sequence.

In linear audio for video, the timeline is usually a multitrack tape locked to the video master by timecode, but sometimes it's multiple audio tracks on the master video itself. Sounds are recorded on tracks as both audio and video are played, but—as with linear video—you can't change the timing of an element without re-recording it.

When all the tracks are assembled the way they should be, they're mixed onto a final mono or stereo master.

Nonlinear Editing

Nonlinear editing revolutionized video production in the late 1980s, but it added only one new concept: the ability to pick up and move whole pieces of previously assembled timeline. It was a crucial difference.

In nonlinear video editing, all of the images are stored in a computer, usually on hard disk (though other random-access media can be used). As far as the computer's concerned, the timeline is really just a database: a list describing what part of its storage will be played back at any moment. When you move scenes around, the nonlinear editor—usually called an NLE—merely rearranges the database (Figures 2 and 3). Only a few bytes of data are involved, so this appears to happen instantly.

When the program is finished, complex effects are created by combining data from different places on the hard disk, then all the images are retrieved according to the database and either shown in real time and recorded to videotape, or copied onto one large file.

At the deepest software level, many nonlinear systems can be thought of as just incredibly fast linear database editors. The databases themselves can even be linear: when you insert or rearrange a scene, the system copies part of the data list from hard drive to temporary storage, rearranges it, and then "dubs" it back.

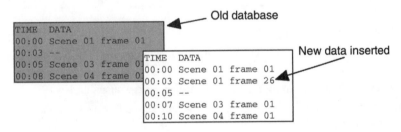

Figure 2: Nonlinear editing is really just database management . . .

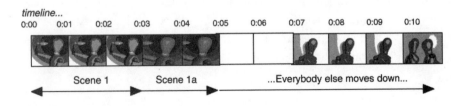

Figure 3: . . . though the result appears to be edited picture.

Nonlinear audio editing works just about the same way, with multiple databases—one for each track—relating to sounds stored on hard disk. Since audio editing isn't frame-based and can be more precise than video, the counting system is more elaborate. Sophisticated systems keeps track of individual samples (see Chapter 2). Effects such as reverb or compression can either be created during the editing process and stored elsewhere on the disk, or be noted in the database and applied on final playback.

Linear Versus Nonlinear for Video Editing

The primary advantages of linear video editing are speed and simplicity. There's no time wasted on digitizing, file transfers, or rendering, so a long program with just a few edits can be put together in little more than the length of the show itself. The equipment is simple: all you need is one or more playback decks, a video recorder, and some way to control the decks and select the signal. The concept is even simpler —cue both decks and press Play on one while you press Record on the other*—even though it may take a lifetime to master the art involved.

The primary disadvantage of linear editing *used to be* loss of quality. Each time an analog tape is copied, it picks up distortion and noise (see Chapter 2). But digital videotape and signal chains don't suffer from this. These days the disadvantages of linear editing are the equipment cost and the time it takes to cue and record each individual edit.

Linear editing may be faster or slower than nonlinear.

➤ Linear wastes very little time on "overhead." There's no need to preload video, render, or dub the final project to a master tape.

➤ But the edits themselves take place in real time, plus a few seconds for cueing and locking.

If a program is long and doesn't have many edits, linear editing will be faster. But if it's short and has complex sequences, nonlinear will be faster.

The primary advantages to nonlinear video editing are that it's easy to make changes to a sequence and that the equipment can be small and inexpensive—all you need is a video recorder and a computer. On the other hand, nonlinear systems have steep learning curves and are subject to setup and configuration troubles.

---

*Okay, that's just the concept. To do this for real also involves preroll, synchronization, vertical-interval switching, and things like that, but an editing computer usually takes care of this dirty work.

Unless you're already an expert or very lucky, or purchase a turnkey system and training seminars, you'll find yourself facing mysterious blank frames, loss of lip sync, or other troubles . . . and you might not be able to tell whether it's your fault, the software's, or some incompatibility in the system.

Implications for Audio

You have to pay more attention to audio during a linear editing session than during a nonlinear one. If the sound quality doesn't match across a cut, it may be almost impossible to correct it after the program is done. Unless you have an automated mixer linked to the video editor, cross-fades have to be done in real time by moving faders while you're watching the picture. Equalization and other corrections have to be applied on the fly, and you can't go back to change them without redoing the edit.

To handle sound properly in a linear edit, you absolutely must have good audio monitors and the time to pay attention to them. You also need a clean audio path, with good wiring and a high-quality mixer. If there's a sound problem and you can't fix it immediately, you may have to live with it forever. On the other hand, you can hear as soon as something goes wrong. And the most common audio problem with nonlinear editing—lost sync—almost never happens in a linear editing suite.

Nonlinear editing give you more flexibility, but this can be a double-edged sword. Although you've got the freedom to put off audio decisions during the visual editing process, this often translates to a carelessness about sound. There's a tendency for visually oriented producers to consider a project done when the pictures are finished and blast through the audio mix without paying attention. Since most NLEs don't let you hear all of the audio effects at full quality until they're rendered in final form, you can miss problems that would be quickly spotted in linear edit sessions.

To make things worse, NLEs are often supplied with miniature monitors and set up in rooms with bad acoustics. The next chapter discusses some of the things you can do about this, but with many NLE setups you couldn't do a good mix if you wanted to!

On the other hand, audio elements don't need to be copied or changed during the nonlinear process. There are fewer places for their quality to be accidentally compromised. You have to get sounds accurately into the computer when you start the project (see Chapter 10); but once you've done that, you don't have to worry about them until it's time to concentrate on the track.

This means you can put off critical mix decisions until you have a chance to think about them, and you can move these decisions to a different editing station . . . or to a separate facility with good monitoring and control equipment.

Audio Options Beyond the NLE

Video-editing software is designed to manipulate pictures, and its audio capabilities—even on the big-name systems—are often minimal. You can add expensive processing plug-ins, but you'll still be limited by the NLE's software. Fortunately, audio and video are kept as separate files within a computer. Edited or raw elements can be exported in standard formats—or even as digital audio tape—without losing any quality. They can be processed or mixed elsewhere and then get married back to the picture.

All this means you've got lots of choices for how to manipulate audio in a nonlinear environment.

Edit and mix within the NLE

This approach usually restricts you to editing on frame lines, which may be too far apart for precise audio edits. It also can limit what mixing and processing tools are available, though many of the plug-ins that work with mainstream audio applications are also usable—with certain limits—in the video software. On the other hand, staying inside the NLE is fast and simple, and you don't need to learn a new program.

Edit in the NLE's computer, but with a separate audio program

This choice gives you a lot more audio-editing power. It's also cheaper than buying a dedicated system: good audio-only software costs just a few hundred dollars and can share plug-in processors with the NLE. Since both the audio editor and the NLE will be using the same drives, only a single set of files is necessary, and you don't have to worry about networking. However, both these kinds of programs demand processing power and a lot of RAM, so it might not be possible to use them simultaneously. And using a separate audio program does nothing to solve problems you may have with the monitors and acoustic environment in your work space.

Edit in a dedicated digital audio workstation

Digital audio workstations (DAWs) are tightly integrated systems, usually with more specialized hardware than you'll find on an NLE. Most high-end systems use a dedicated CPU, often with a customized operating system, and include multiple digital signal processor (DSP) chips to do complex processing in real time. The better systems provide hands-on controls, so you can manipulate multiple tracks simultaneously with your fingers instead of trying to adjust on-screen faders with a mouse. This is essential, since a mouse won't let you do the constant rebalancing between voice, music, and effects that are essential in a good video mix.

Most professional DAWs can share file formats and removable drives with a NLE. In large facilities, audio- and video-editing systems are often networked together and communicate using Ethernet to a central server.

But the biggest advantage to mixing in a DAW may have nothing to do with the hardware or software. Because they're expensive and have a fairly steep learning curve, they're usually installed in rooms with good monitoring facilities and maintained by people who understand audio.

Organizing Postproduction Audio

Polish the video first. It's silly to try to fine-tune a soundtrack if the picture isn't finished. Audio moves in continuous sweeps rather than individual images, so trivial picture edits may require large segments of track to be rebuilt. Audio edits can also help smooth over abrupt picture cuts.

However, don't put off *thinking* about the soundtrack until after the picture is done . . . by then, it's too late to do a good job. There's a definite order that you should approach things in to get the best track with the least amount of bother:

1. Decide which sequences will be driven by nonsync audio, and make sure you have the necessary elements (music for montages, voice-over, and so on).

2. Edit the picture, along with its dialog or any nonsync audio that drives it. If you can't edit the sound smoothly, put the audio across alternating tracks and provide "handles"—a few seconds extra sound at the in- and out-points (Figure 4). These can be used later for correcting sound problems and fixing transitions.

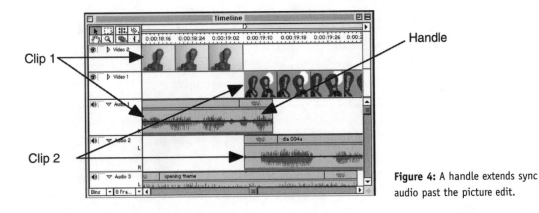

Figure 4: A handle extends sync audio past the picture edit.

3. Drop in any sounds that are necessary for plot development, such as phone bells, explosions, and off-camera dialog. Do this before committing to a final edit, because you might have to extend or shorten a scene to accommodate the sound. Don't obsess about sounds that aren't perfect; it's okay to use what you have as a placeholder and plan to change it later.

4. Get the necessary approvals for the video, make any required changes, and lock the picture. Make sure everyone involved understands that additional picture changes will also affect the cost or complexity of the track.

5. Fine-tune the audio elements. There's also a definite order that makes this more efficient (see Audio Priorities, in a few pages).

6. Mix the track and get *it* approved.

7. Finish the job: layback the track to videotape, or import it back into the nonlinear editor for final rendering.

Titles and other visual effects can be added at the same time the sound is being finished, if they won't have any effect on sync. Obviously, visual effects that are linked to sounds—explosions, flames, or a laser whoosh as the title is revealed—must be in place before the final mix.

Dealing with Nonsync Audio

It's important to have voice-overs and music available before you start cutting, because they influence how the picture is edited. But it's not important to have the same ones you'll use in the final mix.

Scratch tracks

Many producers prefer not to record the voice-over of a long project until the picture is fully cut because any script changes may require another recording session. Sometimes you don't even know what has to be changed until the picture is edited.

But without a narration track, it's difficult to cut the picture. You have to guess how long each line will take, and edit in a sterile environment with no audio reference. This is extra work both for the video editor and for some poor narrator who has to read each line to an arbitrary timing.

Instead, record a temporary narration track in your own voice. Quality isn't important—you can use a cheap multimedia mic and record right at your editing station. What *is* important is that you speak slowly and meaningfully, simulating the pace you'll want from the professional narrator. You can edit precisely to the scratch track; when you place key images and titles to fit against your own reading, chances are they'll still line up against the high-priced talent's version.

Besides, if your client approves a project hearing your amateur narration, think of how blown away they'll be when they hear a professional doing the job.

Temporary music

Hollywood editors often use a "temp track," borrowing a piece of a pop song or even one of the studio's other film scores, and cutting montages and other music-driven sequences to it. When the final score is created, the composer can use the temp as a guide for tempo and feel. Occasionally, a director falls so much in love with the temporary music that they buy the rights to it, and use it in the finished film.

It's probably not a good idea for a corporate or event videographer to borrow existing copyrighted music to use this way. If an unsophisticated client falls in love with the piece, you'll have to tell them they can't afford the rights to use it (copyright law doesn't forgive an infringement just because a client has bad judgment). Besides, it's easy to get so used to hearing a particular piece of music that nothing else—no matter how good—will sound right.

Instead, use a rough version of the actual music you're planning to use. If the video is going to have an original score, get the composer to throw together a demo of the scene's music. If you're buying library music, select the pieces for that scene before you start editing. Don't worry about the roughness of a demo or problems with specific aspects of the library cut; you can fine-tune after the picture is edited. In the meantime, you'll have the right feel and rhythm to cut against, and you won't have to worry about client disappointment in the final mix.

Audio Priorities

Once the picture is cut, it's most efficient to approach the remaining audio operations in a definite order:

1. Clean up the dialog first. It tells the story. Take advantage of cutaways and extreme wide shots to smooth out a performance or fit in an alternate performance.

2. Edit the narration second. It explains what we're seeing. If you've been using a scratch narration track, now's the time to replace it with the real thing. Chapter 11 has some tips on both narration and dialog editing.

3. Replace any hard effects that need fixing. Ignore smaller sync effects for now; you might not need to waste time on them after the music and ambiences are in place.

4. Insert the music. If you're using library cuts, trim them to length. It doesn't take much effort or a musical genius to stretch or shorten a piece of music seamlessly (Chapter 12 teaches you how).

5. Add background ambiences. Don't do this until you've added the music. In a lot of video projects—even big-budget network dramas—music can take the place of ambience.

6. Add whatever smaller sync effects seem to be missing. A lot of times, you'll find that a random noise from an ambience track can be nudged a few frames to take the place of a sync effect.

7. Mix.

8. Dub to the final medium. This may be a videotape or timecode DAT, or a file to be imported back to the NLE or DVD mastering system.

Mixing and Editing Are Separate Functions

Modern DAWs can handle editing and mixing almost simultaneously. You can start mixing a sequence, notice a dialog glitch or misplaced effect and fix it immediately, and then continue mixing where you left off. You can also begin mixing a scene, decide that you don't like one particular cross-fade or level, rewind to where the problem began, and start mixing again. The system will join the various parts of the mix seamlessly. These are great conveniences . . . but only if you don't take advantage of them too often.

Although the computer lets you develop a mix in pieces, it's not a good idea from a human point of view. Audio develops over time. Your viewers watch the scene as a continuous whole, and it's almost always best to mix it the same way. There's more about mixing in Chapter 15.

CHAPTER 9

PostProduction Hardware

R O S E ' S   R U L E S

⇨ The tools you use in video editing affect the quality of your track.* Any damage you do here will be difficult or expensive to fix later.

⇨ When you set up an edit system, it's often more important to pay attention to detail than to spend a lot of money.

⇨ The most important audio equipment you can own is the monitor amplifier and speakers. If these aren't right, you won't be able to get the best performance out of anything else.

Nonlinear editing systems never exist in a vacuum. They need other equipment to be usable. You'll want a set of reliable audio monitors, at least. If you're also going to use this system for input and output—that is, if you're not going to be getting all of your elements as preformatted files, and delivered in a computer format—you'll also need video and audio tape decks, routing and control equipment, and audio wiring. Even the simplest installation requires attention, because how you handle signals will make a difference in what your finished track sounds like.

Monitoring

The quality of your monitoring system doesn't directly influence anything in your soundtrack. Signals don't pass through your speaker or amplifier on their way to the

---

*There's only one exception: if you're importing tracks to an NLE via digital wiring and will be exporting individual edited tracks as files to mix elsewhere.

viewer. But your monitors are the most important piece of audio equipment you can own because signals pass through them on the way to your brain and affect every decision you make.

Before you go out to buy new or better monitors, take a look around your editing room: the environment where you work can have as much of an influence on the sound as the speakers themselves.

Editing Room Acoustics: When Good Speakers Go Bad

You're set to edit your magnum opus. You put up color bars and adjust the monitor so that everything is a mellow shade of rose pink or a shocking green. Then you smear grease on the picture tube, splash some white paint around it, and—just for good measure—adjust a strong light so it glares off the screen (Figure 1).

Figure 1: It's just a cartoon, folks . . . but some people mix with the aural equivalent.

Maybe that's not how you work on pictures, but I've seen a lot of editing rooms where they do exactly that to the track. Badly positioned speakers—in some cases, they don't even face the operator—interact with the room's walls to actually blur the sound. Speakers are chosen because they sound flattering in this blurred environment, rather than because they reveal the truth.

It's not hard to set up a good listening environment. It just requires a little thought and some elementary physics.

As you learned in Chapter 1, the echoes in a room can interfere with a sound in ways that aren't immediately obvious. You don't hear it as an echo, but you do hear cancellations and reinforcements of different pitches in the sound, affecting its color or timbre. And this effect can change drastically, depending on where you are in the room. In many desktop editing environments, the highs you hear directly in front of the video monitor can be different from what a client hears two feet away.

You cannot fix this with an equalizer, even if you care only about a single listening position. That's because the problem can be drastically different at frequencies that are too close together for an equalizer to pick out, and it varies with the distances between speaker, wall, and listener—moving your head six inches can change what you hear. It's even influenced by room temperature.

Soft and hard

The best solution is careful edit room design. By calculating how different wavelengths will cancel or reinforce, you can plan the room dimensions to smooth out the sound. If you're building a new studio from scratch, pick up a book on acoustics and learn how simple changes in the floor plan can make tremendous differences to the sound. (I'd recommend those by F. Alton Everst, such as *Sound Studio Construction on a Budget*. They're understandable and relatively nonmathematical.)

But if it's too late to move the walls—or if for some reason the building's owners disapprove—you can still use some rule-of-thumb acoustic science to correct a bad sounding room. Go back to the second part of Chapter 6 and read some of the ways to improve the sound at a location. Substitute your editing position for the microphone, and the monitor speakers for the actors, and the same techniques will work in the editing suite.

Homemade sound eater

Luxury postproduction facilities have posh treatments and careful acoustic design. But the nonlinear editing rooms in television stations, corporate environments, and kitchen table production companies tend to be random offices with bare walls. Absorption is almost always needed to get these rooms sounding good.

You can buy studio-quality absorbers and diffusers from acoustic consultants for a hefty price. Or you can build reasonably efficient fiberglass absorbers for very little money, using only minimal carpentry skills. The key is to use the right kind of fiberglass. Owens-Corning #703 is a semirigid yellow board designed for sound and is much denser than the pink fluffy stuff sold as home insulation. A carton of 80 square feet, in 2-foot-by-4-foot panels, costs about a hundred dollars at hardware superstores, acoustic suppliers, or ceiling contractors in most big cities.

Figure 2 shows the basic construction. The overall size isn't critical, but try to cover about half of the total area in a stripe from a couple of feet below ear level to a couple of feet above (if you're seated, that's around 2 feet to 6 feet from the floor), on any wall that's causing problems. The worst offenders are usually the wall directly behind your editing position and the side walls from a few feet in front of you to a few feet behind. Tiny scraps of fiberglass can fly around during construction, so wear long sleeves as you do the following:

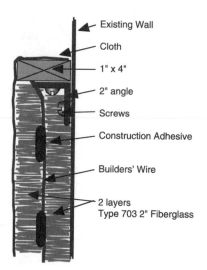

Existing Wall
Cloth
1" x 4"
2" angle
Screws
Construction Adhesive
Builders' Wire
2 layers
Type 703 2" Fiberglass

Figure 2: Basic, low-cost wall-mounted absorber

1. Build a rectangular frame out of 1-inch-by-4-inch pine, cut to fit the wall area. The finished panels won't weigh much, so you can attach the frame to the wall with a couple of small angle brackets and not leave too much damage if you have to move.

2. Lay a 2-inch-thick piece of #703 inside, cut to fit the frame. Friction should hold it in place while you work. Secure the fiberglass with a few lengths of galvanized builders' wire stapled to the inside of the frame.

3. Stick another layer of #703 on top of the first piece. A few dabs of construction adhesive will keep it from sliding around.

4. Cover the whole thing with decorative cloth, burlap, or even brightly printed bed sheets. In commercial buildings you'll probably need flame-retardant cloth, available from upholstery suppliers for a few dollars a yard more than the stuff that burns.

One-by-four pine is less than 3 inches wide—it's one of those ancient lumber-yard traditions—so four inches of fiberglass will be slightly thicker than the frame. If you don't like the way it bulges the cloth, use wood cut to exactly 4 inches. If you want a more professional appearance, replace the top layer and cloth with wedge-shaped foam tiles (available from audiovisual suppliers). The foam wedges don't absorb much better than the fiberglass does, but they look good and their shape provides some diffusion at high frequencies.

Adding more diffusion to a room is even easier: a few shelves filled with random-size books or tape boxes will do an excellent job.

The nearfield solution

The other way to conquer room acoustics relies on the inverse-square law: if a sound has to travel twice as far, it becomes four times softer. Make the distance from speaker-to-ear significantly less than the distance from speaker-to-wall-to-ear, and the echoes will be relatively less important.

That's the secret behind nearfield monitors, the square boxes you often see perched on top of the console in recording studios. These speakers are very close to the engineers' ears, so the engineer hears a lot more of them than of the reflections off distant walls. Nearfields have only a couple of problems:

- By definition, only a small area can be within the "near" field. So the monitors are effective in only one place. Unless you all sit very closely together, the producer, editor, and client will hear something totally different.

- It's next to impossible to get a good sound out of a box that's small enough to fit on the top of a console. Typical cube and small bookshelf speakers are notorious for distortion and limited bandwidth.

One high-tech solution is to integrate smallish speakers with a precisely calibrated amplifier. But it takes a lot of engineering and expensive components to do this right, and the professional versions that actually sound good can cost a few thousand dollars per pair. More modestly priced speaker/amplifier combos—those for many hundred dollars—are often full of compromises that cause uneven response at various frequencies, and distortion at both ends of the band. Speakers like this aren't suitable for professional mixing. Low-cost amplified "multimedia" speakers, costing under a hundred dollars a pair, aren't suitable for anything more than Web surfing.

Choosing Monitor Speakers

If you're going to be mixing with your NLE setup, you need good speakers. These aren't necessarily speakers that "sound good." Most people are partial to speakers with too much bass and a missing midrange because it's flattering to a lot of popular music. Many manufacturers deliberately build their speakers this way. But speakers like this will lead you to make bad decisions in the mix.

Fortunately, there are strategies you can adopt to help you find speakers you can rely on . . . even if you're not blessed with golden ears.

The theoretical case against small speakers

Some people claim you should always mix on tiny speakers because they represent a worst-case scenario: if a track can make it there, it can make it anywhere. But if you think about what those speakers are really telling you, you'll realize they can't be relied on at all. Figure 3 shows the frequency distribution of a typical voice (black) and music (gray) track, as measured in Waves' PAZ psychoacoustic analysis plug-in. The relative heights show how much energy is in either track at any frequency. I've drawn the black box to indicate the accurate range of a typical tiny monitor— between approximately 200 Hz and 7,000 Hz.

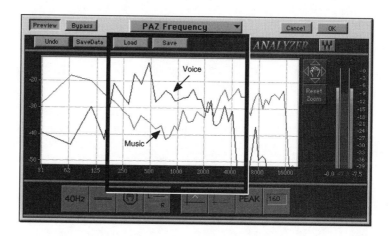

Figure 3: A small speaker can give you the wrong idea about voice/music proportions.

If you just look inside the box you'll think the voice is louder than the music. Play this mix on a speaker that sounds like this, and you'll think it's fine. But if you look outside the box—or hear the mix played on a better loudspeaker—you'll discover there's much more overall energy to the music. The voice would get lost on a good system . . . and you'd never know it on this speaker.

Even if your viewers don't have the best of speakers in their sets, this track is likely to find its way through a number of compressors and other level-control devices before it gets to them. Every time the music hits a loud note, these processors will squash the entire mix down—even if the note is in a range that small speakers would ignore. (TV stations use multiband processors to reduce this problem, but many of them also pass the signal through wide-band compressors with the same unfortunate effect. Cable networks, Internet broadcasters, and DVD authoring stations usually have just the wide-band units.)

It's fine to check a mix on small speakers, but making primary mix decisions on them misplaces the track's priorities: you're sacrificing how voices will be heard on better sets, to favor how music is heard on poorer ones. Video is a dialog-driven medium. If anything is at risk, it should be the music.

The real-world case against small speakers

So far we've dealt with small speakers in the abstract. But once you get to real-world examples, the problem isn't just lost highs and lows—it's also what the speaker does to the middle. Good full-size monitor speakers are accurate over their entire range. Mixes you do on them will sound right on any other good monitor and will at least be predictable on most tiny monitors. But bad speakers are random; corrections that improve the sound on one may make it a lot worse on another.

For example, there's a small powered monitor that's been popular for years. It looks professional, even has XLR connectors, and has been bundled with nonlinear editors. It doesn't sound professional. A speaker-designer friend of mine tested them with lab equipment, and I used what he discovered to retouch our frequency analysis plot. The result is Figure 4 . . . not that Waves' PAZ will ever look like this on your screen, but it does accurately depict how these speakers distort the sound balance.

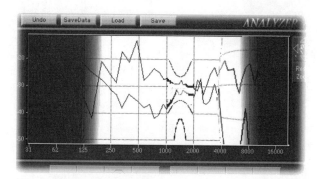

Figure 4: One popular small monitor is this uneven with the frequencies it *can* handle.

The high and low end disappear in the figure because they also do in the speaker. While the manufacturer claims a low frequency limit of 80 Hz, things are very quiet down there. In reality, the bass starts to fall off drastically at 150 Hz and is essentially too soft to be useful by 100 Hz. The opposite happens to the highs: to reach a claimed 13 kHz cutoff, they apply a gigantic boost at 8 kHz . . . so these speakers tempt you to turn the midhighs much lower than is appropriate! To top it all off, there's a major dip between 1 kHz and 2 kHz—probably to make pop music sound better on them. Nobody could do an accurate mix on this speaker.

Subwoofers

Another approach that doesn't work for video mixing is to combine a tiny speaker with a subwoofer. These "satellite" systems are sold by respected speaker companies for unobtrusive home or restaurant music systems. Bass notes aren't very directional and don't get affected as much by room reverberation, so a system like this has great flexibility in how it's mounted. But the thumping bass it provides doesn't tell you what a track will sound like on television. Almost all of these systems split the band in the middle of critical speech frequencies—exactly where most single-element small speakers are most sensitive—and distort or lose signal where you need the most accuracy. They're great for background music in a restaurant . . . and useless for critical listening. The only time they're appropriate is if you're mixing specifically for one of these satellite speaker systems—which might be the case in an interactive kiosk—and the track will never be played anywhere else.

Subwoofers, in and of themselves, are not the problem. Theatrical surround sound systems use them effectively, but they also use full-size speakers for the main channels. This way, the subs can concentrate on much lower frequencies than those in satellite systems. Critical sound in a theatrical surround system is carried by full-range, properly located speakers, and the subwoofer is just used to enhance bass notes.

You might conclude from all of the above that I think computer store multimedia speakers—either stand-alone ones, or those with subwoofers—are useless for video mixing. You'd be right.

Choosing full-size speakers

If you want to know what you're mixing, you need full-size monitors. Your best source is a broadcast or studio supplier, or a high-end audio dealer, rather than an electronics chain or music store.

Read the specs: it's a dead giveaway when a manufacturer brags about a speaker's frequency range, but doesn't say how much the sensitivity varies within that range. Watch out for specifications speakers with built-in amplifiers; some quote impressive numbers and even supply a frequency response graph but note in tiny type that these ratings apply only to the amp.

On the other hand, you can trust your muscles. Try to lift the speaker. Professional speakers use much heavier components, both for rigidity and to generate stronger magnetic fields. If an amplifier is built in, it'll have a large power transformer.

Train your ears to know when a speaker is doing a good job (this will also help you do better mixes). Enlist the aid of a friendly studio engineer, and listen to a good program mix in a studio. The narration should sound natural and close-up, with the consonants perfectly clear. The music should have a sheen or high-end sparkle. Listen for a full bass sound, but don't be swept away by deep bass that gets thrown away in the broadcast process. Get familiar with the relative ratio of voice to music sound on this mix. Then have the engineer make a copy of it on CD.

Go to a dealer where you can audition different speaker systems simultaneously. Pick two stereo speaker pairs, adjust them to the same volume, and switch back and forth while you listen to that CD. Start with the best two pairs the dealer has to offer, and work your way down in quality (or price) until you notice that the disc doesn't sound like it did in the studio any more. Go back up one notch—that's the speaker for you. (If the speaker you choose is out of your budget, don't feel bad. It merely means that you've got better hearing than somebody in your financial league has a right to expect. Settle for the best speakers you can afford, and try to stay aware of what's missing in them.)

Be wary of dealers who won't let you switch between speakers, don't have a way to let you match the volume of two different systems (the speaker that's louder almost always sounds better), or won't let you play your own CD. Relying on well-known manufacturers can help, but it's not infallible; one of the biggest names forbids its dealers from demonstrating their products alongside any others. It's scary, but they sell a lot of speakers.

Speaker setup

Once you've got the speakers, mount them rigidly—loose mounting can absorb bass notes. The tweeters should point toward your listening position and be about at ear level because high frequencies are the most directional. There shouldn't be anything between the entire speaker and the listener; a computer monitor, part of a tower, or even a CD player can reflect high frequencies away from you.

One of the best arrangements for speakers is an equilateral triangle, slightly above ear level and pointed down, as shown in Figure 5. That control room also uses absorption around the front and sides, has a bookshelf diffuser on the back, and uses another technique—splaying the side walls so echoes don't build up between them.

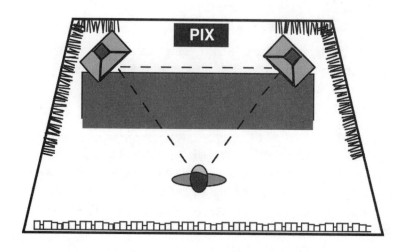

Figure 5: Speakers and you should form an equilateral triangle.

Choosing an Amplifier

Don't skimp on the size of the amplifier, either. Professional ported-design loudspeakers might need only 10 watts per channel for average speech-level mixing (acoustic suspension designs are more power hungry), but that's just the average. Peak requirements are many times higher, and an amp that can't handle the load will sometimes generate a form of distortion that actually damages the speaker elements. Fifty clean watts is an absolute minimum per channel.

Building a good amp is a lot easier than building a good speaker, and higher-end amps from consumer electronics stores can be perfectly adequate for driving your professional speakers—the only major differences between a top hi-fi amp and a studio one are ruggedness and reliability. Again, weight is a good guide: a decent amplifier needs a good power supply, and in consumer amps that always means a heavy power transformer. (Some music mixers prefer the sound of vacuum tube amplifiers. These will be even heavier because of their output transformers. However, tubes present absolutely no advantage—and a lot of disadvantages—in a digital video mixing suite.)

If you're buying the amp at a consumer retailer, it may come with a built-in FM tuner. This isn't a problem in itself, but check to make sure the FM sound doesn't leak through when you're using one of the line inputs. Other features to check:

- The stereo image should stay rock-stable as you raise or lower the volume control, and not drift from side to side. A cheap volume control won't have its channels matched properly across the entire range, and that can fool you into making bad balancing decisions in your mix. It also suggests the manufacturer might have cheapened things elsewhere as well.

- Tone controls are worthless on a monitor amp. All they'll do is stop you from hearing what's really in your mix. Since a consumer amp inevitably comes with tone controls, look for a switch to defeat them . . . or at least a detent to keep their knobs set to a neutral position.

- "Extended bass," "Hyper-bass," and even "Loudness" are tone controls in disguise. They won't do you any good. If an amp comes with these features, make sure you keep them turned off.

Room equalization

Some professional studios have installed equalizers in their monitor amplifiers to boost or cut specific frequencies and smooth out the speaker's performance. Don't even think about trying this with the tone controls in a consumer amp. Their action is much too broad for this and will do more harm than good. In fact, I'd recommend against doing it under any circumstances. Unless you've got very good speakers and carefully tuned acoustics, the necessary correction will add its own distortion—even if you're using a high-quality equalizer. And you can't do this kind of tuning by guess-work. You need precise test equipment.

"Digital" amplifiers

Some monitor amplifiers and amp/speaker combinations come with digital inputs and connect to your editor via USB or a digital audio cable. All this does is move the digital-to-analog conversion circuit from inside your computer's tower to inside the amp. While a computer's audio output might not reach the highest specifications for critical listening, the circuits used today are more than adequate for monitoring and mixing when used with a good analog amp and speakers. While there's nothing inherently wrong with the idea of a digital input in a monitor system, it adds to the cost and limits your selection. Don't bother with it.

The easy way out

Smoothing out the acoustics and buying a high-quality amp and speakers can be expensive. It may be more efficient to just keep the multimedia speakers that came bundled with your NLE—they're good enough for editing—and then rent time in a well-equipped sound studio when it's time to mix.

A useful gadget: mono test switch

One feature that's seldom found on consumer amplifiers, and almost essential for accurate video mixing, is a mono test switch. It combines the left and right channels electrically so you can hear if there are any phase errors that will affect mono compatibility. You can't take this compatibility for granted; bad wiring, asymmetrical processors, and some "three-dimensional" effects can make a good stereo track sound awful in mono. A few stereo music synthesizers completely disappear when their channels are combined. If any of your work will end up on broadcast or cable or in computer media, you'll need to do this kind of checking.

You can build a mono/stereo test switch easily. This gadget sends both channels to one speaker, silencing the other. It can also simultaneously lower the volume, so you'll get a better idea of how a mix will sound at typical listener levels.

You can see how it works by following the schematic in Figure 6. The left and right outputs of your NLE or mixer are combined through the two 4.7 kΩ (4,700 ohms) 1/2-watt or 1/8-watt carbon resistors. They keep the individual outputs from drawing current from each other. They also cause a tiny loss of stereo separation through the monitors, but with most equipment it won't be noticeable. (The

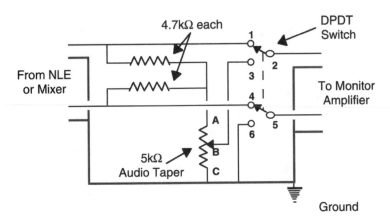

Figure 6: A simple adapter to add the controls most hi-fi amps leave off

resistors are the right value for modern NLEs and prosumer audio gear, but not for tubed or transformer-coupled equipment; if you've got that stuff, you probably already have sophisticated monitor controls.) The 5 kΩ audio-taper potentiometer lets you preset a lower volume for mono listening. The switch is a light-duty double-pole, double-throw toggle. With the switch up, the amplifier sees the stereo outputs of the computer; with it down, one side of the amp sees the mono sum and the other is grounded to stay silent.

The easiest way to deal with input and output cables is to buy 6-foot shielded audio cords with appropriate connectors for your equipment; probably these will be phono plugs for the amplifier and either phono or 1/4-inch phone plugs for the mixer or NLE's sound card. Once you're sure the cords are right for getting a signal into your amp, cut them in half and separate the inner conductor from the outer grounding shield. Cut off an extra few inches to use as hookup wire, unless you have some other light-gauge wire sitting around from a telephone or toy train project.

This circuit isn't complicated to build, but it does require soldering. (There aren't any hazardous voltages, so it's a good project for the beginner. If the very idea of soldering sends hot metal flashes down your spine, enlist a local high school hacker to build the circuit for you.) The gray lines in the schematic represent the cable shields; it's important that these all be connected to each other as well as to the volume control and switch. The ground connection is optional, but may reduce noise if you tie it to a grounding screw on the amplifier. The bold letters and numbers refer to specific terminals on the switch and control, identified in Figure 7. Any light-gauge hookup wire can be used. For best results, build the circuit in a metal box and also connect the ground point to the box; this provides shielding as well as a solid mounting surface for the switch and volume control.

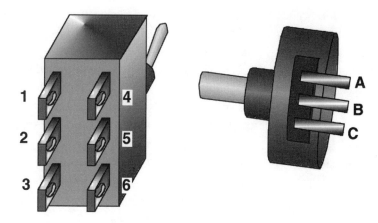

Figure 7: Connection key for Figure 6

All of the parts are available from electronics stores, and the whole thing should cost less than $10. Since there's probably a Radio Shack within a mile of this book as you're reading it, I'll give you their part numbers . . . though parts from professional suppliers may be better quality. The resistors are part #271-1330. The audio-taper potentiometer is #271-1720, and you may select a plastic knob of your choice. You don't have to build this circuit in a box—there are no hazardous voltages—but if you touch any of the connections with a finger, you may hear a loud buzzing in the speakers. If you do want a case to protect against this or to make the project prettier, try #270-238. Radio Shack can also sell you a soldering kit with instructions, #64-2802, if you want to try building it yourself. Don't forget the audio interconnection cables.

Plug one side into your computer's or mixer's line outputs, and the other into a monitor amplifier. With the switch in one position, you'll hear stereo. To check compatibility, flip the switch to the other side and make sure every element still sounds right. To check the mix balance, turn down the volume control until you barely hear the sound. In a well-mixed track, you should still be able to follow the dialog even when it's too soft to catch all the music and sound effects.

The Mixer

Despite their name, mixers aren't just used for combining multiple tracks in a post-production suite. More often, they're used to select and control individual signals, adjusting the volume and possibly adding equalization before they're digitized into the editor. In fact, unless your NLE has multiple-track outputs, you probably won't use the mixer for mixing at all; you'll do that operation in software.

The ability to manipulate a signal when you're digitizing is both a blessing and a curse. You can boost levels and reduce noise or add crispness quickly with analog controls to take advantage of the widest digital range once the signal is in the computer. But if you're going to tweak a track before you digitize, you need some way to repeat those tweaks exactly, if you have to redigitize part of a scene. You also need a way to assure that good recordings aren't harmed by inadvertent tweaking.

The problem is that most analog mixers are ambiguous. You can't set the volume or equalization to precise levels, and you can't take the equalizers out of the circuit when you don't want them. Low-cost mixers, with small controls and sparse calibrations on the panel, are almost impossible to set the same way twice. They can also have problems with signals leaking from channels that appear to be turned off, adding tiny amounts of noise or feedback into your tracks.

Midpriced digital mixers avoid these problems by letting you display and set volume and equalizer settings numerically, and by storing your most common setups for instant recall. Most of them also include other processing, including compression, noise gates, and reverberation (Chapter 14). They often include digital as well as analog inputs and outputs, so you can avoid the potential distortion of another conversion. These mixers are mass-produced for the home music market, bringing their price down to around a thousand dollars. If one has sufficient inputs and outputs, you won't need a patchbay, so it might be the only piece of audio control and processing equipment you need.

Many mixers provide line-level monitor outputs, which are a convenient way to hook up your amplifier and speakers without disrupting the connection to your NLE's input. But even if they don't, the headphone outputs are often clean enough and the right voltage to feed an external monitor amp. Check the manual (or just try it, making sure the amplifier's volume is turned all the way down when you first make the connection).

Mixer alternatives

If you're mixing within your NLE but still want some control over levels and equalization while digitizing, consider a stand-alone equalizer instead. These provide finer control than the basic equalizer knobs on a mixer and are calibrated for easier resetting. A parametric equalizer—with knobs to control tuning as well as frequency—will let you hone in on offending noises without affecting too much else in the track. Hook up the equalizer through a patchbay, so you can bypass it when you want an absolutely clean connection. Processors, including equalizers, are discussed in Chapter 14.

Audio Sources and Recorders

While a lot of your track will probably consist of dialog recorded in the camera, and then imported into an NLE from the camera or a separate video deck, you may also want additional equipment to play back nonsync elements such as music, sound effects, and narration.

Then again, maybe you won't. Chances are your NLE already has a provision for importing stock music and effects from audio CDs, and most sound studios and freelance suppliers can now provide narration and original music on audio CD, or as files on CD-ROM and removable hard drives. So consider all the equipment in this section optional.

CD Players

Library music and sound effects are distributed on audio CDs, the same format as you'd play in a home stereo. These discs are readable in the CD-ROM drives supplied with virtually every computer, and software to convert the sounds to standard WAVE or AIFF files either came with your system or can be downloaded for free from the Internet (search for "ripper" programs). These programs deal with sound as data, so the quality doesn't get degraded by converting it to analog and back, and they can import a long selection in less time than it would take to play it as audio. If you need only a few sounds from CD and don't have a sample rate conversion problem, you can use your computer's disc drive and save the cost of a separate player. On the other hand, unless your production is at a 44.1 kHz sample rate—the standard rate for audio CDs—the software will have to manipulate the data so it plays properly at the new rate. With some programs, this can take extra time and add noise and distortion.

There may be other advantages to using a separate CD player with audio outputs and re-recording into your NLE. It's faster to find specific sounds with a player because discs load more quickly and the dedicated controls make cueing easier. You don't need to leave your editing software and launch another program to make the translation. Some ripper software doesn't let you select just part of a CD track or preview its sound, forcing you to turn an entire track into a large file to extract one small sound . . . or to discover you had chosen the wrong cut. Reasonably priced professional CD players also offer features that may be impossible or require extra processing steps with a CD-ROM drive, including varispeed to change the tempo and timbre of a sound, the ability to cue directly to index points within properly encoded CD tracks, and—though I'm not sure why you'd want them—DJ-style scratching effects.

The best way to record audio from a stand-alone CD player is to use its digital outputs. Professional players come with s/pdif interfaces, which can plug directly or through an optical adapter (Chapter 3) into a properly equipped sound card. When you re-record audio this way, the signal isn't affected by noise or analog conversion distortion. However, if you're using a digital connection, you may have to forego varispeed or scratch effects; these change the sample rate to a nonstandard value, and most sound cards can't deal with that at all. If your production isn't at 44.1 kHz sample rate, you'll be facing the same conversion issues as with a CD-ROM drive.

You can avoid the sample rate problem by using the player's analog outputs. Most players have very high quality output converters, so the limiting factors will be your analog wiring—which should be as direct as possible—and the quality of your NLE's analog inputs. With good equipment, neither of these should present a problem.

You can also use a portable battery-operated CD player to import audio. Look for a unit with a line-level output on the back (many of them have one for connection to a hi-fi system), so you can avoid distortion and variations caused by the headphone amplifier and volume control. While the output converters on a portable player may not be as good as those on a studio deck, running the portable on batteries instead of its AC adapter will completely eliminate power-line hum. If your studio is plagued with ground loops, this may be the cleanest analog connection.

DAT, Mini-Disc, and MDM

DAT tape (originally R-DAT, for Rotary Digital Audio Tape, because the system uses rotating heads similar to those on a VTR) is the standard for interchange among audio studios. Unless you specify otherwise, narrations and original music will probably arrive in this format and post audio facilities will expect you to bring nonsync elements recorded this way. Professional recorders with digital and analog connectors, shuttle wheels for cueing, and the ability to work at 44.1 kHz or 48 kHz sample rate, can be had for around one thousand dollars. More expensive decks add synchronization via blackburst, timecode, or both, and special features like the ability to record individual tracks, 24-bit recording, RAM buffering for instant start, and VTR-like control via RS-422 serial data. These can be essential in a professional studio but are overkill in most NLE environments; for average-length scenes, the DAT system itself will provide better speed control than a typical crystal-locked analog film sound recorder. The only thing needed for synchronization will be a beep or clap before the action begins.

Some DAT recorders also provide a "long-play" 32 kHz recording mode. Don't use it. There's nothing inherently wrong with 32 kHz sampling, but this mode also uses a 12-bit sample depth—they don't tell you that on the front panel—which adds noise and distortion.

The 4 mm tape and cartridges used in DAT recorders are identical to the DDS format used for computer backup, and DDS tapes work fine in audio recorders (though this may ruin them for subsequent data use). However, the data formats are different. Nobody makes software to play or record audio DATs in a computer's DDS drive on either the Windows or Macintosh platform, and the software for more specialized platforms costs more than a stand-alone DAT deck.

Mini-Disc combines the recording flexibility of DAT with the random access of a CD or hard drive and may seem like an ideal medium for postproduction. However, it was introduced under a cloud—early units incorporated a somewhat nasty-sounding lossy compression algorithm, and even modern ones still use some form of data reduction—and never achieved the acceptance of DAT. Their random access lets you edit and cue tightly within the Mini-Disc player itself—something of limited value in postproduction but very handy in news broadcasting and theatrical sound effects, where the format is more widely used.

MDMs (modular digital multitracks) are used extensively in music studios for original recording and in high-end audio post facilities for interchange but seldom find their way into an NLE setup. There are two competing and noninterchangeable formats, Alesis ADAT (used in music) and Tascam DTRS/DA-8 (almost universal in postproduction), so check with the client or other studios you'll be working with before specifying one or the other.

Analog audio media

Audio cassettes are still considered a handy, low-cost way to distribute music demos or voices for auditions. However, their quality is too low and speed too unstable for any professional use in video production.

Quarter-inch (and wider) audio tape is often used in music production to add "analog warmth"—a particular, pleasing form of distortion—but high-quality analog recorders are too unwieldy and expensive for video work, and the distortion builds up quickly over multiple generations. Some Hollywood features are still mixed with analog recordings on film-style perforated stock, but this is for economic reasons—studios prefer to use equipment that's already paid for—rather than any technical advantage.

Some historic documentary sounds, effects, and music may be available only on analog vinyl disks. If you have to play them, check with local studios and radio stations to find some way to transfer their sound to digital. (I still keep a turntable and preamp in the basement, wrapped in plastic, for just such occasions. I haven't unwrapped it in close to a decade.)

The best strategy with any of these analog media is to transfer to digital as soon as possible. Don't try to correct problems at this stage, unless they're being introduced by the playback mechanism—a badly maintained analog tape recorder will add hiss and lose high frequencies, and dirt or dust on a vinyl record can add noise. These problems can permanently damage your source material, so have them fixed before you continue with the transfer. Once the sound is in the digital domain, you can experiment with noise reduction software and equalization and still be able to undo the effects.

Synthesizers and samplers

If you're a skilled musician, you might want to add music-making equipment to your NLE system. The technical requirements for this are documented in tons of books and magazines. They also tend to be somewhat different from the requirements for post-production, so it might be more efficient to build separate setups and let two people play at the same time. A synthesizer can be helpful in the postproduction studio, however, if you need frequent laser zaps and other electronic effects and know how to use the instrument.

Some library music is distributed as MIDI files, a compact data format that describes when and how to play individual notes in a song. But unless you have a full MIDI studio (and know how to produce and mix music), it's not of much use in sophisticated video production. Software-only synthesizers that can play MIDI through a computer's sound card have limited sound quality. However, new music data formats, being developed for Internet use, also include production and sound synthesis information. Don't turn your nose up at music generated completely within a computer until you've heard the latest tools.

Samplers—RAM-based digital audio recorders, with exceptional flexibility to warp the sound quality during playback—are often used in sound design. They can also be helpful in the postproduction suite for sound effects manipulation . . . if you know how to work them.

Other Handy Gear

Software and hardware-based processors—such things as equalizers, compressors, and reverbs—are discussed in Chapter 14. But there are some other gadgets that can help you assure a good soundtrack.

Meters

The on-screen meters in most nonlinear editors range from deceptive to worthless. It takes computing power to make a digital meter that matches broadcast standards, but many programmers seem reluctant even to put calibrations on their nonstandard meters. Figure 8 shows the minimalist record-level indicator in one very popular video editing program; using it as a meaningful guide for setting levels is almost impossible (but see the tips at the end of this chapter).

Figure 8: The record-level meter in one popular program hardly tells you anything.

A proper meter should indicate both the peak level—bursts of sound that can overload a digital circuit, causing crackling noises—and the average level that a listener hears. It should also be calibrated in meaningful units—in a digital studio, that is decibels below full scale (see Chapter 2). Some programs have on-screen meters that are properly calibrated and indicate peak and average levels as different colors (Figure 9); but if your software doesn't, it's worth investing in an accessory external meter.

Figure 9: A good software meter indicates peak and average levels.

To be absolutely accurate, a digital meter should be connected to a digital audio signal—that way, no analog circuitry can have an effect on it. But meters like this are built to precise specifications and are expensive. A good compromise is an LED meter with analog inputs; you can get one that displays both peak and average levels for under $150. Connect it directly to a sound card's constant-level output, so there aren't any volume controls between the signal you're recording and the meter. (If your software or sound card driver has an output level control, leave it at the nominal zero dB or 100% position.)

It's difficult to find a good mechanical meter these days—the kind with a swinging needle. To measure volume properly, a VU (volume unit) meter must have precise ballistics and electrical characteristics. These things have gotten so expensive that even large recording studio consoles don't have them any more. The cheap voltage meters sold as accessories for editing suites don't have the right response to audio waveforms and are too bouncy to use as a reliable indicator while mixing.

Spectrum analyzer

A close cousin to the level meter is the spectrum analyzer, which displays the relative level of each frequency in a signal. Figure 3 showed one software version that can be called up to analyze a file. To be truly useful, though, a spectrum analyzer should be available while you're mixing—and the software version ties up computing cycles and screen space.

High-quality hardware spectrum analyzers, with rows of LEDs that measure the level at every third of an octave, cost many thousands of dollars. Lower-cost accurate analyzers, with just a couple of LEDs for each frequency, are designed for calibrating PA systems and aren't useful for mixing.

But even a less-than-perfect spectrum analyzer can be handy. Once you've learned to correlate what you hear through good monitors with what you see on the analyzer, you've got a way to verify that what you think you're hearing is really there. I keep an octave-band analyzer in my studio (Figure 10), wired up to the monitor circuit, so I can glance at it when I suspect fatigue or a head cold is plugging up my ears. This analyzer, part of a graphic equalizer sold for home stereos, cost less than $100 at a close-out sale. Radio Shack sells a similar unit with a smaller display for under $150. Either one is too noisy to use its equalizer section on a track, but the visual display is sure handy.

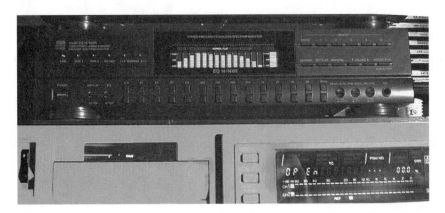

Figure 10: A $100 hi-fi spectrum analyzer sits on top of an expensive timecode DAT deck in my studio.

Tone oscillator

Even though a lineup tone isn't strictly necessary for digital videotape—the digits themselves provide an unambiguous reference—it's still essential for making the digital-to-analog leap in a dub house or broadcast station. A steady tone is also necessary for calibrating equipment, checking stereo balance, and assuring that every device in a mixed analog/digital signal chain is operating at its best level.

You can get a miniature test oscillator, built into an XLR plug, that uses phantom power and puts out a microphone-level signal. The units cost under $75 and are sold for checking PA systems in the field, but they can be plugged into a mixer for postproduction use. More flexible units with line-level outputs and a variety of test signals are available for under a few hundred dollars. One or the other should be a part of any professional studio.

A less flexible alternative is on tracks 12 through 14 of this book's CD. I've recorded one minute of a 1 kHz tone at -20 dBfs (network standard), -12 dBfs (analog "zero" equivalent for processed material), and 0 dBfs (for digital testing). If you transfer the tracks as files directly into your editing software, the levels should be accurate enough to use at the head of your digitally output tapes. You can also play them through a standard CD player as an analog lineup tone.

Phone patch

Sometimes you need to play a library cut or dialog edit to a distant client just for content approval, without needing the quality of a file transfer or overnight courier. You could hold a telephone handset up to a speaker, but the results are hardly professional. You can buy a telephone coupler for a few hundred dollars. Or you can build this $10 version, which sounds just as good (and also lets you record a telephone signal through a line-level input). It's based on a circuit you used to be able to rent from the phone company—back when there was only one phone company to deal with—and under ideal circumstances can sound as good as the connections at radio call-in shows.

The coupler doesn't work into digital phone wiring. But chances are your phones are analog, even if your sophisticated office system includes voice mail and call-forwarding. To find out, turn a phone over and look for a "Ringer Equivalent Number" (REN) value printed on a label; if you see one, the phone wiring is analog. (Sometimes the REN label is hidden under a snap-on mounting bracket, so look carefully.) If you don't see an REN, you can still use the coupler with one of the $50 handset modem adapters sold for business travel . . . but it's hardly worth the effort, since most of those adapters already have an equivalent circuit built in.

The circuit diagram is laughably simple, with only two components (Figure 11). A 1:1 600Ω transformer isolates the computer and phone system from each other, while still letting audio pass through. Radio Shack's tiny version (part #273-1374) isn't exactly high fidelity, but its quality does match that of a telephone line. A .1 μF (microfarad) capacitor (#272-1069) protects the transformer from the constant voltage that's always on a phone line, and keeps the coupler from interfering with normal dialing and hanging up. If you're getting parts from a more comprehensive supplier than

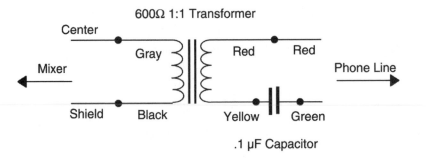

Figure 11: Easy-to-build telephone coupler. The color codes refer to specified Radio Shack parts.

Radio Shack, look for a capacitor with a 100 volt rating; it'll last longer. The only other parts you need are a wire that connects to your telephone line and a cable to plug into your mixer's line-level or headphone output.

This circuit is so easy to build that I threw one together on a piece of scrap cardboard (Figure 12), using cellophane tape and paper clips. The thick black wire on the left comes from the computer's or mixer's line output. Find a cable with an appropriate plug, cut off one end, and use a knife or cutting pliers to pull off the outer covering. You'll see a metal shield—braided or twisted wires, or a foil wrapper—around a single insulated conductor. Separate the shield from the inner wire and twist it together, and then strip back some of the insulation from the end of the inner wire (or buy a #42-2370 cable, which has a phono plug and is already prepared for use). The gray telephone wire on the right is a #279-310, which has a standard modular plug on the other end and can plug into any analog telephone jack. You can also plug this into the "data port" on some telephones. Or use any two-conductor low-voltage wire, and connect to the red and green wires inside the phone jack on your wall.

Follow the color codes in the photo and schematic, and connect the components by twisting their wires tightly together (soldering isn't necessary). Make sure the connections are secured so they don't touch each other, and be sure to cover the wires on the telephone side of the circuit with tape so nobody accidentally touches them; when the phone rings, these carry as much as 125 volts. It's low current, but can give you quite a tickle.

To use the coupler, just plug it into a sound source and a telephone jack. You'll need a regular phone on the same line to dial and monitor the call; the easiest way to hook them both up is to plug a Y-connector (#279-357) into the wall and then plug both the phone and the coupler into it. Raise the source's volume until it just starts to distort in your phone's handset, then back it off a little. It's okay to leave the

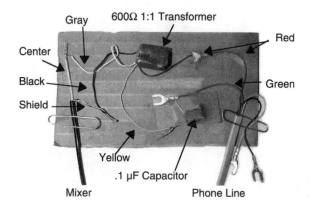

Figure 12: No soldering required. You can build this telephone coupler with paper clips and cellophane tape.

coupler connected between calls, but be aware that anything going through your mixer will also be transmitted into the conversations going on.

If you want to use this coupler to record a telephone conversation, simply plug it into a mixer's line-level input. Your local voice will be some 20 dB louder than the distant caller's, a characteristic of any analog phone system. If you're recording an interview, keep your phone muted during the responses so breaths and other local noises don't overwhelm the distant voice. To record a conversation, you'll need to keep a quick hand on the level control. Or get a true "hybrid" circuit, which balances and nulls out your voice from the phone line. It's too complicated to describe here, but you can buy one for about $500.

Moving Signals Around the Editing Suite

The simplest audio setup for NLEs is a straight digital connection—Firewire, AES/EBU, or s/pdif—between the VTR and the editor. You can import audio, edit and possibly mix it within the editing system, and put the finished track back on videotape without compromising the signal in any way. Hang a monitor amplifier and speakers on the editor's analog outputs, and you're ready to go (Figure 13).

It's possible your setup will be this simple. If so, congratulations. Skip the rest of this chapter and start editing.

But if your NLE has only analog inputs and outputs, things get complicated very quickly. You can run a wire from VTR output to editor input for digitizing, and from editor output to monitor to hear what you're doing; but once the job is edited, you'll have to rearrange things to get the signal from NLE back to tape and from tape to monitor. If you add additional sources such as a DAT or CD player, the complexity

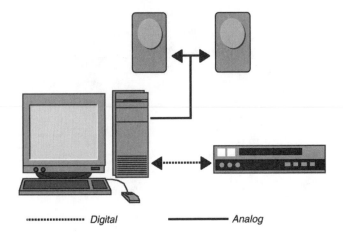

Figure 13: Simple NLE audio wiring with a digital VTR

······················ *Digital*   ——————— *Analog*

grows geometrically. You need some way to choose which signal gets digitized, to dub between media, and to connect the monitor to the right output for each different function (Figure 14).

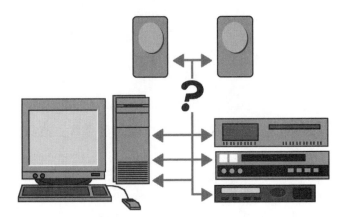

Figure 14: When you add more equipment, things stop being simple.

There are three different ways to deal with this web of connections:

- You can reach behind the equipment when you want to change signal routing, find the right cords, and plug them into the right jacks for the current task. Aside from being inconvenient and confusing—you have to remember how things are wired before you can use them—this puts extra stress on the equipment's connectors and can lead to early failure.

- You can use a routing device, which can be as simple as a low-cost patchbay or switch, or as complex as a microprocessor-based router, to handle the connections for you. Aside from protecting the equipment's connectors, this makes the whole process more straightforward. You don't have to do any reaching, and you can glance at the patchbay or switch to see how things are set up at any moment.

- You can wire everything to a mixer, which then serves as your central audio control. This gives you other options for manipulating the sound, but may also subject your sound to unwanted changes.

The best solution—and the one applied in almost every professional studio—is to use both a patchbay and a mixer. The patchbay supplies flexibility and direct connections when you don't want the sound changed, and the mixer gives you control when you do.

The Patchbay

Audio has been routed with plugs and jacks since the earliest days of the telephone, and a patchbay with dangling cords seems to be a required element in every photo of a recording studio or broadcasting plant. There's a reason: patchbays make it easy to control where the signals go.

In its most basic form, a patchbay is simply a means to extend the jacks from the back panels of your equipment and group them in one convenient place. Even low-cost ones (under $150 for a 32- or 48-point bay) use rugged 1/4-inch balanced phone jacks, which last longer and provide a better connection than the miniature or phono jacks on your equipment. Many brands have jacks on both their front and rear panels, so you don't need to do any soldering to install them; just get cables with appropriate connectors for your equipment on one end and a 1/4-inch plug on the other, plug them into the back of the patchbay, and forget about them. If your equipment has balanced inputs and outputs (Chapter 3), use two-conductor shielded cables with tip/ring/sleeve plugs to preserve the benefits of balancing. If some of your equipment is unbalanced, use standard two-conductor cables for it. In most situations, the balanced jacks in the patchbay will find the right conductors and you won't need separate adapters. Keep unbalanced cables as short as possible to avoid noise pickup.

Most preassembled patchbays have switchable "normals"—circuit paths that are activated when no cord is plugged in. Figure 15 shows how they work.

The contacts in a normaled jack are slightly bent. When there's no plug inserted (Figure 15a), they make contact with a separate jumper that routes the signal someplace else. If that happens to be another normaled jack, as drawn, it's called a "full normaled" patchbay. When you plug in a patchcord (Figure 15b), the contact is

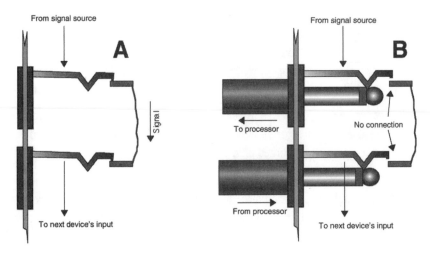

Figure 15: Normaled jacks provide a connection even when nothing's plugged in.

pushed away from the jumper. Signal goes to the plug but nowhere else. Balanced patchbays will have dual contacts and jumpers in the same jack—one for each conductor in the cable—and both are activated by the plug at the same time.

A patchbay can also be "half normaled." Imagine if the top jack in the drawing didn't have a jumper, and there was a wire from its main contact directly to the jumper in the lower jack. You could plug into the top jack to tap the signal coming from the source device, but it would still also be connected through the patchbay to the next device. But in that same arrangement, if you plugged into the lower jack, you'd break the normal connection and substitute just what's on the plug.

Common practice in sound studios is to put signal sources along the top row of a patch bay and destinations along the bottom. A patchbay in a small nonlinear editing suite might be organized like Figure 16. The arrows on the first four sets of jacks indicate a half normal connection.

Since the VTR is normaled to the NLE inputs, and the NLE's outputs are normaled to the monitors, you can digitize and edit without using any patchcords.

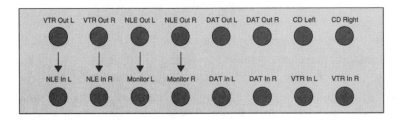

Figure 16: A basic NLE patchbay

When it's time to dump the finished project back to tape, you'd add two cords (Figure 17). The normals to the monitor amp aren't interrupted, so you can still hear the NLE's output. If you want, you could plug two more cords from the VTR's outputs to the monitor inputs and check the signal going to tape; this would break the normaled connection between NLE output and monitor.

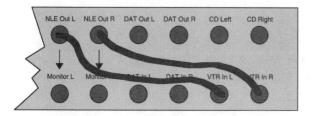

Figure 17: With two patchcords, you're ready to lay the finished project back to tape.

The most flexible configuration is to use a mixer and a patchbay. Connect each source in your studio to a separate mixer input through a normaled jack pair, the mixer's outputs to your NLE's inputs, and the mixer's monitor or headphone outputs to your amplifier (Figure 18). For most operations, all you'll have to do is raise the appropriate faders (leave all of the others down to reduce noise); when you want the cleanest signal or special routing, just grab some patchcords.

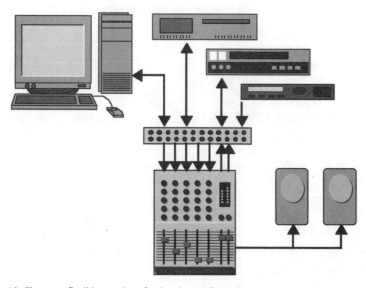

Figure 18: The most flexible—and professional—configuration uses patchbay and mixer together.

Switchers and Routers

Although it's possible to route digital audio through an analog patchbay, it's not recommended. Ordinary patchbays aren't designed to handle the high frequencies of serial digital audio, and the connectors can cause high-frequency reflections that make it harder for your gear to interpret the valid signal. Special patchbays are designed for AES/EBU wiring, and broadcast video patchbays do a decent job with s/pdif, but both these types are expensive solutions.

A few companies make electronic AES/EBU switchers. These route any input to any output—usually in an 8 × 8 or a 16 × 16 matrix—with additional buffering so that a signal can be sent to more than one device. Since they're driven by microprocessors, complex setups can be recalled quickly. Some of them also include reclocking and sample rate conversion. While these routers are also expensive solutions—prices start around $1000—they're the only efficient way to handle signals in a complex all-digital facility.

Less-expensive switchers are also available for both digital and analog audio. The simplest of them are just mechanical switches in a box but can be practical when you just need to select one of a few sources for an input. More elaborate ones can switch audio, video, and machine control simultaneously and are handy when your suite includes more than one video source.

Wiring the Postproduction Suite

The best, highest-quality way to wire your equipment together is to use digital connections for everything except the monitor circuit. Get appropriate cable for the high-frequency digital signal (see Chapter 3), and if you have a lot of gear, use a digital mixer or routing switcher.

If you have to use analog connections, the best plan is to stick with balanced wiring (also in Chapter 3, along with some suggestions for when you have to mix balanced and unbalanced equipment). If everything in your facility is unbalanced, there's no point to using balancing adapters. But there is a way to reduce noise in unbalanced setups, if you're willing to do some soldering:

1. Use the same kind of two-conductor shielded cable as you would for balanced wiring.

2. Connect the "hot" conductor—usually white—to the center pin of the phono or phone plug at each end, or to pin 2 of an unbalanced XLR.

3. Connect the other conductor to the sleeve of a phone plug, outer shell of a phono plug, or to pin 1 of an unbalanced XLR.

4. Now here's the trick: connect the cable's outer braided or foil shield to the sleeve, shell, or pin 1 at one end only (Figure 19). Use shrink-wrap or electrical tape to make sure the shield doesn't touch anything at the other end.

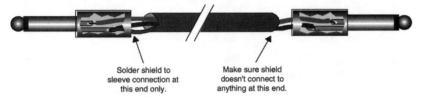

Solder shield to sleeve connection at this end only.

Make sure shield doesn't connect to anything at this end.

Figure 19: You can reduce noise in unbalanced circuits by connecting the shield at one end only (shown here with phone plugs).

5. Be consistent about which end of the shield gets connected: always connect the end at your patchbay and leave the equipment end floating, or always connect the end at the equipment and leave the patchbay end floating.

> ➤ Only do this with two-conductor shielded wire and with a definite ground connection through one of those wires. If you leave the shield disconnected with one-conductor shielded wire, you may get horrible hum.

Practical ground loop elimination

In Chapter 3 we talked about how a ground loop can form and produce hum or noise in a circuit, and how balanced wiring can eliminate almost all of the problem. Unfortunately, much of the equipment in the prosumer realm is unbalanced and not immune to ground loop noise. It's also difficult to chase down loops, since equipment may be interconnected with video, machine control, Ethernet, and MIDI as well as audio cables and power-line grounds—and any of these can form an extra ground path. Finding and fixing a ground loop can be more voodoo than science.

Sometimes you can reduce the effect of a ground loop by tempting the circuit with an even better ground. Heavy-gauge wire has very little electrical resistance, so if you provide a ground path using thick wires it can divert some of the ground loop current from being carried on the signal wires. Get some heavy-gauge wire and run lengths of it from one piece of equipment to another—on audio equipment, there's usually a back-panel screw marked "ground" specifically for this connection; on computers, connect to the outer metal shell of a rear-panel jack. A good wire for this purpose is 8- or 10-gauge electricians' type TW wire, available for a few cents a foot at building supply stores, or automotive primary wire, which is slightly more expensive but also more flexible. You should hear the hum go down as soon as you make the connection. (You might also hear it increase, which means you're just making the ground loop worse. Like I said, sometimes it's voodoo.)

If you can't find an exposed ground connection on a piece of equipment, don't go rooting around inside the cabinet. You might find dangerous voltages instead.

If you can't get rid of a noise-producing extra ground in a power or control cable (or even figure out which cable is the culprit), you can often reduce ground loops in unbalanced equipment by breaking the ground path that takes place across the audio cable:

- Sometimes, just cutting the shield connection can help. Turn down the speakers; then pull a phono plug partway out, so its shell isn't contacting the jack, or use a phone-plug cable where the sleeve isn't connected at all. Turn up the speakers *slowly*. Sometimes this fixes the problem, but other times it makes it much worse.

- You can isolate audio circuits completely by using a transformer. Small stereo isolation transformers, prewired to phono jacks, are available at automobile sound dealers. Radio Shack's version (#270-054) costs about $15. If one of these fixes the problem but the transformer isn't good enough—you'll notice a slight decrease at the extreme high and low frequencies—you can get a higher quality unit from a broadcast or video supply company.

One special hum case occurs when a VTR or monitor is connected to cable television as well as to a computer or audio equipment. The cable company's wiring is connected to the power-line ground in a lot of different places and is a hotbed of ground loops (which don't matter to the high-frequency television signal). But once you complete the circuit to a piece of grounded audio equipment, hum develops. It won't go away when you turn off the VTR but should disappear if you disconnect the television cable.

If you're hearing this kind of hum, you can make a television frequency isolation transformer for under $10. Get a couple of 75Ω to 300Ω antenna transformers—one each of Radio Shack #15-1140 and #15-1523 work well for this—and connect them back-to-back at their screw terminals (Figure 20). Then insert the whole assembly in series with the TV cable, making sure that nothing shorts the cable's shield from one side of the transformer to the other. If the hum doesn't stop, you may have gotten "autoformers" instead of true transformers. Check with an ohm-meter; there should be very high resistance between the screw terminals and either coaxial connection.

This cheap fix may pick up snow or other video junk in marginal conditions, but it won't degrade the audio. If the hum disappears but other problems appear, get a better quality transformer at a high-end stereo store.

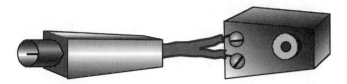

Figure 20: Connect two antenna transformers back-to-back to break cable TV ground loops.

Wiring monitor speakers

Hi-fi enthusiasts claim great benefits to using special braided or oxygen-free cables between the amplifier and speakers. The physics behind these claims is doubtful. Ordinary 18-gauge "zip cord"—the stuff table lamps are wired with, available at any hardware or electronics store—should be sufficient for almost any speaker wiring chore in a digital video studio. If speaker cables are going to be longer than 10 feet or so, you might want to bump up to 16-gauge zip cord, also commonly available.

Two considerations are important when wiring between a speaker and ampli-fier, particularly if they have individual screw or pressure terminals.

* Electrical phase must stay consistent, or else it will be difficult to get a good idea of the bass notes in your mix. One screw or terminal at each speaker and on each channel of the amp will be marked with a + sign or special color. One conductor in the cable will be copper color, or marked with a stripe or ribs in the insulation. Use these identifications to make sure both speakers in a stereo pair are wired exactly the same way. The code doesn't matter—for example, you may choose to connect + on the amp, to the striped conductor in the cable, to the red screw on the speaker—but it has to be the same for the left and right channels.

* The fine copper wires that make up each conductor in the cable can become unwrapped, and a tiny stray wire may bridge two terminals and cause a short. This may damage or blow a fuse inside the amplifier. If possible, tin the wires with a soldering iron to keep them together, or use a high-quality crimp-on lug. If not, be very careful that every strand of wire is held in place by the screw or binding post.

Mixing −10 dBV and +4 dBu Equipment

Even the most professionally wired postproduction suite may have some unbalanced −10 dBV equipment (see Chapter 3), and NLE setups are apt to have a lot of it. Prosumer VTRs, CD players, musical equipment, and sound cards are likely to operate at the lower interconnect voltage. Consumer-grade monitor amplifiers may be totally professional in every respect except their input circuits.

There's no reason the two standards can't coexist in the same facility. Small buffer amplifiers, costing $50–$75 per channel, are available at broadcast and video supply houses. They take a -10 dBV unbalanced signal and provide both amplification and balancing, turning it into +4 dBu balanced. If your facility uses balanced wiring, they can be mounted right at the CD player or other low-level source to give you noise immunity as well as a voltage boost. If you need to integrate a high-level balanced input (such as on a broadcast VTR) into an unbalanced system, it's probably easiest to mount the booster right at the deck and consider it just another prosumer device.

If you have just a few low-level unbalanced inputs (such as a prosumer VTR) in a balanced environment, it's best to use similar buffers or transformers at the decks to turn them into balanced inputs. This way, all the cabling remains balanced and you won't be facing sudden changes in the grounding scheme when you patch into them.

If you have just a few high-level balanced sources in an unbalanced setup, things are even easier: you can build a simple resistive adapter for a few dollars. You'll lose the benefits of balancing at the professional devices, but it's no real loss since you're not using it anywhere else in the room. Figure 21 shows the wiring. Resistors are standard 1/2 watt or 1/4 watt, from Radio Shack or anywhere else. Start without a jumper between pins 3 and 1 on the balanced side. If everything works, fine; if you don't hear a signal, add the jumper. You may find it more flexible to build a variable version of this circuit using a 5 kΩ trimmer or variable resistor: just substitute the

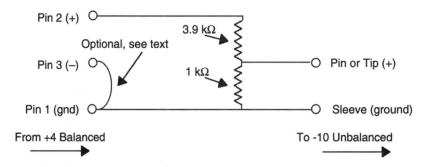

Figure 21: A simple pad to use high-level sources in a prosumer suite

three terminals on the trimmer for the three resistor connection points in the circuit, with the middle trimmer terminal going to the pin of the -10 device. Set it once for a proper level, then ignore it.

Nonaudio Wiring

The digital video-editing suite is a complicated place, and some signals that have nothing to do with audio can still have an effect on your sound.

Digital sync

Digital audio is almost always handled in serial form: a string of ones and zeros is taken as a group, to represent one 16-bit (or higher) digital word. For this to work properly, the equipment has to agree how to find the start of each word . . . because if it can't, unpre dicta blethin gscan happ ento yourso und (like that). Each digital stream is self-clocking—a piece of equipment can look at it and determine where the word should start. But in a complicated facility, many audio signals may be moving simultaneously. If they don't all start their words at exactly the same time, the equipment won't know how to translate them. And audio/video equipment such as digital VTRs have the added burden of keeping the picture and sound words starting together, so they can be recorded or processed predictably.

Word clock

In sound studios, digital audio is often synchronized by routing a separate audio sync signal. This "word clock" is wired like video, using 75Ω cable and BNC connectors. One device is designated as the master clock, and every other piece of equipment is set to sync its own internal circuits to it. The advantage is predictable operation, particularly when multiple audio signals have to be mixed together. Many digital mixers don't need word clock and will buffer each input's data until all the timings match . . . but this adds another processing step and another chance for the signal to get degraded.

Video sync

Equipment designed to handle audio in a video environment, such as professional DAWs and timecode DAT recorders, often gives you the option of synchronizing both their internal timing and their digital words to a video signal. This is the same black-burst, video sync, or "house black" that you should be distributing to your VTR and NLE already; all you have to do is extend it to the additional inputs. It's better than timecode for keeping the internal timing of DATs and DAWs in step, since it's more precise and not subject to audible variations.

Most audio equipment that can handle a video sync signal also provides a separate, synchronized word clock output. So you can use a one blackburst generator for all your video equipment, route its signal to a convenient DAW or DAT recorder, and then distribute synchronized word clock to the audio devices that don't accept video sync. This will keep all the timings accurate and assure the cleanest digital audio processing. You might not even have the choice whether to do this: some digital video devices won't accept digital audio unless it's also locked to blackburst.

Timecode

Even though it's not as good as video sync for controlling internal timing, SMPTE timecode is the standard for tracking individual frames of audio- and videotapes and making sure shots and sounds start when they should. Its data format and standards are discussed in the next chapter, but it also has an implication on edit suite wiring.

SMPTE code is usually distributed as an unbalanced, audiolike signal. Its 1 volt square wave, right in the middle of the audible band, has harmonics that can leak into any nearby audio cables. The result is a constant chirping, very much like the sound of a fax transmission.

For best results, keep SMPTE cables far from audio ones. Don't run the two kinds of signals through the same patchbay. SMPTE is so likely to cause interference that it can even distort itself; if you run two different timecode signals on the dual shielded cables used for stereo wiring, the resulting cross-talk may make both unreadable.

Levels and Digitizing

Some day we'll all speak the same language. Eventually digital video cameras, editing systems, broadcast facilities, and possibly even feature film studios and video games will share the same file systems. Getting sound or picture from one unit to another will be as simple as popping in a data cartridge or logging onto a network.

You can do this now to a limited extent in audio production. A studio or composer can send you narration and music on removable media, ready to run on your NLE . . . if you agree on the file format and medium ahead of time. After you've edited, if you want to mix at an outside facility, you can bring them tracks the same way.

But for most nonlinear production, you're going to have to transfer at least some of the sound from camera tape or DAT to computer file, and then from NLE back to videotape. You also have to make sure that sound on the finished tape is in a reasonable form for the broadcaster or dub house who'll be working with it. This chapter is about the steps you should take to make sure nothing gets lost in the process.

Transfers and Digitizing

When Digitizing Isn't

Editors often use the term "digitizing" to refer to bringing sound or pictures into NLE, but if you're transferring via Firewire or a digital audio link, digitizing doesn't really happen. The signal already exists as ones and zeros. It's merely going from serial data on tape to a data stream on a wire, then into a RAM buffer, and finally to one or more files on a hard drive.

If the file's sample rate and bit depth matches that of the data stream, and you're not making any intentional changes to the sound, this "nondigitizing" process should be completely transparent. Unless there's a timing problem somewhere along the line, the computer won't do anything that can affect the sound. On the other hand, you may need to turn sound at one sample rate or bit depth into a file with different specifications. This can add distortion and noises if done improperly (though most programs handle the process pretty well).

In virtually every case, transferring a sound digitally will work better than using analog wiring. Each analog/digital conversion—even with the best equipment—adds a little bit of distortion. If your digital signal needs equalization or volume changes, it's better to do this in software than to convert it to analog for the processing, even if the analog equalizer you'd use is slightly better than the software version you have. This isn't necessarily the case in music production, where a certain amount of analog "warmth" is often preferred. But by the time a limited-bandwidth video project gets through its multiple generations and broadcast processing, clarity is a lot more important than warmth.

> If your system gives you the option of straight digital transfer—camera or deck to NLE via digital wiring, with no analog in between—use it.

If you need to tweak levels or equalization and you have a good *digital* processor, it's acceptable (and certainly a time saver) to apply this correction while you're transferring. But keep things subtle; it's a lot easier to add additional processing later than to compensate if you go overboard now. Be sure to store the processor's settings so you can reapply them if you have to retransfer.

No matter how good your digital reverb is, don't apply this kind of processing during the initial transfer stage. If a track seems too dry to match the picture—perhaps because a radio mic was very close during a long shot—cherish its purity;

tracks like this are the easiest to edit. Once the show is completely cut, and you've also got music and sound effects in place, you can add appropriate reverb.

Getting the cleanest digital transfers

Even though an all-digital transfer won't introduce noise or conversion distortion, there are still places for audio gremlins to creep in. These generally present themselves as a flutter or roughness to the high frequencies, periodic clicking in the track, a low-level hiss that comes and goes with the signal, or occasional dropouts. They're often the result of impatience or deadline pressures, making you start the transfer before you're sure what each switch and software setting really means. Here are some guidelines for avoiding them.

The following rules also apply after you've digitized an analog signal. If you're going to be moving *any* digital audio signals around your edit suite, pay attention to them.

- Use the right cable.

Hi-fi cords look like s/pdif cables, but can cause dropouts in digital connections. Modem cables look like they should handle multitrack digital audio, but can damage the recorder. If you're not sure you've got the right kind of wire, check the manufacturer's instructions and Chapter 3 of this book.

- Choose an appropriate sync source.

Digital inputs rely on serial data, so they need synchronization to find the start of each word. Consumer gear synchronizes automatically to the input, so this may not be an issue. But professional equipment often gives you a choice of synchronizing to the input, a separate audio or video sync source (see Chapter 9), or internal crystal. Some gear supports only external sync with certain inputs.

If your facility is wired with video or word clock sync, use it whenever possible to prevent problems. You'll have to specify the sample rate or video format for it to work properly. Some digital audio systems require you to set the sync source in two different places—at the internal clock, and at the input module —and will have problems if these settings disagree (it's bad software design, but you may have to live with it).

If you have to dub from a nonsynchronizable source such as a CD player or portable DAT, you may have a choice: set the recorder to sync from its input, or use the recorder's ability to resynchronize (or "reclock") the input. Either will usually work. If the source has an unstable crystal, using the input as a sync source will often be cleaner. But if the source is intentionally out-of-spec—for example, if you've varispeeded a CD, forcing its sample rate to something other than 44.1 kHz—you *must* reclock the signal. If you don't, the effect of varispeeding will disappear when you play the transferred file at the normal rate!

- Plan for as few sample rate conversions as possible.

It's probable that you'll have to change the sample rate of one source signal or another during production. CDs run at 44.1 kHz. Digital videotape often uses 48 kHz. Internet and multimedia audio might come through at 32 kHz or 22.050 kHz. Mixed film/video productions often require a 0.1% sample rate correction.[1] But you can't mix the production—or in most cases, even edit it—until all the rates match.

A little planning here can make a world of difference. Figure out what your final sample rate has to be. If you're going to most digital video formats, 48 kHz will be necessary. If you're mixing for CD-ROM or analog video, 44.1 kHz or lower might be appropriate. Set your NLE to this rate, and convert any nonmatching digital signals as you transfer them. This can eliminate extra processing later on, and any artifacts from the conversion process will be randomized or buried when mixed with additional tracks. You needn't worry about these artifacts, however; although older programs often had problems with sample rate conversion, modern software converts at extremely high frequencies to push glitches and filter problems out of the audible range.

When doing analog production, it makes sense to run tapes at their highest possible quality and not dub to the final format until the master is done. But in digital production, there's no generation loss . . . and absolutely no advantage to preserving a higher sample rate than the finished media.

If you're creating audio for mixed sample rates—for example, if a mix will be released on digital video (48 kHz) and audio CD (44.1 kHz)—it may be advantageous to work at the higher rate. But think things through before deciding. If the video is being broadcast only on analog TV, nothing above 15 kHz will be transmitted . . . so it makes more sense to work at 44.1 kHz, giving the higher-quality CD the advantage of fewer conversions.

There is a small advantage to setting your production to the lowest sample rate that will satisfy every eventual use: lower rates use less file space and can be processed by the computer faster. Although the difference between 48 kHz and

---

[1] This is to compensate for the difference between 24 fps film, which is easily sped up to 30 fps by doubling occasional frames, and NTSC video at 29.97 fps.

44.1 kHz is only about 8%—any savings there will be buried by the much greater storage and processing requirements for video—the difference between 48 kHz and 32 kHz is one-third! If your converters can do a good job at that rate, and you're sure you'll never need anything above 15 kHz, storage and processing savings can be significant in a long program.

- Keep the bit depth as high as possible.

The minimum for professional production is 16-bit audio. Better is 24-bit, not necessarily because the signal can have a greater dynamic range—a consideration in music and feature films, but not in video—but because it's got more margin for operator and software errors.

You may find 12-bit audio adequate for recording gritty documentaries, but it shouldn't be used during production or editing. And 8-bit audio is all but obsolete.

Low bit-depth problems *are* cumulative over multiple generations. Keep your signal at the highest possible number of bits at all times. If your mixing software supports 24-bit audio, use the setting even when mixing 16-bit signals. If you've shot 12-bit audio in the field,* convert it to 16-bit before editing. No quality is lost when you raise a file's sample rate.

Eventually you may have to convert your mix from 24-bit back to 16-bit to fit on a video or CD format. When you do, be sure your software's Dither option (Chapter 2) is turned on. If possible, keep a high-bit version of the file so you don't pick up extra noise if you have to make changes.

- Avoid data compression until the final step.

You may need to run the final mix through AAC, AC-3, or other data reduction algorithms for distribution. If so, keep an uncompressed version. These processes are not reversible—decoding the compressed audio always results in some data loss—so you'll need the original if you have to re-edit or compress the track through a different algorithm. Besides, new processes are constantly being developed. Tomorrow's compression might be a lot cleaner, and you'll want to be able to take advantage of it without being stuck with yesterday's data loss.

Even if your project will never be recut or re-encoded, you still shouldn't compress individual tracks. They'll just have to be decoded when you edit or mix—even if the software does this in the background without telling you—and coding artifacts will build up when they're recompressed. Wait until you've got a mixed track, and then do the whole thing in a single pass.

---

*And you'd better have a darned good reason for using that lower-quality setting.

- Listen!

Whatever you do, keep an ear on what's actually coming out of your NLE or processor rather than what's going in. If an element is being processed in software, play the whole thing back before proceeding. Most digital audio problems will show up on good monitors, if you just listen carefully, and can be undone if you catch them quickly enough.

Dealing with Analog

Often, analog sources such as Betacam or live mics have to be edited, or an NLE isn't equipped for digital input. In these cases it's necessary to digitize, converting the analog signal to digital in the input circuits of the editing system. This introduces a whole new layer where things can go wrong.

The problem is that analog audio can't be controlled with the precision or simple user interface of digital transfers. Until a signal is turned into ones and zeros, the computer has nothing to do with it. Everything is up to you.

➤ The best way to avoid problems with digitizing is to not digitize at all. Use your NLE's digital input for DAT decks and CD players, if it has one. Import CD audio from the computer's CD-ROM drive rather than via its sound card, if it doesn't.

➤ Most recording studios, announcers, and composers can supply tracks as files or audio CD as well as on DAT or analog tape. Ask for media that can be transferred directly rather than digitized.

It takes some thought to set up a good system for digitizing, but once you've done this preliminary work it shouldn't be any trouble to digitize your material cleanly. The place to start is with the analog circuits in your edit suite, before the signal ever gets to the NLE.

Gain-Staging

Everything in your analog signal path has a finite dynamic range. There's only a narrow window between too soft—when the signal is mixed with hiss and other electronic noise—and too loud to handle without distortion. Each piece of equipment has a specific range where it gives you the best performance. Gain-staging is the process of fine-tuning the volume as it passes from one piece of equipment to another, so that the signals always stay in that range. (This also applies to digital signals, but their dynamic range is wider and you don't have to worry about recalibrating at every step—once a signal is digital, its level stays the same no matter what equipment or software you use. So unless you're writing audio processing software, gain-staging is usually thought of as an analog concern.)

Figure 1 shows how things can go wrong in a setup with preamp, equalizer, and compressor . . . but the same problems can occur in a setup with just a preamp and computer input, between the input and output circuits in a mixing board, or any other time a signal has to pass through multiple stages.

Although both signal paths in the figure yield the same volume at the end, the top signal is distorted and noisy . . . and won't sound good in a mix. The problem is that the preamp was set for too much gain in the top path. This forced it to a higher level than its own circuits could handle, causing distortion on its output. It also meant that the equalizer saw too much signal, so its volume had to be turned down. But it was turned down too far, forcing its output down to where part of the signal is obscured by electronic noise. The input to the compressor was then turned up to compensate, amplifying both signal and noise . . . and doing nothing about the distortion.

In the lower path, the preamp is set to a reasonable amount of gain. Its output is just right for the equalizer, which puts out the right amount of signal for the compressor. The result is a signal that's just as loud as the top path's, but a lot better sounding.

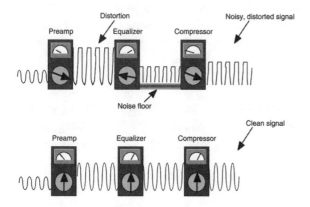

Figure 1: Both signal paths have the same final volume, but the bottom one will sound a lot better.

What makes things worse is that the nice meters and large calibrated knobs I drew don't usually exist in real life. Many consumer and semiprofessional devices don't give you anything more than a flashing overload light. The only way to tell if equipment is working in its proper range is to test a lot of different levels.

Here's a general procedure, though it's worth checking individual product manuals since specific equipment may have other alignment procedures.

1. Start with the first item in your signal chain. Apply a normal signal from the playback of well-recorded original track.

2. Raise the equipment's input volume until the overload light starts flashing, then lower it until the light flashes only on occasional peaks—no more than once every couple of seconds. If analog equipment has a bouncing meter instead of a flashing light, consider one or two units above the zero point—where the meter scale turns red—as the equivalent. If the equipment has an output level control, turn it to the midpoint or detent.

3. Now do the same thing with the next device in the chain. You should end up with its input volume control around the midpoint. If you have to turn it up or down a lot, there's either a mismatch between equipment at −10 dBV and at +4 dBu, or you've gotten microphone- and line-level connections mixed up. If it's the former case, you'll need a buffer or pad (see Chapter 9). If it's the latter, fix the wiring—anything else you do will sacrifice quality.

Digitizing Analog Signals

After you're sure that levels are being handled properly before the signal gets to your computer, you can start to turn the analog signal into data on a file. There are two potential trouble spots here: the quality of the NLE's digitizing circuit, and how well the software's meters are calibrated. You can do something about both of them.

Getting Better Inputs

No matter how fast a processor chip is, or how many audio effects are supplied with the software, the ultimate limit on an NLE's sound quality is the analog circuits. Unfortunately, turning audio into digits is an exacting process that requires expensive components. A computer is simply a very scary place for an analog audio signal:

- The analog circuits in most 16-bit sound cards don't handle more than 10 or 12 bits' worth of volume range, around 72 dB. Even premium cards rarely get 14 bits of performance. Too soft and the signal is compromised by noise; too loud and it's distorted.

- A sound card that *does* have good analog circuits is likely to pick up interference from the logic pulses flying around the motherboard. This reduces the effective volume range even more.

Professional audio systems solve the latter problem by keeping analog audio off the motherboard. Instead of a sound card, they use separate analog converters in a shielded case. These are complete circuits, usually with their own power supplies. Don't confuse them with the external "connection pods" that come with some internal cards.

You can do a similar thing if you want better quality than the onboard converters, and if your system has digital connections (if it doesn't, consider getting a digital-only sound card or digital audio to USB adapter). The converters in even a modestly priced DAT recorder will probably be better than those in a sound card, since the manufacturer is concentrating on audio quality. There's no reason you can't use one as your editing system's analog stage, passing the signal to the NLE via s/pdif or AES/EBU. These decks also have much more reliable metering than NLE software, so you'll be solving two problems at once. Since you probably need a DAT deck in your editing setup anyway, choose one that lets you pass a signal from analog input to digital output without having a tape loaded—some decks only do this while the tape is in Pause or Record mode, which will cause excess wear on the transport and heads when you try to use the deck as an input.

As an alternative, consider a high-quality equalizer/compressor with both digital and analog connections. You can turn off the processing and use it just as an input converter, apply gentle processing (and save the settings) if necessary to clean up field audio tracks, or use it as a final multiband processor in digital input/output mode when transferring the final mix to digital videotape. You can also get the ultra-high quality, 24-bit 96 kHz standalone converters used in professional recording, but these are overkill in the video suite.

You need only one external converter to improve both digitizing and final output: while you're recording or editing, put the converter on the NLE's input and monitor via the system's built-in analog output. When you're ready to mix or send the finished track to tape, switch the converter to the output and use it in digital-to-analog mode.

Calibrating an NLE's Meters

The record-level meters that came with your NLE software are probably inadequate (see Chapter 9), and will lead you to digitize at too low a level. This is a major problem, because even though a digital system may have a theoretical 16-bit range, computer input circuits can sacrifice some of the range and processing errors[2] can destroy even more. You can't afford to throw away any bits. This gets even more important if you're editing material for broadcast, where subsequent processing—

[2]The NLE's, not yours. If it calculates fades or equalization using 16-bit math, there'll be inevitable errors caused by rounding off the lowest possible numbers.

either at an audio post facility or at the TV station—will emphasize any low-level noise and distortion.

Even if you've got a separate hardware meter, you won't have accurate calibration unless it uses a direct digital connection to the NLE. Fortunately, calibrating a software or hardware meter is easy in an editing system. You don't need any additional hardware or technical knowledge, the procedure doesn't take very long, and it'll remain accurate until you specifically change the system.

1. Start by setting the program's input volume control (if it has one) to its nominal position. This is usually the default value and may be marked as 0dB or 50%; in most situations it will result in the cleanest recording. You'll be making volume adjustments as you go along, but do them with an analog output volume control at the source. This is one case where analog is better than digital.

2. If your analog equipment doesn't have an output volume control, or following this procedure makes you turn that control below about 30% of maximum, you'll need an accessory attenuator between the source and your NLE; check the instructions after these steps. Without one, you'll never be able to set the best digitizing level.

3. Find a well-recorded source tape. Play it and adjust the source's output (or accessory attenuator) so the meter swings into its red area only on occasional peaks. The red area might be marked 0db, −6dB, 80%, or some other message at the whim of the manufacturer, but it'll be at the top of the scale right below the overload indication.

4. Once you've adjusted the volume, record 10 or 15 seconds at that level and save the file. Use a name that'll help you remember the peak meter reading for that trial (see Figure 2). Now make two more recordings, one at a somewhat lower output level, and one somewhat higher. Note their peak readings also, and save them with appropriate names.

5. Open the three files and look at their waveforms. See which meter reading gave you the loudest recording without distortion; look for the file with the tallest waves that are still rounded (like Figure 3). If the waves reach the upper or lower boundary of the window or have flattened tops and bottoms (Figure 4), the recording was too loud.

6. It's unlikely that your results will match mine on the first set of recordings. So repeat the process, making finer and finer adjustments centered around the best meter reading from the previous trial. In a few minutes, you'll find the ideal reading. It doesn't matter what the meter says in dB or percentage or arbitrary numbers, so long as you can repeat it. The next time you're digitizing, set the source's volume control so the meter reacts the same way. Dialog, narration, and different kinds of music can cause different meter responses, so you may want to repeat the calibration procedure with various audio sources.

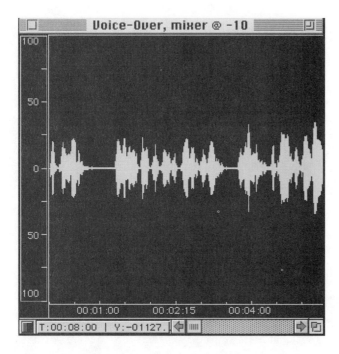

Figure 2: Save the file with a name that'll help you remember its level.

Figure 3: Good recording levels fill the screen without touching top or bottom.

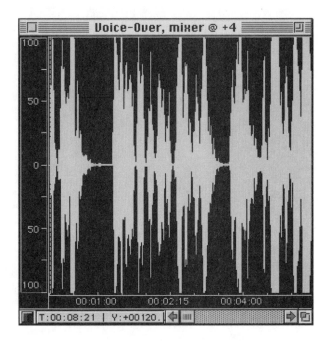

Figure 4: When the digitizing level is too high, tops and bottoms of waves are too loud for the window.

Linear and "Boosted" windows

Some NLE software lets you view an audio clip with a built-in visual distortion that boosts lower volumes so you can see them better (Figure 5). This affects how the softer samples will appear, but won't change the sound or what you're looking for: the best recording level will be the one that fills the window without touching the edges.

Accessory attenuator

If you have to turn the source's output control very close to its lowest level to get a good recording, it's likely you'll be picking up extra noise from the source's output circuits. These usually follow the level control, so turning the knob all the way down has the same effect as bad gain-staging (as with the equalizer in the top of Figure 1). A better solution is to run the output device at its proper nominal volume and insert a simple resistive attenuator between its output and the digitizer's input.

You can buy calibrated attenuators for about $75, but you might prefer to build your own for about $5 using a single 5 k$\Omega$ audio-taper potentiometer (Radio Shack #271-1720) and appropriate connectors. Figure 6 shows how to wire it for balanced and unbalanced circuits, and Figure 7 identifies the connections as they'll appear on most brands of potentiometer. You must use soldered connections to avoid noise

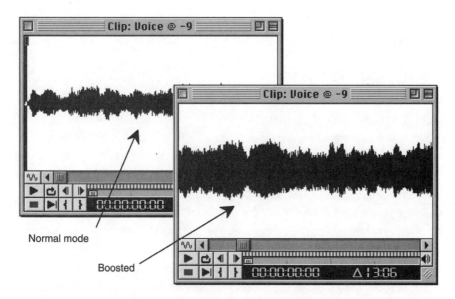

Normal mode

Boosted

Figure 5: Your NLE might let you view a clip "Normal" or "Boosted." It doesn't affect the calibration process.

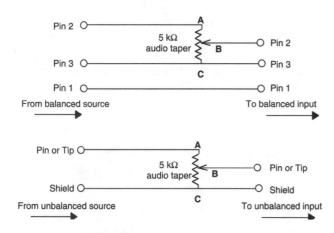

Pin 2

5 kΩ
audio taper

A

B

C

Pin 2

Pin 3

Pin 3

Pin 1

Pin 1

From balanced source

To balanced input

Pin or Tip

5 kΩ
audio taper

A

B

C

Pin or Tip

Shield

Shield

From unbalanced source

To unbalanced input

Figure 6: A simple resistive pad for adjusting digitizing levels

A
B
C

Figure 7: The letters refer to connections in Figure 6.

and may want to put the unit (or a pair of them for stereo) in a metal or plastic box with a large knob so it's easier to check and restore the settings.

Diagnosing Problems

Bad digitizing levels can hide hum or noise in your audio chain. Once you've calibrated the system, digitize another test file at the correct volume. But this time, use a source tape that has some silence or room tone recorded on it as well as normal program material. Play back the file and listen very carefully to the silent part. If there isn't any noise, your system is properly calibrated and you're done.

If there is noise on the test file, digitize that source tape yet again. But this time, pause the tape for a few seconds in the middle of the recording. Play back this file and listen to where you paused. If the noise stopped, it's on the source tape. You may be able to reduce it in software, but only at the cost of losing some of the desired sound. (Most "noise reduction" systems assume noise is most bothersome during pauses and simply turn down the overall volume—or just the treble—when things get soft. But the noise is still there, lurking under the signal and ready to be emphasized by subsequent processors.) Reread the second section of this book, and do a better job of recording next time.

If the noise continues even when the source tape is stopped, it's being generated by the playback deck or digitizing hardware. Here's what you can do about it:

- Hiss is often a question of bad gain-staging.

- Hiss can also be caused by magnetized tape heads in an analog audio or video deck or badly aligned analog equipment. You can get a demagnetizer with instructions at most electronics stores, but for anything else you'll need the help of a technician.

- Random noises—snaps, crackles, and pops—are usually caused by loose connections or bad circuit components. Try cleaning the connectors (a rubber eraser works well, or you can get special cleaning fluids at electronics stores) or replacing the cables. If that doesn't help, it's time to take your equipment to the shop.

- Hum in desktop video setups is almost always the result of ground loops. See Chapter 9.

Once you've tracked down and fixed any noises or hum, make a final test recording at the ideal level you found and look at its waveform. It's unlikely, but you may need to go through the calibration procedure again. Then relax, secure in the knowledge that your analog digitizing chain is properly set up.

Working with Very Low Sample Rates

If a project will end up only on the Internet or in a desktop learning situation, a 22 kHz sample rate may be adequate (and possibly desirable, because its smaller files make it easier to transmit or store). If you need very small voice files, and compression schemes such as IMA or MP3 aren't supported by the playback medium, 11 kHz sampling may even be usable. (On some systems, these rates are actually 22.050 kHz and 11.025 kHz, as submultiples of the standard CD sample rate.)

These very low sample rates have little margin for error. Problems at the upper frequency ranges of a 44.1 kHz file, where there's very little musical information, are easily ignored. But those at the top of a 22 kHz file are immediately obvious in music, and those near the top of an 11 kHz file can cut into the intelligibility of a voice track. Two principles will keep you from getting into trouble.

The first rule is not to digitize at the final sample rate. Audio has to be filtered when it's digitized to keep overly high frequencies from generating false data and accompanying themselves with whistles and squeaks. But the analog filters in most desktop systems aren't very flexible and can have serious problems when switched to low frequencies. Any filter, digital or analog, creates a distortion that gets worse as you approach its limit.

The solution is oversampling, discussed in Chapter 2. Professional equipment usually records in the megaHertz range, with gentle analog filters, and then refilters in the digital domain as it divides the sample rate down. You might not have this option on a desktop system, but you can do the next best thing by recording at the highest frequency your sound card supports and then converting in software. Any good audio program has a "downsampling" function. Use it right after you've digitized a file to save storage space and processing time.

The second rule is to stay away from analog as much as possible. Each time you pass a signal through the analog inputs or outputs of a sound card, it goes back through those nasty filters. Unless you have significant oversampling, the high-frequency response will fall off rapidly. So if you have to leave the digital system to pass through an analog effect or mixer, keep the signal at a high sample rate while you do. Just downsample the final mix.

Metering and Lineup Tones

Audio level meters do more than tell you how loud a mix is, or when you're digitizing at the right level. Used with a lineup tone, they provide repeatability: you can digitize part of a scene today, redigitize other parts of it next year, and all the audio should intercut perfectly. Meters and tone also assure consistency, so the dub house or broadcast station that gets your tapes will have some idea what to expect for volume levels.

Experienced audio professionals usually take tone with a grain of salt. We use them to calibrate gain-staging and are rigorous about providing accurate tones on tapes we send out. But we've all been burned by badly applied tones on tapes we get, so we verify levels against the actual program material before digitizing.

VU meters

The big Bakelite volume unit meter used to be a standard fixture on every piece of audio equipment. These were more than simple voltage meters; although they measured steady tones the way voltmeters did,[3] they responded to quickly varying sounds very much like our ears do. Their ballistics were designed to smooth over very fast volume changes, so they correlated nicely with subjective loudness. They also drew current from the audio line, loading it down, and their rectifiers added a subtle but audible distortion to the signal.

So much for nostalgia. Today there are so few true VU meters being manufactured that they're too expensive to include in most equipment. If they were included, they'd need separate overload indicators, since their damped movements can't catch the sudden peaks that cause digital problems.

Analog voltmeter

The things that *look like* VU meters (Figure 8) in modern analog gear are really simple voltmeters and don't have the same kind of calibrated dynamics. They're too fast to show you average levels but can't respond quickly enough to short transients. On the other hand, they're accurate with steady signals and can be used for lineup tones. If you have a true VU meter and one of these voltmeters on the same signal, you'll notice that the VU is much easier to read because it's not jumping around as much. You'll also notice that if they're both calibrated to the same tone, sudden jumps to +1 on the VU meter might swing as high as +6 on the voltmeter.

---

[3]They were calibrated to power levels across a 600Ω line and actually read out in dBm when the impedances were properly matched. But they were usually isolated from the line with a 3.6 kΩ resistor to reduce their effect on the circuit; this caused a 4 dB loss. That's how +4 dBm came to be the line-level standard. See Chapter 3 for more about dBm.

Figure 8: The "VU" meters in most modern equipment are really low-cost voltmeters.

Peak reading meter

Both digital and analog distort when a signal is too loud. But analog distortion isn't noticeable on very fast peaks, while some digital gear will make a horrible crackling noise if a peak is much longer than a ten-thousandth of a second—the first split second of a gunshot, for example. Even a fast-responding analog voltmeter can't display peaks this fast, so electronic circuits are added to capture the loudest reading and hold it for a few seconds. These circuits can also determine the average volume and generate a voltage that makes a lower-cost voltmeter behave like a proper VU meter. (Building one of these circuits and calibrating it with a specific voltmeter mechanism is still an expensive proposition, however, so you rarely find them outside of recording studios.)

Microprocessors can also measure peak and average voltage. Some audio programs put a relatively reliable combination meter on the computer screen, though the CPU might be too busy during actual recording to respond to very fast peaks. The most accurate audio meters in common use today have dedicated circuit boards with their own processor chips and display both peak and average level, either on a row of LEDs in a stand-alone meter or superimposed on the video monitor. If the circuit is fed with an AES/EBU or s/pdif digital audio stream—Figure 9 shows one like that in my studio—the meter is self-calibrating and absolutely reliable.

How much is zero?

Traditional VU meters were calibrated to 0 dBm—a precise standard—even though the circuits could handle a few decibels above that level with no trouble. So engineers

Figure 9: A combination peak/average meter, calibrated for digital inputs

got used to the idea of "headroom" and would run their equipment so that loud voices or music might exceed zero every few seconds. Lineup tones on the tape or over the network would still be calibrated to zero on the meter, but program peaks might hover around +3 VU.

But digital audio levels aren't measured in volts or dBm; they're expressed as a ratio below "all bits are turned on"—the loudest possible sound you can digitize, since there aren't any bits to show that a sound has gotten louder than that—or decibels below full scale (dBfs). This led to a confusing state of affairs:

- Analog audio meters start at some negative number, around –40 VU, and then are calibrated through zero to a positive number (usually +3 or +6). Zero is the nominal operating level; lineup tones are set to match it, even though some peaks are expected to be louder than zero.

- But digital audio meters start at a negative number and top out at 0 dBfs. Peak levels have to be held below digital zero, and with a safety factor they may be considerably below that. If you set a lineup tone to zero on a digital meter, and then calibrate an analog system to that tone, the peaks will be much too soft.

- Since analog meters read up to +6 VU and digital ones up to 0 dBfs, it would seem logical to make the digital lineup tone precisely –6 dBfs. If you do this, and set the analog meter to zero on that –6 dBfs digital tone, the two meters will agree perfectly . . . *but only for steady tones.* Remember, analog meters show average levels and don't respond to instantaneous changes. Speech that looks perfectly good on the digital meter may only tickle the analog circuits at –18 VU if the meters are calibrated this way.

This is a very real problem. Unfortunately, there can't be a standard solution. That's because the peak-to-average ratio depends on the program material. Live classical music or sporting events may have sudden peaks as high as 18 dB or more above the average level. But heavily processed pop music might have its peaks clamped to 6 dB above average.

So the level for the lineup tone in a digital audio- or videotape will vary according to studio or client standards, but never be zero. Most pop music production uses a −12 dBfs tone. Tones in classical music may be as low as −24 dBfs. Broadcast networks usually quote −20 dBfs for the tone but also specify that no signal should exceed −10dBfs. This leaves an official 10 dB for peaks, with another 10 dB safety margin above it.

Synchronization

Whereas nonlinear editors have internal databases to keep multiple audio and video tracks in sync, you need a more standardized timing reference when you step out of that closed system. SMPTE timecode—developed by the Society of Motion Picture and Television Engineers, and first popularized as an editing and timing reference in the late 1970s—is the universal language to identify specific frames in a videotape. Analog and digital audio systems use it as well, to keep track of which sounds should play against those frames.

Although SMPTE code can also be used as a speed reference, by measuring the length of time from one frame to the next, it's often not precise or stable enough for digital audio or even analog color video. Most systems use blackburst (see Chapter 9) to control the speed, once timecode has been applied to get the frames in sync. Better audio workstations give you a choice of what they'll do if timecode and blackburst aren't moving at the same speed: just report the error and continue relying on blackburst, resync so that timecode agrees, or stop cold and wait for operator intervention.

But if you're going to intervene, you have to understand what timecode is really doing . . .

Understanding Timecode

Prepare to be confused. Of all the techniques we use, SMTPE timecode is the most bewildering. What else can you expect of a system where 29 + 1 = 30 nine times out of ten, and 29 + 1 = 32 the tenth?

Timecode was invented to help video editing. Each frame gets a unique hour:minute:second:frame address, so you can assemble scenes more predictably. It also serves as a common reference to assure that sound, picture, and animation from different systems all fit together. The one thing it *doesn't* do is keep track of time. A minute of it won't precisely equal a minute on anyone's standard clock. An hour of the stuff might equal an hour on your wristwatch . . . or maybe it won't. And the last three sentences aren't true in Europe, Africa, or Australia!

Fortunately, all you need is logic—and a little bit of history—to become a master of time(code).

Once upon a time . . .

The problem started more than 50 years ago. Back in those black and white days, U.S. television scanned at 30 frames per second. This number was chosen both because it was easy to derive a sync signal from the 60 Hz power line that ran into every home, and because any hum introduced into the video circuits of early TVs would stay in sync with the picture and not roll around the screen.

When color TV was invented, more information had to be jammed into the picture to keep track of colors. But broadcasters didn't want to make this more complex signal incompatible with older sets because they'd lose viewers. So they stretched each frame a tiny bit longer—1/10th of a percent, to 29.97 fps—and used the extra time to put in a color reference signal. The new frame rate was close enough to the older standard that monochrome viewers could adjust their sets to compensate. (If you're over 50, you probably remember having to jump up and trim the vertical hold knob whenever a TV station switched from monochrome to color.)

This 29.97 fps system worked fine until timecode was invented. You can see the problem in Figure 10. The top filmstrip represents 30 fps black and white video, with a digital wall clock beneath it. At the end of 29 frames both the video and clock are ready to move on to a new second. But color TV (middle strip) is slightly slower, so it's still playing that 29th frame when it's time for a new second. The timecode numbers can't move until the frame is finished. This tiny error accumulates to the point that an hour's worth of timecode is over an hour and three seconds long. A program that was produced to start at 1:00:00 timecode and end at 1:59:59 would actually finish a few seconds after two o'clock! (To think of it another way: The frame rate was slowed down 1/10th of a percent. An hour is 3,600 seconds, so slowing it down means 3,600 seconds times 0.1%, or 3.6 seconds.)

Broadcasters realized this timecode stuff could cause shows to bump into commercials, costing them money, and howled for a solution.

Dropframe

The broadcasters' solution was to periodically skip a few numbers. At the end of most minutes, the number jumps ahead by two. If your tape is parked at

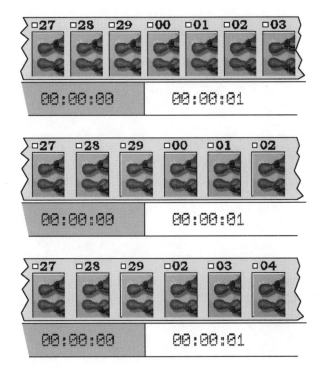

Figure 10: Dropframe is necessary because there aren't an even number of frames per second.

00:01:59:29 (hours: minutes: seconds: frames) and you jog exactly one frame forward, you land on 00:02:00:02. Even though the format is called dropframe, no frames are ever dropped; instead, two numbers per minute are. The bottom strip in Figure 10 shows how it counts.

There are 60 minutes in an hour, so dropping two numbers per minute means 120 will be dropped each hour. But the actual error caused by that 1/10th of a percent slowdown was 3.6 seconds, or 108 frames. Now our timecode hour is 12 frames too short! So to fine-tune the process, six times an hour—once for every minute that ends in zero—counting reverts to normal. Park at 00:09:59:29 and jog one frame, and you land on 00:10:00:00. This puts back two numbers each time, or—*ta-dah!*—12 frames an hour. When you do all this, an hour of dropframe timecode precisely equals an hour of the clock on the wall.

It works, but this crazy counting makes editing more complicated. The duration of a scene frequently doesn't equal the difference between its in-time and its out-time. Editing computers can handle this automatically, but human editors have a hard time getting around it. So television production in NTSC countries uses two timecode formats:

- Nondropframe timecode counts continuously, so it's easier to use when running length isn't critical or for short projects. It's usually preferred in commercial post-production and nonbroadcast media.

- Dropframe timecode is harder to count, but on average it agrees with the clock on the wall. It's preferred by broadcast producers and stations.

I once worked with a producer who insisted his projects were too important to use drop-frame timecode. Every frame of his project was vital, and he didn't want any thrown away.

You know better.

Both dropframe and nondrop run at the same 29.97 fps rate, so tapes are inter-changeable. You can produce your spot using nondrop, and TV stations won't turn it down (they may insist on dropframe for program masters, to make things easier in the control room). Well-designed editing systems even let you mix code formats in the same production.

Those crazy Americans

This nonsense applies only to NTSC[4] countries—North and South America, and parts of industrialized Asia—where color video runs 29.97 fps. In the rest of the world power lines are 50 Hz, so black and white TV evolved at 25 fps. This is slow enough that PAL and SECAM countries didn't have to stretch frames to accommodate color.

Audio programs and nonbroadcast computer systems sometimes use 30 fps timecode, since it's easier to count and modern technology has no problem synchronizing it. By definition, 30 fps timecode has to be nondropframe . . . there's no point skipping numbers since it already matches the clock. You may see "30 fps dropframe" on editing equipment, but the name is the mistaken result of confusing frame rate with counting format.

Table 1 summarizes the code formats.

---

[4]NTSC really stands for National Television Standards Commission, though most broadcast engineers will say it means Never Twice the Same Color.

TABLE 1: Code formats		
Code Type	Frame Rate	Counting Format
24 fps	24 fps (film)	Count to 23, then 1 second 0 frames
25 fps	25 fps	Count to 24, then 1 second 0 frames
29.97 nondrop	29.97 fps	Count to 29, then 1 second 0 frames
29.97 dropframe	29.97 fps	Count to 29, then 1 second 2 frames . . . except once every 10 minutes, don't.
30 fps nondrop	30 fps	Count to 29, then 1 second 0 frames
30 fps dropframe	This rate and format combination seems silly, but some manufacturers support it anyway.	

Timecode Recording and Transmission

Timecode is usually carried as a biphase serial word around 2,400 Hz. The exact frequency depends on the frame rate, but it's always in the middle of the audio range. This way it can be recorded on one of an analog video deck's regular audio tracks or on a specialized audio "address track" that includes circuitry to protect the code's square wave—one of the few times that a true digital signal is recorded as analog data. Since these tracks run parallel to the tape, instead of scanning diagonally like the picture, the code is called Longitudinal Timecode (LTC)—a term that also refers to that signal as it chirps through the studio wires as a digital serial stream.

LTC is rugged, can be read during fast wind, and is easy to deal with. But when it's carried as analog audio on a tape, it disappears when the tape is paused or shuttling slowly. So the same numbers are also frequently written as a series of white dots, as a digital code in the space between pictures. This Vertical Interval Timecode (VITC) lives with the video, so it can be read whenever the image is visible, but gets disrupted when the image is edited. It can also be carried over a studio's video wiring or transmitted on the air along with the picture.

Most professional analog video decks use both forms of code, choosing the most reliable at any given moment, and delivering the result as an LTC signal at the deck's output jack and—on request from the edit controller—over the deck's serial control wires. Most professional digital audio and video decks keep track of timecode as part of their other timing data, readable whether the tape is paused or playing, and deliver it the same way.

As far as the next piece of equipment is concerned, there's almost no difference between analog-recorded LTC, video-recorded VITC, or digitally recorded timecode.

Shuttling timecode

One anomaly makes LTC recorded on an audio track, and LTC translated from VITC or digital data, behave differently at slow speeds. Remember, timecode is transmitted as a serial word; you can't read it until a full word is sent, which takes exactly one frame. At play speed this means the received code is always exactly one frame behind the picture that's playing. Editing systems compensate by adding a frame. This works even if the tape is shuttling at fractional speeds, since the audio track is slowed down the same amount.

But VITC and timecode from digital recorders continue to flash by once per frame, so LTC derived from it is constantly updating . . . even if the video is moving slower than a frame at a time. This means that if the picture is playing at half speed—one frame every 1/15th second—it's one frame late for the first 1/30th second and then it catches up. At quarter speed it's late for only the first frame in four. If a system tries to compensate for timecode delay when the picture is scanning at quarter speed, it'll be wrong 75% of the time. A few pieces of equipment can sort this out, based on how the numbers are counting, but the rest of them expect you to live with the error. Some give you the choice of generating timecode as analog- or digital-style, so you can set whether it has a constant or variable rate to accommodate the next piece of equipment.

Syncing Film with Audio

A lot of broadcast projects are shot on film and edited as digital video on NLEs to get the best combination of image quality and editing flexibility. Since it's not practical to record sound on film the way it is with videotape, separate audio recorders are always used. Sometimes they rely on timecode for synchronization, but many times a simpler (and cheaper) system is employed.

A half century before timecode was invented, Hollywood faced the challenge of keeping sound and picture running at the same speed. Originally, this was done by punching holes in the sound recording medium (first optical film, then heavy-gauge magnetic tape) the same distance apart as they were on the picture. Electric motors on both the camera and sound recorder were driven by common power supplies to run at the same speed. These turned sprockets with teeth that engaged the holes, keeping both media running at the same speed. It was cumbersome and used lots of wiring and heavy motors, but it worked.

As portable cameras and recorders were developed, the system was simplified: a 60 Hz signal derived from the wall current, from a generator inside the camera, or from matching crystals in the camera and recorder, was recorded on standard magnetic tape instead. When the tape was played back, this signal was used for the reference. It either drove the sprocketed recorder's motor, or controlled the playback speed while the signal was dubbed to a fixed-speed recorder (or sometimes videotape).

Pilot tones

High-quality portable analog recorders, particularly the Nagra III and IV series used in film production, often use the Neopilot system for recording that 60 Hz sync signal. But it isn't recorded on a separate track. Instead, the "pilot" signal is recorded with a special tape head that records two simultaneous tracks on top of the audio signal. One of these tracks has its polarity inverted, so that when the top one is writing a positive signal, the bottom is writing a negative; if both tracks are played together, they cancel each other out. The monaural audio signal, on the other hand, is recorded with a normal head across the entire width of the tape. This wide track has a higher quality than if two half-width tracks were used, one for audio and one for pilot.

On playback, a similar Neopilot head is used. Its inverted tracks cancel the full-width audio signal but read the pilot with no trouble. The audio head reads the entire width of the tape and can't see the pilot. It's the tape equivalent of phantom power (Chapter 6)!

You may encounter a "Nagra tape" with location sound in a mixed film/video production. Stereo pilot and timecode-based Nagras use a special timing track that can't even be detected on normal stereo recorders. But tapes from Neopilot mono Nagras—and there are a lot of them still in the field—will have a pronounced 60 Hz hum when played on a stereo deck. The solution is to mix both tracks of the stereo deck together into a mono signal. When they're properly balanced, the hum will disappear.

Editing film sound on a computer

Some student and experimental films attempt to combine techniques—shooting film and editing pictures with traditional splicing, for eventual projection in a theater, while cutting sound on an NLE. It's common to use nonlinear editing on Hollywood features, but this requires special equipment that can sync at 24 fps. But it's also common for a beginning filmmaker to ask, "How can I use my desktop computer and low-cost software to make a track for the 15-minute, 16mm movie I've already cut as film?"

It can be done, but you'll need some luck. And you'll have to spend a few dollars even if you already own the software. Whether you're planning to release the project on film or videotape, the first step is to have a post house or TV station transfer the film to tape. The issue is synchronization, and you have to be sure the projector or film scanner and a timecode generator are both locked to a common blackburst. Even if you're planning to release on film, you can't skip this step or do the job yourself by pointing a camcorder at a screen. You can, however, save a few dollars with a "one-light" transfer if picture quality isn't critical.

Since you're not cutting picture, you don't need NLE software. Most audio programs can play back a video file while you're working, or sync to timecode from a VCR. Many relatively low-cost programs use MIDI timecode, and SMPTE-to-MIDI converters are available at music stores. Edit individual elements any way you want while you're looking at picture, but don't attempt to mix them to a single track unless you're feeling very lucky.

The problem is most low-cost programs (and some embarrassingly expensive ones) don't really sync to timecode; they merely start segments of audio on specific frame numbers. A very long section, such as a completed mix, can drift noticeably out of sync even if it's been started on time.

One solution is to mix back to your videotape, syncing the audio program to timecode on the tape and hopefully doing the entire thing in one pass. Now, at least, you've got sound and picture in sync on tape.

But if your final output must be a composite film with optical or magnetic track, and you're working in an NTSC country, things get trickier. The reference video you've used as a reference when building sound—the one you paid good money for at a post house—runs off-speed by a tenth of a percent, the same factor that makes dropframe necessary. Audio-for-video professionals know how to speed things up to compensate, and professional DAT players have the necessary adjustment built in. Film technicians might not have encountered this problem, however, so check with the optical sound facility or film lab before making the final transfer.

Or use this shortcut: edit individual tracks in a computer, and even do submixes if you want. Then transfer them all to mag film, and do some creative cutting on a flatbed editor before mixing film-style. Over the course of a 15-minute project, you'll have to delete about 21 frames to compensate for that 30 fps to NTSC pulldown . . . surely a piece of cake for someone who's trying to splice together an entire film.

Editing Voices

Being a good video editor doesn't automatically make you a good dialog editor. The principles are different. But if you're good at cutting pictures, you already have one skill that's absolutely necessary for cutting sound: you pay attention to details. It just might not be obvious which details are important.

For example, one good trick for editing picture is to let on-screen movements bridge over a cut. If Sue reaches for a door at the end of scene 1a, scene 1b can be a close-up of her hand turning the knob. This continuous motion helps the viewer connect the scenes, so we see one action even though it was shot in two takes.

Voice editing follows a different rule: you almost never want to edit across a continuous sound. If shot 1a's track ends with Sue saying, "I'm glad to se" and 2a begins with a different take of "e you, George"—that continuing /ee/ sound being the audio equivalent of when she reached for the doorknob—the audio edit will jump out at us. If I had to edit those two audio takes together, I'd cut on the /t/ in "to", the /s/ in "see," or even the tiny /d/ that starts the word "George."

This chapter is about finding those other editing points, and why they're better. These are the tricks a dialog editor learns . . . such as, did you know there's a /d/ in the front of "George"? Go ahead. Say the name aloud slowly. It starts with exactly the same tongue movement, producing exactly the same sound, as the /d/ in "dog." The only difference is that in the man's name, it's followed by a buzzing /zh/ (like the one in "leisure"). The science behind this—how mouth movements and breath create individual specific sounds (phonemes), and how they blend together into the words we recognize—is phonetics. It's handy stuff for a voice editor to know.

There's an official way to write these sounds. According to the International Phonetic Alphabet, the /ee/ sound in "see" should really be written /i/. The /t/, /s/, and /d/ symbols mean what you'd think, but the symbols for /zh/ and many other sounds don't even exist in normal typefaces because there are more phonemes than there are letters.

Unfortunately, the phonetic alphabet can look like hieroglyphics to the untrained (see Figure 1), so I'll use a simplified version in this book.

ðæts maɪ neɪm dʒeɪ

Figure 1: That's my name, Jay, in the International Phonetic Alphabet. Even if you can't read it, it's important to recognize that each character represents an individual sound. There are 15 separate, editable sounds in the four syllables of "that's my name, Jay."

In most of this chapter we'll use *dialog* to refer to any spoken words, whether it's conversations between on-camera actors, talking heads, location interviews, or voice-over. The editing techniques are the same. The only difference is that you've got more freedom when you don't have to worry about lip sync, so we'll use that as the basis for our examples.

The Right Tools for Editing Voice

Once you understand how voices should be edited, you can use these techniques for the rest of your career. The principles are absolutely portable, and they work because of how we listen, not because of special equipment or software. I use a

DAW now because it's faster, but years ago I was cutting exactly the same way on 1/4-inch tape and 35mm magnetic film.

However, you should be aware there are easier environments to edit voice than most NLEs, which force you to edit on frame boundaries. A /t/ sound lasts less than a third of a frame, so one-frame resolution in a video program means you can't hone in on it accurately. Audio workstations and analog tape have essentially infinite resolution; you can cut from any place to any other place, regardless of frame boundaries. Even 35mm film sound is more than three times more precise than an NLE; you can cut from any set of perforations to any other, and there are four sets of perfs per frame, for an edit resolution of 1/96th of a second.

If you're going to be doing serious voice or music editing, I urge you to get a separate two-track audio-editing program to use along with your NLE. They speak the same file format, so you can move sounds between the two programs freely. Many of them also play video in sync, so you can watch a clip while you're editing. Even if your NLE has better than one-frame resolution—some let you nudge audio in- and out-points very precisely—it still probably forces you to treat each edit as two separate clips. This is much less efficient than audio programs, which treat sound as a continuous stream so you can cut and paste with word processor ease. The time you'll save will offset the couple of hundred dollars an audio-editing program costs.

Scrubbing, jogging, and shuttling

Whether you're working in an audio program or an NLE, anything more sophisticated than basic paragraph-by-paragraph assembly requires the ability to mark edits while actually listening to the sounds at various speeds. Audio folks call the process "scrubbing." Editing programs may have two different scrub modes, roughly equivalent to shuttle and jog modes on a VTR. Normal tapelike scrubbing is similar to shuttling: the sound moves forwards or backwards, either at a constant rate or in response to a mouse being dragged or a knob being turned. As you speed up, the sound gets higher in pitch; as you slow down, the sound gets deeper, but it's easier to pick out separate phonemes because they're farther apart. Some programs also offer dynamic scrubbing, which is similar to video jogging; as you move the mouse slowly across the audio, you hear short segments of sound—ranging in length from about a third of a frame to a half-second—continuously looping at normal speed. Since sound is always played at its normal pitch, it's easier to recognize where vowels or musical notes change. Figure 2 is a graphic representation of these two modes. Dynamic scrubbing continuously repeats a short, moving loop so you can hear its natural pitch; tapelike scrubbing slows down each sound, but you can hear their precise beginnings and endings. Track 15 of the CD lets you hear the difference.

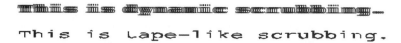

Figure 2: Dynamic and tapelike scrubbing modes

Editing I: Cutting in Silences

Nobody . . . talks . . . like . . . this. Speech is made of continuous sound, with constantly changing volume and pitches, punctuated by brief pauses when you breathe. Dub track 16 of this book's CD into your editor—or read the preceding two sentences into a microphone—and look at it on a waveform or clip display. It'll probably look like Figure 3. Play through the clip, and notice how individual sounds line up with the display. Then save the clip: we'll be editing it a lot, and you'll want to keep coming back to this original version.

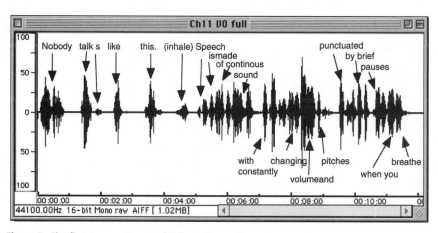

Figure 3: The first two sentences of this section

I added callouts to make the picture easier to interpret. The hills and valleys represent where the track gets softer or louder.[1] Notice how some words share a broad hill ("volume and"), while other single-syllable words might have two separate hills of their own ("talks"). In the latter case, there's one loud burst for the /t/, a quieter stretch for /al/, a short pause while the lower lip closes against the teeth, and then the louder friction of the /ks/.

If you wanted to edit between those takes, you could mark your cuts any time in the silences before each of the first four words or in the pauses after "sound" and "pitches." But you'd have to be careful if you marked the pause between the first

[1]Read more about audio envelopes in Chapter 1.

and second sentence, because it's not really silence. That's where the announcer breathes. If you try to cut in the middle of that breath, you'll disturb its natural rise and fall—calling attention to the edit. You have to cut completely around it. Try it both ways, or listen to my version of that sloppy cut on track 17 on the CD. (There's more about breath editing later in this chapter.)

The point is that it's very difficult to do a smooth edit in the middle of a continuous sound. Sustained vowels and long consonants (such as the /z/ in the middle of "pauses") are continuous, but so is room tone and the breath between words. In fact, it's the first rule of editing:

> ➤ Never cut away from the middle of one long sound into silence or into the middle of another.

But like every rule, there are exceptions. If you fool the ear into thinking that the first sound continued, you can get away with this kind of edit. We'll discuss how to do this with music in the next chapter. To do it when you're editing voice, you have to pay attention to how individual sounds start.

Editing II: Sounds with Hard Attacks

Notice how the left sides of some hills in Figure 3 are very steep. These are the beginnings of sounds that get suddenly loud: the /t/ at the start of "talks" and in the middle of "continuous," the /k/ at the start of "continuous," or the /p/ in "punctuated" or "pitches." One of the characteristics of sudden loud sounds is that

Spelling errors?

There's no *z* in "pauses," and no *k* in "continuous" . . . so why are they written this way in the book?

Phonetics—even the simplified version in this book—depends on accurately hearing and depicting actual sounds. It has nothing to do with the letters in a word.

The *s* in the middle of "pauses" has a buzzing to it, just like the /z/ in "zoo." If you try saying it like the /s/ in "sue," you get a totally different word: "paw-sis." Try it. You'll find other cases where the letter *s* turns to /z/ at the end of "boys" and "eggs."

And why is the *c* in "continuous" written as /k/? It's certainly not the same sound as the *c* in "certainly," which would have to be written /s/. In fact, there's no character in phonetics for the letter *c* because it's always sounded like some other consonant.

they mask other, softer sounds that might be going on at the same time or immediately before it. So if you edit from a softer sound to a louder one, the loud sound distracts your ear from any discontinuities caused by the edit itself.

Figure 4 shows how sudden loud sounds can distract the ear in an actual edit. The left side of the figure is zoomed in so you can see how the waveform abruptly changes direction; this would normally cause a click. But because it's part of a cut from a softer sound to a much louder one, as you can see when the screen is zoomed out (right), nobody hears the problem.

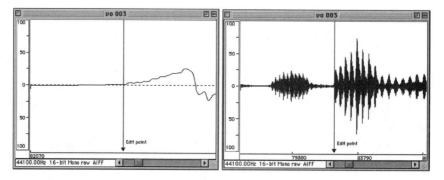

Figure 4: There's a jump in this edit (zoomed in on the left), but because the cut is to a louder sound, you'll never hear the problem.

This is the key to the second rule of editing:

➤ You can generally cut from any continuous soft sound into one with a hard attack.

An Editing Exercise: Cutting Where There's No Pause

You can use that rule to change the material you just put into your NLE, deleting "continuous sound with" so it reads

> Narr: Speech is made of |constantly changing volume and pitches, punctuated by brief pauses when you breathe.

The | indicates where the cut should be.

1. Scrub forward in your editor until you hear the sharp /k/ sound at the beginning of "continuous," and make a mark.

2. Continue scrubbing to the /k/ at the beginning of "constantly," and make another mark.

3. If you're using an audio program, select between the two marks (Figure 5) and delete. You're done. If you're trying this in an NLE, make a duplicate copy of the clip; use the first mark as the out-point of the first clip and the second mark as the in-point of the second, and slide them so they snap together (shown on two separate audio tracks in Figure 6 for clarity). Some NLEs let you use timeline tools, such as a razor blade, to separate clips into pieces without opening a separate window.

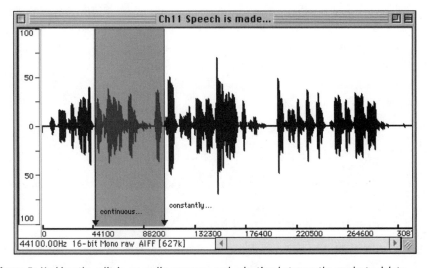

Figure 5: Marking the edit in an audio program, and selecting between the marks to delete

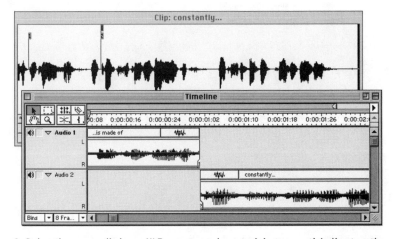

Figure 6: Doing the same edit in an NLE means you have to join two partial clips together.

Play it back, and your edit should sound just like my version (track 18 on the CD).

In fact, we've cut away from one phoneme (the /k/ in "continuous") and into an identical phoneme in a different word (/k/ in "constantly"). If this were video editing, the equivalent—matching one action to another—would assure a smooth cut. The same rule holds for sound:

➤ You can almost always cut away from the start of a sound in one word and into the start of that same sound in another word.

But the cut-into-something-hard rule is more powerful. We could go from virtually anything to a hard sound and it would be fine.

Here's proof (and a chance to practice another technique), cutting away from a /k/ and into a /p/ :

```
Narr:    Speech is made of |pauses when you breathe.
```

1. Go ahead. Reload the original clip and mark the /k/ in "continuous."

2. Mark the /p/ in "pauses" for the other side of the edit. If you scrub slowly, you'll be able to hear precisely where the buzzing /v/ in "of" ends, then a tiny break, and then the start of the /p/.

3. Cut them together, and it should be as smooth as my version on track 19 of the CD.

Practice a few times on other voice tracks, and you'll be ready for truly advanced voice editing.

Editing III: Hearing Phonemes

So far, you've made edits by finding and marking hard attacks. But speech is made up of sounds, not just sudden attacks. Once you learn to recognize individual phonemes and can find the beginning and end of them, you've got a lot more flexibility in how you edit.

An Even More Impressive Exercise

We'll start with a slightly more complicated edit, finding the boundary between /z/ and /m/ in "speech is made" so we can turn the line into

```
Narr:    Speech is |punctuated by brief pauses when
         you breathe.
```

1. Reload the clip, and start scrubbing from the front. You'll hear a recognizable /tch/ at the very end of "speech." At the end of it is the beginning of the word "is".

2. Keep scrubbing forward, and you'll hear a hissing or whistling—depending on how fast you're scrubbing—at the start of the /z/ that finishes "is." Scrub some more, very slowly, and stop as soon as that whistle ends. Mark it. That's the end of /z/ and the beginning of /m/ in "made."

3. Now mark the /p/ at the start of "punctuated"—just like you did in the previous exercise—and make the edit between them.

The result will sound like track 20 on the CD. If it doesn't, you probably scrubbed a little bit too far after the end of the /z/. Undo and try again.

Fooling the Ear

If you can't find something hard to cut on, or identical sounds to cut between, you can sometimes fool the ear into thinking an edit is smoother than it really is:

> ➤ Cutting away from the start of one sound, and into the start of a similar sound, often works.

That's because in normal speech, the end of one sound is often influenced by the sound it's going into. The mouth has to get into the right shape for the next phoneme, and it starts moving slightly before the phoneme actually starts.

Try it yourself:

```
Narr:    Speech is made of continuous sound, with
         constantly changing volume and pitches |when
         you breathe.
```

1. Find the /s/ at the end of "pitches." Do this by playing or scrubbing until you hear the word "pitches," start, and then scrubbing very slowly. You'll notice the /tch/ in the middle of the "pitches," then the /i/, then a hiss as the /s/ starts. It's similar, but not identical, to the buzzing /z/. Continue slowly to the end of the hiss; that's the end of the phoneme. Mark it.

2. Move ahead a few seconds to the word "pauses." Mark the end of the final / z /, just like you did with the word "is."

3. Edit the two marks together. If it sounds a tiny bit awkward, you've probably left a brief pause after the / s /. Trim a tiny bit off that edit, and try again. Track 21 of the CD shows this edit with and without the pause, so you can hear the difference.

There's even a science to determining when sounds are similar. Read on:

Phonemes Come in Families

There are 46 phonemes in normal American English, but as an editor you really only need to know about a few categories of them: two kinds of consonants and two ways of making them, the vowels and a few special consonants that glide between vowels, and some common sounds that are really combinations of two others (such as the / d / and / zh / that make up the letter *j*).

Voiced and unvoiced consonants

You've probably noticed that / s / (as at the end of "tots") and / z / (at the end of "toys") have similar, but not identical, sounds. In fact, you form your lips and tongue exactly the same way to make them. The only difference is that / z / has a buzzing from your vocal cords, while / s / is made just by exhaling—your throat doesn't buzz at all. / z / is called a voiced consonant; / s / is unvoiced.

As an editor, it's important to know this distinction:

- Unvoiced consonants have very little to identify who's speaking. Almost none of a specific character's voice is carried in these sounds. This means that except for matters of room acoustics or background noise, you can often substitute one actor's unvoiced consonant for the same consonant from a different actor. Believe it or not, you can take an / s / from one of Sue's lines and put it in a similar word while George is talking, and it'll sound fine!

- You can sometimes swap voiced and unvoiced consonants when you need to create new words. If George said "boy" when the script required "boys," but the only final *s* you have in his voice is from the word "tots," you might still be able to cut them together. The result will sound slightly foreign, "boysss" with a hissing ending, but may work in context. (You can't use one of Sue's / z / sounds for a George / s / because voiced consonants include a lot of the sound of a particular person's voice.)

Other voiced/unvoiced pairs include

/v/ (as in "very")	/f/ (as in "ferry")
/zh/ ("seizure")	/sh/ ("sea shore")
/g/ ("gut")	/k/ ("cut")
/d/ ("dip")	/t/ ("tip")
/b/ ("bark")	/p/ ("park")
/th/ ("then")	/th/ ("thin")

This last pair is hard to notate without using the phonetic alphabet, since English makes no spelling distinction between them. The first would be notated as a lower-case *d* with a line through it (the first character in Figure 1), while the second is a Greek *theta* (an *O* with a horizontal line through the middle).

Voiced/unvoiced pairs of consonants are very similar, and you can often edit between them, because the mouth makes an identical shape for them. But sounds also come in more general families, based on the physics of how they make noise, and knowing this can also help you find a place to edit.

Fricatives

The sounds /z/ and /s/, /v/ and /f/, /zh/ and /sh/, and the two /th/ sounds are all made by forcing air through a small opening formed by your tongue held close to some other part of your mouth. This air friction makes various hisses, whose high frequencies stand out when you scrub through a track slowly. Learn to identify this hiss (as when you found the end of the word "is"), and you'll be able to spot the start and end of these consonants quickly.

/h/ is also a fricative, but the mouth is held open and the friction happens between moving air and the sides of the throat. It also has a hissing sound, but a much quieter one.

Plosives

The sounds /b/, /p/, /g/, /k/, /d/, and /t/ are formed by letting air pressure build up and then releasing it quickly. Because of this burst of pressure, any plosive can cause a popping sound when it's delivered too close to the mic.

The only way to make a plosive is by shutting off the flow of breath momentarily, either by closing the lips (/b/) or by sealing the tongue against part of the roof of the mouth (/g/, /d/). This makes life easy for the dialog editor:

- When a plosive starts a syllable, there'll be a tiny pause before it. Listen for that silence, and you've found the exact beginning of the syllable. Some trained announcers start their voices buzzing before the pop of an initial /b/ or /g/; if you scrub slowly, you'll hear a frame or two of /m/ at the front of "boy." You can almost always cut this buzzing out without affecting the word.

- When a plosive ends a syllable, it actually has two parts: the closure and then the release. Say the word "cat" slowly, and you'll hear two distinct sounds: /kaa/, then a brief pause and a short /tih/. If the same plosive consonant happens twice in a row (as between the words in "that Tom!"), you can almost always run them together (/thah tom/). Overly formal or nervous speakers will separate the two plosives (/thaht tom/); if you cut out one of the two sounds, the speaker will appear more relaxed.

Glottal and nasals

The sounds /h/, /n/, /m/, and the /ng/ at the end of "ring" are four completely different, long consonants. They can often be shortened by cutting out their middles, but they can't be substituted for anything else.

Vowels and intervowels

Although there are five vowels in written English, there are a dozen in the spoken language. The important thing for an editor is learning to distinguish them because they can't be substituted for one another. For example, *a* is completely different in "cake," "cat," "tar," "tall," and "alone." If you're looking for an alternate syllable to fix a badly recorded word with an *a* in it, you can't just search for that letter in the script.

Vowels are, obviously, always voiced. They are always formed by buzzing the vocal cords and changing the resonant shapes of the mouth. They have no unvoiced equivalent.

The consonants /w/ and /y/ always appear with a vowel after them, and their very ends are modified by the vowel they're gliding into. If you need to fix a badly recorded /w/ in "whale," chances are the /w/ in "water" won't work well because the vowel is different.

The consonants /l/ and /r/ always appear with a vowel on one side, the other, or both. They're not influenced as much by the vowels next to them, but will be different depending on whether they're leading into one or following it.

Diphthongs

Some common sounds are always made of two phonemes joined together. Learn to listen for them because they give you twice as many editing options as single phonemes:

> ➤ You can frequently isolate a single sound from a diphthong to use elsewhere. You can almost always cut from the middle of one diphthong to the middle of another, or to the start of a different sound.

There are two consonant diphthongs, /t sh/ (as in "church") and its cognate /d zh/ ("George").

There are five vowel diphthongs: /aah ih/ ("eye"), /aw ih/ ("toy"), /ah oo/ ("loud"), /ay ih/ ("aim"), and /oo uu/ ("open"). This is advanced stuff. Diphthongs in vowels are often hard to hear and take a very precise hand to edit, but they're really there.

Intonation

Voiced sounds have pitch, and people vary this pitch as they speak to express emotions. As you get more into dialog editing, you'll be amazed how *little* attention you have to pay to this factor. If you're cutting between takes of the same copy, or changing words in a performance by a trained actor or narrator, the pitch will be remarkably consistent. Any slight variations you cause by editing will probably sound like natural intonation, particularly if the edit is smooth and the viewer is following the content. Wide variations will be immediately apparent, so you can undo the edit and try something else. One of the things you should try is a few percent of pitch manipulation or varispeed, if your editing system has this feature. A pitch shift—no more than 3% higher or lower—may be all you need to join two unfriendly phonemes.

Projection Levels

A performer's projection level affects more than how loud they are. As you raise your voice, the throat tightens and the vocal buzz that forms voiced sounds loses some of its lower frequencies. At the same time, most trained speakers will also push their voices "into the mask," directing more energy to resonating cavities in the front of the face and adding high harmonics. You can't compensate for these timbral changes by simply adjusting volume. In most cases you can't compensate for them at all, and editing between two takes of widely varying projection levels can be difficult.

The envelopes (Chapter 1) of individual words also frequently change as projection levels raise. The beginnings of individual words get stressed more, to separate them, than they'd be in normal speech.

> ➤ If you must cut between two takes with different projection, keep the takes on two separate tracks as you move their phonemes around. Then experiment with volume and equalization to make them match. A little reverb on the softer track can also help. Once the sound matches, mix the two tracks to a single composite voice.

Editing IV: the Tricks

Breathless

Go back to track 16 on the CD, the one you loaded at the start of this chapter, or look at Figure 3. There's a big puff of air in the middle. Most announcers will take a gigantic breath between paragraphs, and many loud fast ones throughout the paragraph. These noises don't communicate anything other than "I'm reading from a script," and—unless you're trying for a comedy effect—should come out of voice-over tracks. Breaths in front of a take are easy to get rid of—just move the in-point a little later. But those catch-breaths during a read are more troublesome. While you can spot breaths on a waveform and hear them when you scrub, you can't just cut them out—that would pull the surrounding words too close together. You also can't just erase them because that'll leave the words too far apart.

In general, a breath in a voice-over can almost always be replaced by a pause *two-thirds* its length. If it takes one second for the announcer to gasp, use 20 frames of silence instead. The result sounds cleaner, more energetic, and completely natural. This ratio has worked for me in thousands of projects with hundreds of different announcers. Even though I edit by ear—erasing the entire pause, playing the line, and marking where I think the next phrase should start—it almost always turns out to be two-thirds. I have no idea why the number is magic.

If you're starting with a clean voice-over recording, and it will be used on a sound-limited medium such as broadcast TV or mixed with music, you can replace breaths with digital silence. But if it'll be played at theatrical levels, use room tone; otherwise, the finished edit will sound choppy. On-camera breaths are trickier, since the two-thirds trick would destroy sync. Even replacing the whole breath with room tone may be a mistake: if we see the talent's mouth open, we should hear something.

Simply Shocking!

Amateur announcers and real-life interview subjects don't take the big breaths, but often do something worse: they unconsciously let their breath build up, then blast it out when they talk. It causes a little click if the phrase starts with a vowel. These *glottal shocks* are a natural result of nervousness in the throat, so we all get used to associating them with that condition. Your listeners won't know why, but they'll know your track is somehow hesitant and unconvincing.

Glottal shocks often follow long pauses, when a speakers is unsure and looking for "just the right word." If you try to shorten this pause but don't take care of the shock, your editing won't sound natural. It's easy to get rid of the pesky things, but only if you zoom in. Deleting about a hundredth of a second, at the start of a word, is usually enough to turn a speaker from nervous to confident.

Extensions

Frequently you'll need to start or end a voice segment on a particular syllable, even though the speaker might have more to say before or after the clip. If they didn't pause exactly where you want to edit, even the most accurate edit will sound abrupt as they suddenly start or stop talking.

Add a little room tone or natural background noise, butted right up to the edit. This will make it sound as though the performer—and not your editing system—made the pause.

Snap, Crackle . . .

When the clock rolls 'round to winter, you can hear the announcers start ticking. You get annoying clicks and snaps in their voices, particularly when they're close-miked and saying sounds that require the tongue to touch the roof of the mouth (like /l/ or /k/). It's caused by central heating drying up their mouths. This thickens the saliva, which starts to stick and stretch and . . . well, the sound it makes is just as disgusting as the description.

Cutting out the snap can destroy the rhythm of the word. Erasing it—or replacing it with silence—can leave a noticeable hole.

But you can usually replace the snap with a tiny snippet of the vowel immediately before or after it. Locate a snap, select about the same length of audio right next to it— it'll be less than a frame—copy, and paste it over the snap. Depending on the program, you may need to use a Replace or Overdub function; you want the new sound to fit over the snap, rather than move the snap later.

Because the snaps are so fast, it's almost impossible to fix them in a frame-based NLE. Hand the announcer a glass of water, and re-record.

Speak with Forked Tongue

On the other hand, some voice tricks are easy in a multitrack environment like an NLE . One of the neatest is *mnemonic speech*, an effect invented by pioneer sound designer Tony Schwartz. You've probably heard it in commercials: an announcer starts talking, and while he's finishing one phrase he's also starting the next. Two words, from the same voice, at the same time. If it's done well, you're not aware of an overlap, but you do get a sense of energy and urgency. (If it's done badly, you get a clichéd dragway ad.)

You can blast through mnemonic cutting quickly by setting markers in the track at the start of each phrase. Then break the clip at the markers, and move the individual sections onto alternate tracks. Finally, slide the sections so they overlap by a few frames. It's not necessary to fade at the start or end of each phrase . . . the natural flow of the voice will have the same effect as a cross-fade!

Figure 7 shows how the tracks will look in an NLE. Track 22 of the CD lets you hear them.

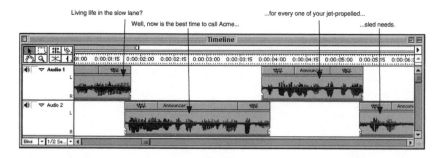

Figure 7: Mnemonic speech lets you hear two things in the same voice at the same time.

Editing V: Keeping Track of Sync

So far all of the voice editing we've talked about has been without pictures. Surprisingly, cutting sync dialog isn't very different. An NLE should take care of synchronization automatically; you can move and mark either sound or picture, and if the software knows the two belong together, they should both stay together. Two rules will keep you out of most trouble:

➤ As soon as you import or digitize synced audio and video, lock their tracks together in the software.

➤ Always keep a copy of the original, unedited take so you can check what proper sync is supposed to look like . . . or, when things get really bad, re-import them and start over.

Keeping things in sync in most audio-editing programs is a little trickier. Once you've loaded the audio/video file, the sound portion can be edited any way you want. If you do anything that changes its length—inserting or deleting sounds, or changing their tempo—sync will get lost. Minor changes shouldn't cause any trouble if you keep this in mind:

> ➤ To edit audio-for-video without affecting sync, stick with operations that don't affect overall length: use Replace rather than Insert, or Erase rather than Cut.

It's just a tiny bit more work to delete specific sounds in a sync track, or close up the gaps between words, without affecting sync after the edit. If we wanted to shorten the silence between "continuous sound" and "with constantly," we could mark both sides of the silence and then cut between the marks (Figure 8). That, obviously, also moves the "punctuated by brief pauses" phrase and could cause us to lose sync.

But if we want to close up those two words without affecting the overall length, we just need to add a third mark at the start of the next phrase.

1. Select between the second and third mark—the phrase that immediately follows the desired edit (Figure 9).

2. Use the program's Copy function instead of Cut.

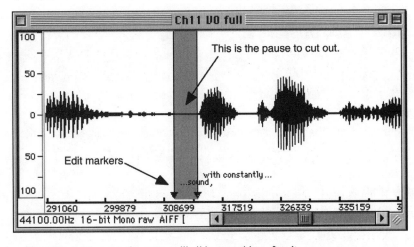

Figure 8: Cutting out the pause will slide everything after it.

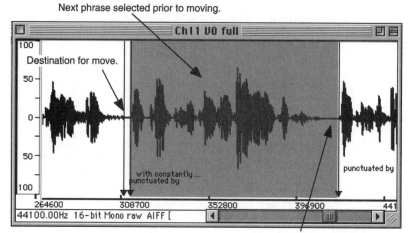

Figure 9: To preserve the sync of later elements, mark the next phrase and move it earlier.

3. Locate to the first mark—the beginning of the edit—and use the program's Replace or Paste Over function. This moves the phrase closer to the one that preceded it, closing up the words.

4. Check the end of the newly replaced region. If there was a long pause after the section you moved, it'll probably be fine. But if there wasn't much of a pause, you may hear the last syllables of the moved section twice. Erase the extra, or paste some room tone over it.

Some audio programs simplify steps 2 and 3 with a single "move" command.

Parallel Track Operations

Sometimes, it's handy to move an audio element from one track to another without changing when it occurs. NLEs make this easy: you can use the Razor or similar tool to cut into the clip, and then move it to the next track while staying aligned to the frame line. If you want to do the same thing in an audio-only program or workstation, you may need to plant a marker at the edit, and use the same marker both as the start of a Cut operation and the destination for a Replace.

Track splitting

If two people have dialog during the same shot, they might get picked up slightly differently because of the mic angle. A little equalization on just one of the characters can help. Rather than switching the processor in and out as they exchange lines, you can split their lines onto different tracks (Figure 10). Then it's a simple matter to apply the equalization to the entire track during the mix. This is also handy for special effects if you want to deepen or add echo to just one voice.

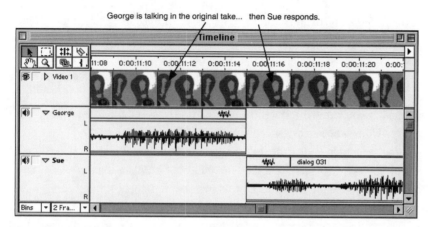

Figure 10: Splitting dialog into multiple tracks so you can process them differently

Be careful, when adding the processing, that there isn't too obvious a jump in any background as they exchange lines.

Switching between mics

Use a similar technique if a scene has been shot with both boom and lav. Put both mics on their own tracks in sync with picture. When you want to avoid a noise on the primary mic (clothing rustles on the lav, or off-mic sounds on the boom), use the Razor or similar tool to make cuts on both tracks on either side of the noise. Remove the noisy section of the primary mic's track, and everything up to the noise on the secondary mic's track.

Continue through the scene this way. When you reach the end, throw away the last segment on the secondary mic's track. Then apply whatever reverberation is necessary to make the lav match the boom (Chapter 14), touch up the equalization on one or the other track, and they should play back as a perfect noise-free whole.

Sync Problems

Lip sync sometimes drifts. Mouths will flap but their sounds will be slightly earlier or later, making everything seem like a badly dubbed foreign film.

Sync problems are often the result of setup errors in the editing system, either at the board or interrupt level within the editing computer or because blackburst signals aren't being properly used (Chapter 10). Sometimes these manifest themselves as problems in a rendered output but not during preview, or during long playbacks but not short ones. There are as many possible causes as there are systems, so you'll need a technician or manufacturer's support line to diagnose and fix the problem. But once it's solved, it should stay solved.

Sometimes sync problems are the result of user errors, such as forgetting to lock tracks together or setting the wrong timecode or reference standard. Some NLEs make certain operations, such as L-cuts, difficult and prone to error. If sync seems unstable, but you know the system is set up properly, check the manufacturer's FAQ or ask an editor who's experienced with your software.

If you're moving tracks from one program to another within the same computer, or exporting them as files to another computer but bringing them back before the final output, sync should stay accurate down to the sample level. The only times you'll encounter problems are if you're doing something that intentionally changes the file's length (editing it or changing the tempo), or a process adds or subtracts samples inadvertently (badly done sample rate conversion, redigitizing, or reclocking real-time digital audio).

Knowing the cause doesn't help much, however, if you've already lost sync.

Fixing sync

Lip sync can be a strange thing. Before you start sliding things around, verify that they're really out. A few techniques are helpful when checking lip sync:

- Give yourself the advantage of a large picture monitor and smooth movement. It's hard to detect lip sync on a 240 × 320 pixel screen, and almost impossible to spot it at 15 fps. Speaker placement also makes a difference: a speaker next to the picture monitor will always sound like it's in better sync than one on the other side of the room.

- Shuttle audio and video at about half speed. This is fast enough that you can understand the sound, while being slow enough to spot lip movements in the picture.

- Look for plosives that build up sound behind the lips (/b/ or /p/). The first frame where the lips are parted should exactly match the first frame of sound.

- Try changing things and see if they get better or worse. Move the audio a frame earlier and watch the sequence. If that doesn't immediately look better, move it two frames later (so it's now one frame later than it originally was). If *that* doesn't help either, the problem isn't lip sync.

These same techniques can be used for fixing sync. Slide things until they're better, staying aware that sometimes a whole track may require correction, although other times only a few clips will be out. Some performances and shooting situations result in soft or difficult-to-spot lip sync. If a scene seems to be out of sync, but nothing you do makes it look any better, shrug and hope for the best.

> ➤ It's always better to err on the side of the track being a frame late, rather than a frame early. In the real world it takes longer for sound to reach us than images.

Sometimes a track will start in sync and then slowly drift farther and farther out. This is almost always because sound and picture are playing at slightly different rates, usually because of a setup error. Check the program's or equipment's settings.

If that doesn't fix it, go to the end of the program and use some of the techniques above to see how far out of sync the track has gotten. Then convert the length of the program into frames. Take a calculator and divide the length of the program *plus* the error into the length of the program. Apply the result, as a percentage speed correction, to the track. This is a slightly Rube Goldberg–ish solution that doesn't address the original cause of the problem, but it works. And believe it or not, for a while one of the biggest names in NLE software was proposing it on their Web site as a workaround for a known sync problem in their software!

A Final Exercise

Okay. You've read this chapter, you've practiced with the examples, and you've gotten pretty good at this voice-cutting stuff. Here's a challenge:

Track 23 of this book's CD is a famous sound bite from the last U.S. president of the twentieth century. Using that short bite as the only source—and nothing from anything else he ever said—turn it around so he admits the very thing he's denying here.

Don't settle for just deleting the "not." If you swap a few phonemes, you can change the "have" to "had" . . . and "I did" to "I've." It'll be an impressive demonstration of editing prowess. (At least it was at the 1999 NAB Convention, when I did it for a live audience.)

Working with Music

Was *The Jazz Singer* the first Hollywood movie with a musical score?

Not by a decade. Long before Al Jolson's 1927 hit, producers were shipping full scores for orchestras to play live during their blockbusters. And these were considerably more inventive than the tinny piano you might associate with *Perils of Pauline.* For example, the theme song that ran for decades on the popular *Amos 'n Andy* show was originally written for D. W. Griffith's 1915 epic, *Birth of a Nation.*

And if you think the idea of using pop music to cross-promote a movie is a new invention, you're off by three quarters of a century. Early Hollywood moguls commissioned sheet music and radio hits just to remind people of the names of their pictures. This gave us "Ramona" and "Jeannine, I Dream of Lilac Time"—pop standards that can still be found in catalogs—along with such monstrosities as "Woman Disputed, I Love You" and "Red Man, Why Are You Blue?"[1]

The point is, music has always been an essential part of moving pictures. And it can be just as important to your video.

[1] Let us review the preceding two paragraphs: a movie about a Jew in blackface, another movie glorifying the Klan, an overtly racist radio show that held the nation's attention for decades, and some random offensiveness against women and Native Americans. I hope we made a tiny amount of social progress during the century.

Music can add the right seriousness, importance, or excitement to a presentation. It can tie a video together when the pictures don't match, or delineate sections when the topic changes. It can provide a driving rhythm for montages, or tug at the viewer's heart because . . . "we're a people company." A grand theme, sweeping to a conclusion, can even let a suffering audience know a too-long corporate epic is about to end . . . so they should start paying attention again. No matter what kind of video you're producing, chances are you can find effective, interesting music for it without breaking your budget or the copyright laws.

Deciding What Music You'll Need

You don't need a musical education or any particular instrumental chops to use music effectively. Many films and TV series are scored by people who can't even read musical note. What's needed is the ability to look at a script or roughcut, tell just what kind of music is needed, and then describe it in useful terms: your computer's keyboard is a lot more useful tool for this than a piano's.

A feature film's music director frequently hires someone else to write the themes, and many features even use the same production music libraries that are available for your video. If you want to use music effectively, you have to start thinking like a music director yourself. You can do it (even if your musical background is so limited you think MIDI is just French for midday). What's most important is your understanding of the emotional flow of the video. After that, it's just a question of listing the music and deciding where to get it.

Start, with spotting notes, even for something as simple as a wedding album or the CEOs annual Message to the Troops. Read down the script or watch a roughcut, and note what kind of music you need along with the page or time where it belongs (Figure 1). Write down what the music is trying to convey (words like "inspirational," or "building to a limitless future" are more helpful than "music under"), and anything that strikes you about the orchestration, tempo, or style. If you don't know a precise musical term, don't worry. "Fast" or "sweet" communicate just as well as their Italian equivalents. You can also make notes by referring to musical groups, specific songs, classical forms, or anything else that serves as a specific reminder. Even "like the stabbing in *Psycho*" is enough to get your point across. Include how long each piece will be on screen and any internal transitions.

This list is important even if you're the only one who'll be referring to it, or if you'll be pulling all the music yourself from a small library. Having it (or equivalent notes on the script itself) will save you a lot of time later.

Don't specify one long piece of music when two short ones will do. A composer of original music will usually work for a set fee based on how much music you need,

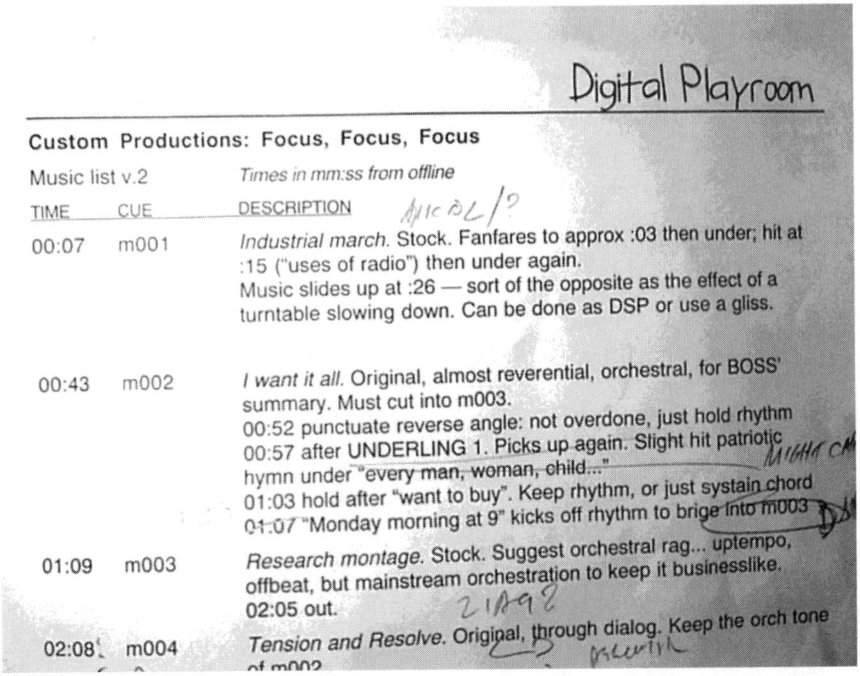

Digital Playroom

Custom Productions: Focus, Focus, Focus

Music list v.2 — *Times in mm:ss from offline*

TIME	CUE	DESCRIPTION
00:07	m001	*Industrial march.* Stock. Fanfares to approx :03 then under; hit at :15 ("uses of radio") then under again. Music slides up at :26 — sort of the opposite as the effect of a turntable slowing down. Can be done as DSP or use a gliss.
00:43	m002	*I want it all.* Original, almost reverential, orchestral, for BOSS' summary. Must cut into m003. 00:52 punctuate reverse angle: not overdone, just hold rhythm 00:57 after UNDERLING 1. Picks up again. Slight hit patriotic hymn under "every man, woman, child..." 01:03 hold after "want to buy". Keep rhythm, or just systain chord 01:07 "Monday morning at 9" kicks off rhythm to brige into m003
01:09	m003	*Research montage.* Stock. Suggest orchestral rag... uptempo, offbeat, but mainstream orchestration to keep it businesslike. 02:05 out.
02:08	m004	*Tension and Resolve.* Original, through dialog. Keep the orch tone of m002

Figure 1: A music spotting list. This one is very specific, since some of the cues will be composed to fit.

not how many individual melodies there are. If you're getting music from a library, you've probably either paid buyout fees or will be purchasing a blanket license that covers the entire show. So it doesn't cost extra to change the music according to the dynamics of the video. Give the viewer a break from time to time—put in a different piece, ~~or even si~~lence. Twenty minutes of the same music, endlessly repeated, isn't interesting even in elevators.

If you're listing multiple cues, indicate which should be related ("peaceful theme :45, based on earlier march #7") and which should sound different. Obviously, this will be a big help for a composer you hire. It also can be useful if you're getting stock music from a library, since some library cues are organized into suites of related themes.

Source Music

Source, or diegetic, music is part of the scene rather than the underscore (Chapter 4). But it's gathered during the scoring session and edited and mixed along with other music. So this is the time to also make notes on music that should be coming from on-screen performers or props like TV sets.

Sources of Music

Finding really great music isn't hard—all you need is time or money. Here are some ways to save both.

Original Music

The easiest (and most expensive) way to get music is to hire a composer. While John Williams[2] doesn't come cheap, you may find a Williams Wannabe at a local music school or recording studio. There's been an explosion of low-cost, high-quality musical and digital recording equipment over the last two decades, and a skilled musician can turn out a fully professional score without a major investment in facilities or session players. Good original scores can now be had for anywhere from a couple of hundred to just under a thousand dollars per finished minute, depending on the level of production required. Episodic TV dramas are often done on a contract basis for under ten thousand dollars per show.

A lot of composers maintain Web sites, and an Internet search for "original music" with "video" will turn up hundreds of qualified sites. Unfortunately, ownership of a Web site—even one with fancy graphics and a picture of a studio—is no guarantee of quality. Once you've found some likely candidates, you have to evaluate their work. Ask to hear some of their past scores, ideally both as excerpts from the finished videos that used their music and the unmixed music tracks as supplied to the producer. This not only gives you a handle on their musical abilities; it also lets you verify that they've actually done this kind of work before.

There are four things to listen for when evaluating a music demo:

- Was it composed well? Is the music appealing, does it match the mood of the video, and does it stay interesting for its entire length? If a piece is supposed to be something other than electronic instruments, does it sound real? Making artificial strings or horns sound real requires serious composing and arranging skill—you have to know what those instruments *should* be playing—as well as good production.

- Was it produced well? Play it in stereo on good speakers. Hum and pops, badly tuned instruments, and a lack of clarity in the mix are signs of amateur production. This can indicate the composer doesn't have real-world experience or lacks the necessary equipment to do a good job for you. If the music wasn't produced at all—if the composer is providing self-playing MIDI files—you're going to be saddled with the chore of turning them into usable music. It can be expensive to do this well.

---

[2]Neither the Hollywood composer nor the English classical guitarist.

- Was it performed well? Music software makes it easy to fake an acceptable performance by fixing wrong notes, evening out the tempo or dynamics, and even adding an artificial "human" randomness. But there's a big difference between acceptable and good performances, particularly in how expressively a line is played. Listen particularly to solos. Do you get a sense of a personality in the performance?

- Is the style of music appropriate for your project? I put this last both because it's probably the easiest for you to evaluate—you know what you like—but also because it can be the least important. An experienced professional with good scoring chops can usually master a number of styles and may have done the kind of music you're looking for even if it's not included on a demo.

Formerly Original Music

Stock music used to be a curse. When I started out, using a music library often meant you gave up quality to get economy and speed. Selections were heavily weighted toward small pop and dance bands because they were cheaper to produce, but that limited what could be written. Orchestras were small, unrehearsed, and frequently out of tune. The few good cuts that did exist tended to be overused—I've judged business film festivals where three entries had the same theme song. It took a highly skilled music editor to blend a few different pieces into something that sounded new. But despite its limitations, stock music was often the only option. We had a library of over a thousand stock LPs in my studio, before the business changed entirely.

Digital recording, computers and samplers[3] created the revolution. Composers could write and arrange full scores on their desktops, review and change what they'd written while listening to synthesized versions, and then walk into a studio and combine a few live players with better-quality synthesizers and sampled backup groups. Soon it wasn't even necessary to walk into a studio at all for some recordings; you could do the whole project in your living room. The overflow of desktop composers raised the standard for all library music. Bigger libraries started to concentrate on fuller sounds and more of the acoustic or vocal textures that couldn't be synthesized.

At the same time, the explosion of media—all those cable channels and high-end videos—meant a lot more original music was being created. The composers often retained the right to sell remixed or generic versions of their works to a library after a period of exclusivity passed.

---

[3]Instruments that play recordings of acoustic instruments—even choirs—from their keyboards while remaining responsive to subtleties in the playing style. Kurzweil made the first successful studio version, in the mid-1980s.

Bottom line: an explosion of good stock music, starting in the early 1990s. A lot of what you can get today is excellent. You'll hear it in national commercials, network programs, and Hollywood features. There's also a lot more music to choose from. The bigger houses release as many as a dozen new CDs a month, and a Web search will turn up more than a hundred small libraries. (Many of the smallest libraries are one-person operations. Their work can suffer from the same limitations as low-end original scoring, so you should evaluate their libraries with the same criteria.)

What was formerly a major difference between library and original music—precise fit to the picture—isn't as big a consideration any more. A good audio editor with a digital workstation can bend existing music tracks to hit picture as well as most of the classic Hollywood score. Even if you're a musical klutz, you can learn to cut music smoothly and accurately using just desktop audio or NLE software. I'll teach you later in this chapter.

Contact information for many music libraries appears in the tutorials section of my Web site, at www.dplay.com.

Paying for library music

Publishers make their money by selling the same recording over and over. You can buy the rights to use it in your project for a tiny fraction of the cost of an equivalent original piece. Another producer might buy the same song tomorrow, but the selections are so wide these days, and there are so many options for customizing music, that there's little chance a customer will recognize your corporate theme on a competitors' video.

Library music is sold two different ways. The rates depend both on how the publisher chooses to do business and how you plan to use the music, but they're surprisingly consistent within those two categories.

Needle-drop

The better libraries usually work on a needle-drop basis. The term comes from the original payment scheme, where a fee was charged each time a technician dropped the tone arm to dub from the record to a film for editing. A really good piece may be licensed thousands of times in its life, so publishers find it profitable to create quality product.

Needle-drop libraries charge minimal prices for their CDs—$12–$15 each—and will occasionally give or loan them to good customers. They make their money charging $60–$90 per song for a business video, up to $700 or so for unlimited use in broadcast media and productions for sale. Rates can be negotiable, depending on your standing with the publisher, and you don't pay anything other than the disk fee until you decide to use a particular piece.

These libraries also offer "production blankets"—you can use their entire catalog, in as many snippets as you want—based on the total length of your project. A blanket for a 10-minute corporate video may cost about $300, and typically buys about half a dozen different pieces. Blanket licenses from larger publishers may cost more because the music selection is wider. You can also buy annual blankets for some of the needle-drop libraries; they cover everything you produce for a prepaid annual fee. Prices vary widely depending on the size of the library and what media you produce for.

When you use a needle-drop selection, you're responsible for reporting the usage—including details about the song, the project, and the medium—to the publisher. They'll supply you with forms or an online site for this purpose, and most will accept a printout from production management software. Depending on your arrangement with them, they then send you an invoice or a license granting a nonexclusive right to use that music, forever, in that particular program.

Buyout

Many of the newer libraries sell their music on a buyout basis. You pay a relatively stiff price to purchase the CD, but have the right to use anything on it, in any of your productions. Prices vary but are usually between $75–$175, with substantial discounts for multidisc sales. Essentially, you're investing that you will use the songs on that CD enough times to justify the cost. As with any investment, you can get burned; there is absolutely no correlation between price and quality. The incentive is for a publisher to turn out as many CDs as possible, and unscrupulous or undercapitalized ones will tend to pad their discs with multiple edited or extra-long looped versions of the same piece—things you can do just as easily (and much more efficiently) on an NLE. Quite a few buyout cuts sound like they were ad-libbed by a single keyboard player, over loops that *they* bought from a sampling library.[4] On the other hand, some buyout libraries are incredible bargains. If you do a lot of video and don't need Hollywood production quality, this may be the right choice.

I recommend that you never purchase a buyout CD from a library you haven't worked with before, until you've had a chance to evaluate the actual discs. A five-minute demo may sound impressive as a montage, but it would be a shame to discover

---

[4]Yes, musicians also buy library music—CDs of prerecorded rhythm sections, playing short musical phrases, that they then use as backup elements for their own songs. The practice started with rap and popular dance music and has extended to video music producers as well.

there's only five minutes of usable music in the entire library. Reputable music houses will provide evaluation copies, on short-term loan, to reputable producers.

Performing rights societies

Most library music is covered by ASCAP or BMI, the major organizations who see that composers get compensated when their music is played on radio or TV. This absolutely doesn't mean that a TV station's annual ASCAP or BMI fee lets you use their music in productions you create, even if they're exclusively for that station.[5] The societies keep track of how each member's music is played on the air, so if you've been hired by a broadcaster, you might be required to assemble a list of what music you used, how long each piece is heard, who wrote and published it, and which society that publisher belongs to (Figure 2). For more details, check the societies' Web sites at www.ascap.com and www.bmi.com.

Digital Playroom

History Channel / "The Big Dig" (Tera Media) 48:00   JR# 4033

APPROX LENGTH	TITLE	COMPOSER	PUBLISHER
:30	Boston Patriots	Kelly Bryarly	Omnistyles (BMI)
1:00	Chiller	Steve Shapiro	Omnistyles (BMI)
1:30	Evening Concert	Mike Carubia	Franklin-Douglas (ASCAP)
3:30	Heritage Suite Finale	John Manchester	Franklin-Douglas (ASCAP)
1:30	Heritage Suite Opening	John Manchester	Franklin-Douglas (ASCAP)
2:30	Horse Country	John Manchester	Franklin-Douglas (ASCAP)
2:30	Killer Instinct	Brian Morris	Franklin-Douglas (ASCAP)
:45	Opec Summit	Derek Richards	Franklin-Douglas (ASCAP)
1:00	Opening Day	Vic Sepanski	Franklin-Douglas (ASCAP)
:45	Opening Night	Doug Wood	Franklin-Douglas (ASCAP)

Figure 2: Information a broadcaster might require for reporting usage to ASCAP and BMI

---

[5]A client or station manager may attempt to convince you that it does, and that it's perfectly legal to use anything you want without paying additional fees. This just isn't true, as has been tested in court many times. The annual ASCAP and BMI fees pay the composers for playing their songs on the air as entertainment. Any copying or editing of a particular recording into a video, or using it as a background for something else, is specifically not covered.

The rights societies have been attempting to define Web sites and other new media as public performances. This may be an issue if your video is included somewhere as streaming media.

Using Commercial Recordings

As a producer, what are your rights regarding music from CDs you buy at a record store? Like the cops say, "You have the right to remain silent." Only three choices are guaranteed to keep you out of trouble: compose and perform the music yourself, get permission from the people who did, or don't use the music.

Copyright is a fact of life.

- Virtually any use of a music recording in any video, for any purpose other than your own personal entertainment in your home, requires written permission.

- It doesn't matter whether you work for a charitable or educational institution, have no budget, don't charge admission, or even intend the piece to promote the musician. You need permission.

- It doesn't matter whether the song is classical or in the public domain—if the performance is on CD, it's almost certainly protected by copyright. You need permission.

- It doesn't matter if you used less than eight bars: brevity was never a reliable defense in copyright cases and was specifically eliminated by Congress a quarter century ago. You need permission.

- It doesn't matter if you claim the wedding videographer's defense that "My clients will buy a copy of the CD, and I'll use that copy in the wedding album I produce." They may be a lovely couple, but when they bought the disc they didn't buy the right to synchronize it. You need permission.

Get the message? The doctrine of "fair use" has very limited application. Unless you're quoting a brief selection in a legitimate critical review of the performance, it probably doesn't apply. Check with a lawyer before making any assumptions about it.

You *can* assume any music written after the first two decades of the 20th century is under copyright, and recent changes in the copyright laws will protect newer pieces a lot longer. Classical works and pop standards may be old enough for their copyrights to have expired, but newer editions and arrangements are still protected. But even if you stick to 17th century Baroque composers, the recording of the performance itself is probably protected. Look for the sound-recording copyright symbol, the letter *P* in a circle, somewhere on the disc or label. Publishers and record labels have large and hungry business departments, and they almost always win in court. Sometimes they even pay their composers and performers, which is the whole point of the exercise.

It's entirely possible you'll sneak under the publishers' radar. Despite urban legends about lawyers coming after Boy Scouts for singing protected songs at a campfire, many casual uses are never spotted by the copyright owners. But that doesn't make it legal, and it doesn't reduce their right to come after you in the future.

The perils of pop

Even if you're not afraid of lawyers or bad karma, it's probably not a good idea to use a piece of current pop music under a video. Music is a powerful associative tool, and psychologists have found that people will pay more attention to the tune already know, from the radio—and think about what happened last time they heard it—than to the new information in your video. The reason national advertisers can get away with using rock classics in their spots is that they run their ads so many times that their message starts to overpower the memories. (And of course, they've gotten permission.)

But if you honestly believe a commercial recording might be appropriate for your project, don't be afraid to ask if you can use it. Record company promotion departments can be surprisingly generous at times—particularly if good causes are involved—and I've been able to get the rights to use sections of a Beatles song in a promo for PBS, and a recording of Leonard Bernstein conducting the New York Philharmonic in a documentary for a music school, for free. Even if the cause is less than noble, you may be able to secure limited-audience rights for a reasonable amount. It doesn't hurt to ask.

If it turns out that rights to a commercial recording aren't available or are too expensive, many music libraries have a good selection of "soundalikes" you can use at their regular rates. These won't sound *exactly* like the original recording—that could also be a violation of copyright—but are close enough to get the message across. If you want to make your own recording of a popular song, you can get clearance through the Harry Fox Agency, the licensing arm of the National Music Publishers' Association, at www.nmpa.org/hfa.html.

Sources for source music

Some of the music libraries have excellent collections of contemporary and new recordings of generic "era" music—such as big-band, swing, or classic rock—designed to be coming from on-screen radios and TVs. If you want an authentic older style, perhaps because your characters are watching an old movie or documentary, check the archive sections of the larger needle-drop houses. Some of those companies were around in the 1940s and 1950s and will license you the same music on CD that they sold on 78s back then. They may also have appropriate music for elevators and supermarkets; between the 1950s and 1970s, some background music services bought from the same sources . . . and I wouldn't be surprised if those same tapes are still in use today.

A few of the buyout libraries have vocal cuts with the same musical and production values as current pop styles. They probably *were* failed pop songs that the composer is trying to recoup some investment from, but we don't care.

Needle-drop libraries are frequently very good with solo piano, jazz combo, and big band sounds for a restaurant or club. But on-screen small rock groups for a club or dance can be problematic; most library music is too well performed, or has too much of a studio sound, to be convincing. Ask the library if they have any demo or scratch tracks they'd be willing to license . . . or find a local band, and ask if they have any tapes of live performances of their original music you can use.

It almost always helps to start in the middle of a source cue, rather than at the front. Unless your characters are psychic, they won't be able to turn on their radios at the start of a song or walk into a club at the precise beginning of a set.

Source music always needs equalization and reverb—often with drastic settings—to make it match the ambience of a scene (see Chapter 14).

Mix and Match

You can use Hollywood's trick of mixing original and library music in your own limited-budget video, hiring a composer for specialty pieces but blending them with stock elements where it will save money. For a 10-minute humorous film about advertising, I needed (and couldn't afford) an almost continuous score. Parts of it had to be precisely timed to on-screen actions and specific words of the script but could have the sound of a small group or sampled chamber orchestra. Other cues required a full orchestra or styles of playing that are difficult to synthesize. Still others were just to set a background or location and could be easily found in a library.

We created a spotting list (part of it is shown in Figure 1) detailing 25 different musical elements ranging from a few seconds' length to slightly less than a minute. Each was designed for a particular part of the video. Then we selected 18 of the cues from a good needle-drop library and made sure they could be edited to fit picture. Finally I gave those cues and the spotting notes to a local composer, along with reference video. She wrote and recorded the other pieces, fitting precise word or visual cues. She didn't have to charge us for 10 minutes of original music, but—since she was using the library cuts as a guide—her pieces blended with the others into a seamless whole.

Non-CD libraries

Some libraries are sold as CD-ROM, allegedly because that medium is "computer-ready" or because they can offer 48 kHz sampling for "better-than-CD" sound. This is hype. Any desktop computer can be equipped to pull sound digitally, as a file, from standard audio CDs with absolutely no quality loss. And unless a 48 kHz sampled recording is both created and played back on high-end studio equipment, there won't be any audible difference between it and a 44.1 kHz CD. In fact, the predigitized music and effects CD-ROMs I've seen at computer stores sound like they were recorded through generic sound cards with no studio production . . . sort of "worse-than-CD" sound.

CD-ROM can be useful if you need a lot of music on a single disk, recorded in mono or at lower sample rates. They sometimes include a utility to rearrange intros and verses at will, or to automatically edit a cue to a specific length. These utilities can get fairly elaborate and may be sold as stand-alone self-editing programs to use with specially encoded CDs. The music included with them is usually of average buyout quality—nothing particularly creative, but nothing disgusting—so you may consider using this scheme as your sole music source. The disadvantage is there's only a limited selection of music that's been encoded to work with any particular self-editing program. Music editing isn't difficult once you've been shown the basic principles (that's the second half of this chapter), so I'm not convinced these programs are a wonderful investment.

Some libraries are distributed via the Internet. You make your selection from a Web page, listening to low-resolution samples, and then purchase the cut online. It's downloaded to you as a compressed file. This is lossy compression (Chapter 2), so the cue will never sound as good as a CD recording. But if the compression is done well, and isn't more radical than 12:1 or so (about 850 kilobytes per stereo minute), the quality should be perfectly usable. And it's hard to beat the 24-hour accessibility of an online library.

You may also consider buying music as MIDI files (see sidebar). These can be cheaper and a lot more flexible to edit, but the burden is on you to turn them into usable music tracks for a video. You'll need additional software, equipment, and musical skills. But if you know what you're doing, you can create acceptable tracks—certainly as good as the basic buyout libraries.

What's this MIDI?

MIDI (Musical Instrument Digital Interface) is actually a local area network (LAN) standardized by synthesizer manufacturers in the early 1980s. It works like other LANs in that messages are constantly flowing across the network, and each node pays attention only to the ones that are addressed to it. Unlike Ethernet, the networks are wired in a daisy chain—computer to synth A, synth A to synth B—rather than with a common hub. Cables use two conductors of a five-pin DIN connector and carry messages in one direction only.

The messages themselves are primarily musical instructions: *Play middle C, turn C off and play the E above it,* and so on. Obviously, enough messages equals a tune. Other MIDI messages may control volume, pitchbend, continuous pressure on sustained notes, what sound is assigned to each address (such as *piano on channel one, trumpet on channel two*), and special messages reserved by the manufacturer. Since MIDI is so ubiquitous a network standard, various manufacturers have also adopted it to control tape decks or processors, or to pass text messages.

Addressing can get convoluted. The original MIDI specification called for only 16 unique addresses, called "channels." Today's synths make different sounds simultaneously, and each may need up to a dozen channels to sort them out. This doesn't leave many for the next instrument down the line. On the other hand, multiple synths may be assigned to the same channel, so they respond to the same commands and thicken the sound.

For this reason, many MIDI music studios use multiple networks. MIDI interfaces connect each of the controlling computer's serial ports to as many as eight separate networks, called "cables." A computer with two serial ports can then control up to 16 simultaneous sounds on each of 16 cables. Sequencer programs control what messages are sent and try to keep track of overall timing . . . but this can be a problem in fast passages with lots of instruments, when the number of simultaneous musical messages exceeds MIDI's low-speed data capability.

The programs can also edit melodies, create their own harmony or rhythmic variations, and even print sheet music. Computer MIDI files follow a standard format, so files can be imported by different programs to play approximately the same song. Since they represent just the note commands, rather than digital audio, they can be quite compact: A MIDI version of a 60-second clip theme might need only 16 kilobytes, whereas a CD-quality recording of that same theme, played on the same synths, would eat more than 10 meg. Of course, the CD version can also include hot session players, studio mixing effects, and human vocals—all impossible to encode in a MIDI file. It also doesn't need a rack full of equipment and serious production expertise to get the best sounds.

Selecting Music from a Library

Grab your notes, the script, and—if possible—the rough video edit, narration tracks, or anything else that will have to work with the music. Then head for the library.

If your facility doesn't have its own selection of discs, check larger local recording or video houses; you can probably rent time in their libraries. Bigger music publishers often have offices in major production cities, with expert librarians on tap; they charge only a nominal amount for this service because it helps them sell licenses.

Obviously, you'll want to listen to the songs you're considering. (Maybe it isn't obvious. Some libraries expect you to select—and pay for—cuts based on their text descriptions. Avoid them.) But before you listen, look at the discs. The titles won't tell you much—*Our Wedding* could be Mendelssohn or Wagner, a medley of waltzes, or even slapstick—but the descriptions can be useful. The better libraries use wordings like *brooding strings; panic stabs at :19 and :23*. Some more marginal libraries describe everything as *Great! The perfect music for financial, high tech, extreme sports, and retail* . . . uh-huh.

Check the composer, too. Bigger libraries have stables of freelancers with different styles. Two or three pieces by the same composer, even if they're on different discs, might fit perfectly as a suite. You may also find yourself enjoying the style of one particular composer and look specifically for that name.

Then start listening, and make notes on which music is best for each place in your video. A few publishers also have automated listening lines; you can punch in numbers from their catalog and hear cues by phone, or search a similar service and listen to low-resolution samples from a Web site. Midsized libraries often have searchable CD-ROM databases of their entire catalog, including excerpts from each cut (Figure 3). These are a valuable time-saver. But no matter how you're listening, turn off the sound the moment you've gotten a feel for a potentially usable cut, and make some notes.

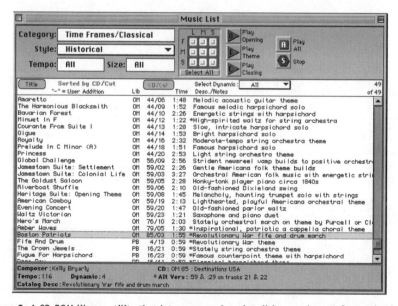

Figure 3: A CD-ROM library utility that lets you search and audition music cues from a database. This one is from Omnimusic.

Not listening is an important part of choosing music. Use the pause control a lot, and take frequent breaks. Human brains turn to oatmeal after extended library music sessions—remember, most of this is music that was never designed to be in the foreground—so stop the music every 15 minutes or so, and do something else. This will make it easier to distinguish and evaluate individual pieces.

Selective listening is an important part of the process as well. The melody of a library cut often starts some 10 seconds after the intro, but there may be variations later on. If you think a piece has some merit but you don't like precisely what you're hearing, skip forward and listen for the texture to change. Include, in your notes, what parts you liked and which you'd rather avoid.

Once you've got a short list, go back and explore those pieces again. Mix the voice with music while you're listening, or play the cut while you watch video. If you don't have a mixer in the music library, put the narration on a boombox next to the CD player. Or make copies of your potential selections, and bring them back into the NLE or video suite for previewing. It's important to try the music under real circumstances.

➤ When you think you've found the right music, keep playing the video or announcer and turn the music off. You should immediately feel, in your gut, that something's missing. If you don't, the music isn't contributing anything to the project.

Don't worry too much about synchronizing specific hits or meeting a particular length while you're auditioning. You'll be able to do all that when you edit.

No matter what you do, don't forget that music is an artistic element. No set of rules, catalog descriptions, or software can replace your best directorial judgment. Don't be afraid to go against type—I once scored a PBS documentary about jogging by using Bach fugues—and don't be afraid to make a statement. (Just be sure it's the same statement your client wants to make.)

Music Editing

No book will ever turn me into a truly good video editor. I lack the visual design skills. But over the years I've learned some rules of thumb (cut on motion, respect the axis . . . oh, *you* know) to make my rare video sessions a less painful experience. It's the same thing with music editing. Unless you're born with musical sensibilities and have learned how chords and beats go together to make a song, you'll never be a truly gifted music cutter.

But most of the time, what makes bad music editing not work has nothing to do with chords or melody. It's simply a broken rhythm. Every mainstream piece of music since the late Renaissance has a constant heartbeat, with accents in a regular pattern. The tempo can change, or different beats might get accented, but only according to specific rules. We learn those rules subconsciously, starting with the first lullaby our mothers sing us. If an edit breaks a rule, we know something is wrong . . . even if we don't know precisely what.

On the other hand, the rules about that heartbeat are simple. You can learn how to deal with it even if you can't carry a tune in a boombox. Use some simple techniques, and you'll soon be cutting like a pro . . . and making generic library pieces fit like a custom score.

Learn to Trust Your Ears

The first step is to forget what you've been told about looking at waveforms. Music editing requires knowing exactly where the heartbeat starts, and there's nothing in a visual waveform—no matter how tightly you zoom in—guaranteed to tell you where it is. All you'll ever find by eye is where the drums are hit loudest, and that may or may not be related to the start of a rhythmic phrase (in most rock and pop music, it isn't). Besides, if you're cutting orchestral music, there aren't any drum hits. If you're cutting salsa, there are too many (Figure 4). Remember: all sound exists as changes of pressure over time. The best way to experience it is by taking time, not by looking at a snapshot.

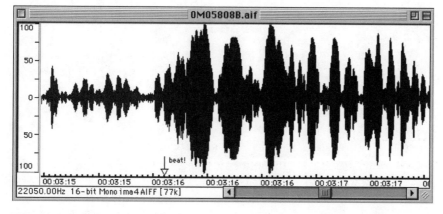

Figure 4: Beat it! You'd never find this downbeat by eye. I marked it for you, but only after listening to the music in real time.

Learn to Count

The most important technique is to learn to count along while you listen. Once you can count in rhythm, you'll be able to mark edits quickly and accurately on the fly . . . without bothering to redraw a screen. In fact, you can apply the same editing technique to computers that don't have particularly accurate zooms, or even nonvisual systems like Mini-Disc and CMX-style edit controllers.

Most of the music you'll ever use—or hear—is made up of evenly spaced beats organized into groups. Usually there are four of them in a group, though occasionally there may be two, three, or six.[6] We'll cover those other numbers later. For now, let's stick to four.

Four beats make up a *bar* or *measure*. There is always a strong emphasis on the first beat of the bar, and a slightly weaker one on the third. This four-beat pattern keeps on ticking no matter what the melody or lyrics are doing, though most melodies are based on groups of four or eight of these bars. The pattern can change tempo, speeding up or slowing down, but it does so smoothly or without breaking the pattern.

> ➤ If you don't respect the four-beat pattern, your music edits will probably sound wrong. If you do respect it, there's a good chance the chords and melody will fall into place.

The trick is to learn to count those four beats at the same time you're deciding where to edit. It isn't hard. All you need is enough eye-hand coordination to tap your edit system's marking buttons at the right time. It's like dancing with your fingers instead of your feet.

We'll learn how with a little Stephen Foster ditty. Everybody sing! *Camptown ladies sing this song, Doo-dah! Doo-dah! Camptown racetrack five miles long, oh the doo-dah-day!*

While you're singing, tap your finger along with the beat. Short syllables get one tap each. "Song" is held twice as long, so it gets two taps. The "Dahs" are held longest of all, three taps. If we print a dot for each finger tap, it looks like Figure 5. Notice how no matter what the words are doing, the dots are evenly spaced. The tapping should have a similarly constant rhythm.

---

[6]And sometimes five, seven, or other numbers, but those are extremely rare in production music. Once you master the more common four-beat system, you'll find this oddly counted music easier to edit.

Figure 5: "Camptown Ladies," with one dot per beat

Figure 6: The same song, counting 1–4 with the beat

Now sing it again, but this time count from one to four while you're tapping. (If you can't sing, tap, and count at the same time, recruit a friend to sing for you.) The loudest syllable will always be "one," like in Figure 6.

We're using "Camptown Ladies" because almost everybody knows it.[7] Think about the pattern of stresses in the lyric: the strongest syllables in the first line are *Camp, sing,* and the two *Doos* on one. The next strongest are *Lad* and *song* on three. This 1-3 stress pattern holds for almost every song in the most common time signatures. ("Camptown" was actually written in 2/4 time, but you can still count it in fours.) Practice counting along with songs on the radio, and it'll become second nature.

The "one" in each count is the downbeat. It's called that because if you're conducting an orchestra playing the song, this is the only time in each measure that your hand moves in a downward direction. (The movements of a conductor's hand follow a centuries-old tradition. There's a specific direction for each beat of the measure, depending on how many beats there are overall. Experienced music editors often conduct their audio workstations while they're playing a cue, following the same hand patterns, so they can feel the metric structure instead of having to count it.)

Listen for the accented syllables of any melody. These aren't necessarily the loudest drum hits; pop styles often accent the second and fourth beats of each measure, to make them more danceable. (If you want to sing "Camptown" in a hoedown style, clap your hands on 2 and 4. Try it!) Don't be fooled by the drummer on these backbeats; it's just rhythmic embellishment. If you sing along with the melody, you'll always be able to find the downbeat.

Some songs don't start on their loudest syllable, so you have to start counting on a different number. Others can have a few short notes sharing a beat. Figure 7 is another Stephen Foster song to illustrate both situations. The "Oh I" shares one

---

[7] . . . and it's in the public domain. We're not using anybody else's performance, so no permission is necessary.

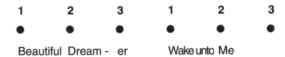

4	1	2	3	4	1	2	3	4	1	2	3	4	1	2	3
•	•	•	•	•	•	•	•	•	•	•	•	•	•	•	•

Oh I come from Al- a- bam- a   with my ban- jo on my knee

Figure 7: This song starts on the number 4, with two syllables sharing that beat.

1	2	3	1	2	3
•	•	•	•	•	•

Beautiful Dream - er   Wake unto Me

Figure 8: This song uses patterns of three syllables, within three beats to a measure.

beat. The syllables "come" and "bam" are much louder than any others around them, so they get the number 1.

A few songs move in threes instead of fours. The principle's the same, as you can see in Figure 8. The three fast syllables in "Beautiful" occupy just one count—the same way that "Dream" does. "Beau" and "Wake" are definitely the accented syllables and get the 1.

Cutting by Counting

Once you've learned to count accurately with the music, the editing part is simple. All you have to do is match the numbers. Start by loading track 24 of the book's CD into your editing system. This is one of a number of pieces written specifically for this book by Doug Wood, president of the Omnimusic Library,[8] and it's designed to be typical of the kind of straight corporate or documentary theme you'd find in most libraries. It counts in 4.

If you're using a desktop NLE, follow the steps below. If you've got a different kind of system, the procedure will be only slightly different. Read along through these instructions, and we'll cover the differences later.

- Open the music in a clip window, start playing it, and count along. You might want to play it a few times before proceeding to get used to the tempo.

- Start tapping the marking button very lightly on each count. When you get to each "one," tap hard enough to actually make a mark. Depending on your system, you might then have to switch to a different button to mark the next "one" without erasing the first. When you're done, you should have a bunch of marks looking something like the gray flags in Figure 9.

---

[8]And, of course, protected by copyright. But you can license similar pieces—as well as a lot more—from Omnimusic (www.omnimusic.com).

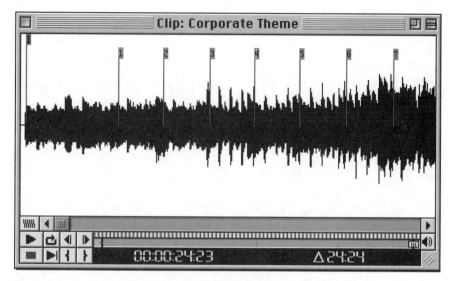

Figure 9: Tap hard enough to make a mark each time you count the number 1.

Copy the clip to a timeline, and you're ready to edit. If you want to shorten the piece, cut out the space between two marks and butt the pieces together. In Figure 10, we cut from Marker 2 to Marker 4, pulling out about three seconds. (Because of the way chords flow in most music, it usually sounds better to cut from an even number to another even one, or from an odd number to another odd one.) If we wanted to extend the music, we could have taken that stretch between Marker 2 and Marker 4 and laid it into the timeline twice.

This is a very short edit—there's only about three seconds between the markers—but the technique works for edits of any length. If you need to edit longer stretches of music, make the marks farther apart . . . say, every fourth "one."

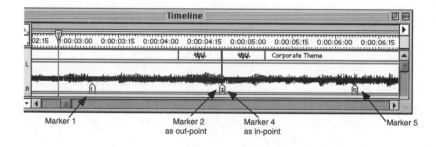

Figure 10: Shortening a cue by cutting from one numbered mark to another

Editing off the marks

As you listen through the sample corporate piece on the CD, notice how the horn melody begins around 12 seconds in. It actually starts on a "4," one beat ahead of the downbeat. But you'll still use those markers you made to cut the song accurately, and start that melody anywhere you want.

- Move the entire clip to one track of the timeline. Play through it, and notice the marker number *just after* you'd like the melody to start. For the sake of this example, we'll say it's Marker 3.

- Go back to the clip, and notice which marker occurs just after the melody's actual start. If your clip looks like our Figure 9, it'll be Marker 7. Slide the clip onto another track, lining up Marker 7 against Marker 3 (as in Figure 11). In most editing programs, you can temporarily call Marker 7 the in-point, and it'll align itself against the other marker automatically. Then slide the in-point forward to include the start of the melody.

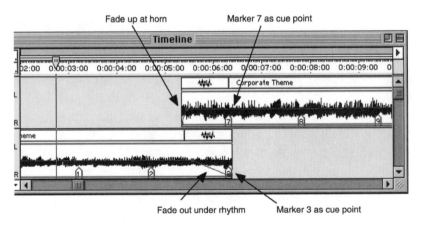

Figure 11: An edit can be before or after a marker, but the markers still have to line up.

In Figure 11, we built the edit on two tracks and added a quick fade up to make the entrance of the horn melody smoother. But you can do a similar edit on a single track, making a butt cut from one marker to the other, and then rolling the edit point forward to pick up the melody. The important thing is that, no matter where you make the edit, you still preserve that constant heartbeat—the length of time from one downbeat to the next has to stay the same.

When it doesn't sound good . . .

If you hear a little hiccup at the edit, chances are you didn't mark the downbeat accurately. This is usually because you were too conscious of tapping the marking button and stiffened your hand up slightly when it was time to press. Editing is like a lot of other physical activities: it helps to stay loose and relaxed. Practice counting aloud as you make the lighter and heavier taps.

If you want to verify that you've made the marks accurately, put copies of the clip on two adjacent tracks, with the first marker on one track lined up to a later marker on the other. Play them both simultaneously: if the marks were correct, you won't hear any stuttering in the drums.

Practice counting along with the beat while you're reviewing an edit as well. If the edit is accurate, your "one" should line up perfectly before and after the cut. If you have to adjust slightly while you're counting, one or both of the edit points were off the beat.

An edit can also sound odd because the chords or melody doesn't match. (This is more likely to occur when the song is strung out along two simultaneous tracks, like Figure 11.) Try moving one of the points an odd number of measures earlier or later. For example, if you cut Marker 3 to Marker 6 and don't like the result, you may have much better luck coming in on Marker 5, 7, or 9.

As you cut more music, you'll develop a better feel for how chords change and melodies develop, and you'll have fewer awkward edits. But don't expect to ever outgrow the idea of counting along with the rhythm. It's one of the most powerful techniques you can use.

Adapting to other systems

If your system edits sound by cutting or pasting sections, the process is very similar. Plant markers on the downbeats, then stop the playback and select an area from one marker to another. Use the cut command if you want to shorten the cue. If you want to lengthen it, use the copy command. Then place the insertion point on another marker, and paste.

If you're using a traditional multimachine online editor with in- and out-points, you just have to mark more carefully. Copy the first part of the cue, at least past the edit point, onto the master tape. Play it back, tapping the Record-in button on down-beats, until you mark the desired record-in point. Now play back the source tape, marking the source-in the same way. Preview the edit and the beat should be constant. Then if you want, multitrim to pick up the melody.

More practice

Not every cue is going to be as straightforward as our corporate theme. Here are two more selections for you to practice on, also both written by Doug Wood.[9]

Track 25 is a jazzier piece that counts in 4, with a syncopated melody and drum tracks that seldom line up with the downbeat. But when you mark those downbeats, the marks should have perfectly even spacing; while the melody is all over the place, the tempo never changes (Figure 12). The edit technique that worked for the straighter corporate piece—lining up downbeats and then sliding the edit to catch a piece of melody—is just as applicable here.

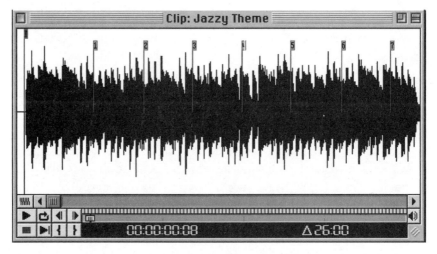

Figure 12: A more syncopated piece. The downbeats are regular, even though the drums and melody aren't.

Track 26 is a waltz played on a string orchestra. You have to count it in threes, rather than fours, but the principle is the same and the downbeats just as regular (Figure 13). Since the melody starts ahead of the beat, the best way to edit this is on multiple tracks (Figure 14); I left track B extended up to Marker 5 so you could see how the markers still line up.

Strings, particularly when played in echoey halls, can take a moment to build up their sound. Since the notes change slowly compared to other instruments, butt cuts—even when on the right beat—can sound abrupt. The best solution is often

---

[9]Once again, remember this music is protected by copyright. You have permission to copy the music to practice editing techniques, but you must contact Omnimusic if you want to use it in a production

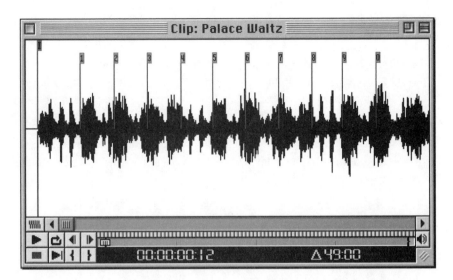

Figure 13: Shall we waltz? You can see how the melody is ahead of most downbeats. If you look between Markers 4 and 5, and between 8 and 9, you can see the definite one-two-three structure.

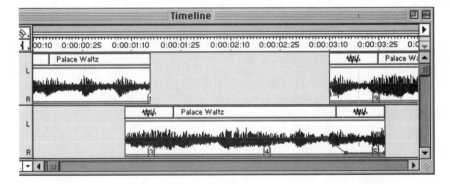

Figure 14: Strings usually do best with quick overlaps.

to overlap the start of one note with the end of another (as in the first edit of Figure 14) or do a quick cross-fade (as in the second edit of that figure). Note the time ruler: neither overlap is longer than a quarter second.

Matching Picture

Once you get comfortable editing this way, each individual cut will take very little time to execute. Then you'll be ready to create custom scores, adding or subtracting measures so that musical climaxes and changes match changes in the video. A few things will help you achieve that perfect marriage of music and picture:

- If a downbeat is almost lined up with an important visual cue, try shifting the entire music track a few frames. The earlier edits may still appear to be in sync after they've been moved slightly, and it'll be easier to catch that golden moment.

- Don't be afraid to speed up or slow down the entire piece slightly, even if it means changing the pitch. Acoustic tracks can be shifted about 3% faster or slower before their timbre sounds wrong, but electronic ones can be shifted as much as 10% and still sound reasonable.

- If your software can change the tempo without affecting the pitch, you can do more radical manipulation—as much as 20% either way on a good audio work-station. You can also change the tempo for just part of a cue, or squeeze or stretch only a couple of bars to fit a video sequence, if the pitch doesn't change.

- If a piece has prominent drums, don't worry about matching the video perfectly. Add a matching drum sound effect on a different track, to sound as if the drummer was deliberately playing ahead of or behind the beat to match picture. This works with orchestral percussion as well as with jazz and rock.

A final tip

Reverberation can cause problems with sound pickup when you're shooting, but it's great stuff to have when you're editing music. A little reverb, faded up right before a cut and out right after, can make up for sounds that got lost because they extended over the barline. And if you have to fade the end of a piece quickly to match a visual fade, a little reverb can help make it sound like the musicians stopped playing on cue.

CHAPTER 13

Sound Effects

R O S E ' S   R U L E S

⇨ They're called sound *effects*, not sound reality, because they seldom follow real-world rules.

⇨ Sound effects can be the lowest-cost way to add a professional flavor to your video. But, like any other seasoning, it doesn't make sense to add them until the other ingredients are in.

We Don't Need No Stinkin' Reality

Just like music, sound effects have been a part of movies since the earliest silent blockbusters. Theater organs often included a "toy counter"—bells, bird whistles, ratchets, gun shots, and anything else that could be rigged to an organ key, designed to add convincing realism to a film. Of course, realism has more to do with convention than reality. While it's tempting to laugh at early audiences being thrilled by bird whistles accompanying grainy black-and-white panoramas, today's practices aren't much more realistic.

For example, when Gene Roddenberry first tested the opening of *Star Trek*[1] in the late 1960s, the Enterprise didn't make a sound as it flew past the camera. Space is a vacuum as well as a final frontier, so there couldn't be any noise out there. But

---

[1]The original TV series, also known as *Star Trek: Who Knew It Would Become a Dynasty?*

by the time the series got to television, the ship's engines had a satisfying *woosh*. Roddenberry rewrote the laws of physics to make a scale-model spaceship more exciting. Today, Hollywood rockets scream by in digital surround . . . but the sound isn't any more realistic than those original organ key gunshots.

In Hollywood, reality means, "If you can see it, you must hear it." Feature films have teams of sound editors, often spending a week on effects for each 10-minute reel. Everything is foleyed or has effects cut to it, and sound effects supervisors will walk into a mix with synchronized tracks for every rustling leaf and buzzing fly in a scene, not to mention the sounds of fantasy light swords and laser bombs. It's overkill—many of these sounds never make it to the final track—but still follows the "see it, hear it" rule.

Your video's budget may be more modest, but properly chosen and applied sound effects can add realism to stock footage or scenes shot on a limited set. They can heighten drama, provide comic relief, and command attention. A good stereo ambience, played through properly placed speakers, can even capture the space around a video screen or kiosk and isolate the user. The trick is planning how to use effects most efficiently. Unless you've got the resources to edit a specific effect for every leaf rustle and fly buzz, it makes sense to concentrate on the ones that'll make a difference.

In fact, the first step in creating a good effects track is to ignore it. Concentrate on the dialog and the music first. A lot of times, scenes that were crying out for effects will be completely covered by the score.

Pioneer sound designer Tony Schwartz once said, sound effects are a waste of time. According to him, those random footsteps and rattles can never sound like real life. They get in the way more than they help. He prefers *effective sounds*—noises that might be unrelated to the story line, but trigger the audience's own memories. I work in a slightly more commercial atmosphere than Dr. Schwartz, with more conventional clients, but I've found his rule to be more valid than Hollywood's "see it, hear it":

The only important characteristic of a sound effect is how it makes the viewer feel. It doesn't matter where you get it,[2] what the label said, or what frames it's applied to. If an effect feels right, it *is* right. If not, change or lose it.

---

[2]Assuming a healthy respect for copyright, of course.

Choosing sound effects can be a much more casual process than choosing music. Music selection usually involves a separate auditioning session, so you can concentrate on individual cues and select them without the distractions of trying to edit them together. It's usually most efficient to grab sound effects as you need them. That's because sound effects aren't presented as an abstraction. Until you've placed one against picture, you can't tell if it's going to work. And if you're going to that trouble, you might as well edit it accurately and move on to the next effect.

It may not be possible to do your sound effects spotting, auditioning, and editing at the same time. If you don't already have a sound effects library, you'll have to record sounds specially or get them from an outside source. You'll need to plan the effects, make a list, audition them at a library or over the Web, assemble the source material, and then cut it into the show—exactly the same process you'd follow for music. But believe me, it's a lot better if you start building your own effects library from the very first project. Get a couple of general-purpose CDs for the most common effects. Any time you have to record or buy a specific sound, make a digital dub for the library. Keep a database (Figure 1), and you'll be amazed how quickly that library grows. The extra effort will pay off with every new project that needs effects.

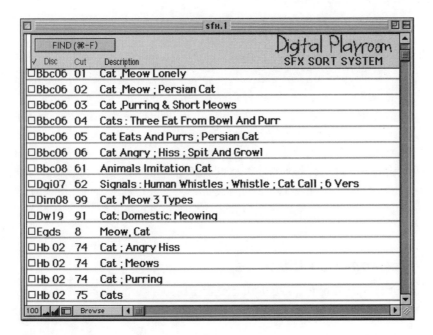

Figure 1: Keep a database because your library will grow quickly.

Sources for Sound Effects

Although audio professionals spend thousands of dollars on immense sound collections on audio CDs or networked hard drives, it's easy to start more modestly. In fact, you already have: the example sound effects on this book's CD can be used in your productions, courtesy of The Hollywood Edge.

You can add about a hundred more effects to your library for free by requesting Hollywood Edge's sound effects demo. Along with a short sales pitch, this CD includes separately indexed effects and the right to use them in productions. It's an odd mix—everything from jungle ambiences to cartoon boings to alcoholics on a street corner—but the effects are clean, well recorded, and absolutely usable. (It's also a good marketing ploy. The CD is an introduction to Hollywood Edge's excellent commercial libraries, and I've bought many of their pro CDs based on it.)

If you're a legitimate producer or potential customer, contact them for a copy: 800/292-3755 or 323/603-3252, or www.hollywoodedge.com.[3]

Where Not to Get Effects

You may find sound effects CDs at a record store, at normal retail prices. They might not be a bargain.

In 1978, U.S. law was changed to allow copyrights on sound effects. Prior to that, you could get a pre-recorded effect almost anywhere and use it with impunity. Today, most digital recordings are protected. Professional libraries include a license to use their sounds in all your productions. Almost all of them cover a/v, broadcast, and theatrical use; some also include using the effects in software for sale.

But most record store discs are legal for personal use only. A few don't carry any copyright notice or have wording like "Your imagination is your only limit." These may be safe, but they can still make you sorry. I've heard some retail CDs that were merely copies of pre-1978 vinyl libraries, complete with record scratches and surface noise!

Professional CD Libraries

Most of the prerecorded sound effects used by professionals come from a few specialized publishers like Hollywood Edge. Their sounds are recorded digitally,

---

[3]They assured me there'd be plenty of discs available when I wrote this book. But the usual fine print must apply: the offer can be withdrawn at any time, and neither Hollywood Edge, Miller Freeman Books, or your humble author are responsible if you can't get a copy.

without echo whenever possible, with a minimum of processing so that you've got the most flexibility to tweak them in your mix. They're then organized onto CDs and grouped into libraries. A specialized foley library might have four or five discs of nothing but footsteps. A category library might have sounds that relate just to the old West (stagecoaches, blacksmith sounds, old guns). A generalized library might include 10–40 discs with enough different sounds to cover most production needs.

Depending on how specialized a library is, how easy the sounds were to record, and how many discs are in a set, professional sound effects CDs will cost between $30 and $75 each. They include the right to use the sound in any way (except reselling it as a sound effect) and may also include catalog files that can be integrated into a database. Most of the publishers are accessible individually on the Web; a few resellers like Gefen Systems (www.gefen.com) represent all the major publishers and serve as a clearing house for sound effects information. Contact information for the large suppliers appears in the tutorial section of my Web site, www.dplay.com.

CD-ROM Libraries

If you don't need full broadcast rights and the highest quality, you can get compressed or low sample rate versions of some professional libraries on CD-ROM. These discs include browser and decompression software, usually for both Mac and Windows, along with the right to include the sounds in corporate presentations and Web sites. The discs sell for about the same prices as standard sound effects CDs, but because they're recorded as compressed files instead of stereo audio tracks, they can include many times more sounds. The more expensive ones may have as many as 2,000 separate tracks, either as 22 kHz 16-bit mono or as data-compressed full-resolution stereo.

Just like with audio sound effects CDs, you have to be careful about the source. Low-cost computer store CD-ROMs may include 8-bit sounds, badly digitized vinyl effects, or other unusable tracks. The better ones are sold by professional sound effects sources, and their labels indicate which large effects library the sounds came from.

SFX on the Internet

If you really want bad sound effects, don't bother with low-cost CD-ROMs. You can find almost any sound you can think of, free, somewhere on the Web. Many audio enthusiasts have put up pages of effects they've digitized from VHS movies and TV shows. Sound quality is poor to awful, and using the sounds will almost certainly violate someone's copyright. Still, some of them are fun to listen to . . . and listening is perfectly legal. These sites pop in and out of existence unpredictably, but your favorite search engine will probably find you a few dozen.

On the other hand, you can also buy professional-quality sound effects over the Internet. Services like Sound Dogs (www.sounddogs.com), a large Hollywood effects company, have put big chunks of their catalog on the Web (Figure 2). You can search and audition the sounds in very low resolution. When you find one you like, enter a credit card number—cost varies with length, but most hard effects are under $5— and within a few minutes the system will e-mail back a password for an ftp site where the sounds are waiting. The scheme is too complicated and time-consuming to replace having your own CDs on hand, but is great when you need a couple of specialized effects during a late-night editing session.

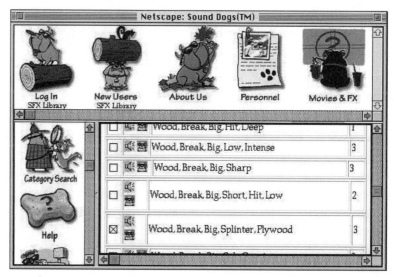

Figure 2: You can buy high-quality sound effects over the Internet from www.sounddogs.com (who says a professional site has to look serious?).

Rolling Your Own

If an effect has to match an on-screen action, the best way to get it may be to record your characters or a production assistant doing the action right after you finish shooting. You'll have the microphone, recorder, and all the necessary props right there. You can also record usable effects in a studio, in your editing suite, and out in the real world. Chapter 8 has specific tips for this kind of recording.

Choosing Effects

So you've got a hundred or a thousand effects in front of you, in a collection of discs or on the screen. Here's how to choose the right ones.

- Try to hear them in your head before you look. This is a reality check to make sure the sound can actually exist. (A major ad agency once asked me for the sound of a flashing neon sign, as heard from across a busy street. I resisted the temptation to ask them what color.)

- It can also help you break the sound into easily found components. A "Cellblock Door" can be just a jingling key ring and a sliding metal gate, slowed and mixed with a heavy echo.

- Hard sounds (Chapter 4) are caused by physical actions. So if you can't find something in the catalog that's a perfect match, look for something else that moves in the same way. A golf club, arrow, and leather whip make a very similar *wsssh* in the air. An electric car window motor may work perfectly as a robot arm, laser printer, or spaceship door. You can occasionally make outlandish substitutions if the sound you're using isn't immediately identifiable and there's enough of a visual cue to suggest what it should be. When a cable network needed promos for the movie *Mouse Hunt*, I used a rubbed balloon's squeaks against images of the star rodent.

- Don't rely too much on the name; you actually have to listen before deciding. "Police Car" could be an old-fashioned siren or a modern whooper, near or far, with or without an engine; or it could be a high-speed chase, or even a two-way radio. The better libraries use long, detailed descriptions, but details are no substitute for listening.

- Pay attention to the environment around the effect while you listen. A car door has a lot of different slams depending on whether it's outdoors or inside a parking garage, how much of a hurry the slammer is in, and how far away we are from the car. Exterior sounds can often be used for interiors if they're clean and you add echo . . . but it's almost impossible to make an interior sound match an outdoor shot. You can add distance to an exterior sound by using an equalizer to roll off the high midrange (Chapter 14).

- You can loop or repeat relatively short backgrounds to cover longer scenes. Twenty or thirty seconds' worth of original sound is usually sufficient, but see the note about looping backgrounds later in this chapter.

- Foreign cities often provide the best American walla. Check your library for street scenes or crowds recorded in other languages. Mixed properly, they'll fill out a scene without interfering with principal dialog. And it's a lot harder to tell when they've been looped.

Sound Effects Palettes

Hard effects generally fall into one of three categories: those made by mechanical actions (usually wood or metal, but also such things as rock scrapes); those from organic sources (crowd noises, animals, fantasy monsters); and those from electronic circuits.

It may seem strange, but I've found that montages and mixed effects often work best if you stay within the same source category, making exceptions only for accents. It's a lot like an artist staying in a single palette of earth tones or cool pastels.

Placing Sound Effects

The easiest way to simplify sound effects placement is to ignore a lot of it. In Hollywood, almost every action is matched by an effect, down to the tiniest foley. But on the small screen, you can often limit your efforts to just those sounds that advance the plot.

- Place the music before you worry about effects. TV mixes aren't very subtle, and if the music's going to be loud, you might not be able to hear anything else.

- Place ambiences before you worry about hard effects. Often a random movement in a background sound will work perfectly for an on-screen action if you merely move it a few frames.

- Don't worry about the little sounds—clothing rustles or pencil scratches—until you're sure they're necessary. Video sound isn't a subtle medium, and these effects may be needed only during intimate scenes that don't have any other sound.

- Always do effects spotting with the narration and/or dialog tracks up. Television is driven by dialog, and words have to take priority over other sounds. (Of course, you'll want to mute any voices while you're actually placing and trimming the effect.)

Planning Effects

It's important to look over the entire sequence while you're getting an idea for effects, so you can respect the dramatic arc of the scene. The effects that are part of the plot—explosions, screams, or even off-screen gasps—are most important and can help viewers forget that other sounds may be missing.

Don't make sound effects compete with each other. There's been a trend in Hollywood action pictures to mix a continuous wall of sound, with everything at maximum volume. This may be fine in a theater, but video has a more limited range that can't handle two sounds of the same volume and timbre at the same time. A simultaneous gunshot and car crash may sound great on large studio monitors, when you know what you're listening to, but viewers will have a hard time sorting them out. Even some softer combinations, such as a cricket background mixed with a campfire, can turn to mush on many sets because the sounds are so similar.

Unfamiliar sounds work best when we know what they're supposed to be, either because we can see what's making the noise or because a character refers to it. It's best to approach this kind of issue when you're first planning the video. Chapter 4 has some tips.

Give some thought to track layout also, when you're planning effects. Leave some dead space between effects on the same track; if they're butted up against each other, they'll be difficult to keep track of on a timeline and almost impossible to control during the mix. If you keep similar sounds on the same track, you won't have to be constantly changing global echo or equalization settings.

After you've done this a few times, you'll evolve a few standard track layouts. I usually put voice-over—if any—on the top track, dialog on the next one or two (depending on how I've split it), hard effect tracks below them, then background effects, and finally music tracks on the bottom. It makes mixing faster because the same kinds of sound always appear in the same place on my screen and on the same channels of my console. It also makes life simpler when the producer asks for dialog, effect, and music stems for foreign-language release.

Backgrounds

It's a good idea to edit background or ambience tracks first. A lot of times, they'll eliminate the need for more elaborate effects work. Since the mind associates what it hears with what it sees, random sounds in a stock recording can appear to match specific on-screen actions. I usually find a few clunks and rattles in a background that serve as perfect foley or hard effect replacements just by sliding them a few frames.

Backgrounds are also easiest to put in, since you can spot their start and end points just by looking at an EDL or timeline. Many sound editors extend their backgrounds slightly past the video out-point, so they can be faded during the mix to cover abrupt picture transitions.

Looping

If a background sound isn't long enough to cover a scene, put it in more than once. You might hear a slight break in the sound where two copies are spliced together, but there are ways to disguise where the "loop"[4] joins:

- Place the splice under a hard effect or loud dialog line.

- Slide the splice to where the camera angle changes.

- Put the repeats on alternate tracks and let them overlap for a few seconds, with a cross-fade between them (Figure 3). This will usually make the splice imperceptible. Track 27 of this book's CD has a cricket background you can try this with.

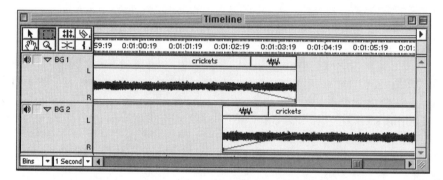

Figure 3: The same sound repeated on alternating tracks. Note the cross-fade where they overlap.

- Some backgrounds, such as traffic, change pitch or timbre as they develop. Others, such as seawash, have a definite rhythm. In either case a repeating loop would be obvious because the sound is different at each end of the loop, and cross-fading would mean we hear the different parts simultaneously. Hollywood's trick for that is the "flip loop," shown in Figure 4. At the top is an original helicopter background. Looping it (Figure 4B) makes an obvious joint. Instead, we take the original sound and reverse it[5]—instead of going from soft to loud as the original did, the copy now goes from loud to soft. We then splice that onto the original (Figure 4C); there's no change at the joint, so it doesn't jump out at us. The combined version starts and ends at the same level, so we can loop it imperceptibly. You'd be amazed how many background sounds can be played backwards and still sound right. Track 28 of the CD has some ocean waves you can try this with.

[4]The term came from the practice of cutting film backgrounds into long loops—often several feet in diameter—that would continuously pass through the player.

[5]In some programs, you do this by applying a speed of -100%; in others, apply a "Reverse" effect.

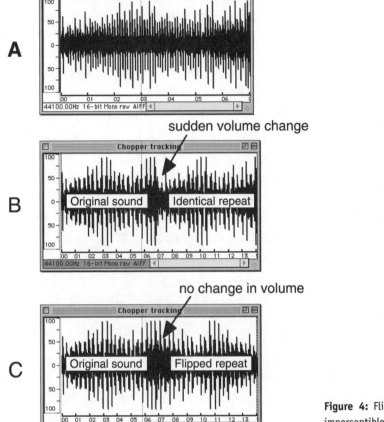

Figure 4: Flipping the loop makes the joint imperceptible.

Making backgrounds seem fuller

If a background is going to be mixed with dialog, any midrange sounds in it will compete with the voices. Since most background recordings—and real-world environments—have a lot of midrange in them, you'll have to turn the track down during the mix, or equalize it so it almost disappears.

A good solution is to find two different backgrounds—one predominantly high-pitched, the other low—and use both under a scene. For example, instead of using a single busy street background, combine rumbling start-and-stop traffic with pedestrian footsteps. The result can sound bigger without interfering with dialog.

Stereo effects can seem much wider if you spread their tracks apart. Delay one side of the stereo signal several seconds, but fade both sides in and out together. This is easily done in an audio workstation; in an NLE you may have to use two separate stereo tracks, with matching fades, and mute one side of each. If the result is too wide, pan each side slightly toward the center. Check the result in mono when you're done to make sure you haven't introduced a hollow flanging sound.

Adding Hard Effects

After the backgrounds are in place, play back the sequence and see what effects still seem to be missing. This probably won't be too long a list: television can ignore most of the foley, which gets lost through a small speaker anyway. You'll probably also find that some hard effects were picked up with on-camera audio and just need to be boosted in the mix. While you're working at this stage, make sure you preview at the same frame rate as the finished product. A preview at 10 fps may be a lot faster to render than at 30 fps but can leave you with a three-frame error—an eternity for sync sound.

Usually you can insert a hard effect right on the same frame where you see an action. As soon as something happens, viewers expect to hear it. Who cares if the collapsing building is a few hundred feet away, and its sound would take half a second to reach us? If a sound is big enough, convention dictates that it will travel instantly through anything at all. So when a laser death-cannon destroys the rebel home planet, we hear the explosion immediately . . . even though the planet is a few thousand kilometers away, through the vacuum of space.

Some effects can be placed intuitively (it doesn't take much imagination to find the exact frame where a punch lands or a car crashes). You may be surprised how easy it is to place other effects, once you scan at the single-frame level. Guns, for example, almost always have a one-frame barrel flash exactly when they're fired, as in Figure 5. The mechanics will vary depending on the system you're using, but most NLEs let you mark a key frame with a single button and will snap sounds to it.

Sometimes, the editing rhythm is so fast you can't find an appropriate frame. Consider the battle sequence in Figure 6. We see a mortar fire on 10:47:07 . . . but by the time we cut to the target, it's already exploded. There's no frame where it hits! This also happens frequently in fight scenes, with a cut from one shot with a fist flying, to a reverse angle where the punch has already landed. If this is the case,

Figure 5: You can tell by the flash that the gun was fired at exactly 01:11:14.

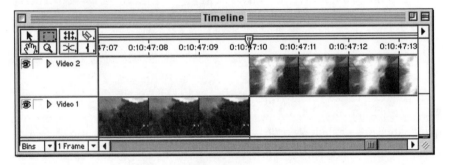

Figure 6: This mortar did a lot of damage, even though there isn't any frame where it lands.

place the sound ahead of its visual by a frame (starting the explosion around 10:47:09). The sound can even help smooth the visual discontinuity.

If the video is moving very quickly, there may not be enough time for big effects to die out either. In this sequence, it would be perfectly reasonable for the picture to cut to distant headquarters half a second or so later. That's too short for the sound of an explosion to register. The best you could do is keep the explosion over the cut to the interior, but fade it quickly into the first dialog.

As you're placing effects, consider that many should be cued to their middle instead of their front. Figure 7 shows a typical explosion. There's a rumble at the

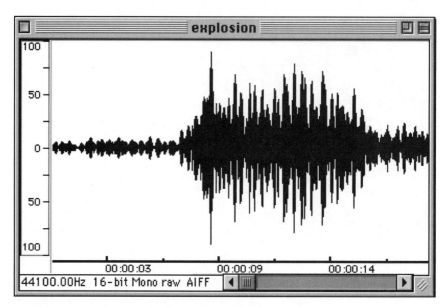

Figure 7: Things don't start exploding until about eight frames in.

start of the sound, before we hear the big crunch. Obviously, the crunch is what we'd line up against 10:47:09 in the sequence above. Also consider that many sounds are based on multiple actions, and a prerecorded effect may need some trimming to fit. For example, "closing a door" consists of a hinge squeal, a latch strike and release, and a rattle against the frame. While you might be able to place most of it with one edit, you'll probably have to slide the squeal depending on how quickly the door is closing.

A few technical tricks can help as you're working with effects.

- Try to leave all your effects at full volume as you drop them in, and save any adjustments for the finished mix. This is particularly important on desktop systems with limited resolution, and it also makes it easier to add echo and other processes cleanly.

- Don't be afraid to vary the speed. A small increase can add excitement to a sound. A large decrease can make a sound bigger. (Slowing an effect in software usually gives you a richer result than the same slowdown on analog tape because artifacts create a false but effective treble.)

- Try the slowing-down trick on an impact like a car crash or explosion, and then mix it with the original to make the sound much bigger. Add a fade to the end of the slower copy, so they both end at the same time. There's a crash on track 29 of this book's CD for you to try this with, followed by the same effect with this process added.

- You can add a *feeling* of speed to steady sounds like auto engines by applying a flanging effect (Chapter 14). If you don't have a flange filter, put the sound on two tracks, delay one track a few frames, speed the delayed one up so it ends in sync with the other, and mix both tracks together.

- Use pitch shift on just one side of a stereo effect to make it bigger. You'll usually want less than a 3% change, but the right amount depends on the sound. Try different settings and check the result on mono speakers as well as in stereo.

- Make hard effects, such as explosions or door slams, wider in stereo by changing the pitch or speed of just one channel a few percent. If you're mixing for broadcast or home video, compatibility is important, so check the result in mono before committing. Try this on the splash effect, track 30 of the CD.

CHAPTER 14

Processing

R O S E ' S   R U L E S

➪ Good effects processing is like good video editing. It improves how your message comes across, but the viewer is seldom aware of what you've done.

➪ Two things separate a good soundtrack from a poor one: the quality of the original recording, and how well it's been processed. It's probably too late to do anything about the former.

Few audio tools are as useful or abused as effects processors. A professional studio will have thousands of dollars invested in these units. They use them to change the tonal balance of a sound, change its dynamics, manipulate its apparent environment, or even change the sound into something totally different. In every case, the real goal is improving communication by making the track easier to understand or a dramatic premise easier to accept.

But for these processors to do any good at all, you have to know what's going on inside them. You can't just grab a knob and twist until it sounds good . . . that's as likely to harm one aspect of the track as improve another. Learning how to use processors properly isn't difficult. All it takes is a little knowledge of how sound works, some imagination, and the next few pages.

The previous chapter was about sound effects—recordings you add to a track to heighten its realism. This one is about effects processors like equalizers and compressors. In a busy studio, both the recordings and the processors are referred to simply as *effects*. Which kind you mean should be obvious from the context.

How Any Effect Can Wreck a Sound

A couple of warnings before we begin. These apply to every kind of processor, from hardware-based analog units to NLE plug-in software, but are particularly important in the desktop environment.

Watch Out for Overloads

Somewhere, inside virtually any effects processor, the signal level has to get boosted. If you boost things too high, the system will distort—adding fuzziness to an analog signal, or crackling to a digital one. The amount of boost is often controlled by something other than a volume knob, and the distortion might not show up until the loudest part of a track, so it can be easy to cause serious damage without noticing. Pay attention to OVERLOAD or CLIP indicators on the front panel or control screen, and listen for distortion while you're previewing an effect. If you hear a problem, turn down the input or output volume control—which one you adjust depends on how the particular effect was designed; if you're not sure, try the output control first.

Watch Out for Sounds That Are Too Soft

If you're working in an NLE, your system probably has only 16-bit resolution. This isn't a problem when you're editing, but can affect sound quality as you add effects and cross-fades. These processes use a lot of math, multiplying and dividing parts of the signal by various factors. Each calculation requires additional bits to reflect the softest or loudest sounds accurately.

If a system doesn't have enough bits for the loudest sounds, you get the distortion described above and can turn down the volume. But if it doesn't have enough bits for the softest ones, it will add subtle noises that aren't apparent until you play the final mix on a good speaker. Each additional processing step makes things worse.

Professionals use 24- or 32-bit effects to guard against this. The best you can do in a 16-bit NLE is make sure you've digitized or recorded at a good level (Chapter 10), and avoid doing anything that'll permanently reduce a sound's volume until the final mix stage.

Take Advantage of Presets

Almost every software-based processor comes with a library of prebuilt settings, often with names like "vocal enhance" or "small room reverb." They're written by people who know the software and what each of its controls can do. Load them, listen to what they do to your tracks, and see what happens to the sound as you change each knob.

Once you learn how to use an effect, think of the factory presets as a starting place. Load them, tweak the controls until they work best with your elements, and then save the result as your own new preset. Also, save the settings you come up with for one-time situations like correcting a particularly noisy location. If you ever have to go back to the original tape, you'll have no trouble matching the sound quality.

There are a lot more musicians buying effects than videographers, so some of the presets in equalizers and reverbs will be designed for that kind of production.[1] They're not much good in video production, but you can still learn from how they've been put together.

Be Wary of Commitment

Many software effects are destructive: they change the file, and the original unprocessed sound is lost. (Some NLE filters are nondestructive and are only applied when the tracks are mixed together.) Before you apply a destructive effect, make sure there's a clean copy elsewhere on your hard drive or on the original camera tape or DAT. It will be invaluable if you have to re-edit, if you have to use the elements in some other project, or when you discover that you had one of the many effects knobs in the wrong position.

Each Effect Affects the Next

If you're applying multiple effects to a track, the order in which you use them can make a major difference. We'll discuss how to take advantage of this at the end of this chapter.

Software-Based Processing Takes Time

Effects use a lot of math, and this can tie up your CPU when it's time to apply them in an NLE or software-based audio editor. Leave effects turned off to speed up editing and previewing. When you're creating material for analog broadcast, use 32 kHz sampling rather than 48 kHz if your system can do the conversion well. The on-air sound will be the same (see Chapter 2), and the final audio rendering will be one-third faster.

Professional audio workstations use separate processing chips so they can apply effects without taking time to do the math.

---

[1] Frequency ranges are much wider in music, but they don't care about the midrange as much as we do. Reverbs are often too big to simulate normal interior spaces.

Equalizers

These ubiquitous audio processors were invented to boost the highs that got lost over long telephone lines, and their name comes from the fact that they made a line equally efficient at all frequencies. Some brilliant sound engineer brought them into an early film mixing suite to equalize the sound from multiple microphones. They're now considered an essential part of any audio production facility.

What an equalizer does is the same whether it's a multiknob wonder in a recording studio, a couple of on-screen sliders in your NLE, or the tone controls on your car radio: it emphasizes or suppresses parts of the audio spectrum, picking out the elements of the signal that will be most useful. The only difference between individual equalizers—other than the noise or distortion a specific model introduces—is how precisely they let you specify the frequency and amount you want it boosted or lowered. Precision is important because sounds you want to keep can be close to the ones you want to lose. But precision requires complexity, and a good equalizer is a lot more than a simple bass and treble control.

Once you learn how, you can use the equalizer to do the following:

- Increase intelligibility of a voice track.

- Make music more exciting under a montage.

- Tailor both the voice and the music so you can make both of them seem louder in the mix.

- Fix some types of distortion, and correct for boominess or power-line hum.

- Simulate telephones, intercoms, and awful multimedia speakers.

  But equalizers have their limits:

- They can't eliminate complex noises like air conditioner motors or timecode buzz.

- They can't turn lightweight voices into deep-voiced giants.

- They can't eliminate the soloist from a piece of music (you need a phase technique to do this).

- They can't compensate for awful multimedia speakers.

Equalizer Types

There are dozens of different equalizer types in equipment catalogs and software specs, but they're really just combinations of three basic functions.

Peaking equalizers affect the volume of the sound around a particular frequency. They'll always have a level control, most of them have frequency controls, and a few also let you adjust the bandwidth (or Q). The Q determines how sharply the equalizer chooses its frequencies. A very high Q can emphasize a single note while not affecting notes next to it; a low Q lets you control an octave or more at once. Figures 1 and 2 show the response curve of a typical peaking equalizer. (All the equalizer curves in this chapter were lifted from screenshots of Waves' Renaissance plug-ins. You can see what the program's full screen looks like in Figure 6.)

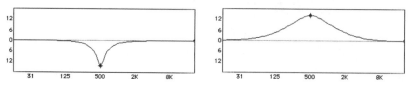

Figure 1: Equalizers set for 12 dB loss (left) and boost (right) at 500 Hz, with a low Q

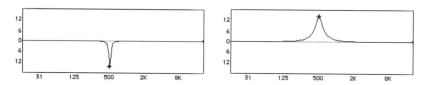

Figure 2: The same equalizers with a high Q

As the Q gets higher and the equalizer gets more selective, it will add subtle distortion to frequencies just outside its range. This is a fact of equalizer life and has nothing to do with the particular brand or design. A very high-Q boost can be so sharp it resonates, ringing like a bell when its exact frequency is struck. A similarly high Q, set to cut instead of boost, can pick out some kinds of noises and eliminate them completely from a dialog track. This is most effective if the noise doesn't have many harmonics, such as some power-line hums, or starts at a very high frequency. (The buzz you get from a ground loop, or the whine of SMTPE code leakage, has too many harmonics to be eliminated this way.)

A peaking equalizer, set for a low Q and gentle dip around 200 Hz, can help dialog recordings that have too much boominess because of room reverb. A moderate Q and boost around the 5 kHz range can increase the perceived brightness of a track without increasing the noise.

A graphic equalizer is really just a bunch of peaking equalizers with fixed frequencies and overlapping bandwidths (Figure 3 shows one from Bias' Deck, a multitrack music program). Graphics are the easiest kind of equalizer to use, since the knobs draw a graph of the volume at different frequencies. But they're also the least

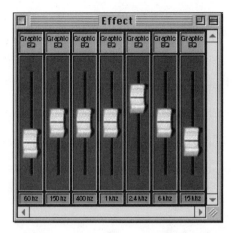

Figure 3: A graphic equalizer is just a bunch of peaking equalizers with fixed frequencies and Qs.

useful because factory-set frequencies on a graphic are seldom the best ones for an application, and the Q is predetermined by the number of bands and can't be adjusted.

Shelving equalizers (Figure 4) apply a controllable amount of boost or cut to sounds above or below the specified frequency. They always have a level control and may have frequency and Q controls. The bass and treble controls on your stereo are fixed-frequency shelving equalizers. Shelving equalizers are most useful when you want to apply a broad, gentle correction; but too much of a shelf can run the risk of boosting noises at the extremes of the spectrum.

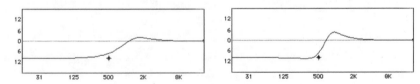

Figure 4: Low-frequency shelving equalizers set for -10 dB below 500 Hz, with low Q (left) and high Q (right)

Cutoff filters (Figure 5) are extreme shelving equalizers, throwing away any sound above (when they're high-cut) or below (low-cut) the cutoff frequency. Their design lets them have much sharper slopes than shelving equalizers, without the disadvantages of a high Q. In fact, cutoff filters don't have level or Q controls; they can be used only to reject sounds beyond a desired frequency. They're useful for noise control and removing parts of a sound that can interfere with the mix. A low-cut at one frequency can be followed by a high-cut at a higher frequency to make a bandpass filter; only those sounds between the two frequencies will pass through. Bandpasses are useful for special effects, such as simulating a telephone conversation.

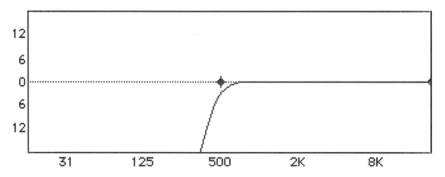

Figure 5: Low-cut cutoff filter at 500 Hz

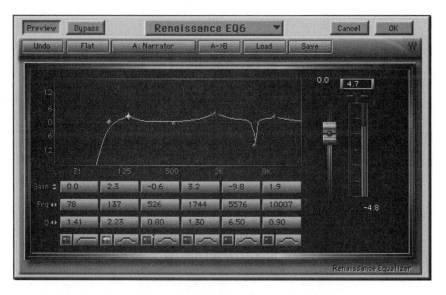

Figure 6: A parametric equalizer set for one cut and five shelving sections

A parametric equalizer gives you complete control, usually with three or more peaking sections, and individual controls for frequency, level, and Q. A software-based parametric like Waves' Renaissance (shown in its entirety in Figure 6) lets you change the function of each section, so you can have cutoffs, shelving, and peaking at the same time.

Learning the Bands

The best tool for learning how to equalize is the equalizer itself. Grab a short voice clip, such as track 30 on the book's CD, and set it to play continuously. Start with all of the level controls in their neutral position (usually marked 0 dB) and the Q around 7. Pick a section, raise its level about 6 dB, and listen to the audio while you sweep the frequency control very slowly. The changes will be subtle as you move from one frequency to the next, but try to give a name to what you hear: *boomy, powerful, harsh, bright*—whatever comes to mind. Then turn the section's level as far down as it'll go, and sweep through its frequencies again. Lowering a few frequencies can make some signals sound better. Then try the whole thing again with some music (tracks 24 through 26 on the CD). You'll hear different effects depending on the type of material.

Ears get used to equalization very quickly, so keep going back to the unequalized sound as a reference, and don't spend more than 10 or 15 minutes at a time on this exercise. Do this a few times, and you'll start to learn exactly where to set those equalizer knobs for the sound you want.

Overequalization

Once you learn how to hear subtle differences, you can avoid the most common equalizer mistake: setting the knobs too high. Equalizers are volume controls, and too much volume causes problems—particularly in digital systems. Check volumes along the entire equalized track. A 12 dB boost at 5 kHz may help the strings at the start of a piece of music, but it'll cause an awful clatter when the cymbal comes in. (Far better to use a 6 dB boost around 10 kHz.)

As a general rule, don't raise any control higher than 6 dB—one bit, in digital terms—and remember that overlapping bands have their levels added together. Save the more radical settings for special effects, or to rescue badly recorded tracks.

You usually shouldn't turn all the knobs in the same direction. If everything's boosted, the signal won't sound better—just more distorted.

The logical extension of these two rules is to remember that equalizers can be turned down as well as up. If a voice is getting lost under the music track, don't look for a way to boost it. Instead, dip the music around 1.5–2 kHz. The overall mix will be cleaner and more natural sounding.

Equalizer Tips

If you're in a hurry, these ideas can help you get started, but don't treat the settings as gospel. Every track is slightly different, and every equalizer contributes its own sound.

- Strengthen an announcer. Cut off everything below 90 Hz—those frequencies are just wasting power. Then try a gentle peak (3 dB, Q = 7) around 240 Hz for warmth, and a similar boost around 1.8 kHz for intelligibility. A sharp dip (–p18 dB, Q = 100) around 5 kHz can help sibilance.

- If there's no voice, you can make the music sound more exciting: boost the bass notes (6 dB, Q = 7) around 100 Hz, and add a 6 dB high-frequency shelf around 3 kHz.

- Actual telephone conversations are cut sharply at 350 Hz and 3.5 kHz so the phone company can squeeze more calls down a digital line. But an equalizer's filters at those frequencies may be too gentle. Try moving the settings closer, such as 500 Hz and 3.2 kHz—and if you're using a filter with enough sections, stack two cutoffs at each end. A sharp peak (10 dB with Q = 100) at 1.2 kHz can also help by adding the characteristic metallic feeling.

- Tune out hum or whistles. The best way to adjust a very sharp dip (maximum attenuation and Q) is to turn it into a boost first. Set it for +12 dB, and sweep the frequency around the noise until you hear a definite peak—most equalizers will distort or crackle at the right setting. Then turn the attenuation all the way down. This is much more accurate than relying on the front-panel calibration or trying to hear the subtle differences as you move a dip around.

- Reduce distortion. If a natural sound doesn't have many harmonics (Chapter 1), such as an acoustic guitar, you can often clean up bad recordings by applying a sharp high-frequency cutoff filter. This not only eliminates hiss; it also reduces the artificial harmonics that a bad analog recording can generate. Start with the equalizer as low as 5 kHz, and then slowly raise its cutoff frequency until the recording doesn't seem muddy.

Compressors

In the real world, the difference between loud and soft adds excitement to what we hear. But in the electronic world of a video track, loud causes distortion and soft gets lost in electronic noise. Used properly, a compressor can control those pesky level changes—and make a track sound louder—without affecting its dynamic feel. But used the wrong way, a compressor can turn tracks into bland, unlistenable mush.

It's easy to misuse these things. That's because the best compressors have a daunting array of knobs with relatively nonintuitive names. You need this control to properly shape your sound, because every element in a track has its own dynamic footprint and should be handled differently. Once you understand exactly how a compressor does its magic, you'll reach for the right knob every time.

What Happens Inside a Compressor

You can understand how a compressor works by using a little visual math; but don't worry, there's no calculating involved. The graphs starting with Figure 7 are a map of how volumes can be affected by a circuit. Incoming sound (the vertical axis) travels to the black diagonal line (the RATIO knob on a compressor) and is reflected down to the output. So in Figure 7, a loud sound at the input (dotted line a) crosses the ratio line and becomes a loud sound at the output. A soft sound (dotted line c) stays soft when it comes out. This trivial graph isn't a compressor at all. The slope of the diagonal line is one unit up for each unit sideways, or a ratio of 1:1.

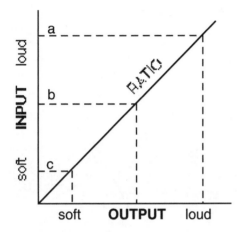

Figure 7: A compressor with a ratio of 1:1

But in Figure 8, we've turned the RATIO knob to 3:1, tilting the diagonal three units up for each unit sideways. A loud incoming sound crosses the diagonal sooner and is reflected down to be only medium-loud at the output. The softer input of the bottom dotted line is reflected later and becomes louder at the output. What was a large volume range going in becomes a small one coming out. Ratios can get as high as 100:1 when a compressor is being used to control peak levels.

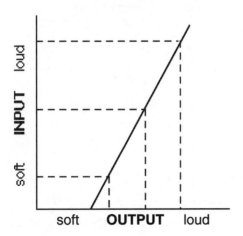

Figure 8: A compressor with a ratio of 3:1

The compressor in Figure 8 also boosts things that *should* stay soft, like room noise, so we fix the problem by putting a little kink in the ratio. Figure 9 shows how it works. Below the bend, the ratio is still 1:1 . . . and soft sounds aren't affected. The location of this bend is usually set by a THRESHOLD control, and its abruptness may be adjusted by a KNEE control. Some compressors have a fixed threshold and let you adjust the overall INPUT level around it. The effect is the same.

You'll notice that the outputs of Figures 8 and 9 don't get very loud. They've been lowered by the action of the ratio slope, so we compensate with an OUTPUT or MAKEUP GAIN control (Figure 10), which preserves compression while making the entire signal louder.

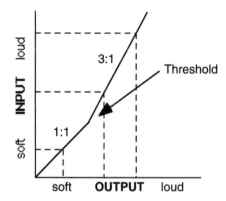

Figure 9: Adding a threshold control, so soft sounds aren't boosted

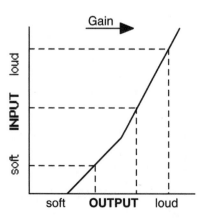

Figure 10: Adding makeup gain, so loud sounds stay loud

You might also see a GATE adjustment to control noise. Signals softer than its setting are totally cut off. You can see this in Figure 11, where a very soft signal doesn't make it to the output at all. A noise gate is a processor with this function only, and no gain reduction circuit. It works like a fast on-off switch, totally silencing a signal when it falls below the THRESHOLD but leaving it unaffected when it gets louder. This total silence can sound unnatural, so noise gates often have BYPASS or THROUGH controls to let a little signal through when they're in the off condition.

Some compressors have a "gated compression" feature, which isn't the same as a noise gate. In a real compressor circuit, the slope of our drawings is replaced by an amplifier with continuously-variable gain. Gated compression freezes the gain of that amplifier whenever the input drops below a preset level, so soft sounds can pass through it without being boosted unnaturally.

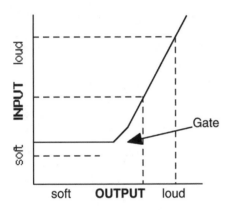

Figure 11: A gate sees that sounds softer than its threshold never reach the output at all.

Using the Compressor

- The best way to adjust a compressor is by ear, with a sample of the actual program material. If you can, keep looping the same 5- or 10-second section so you can be sure you're hearing differences in the compression rather than changes in the source. Adjust only one knob at a time, until you're sure of its effect.

- Good compressors also have a GAIN REDUCTION meter to tell you how much the signal is being lowered. Keep an eye on it. The meter should be bouncing in time with the input. If the meter stays at a fixed value, the threshold or time constants (see below) are set wrong, or you're overloading the input. In either case, the compressor isn't doing much to the signal other than providing distortion.

- If you set a high THRESHOLD (or low INPUT), high RATIO, and sharp or hard KNEE, the compressor will just regulate extreme peaks to avoid overloads. This setting preserves most of the dynamic range, and is often used during original recording. There's an example on track 32 of this book's CD. Listen carefully because the effect is subtle.

- On the other hand, a lower THRESHOLD and RATIO squeezes the volumes together, making a narration stronger or music easier to mix. Since this affects the overall feel of a track, it's best left for postproduction. Hear it on track 33.

- High ratios tend to emphasize any distortion in the sound. Even the distortion of an extra analog-to-digital conversion can become audible in a heavily compressed track.

- Don't obsess about MAKEUP GAIN while you're adjusting other knobs. After you've got things set the way you want, fine-tune the makeup to get a good level on the compressor's output.

Compression in the Fourth Dimension

Those graphs can't illustrate one important aspect of compression: time. Remember *envelopes* from Chapter 1? A compressor has to be set so it responds to the volume of a sound (gray wavy line in Figure 12), but not be so fast that it reacts to individual waves. This requires two additional controls: ATTACK determines how long it

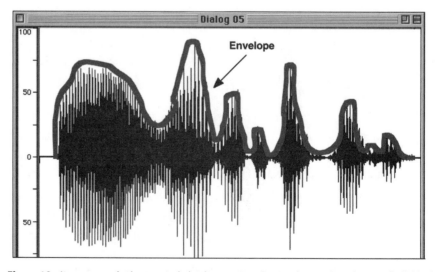

Figure 12: A compressor's time controls let it pay attention to the envelope but not individual waves.

takes to pull the volume down when the input crosses the threshold; DECAY sets how long it takes to recover normal volumes after the input goes down. If there's a gate, it might have its own time controls.

- A fast ATTACK will protect you from momentary distortion or digital overloads, particularly with percussive sounds or sharp consonants. But too fast an attack can destroy the impact of these sounds.

- A fast DECAY can extend echoes and other sustained sounds by making them louder as they're fading out. (A guitarist's sustain pedal is really a compressor with a fast decay.) You can often increase the effect of reverberation in a recording by compressing it and changing the decay time.

- If both settings are too fast, low-pitched sounds will distort as the compressor tries to smooth out waves instead of the envelope. The fundamental wavelength of a male narrator's voice—around 10 milliseconds—is within the range of most compressors.

- A slow ATTACK lets the initial hit of a musical instrument show through in a mix, while keeping the overall track under control. Too slow an attack on a voice track can result in a spitty sound because vowel sounds will be lowered more than initial consonants.

Figure 13 shows how these time settings can change a sound effect. The first envelope (A) is a .357 Magnum shot at medium range, with no compression. B is the same shot with a slow attack and decay; only the initial sound gets through, so the result is more of a pile-driver clank than a bang. C has a very fast attack and decay; the hit is suppressed and the reverb emphasized, making it sound more like a big explosion. Track 34 of the CD lets you hear all three versions.

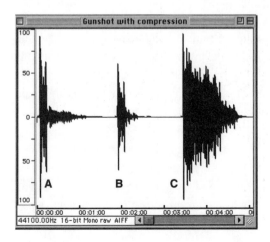

Figure 13: Changing the attack and decay controls can completely change a sound.

Sidechains

Compressors adjust their timing by applying filters to a control voltage, which is basically just a DC version of the input signal. By connecting other circuits to this voltage—called a SIDECHAIN—they can add some useful functions:

- The left and right sidechains of a stereo compressor can be linked together so that both channels are controlled identically, and the stereo image is preserved. Or they can be unlinked to make the whole image swing away from any loud off-center sounds.

- The sidechain can be filtered to make the compressor react more to specific frequencies. Tuning it for sibilance turns a compressor into a de-esser.

- The sidechain can be patched to a different signal entirely. Put a compressor on a music track but give it the narration for a sidechain, and the music will automatically fade down whenever the narrator talks.

- You can even make a compressor predict the future by putting a delay in the main signal path but none in the sidechain. A gunshot, for example, will cause the overall track to fade down before the gun is fired . . . so the impact is preserved, without any overload.

Compressor Variations

Multiband compressors

A compressor reacts to volume changes across the entire bandwidth of the signal; a loud sound at any frequency, low or high, will make it turn down the volume. This works fine for many applications. But imagine a mixed track with a narrator speaking over music that has a strong bass drum beat. Each time the drum is hit, a compressor would turn the entire track down, and the narrator would get momentarily softer. The solution is to break the audio signal into multiple bands by using cutoff and bandpass filters. Each band is processed through its own compressor, usually with different timings to be most effective while avoiding distortion, and then the multiple outputs are mixed together. In our imaginary mix, the bass drum would only trigger the low-frequency compressor, and the announcer's voice—primarily midrange—wouldn't be affected.

Radio stations pioneered the use of extreme equalization and multiband compression to make their music appear louder than the competition's. The extreme highs and lows are boosted and then compressed separately so they blast through on good receivers, while the midrange has its own compression to stay as loud as possible on smaller radios. Five separate bands are typically used.

Following the same principle, hardware-based combination equalizers and multi-band compressors are sold as final "loudness" generators in music production. You may find these units effective in video mixes as well,[2] if you watch out for two things:

- Every other part of your signal chain has to be absolutely clean. The extreme processing emphasizes noise and distortion that would normally be hidden by midrange signals.

- You must build your own presets. The factory-set frequency bands and compression characteristics are designed for rock music, not for soundtracks where the midrange is most important.

Multiband compression can destroy many of the masking cues used by data reduction algorithms like MP3 and AAC (Chapter 2). If you're going to be combining these techniques, plan to spend a lot of time fine-tuning how they interact.

Noise reducers

You can use a noise gate to clean up a recording, but it can have broadband problems similar to the one described above: high-frequency hiss will click in and out as the gate is triggered by midrange sounds like dialog. One solution is to use a three- or five-band noise gate, with multiple filters and gating circuits similar to a multiband compressor. Another is to use a high-cut filter whose frequency is determined by a level detector; the highest frequency that can pass through constantly changes, based on how much high frequency exists in the original signal. This can clean up hiss without sounding as processed as a multiband gate, because moderately high-frequency signals won't make the hiss cut in and out. Similar processors, with sliding low-cut filters, can be used to reduce rumble.

Reverberation

Real rooms have walls that bounce sound back to us. Recording studios don't, because the walls have been treated to reduce reflections. Lavaliere mics—even in real rooms—tend to ignore reflections from the walls because they're so much closer to the speakers' mouths. In both cases, the reverb-free sound can seem artificial.

This may be a good thing, if a spokesperson is talking directly to camera or a narrator lives in the nonspace of a voice-over. But reverb is essential if you want dramatic dialog to seem like it's taking place in a real room. It can be the real reverb of the room, picked up by a boom mic along with the voices. Or it can be artificially

---

[2] I use one on just about everything.

generated, to make lavs and studio ADR sessions feel like they're taking place in the room we see on camera.

Today's digital reverberators use memory to delay part of the sound and send it back a fraction of a second later. There may be dozens of delays, each representing a different reflecting surface in an imaginary room. Since real surfaces reflect highs and lows differently—a thin windowpane may reflect highs and absorb lows, while a bookshelf does the opposite—equalizers are included for the delays. To adjust the sound of a reverb, you have to control these delays and equalizers.

Real Reflections

The speed of sound might be impressive for an airplane, but in terms of human perception it's pretty slow stuff. Sound travels about 1100 feet per second, depending on air temperature.[3] That means it takes about 1/30th of a video frame to move one foot. It can take a couple of frames for a drumbeat to reach the back of a large concert hall by the most direct path. When you sit in that hall you also hear the drum over other paths, each taking a different length of time—that's reverb.

Figure 14 shows how it works. Imagine a concert hall roughly 45 feet wide by 70 feet deep. You're about 20 feet from the drum. There's no way you can hear that drum sooner than 20 milliseconds after it's played—two-thirds of a frame—because it takes that long for the first sound to reach you. I drew that direct 20-foot path as a straight line between the drum and you.

But sound also bounces off the side walls and then to your ears. I've drawn two of the possible paths as dashed lines. The lower one is about 40 feet long, and the upper one is almost 60 feet. You hear a second drumbeat at 40 ms, and a third at 60 ms. If these were the only paths, you'd hear a drum and two distinct echoes. A

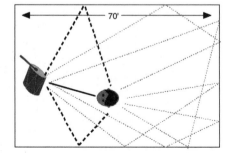

Figure 14: Reverb paths in a concert hall. It's the longer (dotted gray) paths that give the room its rich sound.

[3]There was an exhaustive discussion of this in Chapter 1.

well-designed concert hall has plenty of other relatively direct paths, so these early echoes are mixed with others, and you hear a richer sound instead.

Sound fills the room. Reflections bounce off the back wall, off the side to the back and to the ceiling, from one side to another, and so on. All of these paths—the dotted gray lines—eventually reach your ears, but you hear so many of them that they merge into a barrage of late reflections. The longer the path, the softer the sound gets; in a well-designed hall, it can take many seconds to die out.

Of course, there are other factors. A concert hall, a gymnasium, and a shopping mall can all have the same size and shape but sound completely different. That's because multiple surfaces determine how far apart the reflections are when they reach you. Also, their shape and the material of each surface affects the tone of the reverb: Hard surfaces reflect more highs. Complex shapes disperse the highs and reflect more lows.

A good reverb device lets you adjust

- The timing and number of early reflections (up to about 1/10th of a second)

- The density of late reflections and how quickly they build

- The relative bass and treble of late reflections

- How long it takes late reflections to die out

- The relative levels of initial sound and early and late reflections

By controlling those factors, you can simulate just about any acoustic space. Figure 15 shows some of the controls in one good software reverb, Waves' TrueVerb plug-in. You can see individual early reflections over the first 50 ms, and then a fairly

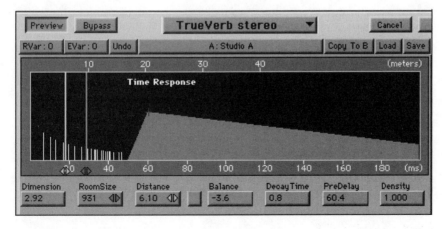

Figure 15: Waves' TrueVerb includes a graph of the reflections it generates.

fast decay of late reflections in this relatively small but rich-sounding room. (A separate panel lets you equalize the late reflections and control the overall mix.)

Evaluating Reverb Units

Accurately simulating every one of the thousands of different surfaces in a real room requires too much processing to be practical. Fortunately, it isn't necessary; we could never distinguish all those echoes in any case. Instead, reverb designers rely on how we hear and give us just enough reflections to think that a space is real. This is as much art as science and is limited by how much processing power is available, which is why different brands of reverb unit will have totally different sounds. A basic echo—the kind you might find thrown in with a video-editing program—will sound very different than a well-written plug-in on the same computer. And modern studio reverbs use dedicated DSP chips for the best simulations.

You can judge the quality of a reverb by playing a sharp, nonpitched sound with an abrupt ending—like the burst of white noise on track 35 of the CD—through the reverb. You shouldn't be able to hear individual early reflections, and there shouldn't be any flutter or vibration in the initial sound. There shouldn't be any particular pitch to the late reflections. The tail of the echo should die out smoothly, rather than suddenly stopping. Even if a reverb device has excellent characteristics, it might not be right for video production. Most are designed for music, with long echoes that simulate a concert hall rather than the very short echoes of a small room where dialog takes place.

Practical Reverb

The first place to control reverb is at the original recording, using the tips in the third section of this book. If you don't have a skilled recordist on your crew, it makes sense to avoid original reverb all together. Most shooting areas are more echoey than the small space implied by the lens. If you record a tight track with a lav, you can add visually appropriate reverb at the mix. This also makes it easier to match the reverb on foley elements.

I believe reverb doesn't belong in voice-overs. Reverb implies a room around the voice, and a voice-over exists in limbo where it can talk intimately to us or reflect a character's inner thoughts. Unless you've visually established a place for the voice-over to be coming from, keep it as clean as possible. Don't make the mistake of thinking that reverb makes a voice bigger; all it does is move it farther away.

Be careful using reverb in a clip-based editing program. If the reverb is applied as a "filter," it can last only as long as the edited clip. Add some silence at the end of the clip so late reflections have time to die out. This may require rendering a new audio element that includes the silence. Also, consider that reverbs exist in three-dimensional space. If your project is stereo, make sure that reverb—even on mono dialog clips—has a stereo path to the final mix. This may mean putting the same clip on two tracks at once.

Beyond Reverb

Echo isn't just for simulating rooms. Add it to sound effects and synthesized elements to make them richer. If you have to cut the end of an effect or piece of music to eliminate other sounds, add some echo to let it end gracefully. Reverb can also help smooth over awkward edits within a piece of music.

One classic studio production trick is "preverb": echoes that come before an element instead of after it. Add some silence before a clip, and then reverse the whole thing so it plays backwards. Apply a nice, rich reverb. Then reverse the reverberated clip. The echoes will build up magically into the desired sound, which lends an eerie sound to voices and can be interesting on percussive effects (track 36).

Always think about why the reverb is there. Early Hollywood films added echo to exteriors to make them more "outdoorsy." But if a sound doesn't have something hard to bounce off—a nearby canyon or buildings—there can't be an echo. These tracks felt artifical, and Hollywood quickly abandoned the practice.

Other Delay-Based Effects

The same digital delays that are at the heart of reverb units can also be used for special effects. Multiple short delays, with constantly changing delay times, can be combined to make one instrument or voice sound like many; this is called a *chorus* effect. A single longer delay, with a slower change in its delay time, can be combined with the original signal; as it does, different frequencies will be canceled or reinforced based on the delay time. This *flanging* effect is used often in pop music production and can also add a sense of motion to sound effects. Chorus and flange don't need as much processing as a true reverb, so even low-cost units and simple software plug-ins can be useful.

Pitch shifters use the same memory function as a delay but read the audio data out at a different rate than it was written. This raises or lowers the pitch by changing the timing of each sound wave, just like changing the speed on a tape playback. Unlike varispeed tape, however, the long-term timing isn't affected. Instead, many times a second, the software repeats or eliminates waves to compensate for the speed variation. Depending on how well the software is written, it may do a very good job of figuring out which waves can be manipulated without our noticing.

Combining Effects

It takes a lot of processing to make a really good soundtrack. Voices are usually equalized and then compressed, even in dramatic scenes, so they're easier to understand. Hard effects are almost always equalized to give them more impact, and then compressed to control their overall level; a gate may be added so they begin or end cleanly. Backgrounds are usually equalized so they don't interfere with the voice, and compressed to a constant level so they'll be easier to mix. A whole dramatic scene may have reverb added, or individual elements might get their own reverb so they match better.

Music should be equalized so it doesn't interfere with voice, but while compression on a music track can make it easier to mix, it can also destroy the dynamic rhythm of the score. Sometimes a little additional reverb, following the equalization, is all a music track needs to be mixable.

Source music, on the other hand, usually needs a lot of processing before it belongs to a scene. If a song is supposed to be heard through a radio or other speaker, use a low-cut at 200 Hz and a high-cut somewhere around 7 kHz, followed by some heavy compression and then reverb with very fast early reflections and a quick decay. This may be more radical than many real-world radio speakers, but the point is to sound more like a speaker than the scene's dialog—which, of course, the viewer is already hearing through a speaker.

If a broadcast mix includes dialog and music, I usually add a little low-midrange peak to bring out the voices, followed by a multiband compressor with fast attacks and decays to bring up the lower-level sounds.

In general, it's most efficient to apply equalization before compression. The equalizer affects how loud the signal will be at various frequencies, which compression can then control. If you compress before equalizing, the compressor might be reacting to extreme high- or low-frequency sounds that'll never make it to the final mix. It's usually best to apply gating—if any—before the compressor, so the gate has a wider range of levels to work with.

Reverberation can be added before or after the other processes. Equalizing before a reverb will affect the source sound without changing the acoustics of the simulated room; equalizing afterwards will make the room's walls harder or softer. Low-frequency sounds can travel greater distances, so shelving out some of the highs can make a long reverb seem slightly bigger. If you compress after a reverb, it'll change how long it takes late reflections to decay and make the reverb last longer.

CHAPTER 15

The Mix

R O S E ' S R U L E S

➥ Most of the elements of a video have very short lives. Camera shots, visual effects and audio edits don't last more than a few seconds at best. The mix is one of the operations where you can approach your project as a continuous whole.

➥ A good mix can fix less-than-perfect elements and mask awkward edits. But no matter how good your individual tracks are, they won't survive a bad mix.

There's a producer who likes to come to my studio to finish her projects. Well, actually she likes to stand outside the studio and watch me through a half-open doorway. She figures if a mix sounds good under those circumstances, it'll work well on the air. Considering how most people hear TV, she may be right.

No two television sets have the same sound quality. Even identical models will sound different, depending on their placement in the room. Different furnishings and room treatments also affect the sound—a comfortable couch really does make television better—and television audio has to be heard over everything from air conditioners and vacuum cleaners to crying babies. It's no wonder my friend runs out of the room in search of a good mix.

But she's the producer. My job as sound engineer is to be as intimate with the mix as possible. That means monitoring on high-quality speakers to hear even the tiniest variation in the sound, keeping the speakers in the nearfield so room acoustics aren't an influence, and making sure the monitoring levels are controlled so my ears don't get fooled.[1] Mixing is a physical activity as well, with fingers constantly tweaking the faders, and eyes constantly darting between video monitor, calibrated level meter, and spectrum analyzer.

Yes, it can be a little stressful. But it's worth it because the mix is our last chance to get things right.

Setting Up for the Mix

Since mixing can be an intense experience, it makes sense to organize things to let you work as efficiently as possible. This requires both equipment and preparation. Most of the equipment—monitor speakers, level meters, and effects processors—has been covered in Chapters 9 and 14.

Do You Need a Mixing Console?

Most postproduction mixes are done either on digital consoles hooked up to multiple outputs of an audio workstation, or on a consolelike controller for the workstation itself. Both systems look similar: there's a panel with sliding faders for each track, some knobs to control effects, and a computer screen. They're both operated about the same way, too: the beginning of each track is previewed while equalizers and other processors are adjusted, faders are preset to a good starting mix, and then everything is recued and rolled. The levels are then adjusted as the scene plays through. If there's a mistake or you want to change something, you back up and fix it.

Mixing for video has to be dynamic. The relationship between sounds depends on what the sounds are doing at the moment, not on where their tracks' faders have been set. So you have to constantly tweak those faders to keep the most important sounds on top of the mix, without pushing other sounds so low that they won't make it through the limited dynamic range of most video playbacks. If a system has mix automation, you can refine and store the fader movements and then have the computer play them all back to mix the scene for you. If not, common practice is to record the mixed audio back into the workstation; pickups and remixes are edited onto the existing mix as you do them.

It's almost never a good idea to set the faders in a fixed position, start the mix, and not change them until the final fadeout.

---

[1]These techniques are detailed in Chapter 9.

Mixing without a mixer

If your setup limits you to using "rubber bands" or volume handles superimposed on tracks in a timeline, it's going to be difficult—or at least very time-consuming—to do a good mix. Figure 1 shows 20 seconds of a work in progress. Although there's a lot of movement in those volume lines, it isn't anywhere near finished. We need to trim the background so it doesn't interfere with other effects, swell the music at the climax, and then fine-tune the whole thing so we're not aware of the mix when we concentrate on the drama. What takes the most time is the mouse-to-ear connection; each adjustment requires you to find a handle, click on it, drag, and then play over the section to decide if you like the result.

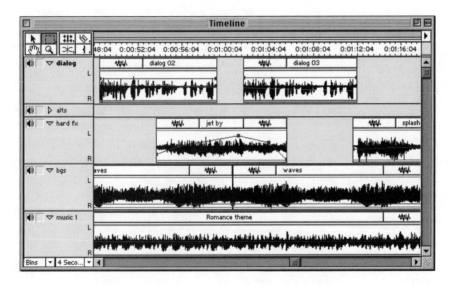

Figure 1: It can take a long time to fine-tune all those rubber bands.

An on-screen "virtual mixing console" will also be time-consuming. You have to reach for the right control point with a mouse, without being able to see any obvious relationship between that controller and the sounds it controls.

If you have to mix more than one or two simple projects in a computer, it's worth investing in an accessory hardware controller with sliders that let you take a "hands-on" approach. If your NLE software doesn't support one, consider getting a separate audio program that does.

If you must mix with a mouse, you'll save time if you get used to doing a screen full of settings at once. Play back, change every track that needed adjustment, check your changes, and move on.

Many producers choose a middle ground, using their mouse-based NLEs for the simplest projects and taking the complex ones to a separate audio studio. There are some tips for those out-of-house mixes later in this chapter.

Track Layout

It makes sense to adopt a consistent format for track layouts, with dialog always on certain tracks and music on others. But you might have to make compromises from time to time. One scene might require three tracks for voices, while the next has many tracks of overlapping effects. Unless you have unlimited tracks (and unlimited console faders to control them), some tracks may end up being used for more than one kind of element.

If you must put different kinds of sounds on the same track, try to choose sounds whose stereo panning, equalization, and other effects will be the same. This way you can apply the effects once, then concentrate on level changes during the mix, instead of having to stop and reset things. Leave some room between adjacent elements on a track, particularly if they'll need different fader settings.

Before You Mix, Don't

Wine tasters rinse their mouths out with water between critical sips so that they can detect every subtle aspect of the vintage they're examining. You should cleanse your ears for the same reason. Don't listen to anything for a few minutes before starting a mix.

Chances are, you've just spent a few hours editing individual elements against the picture. It's only natural that you'll be extra aware of each one of those gems of editorial art and want them to sparkle in the finished product . . . even if they get in the way of your message. Plan for some breathing room between when you build the track and when you mix it. If you can't wait overnight or take a meal break, at least go for a short walk. Don't begrudge the extra few minutes this takes; it can save your having to come back for a remix. Even though I charge by the hour, I'll willingly stop the clock and lose a few bucks to take this kind of a break. It always results in a better mix.

The Mix

A soundtrack can be thought of as a physical space, with mixing simply being the process of putting everything in its place. Things can be close to you or far away, and they can spread (to a limited extent, depending on the final delivery medium) across the left-to-right axis. But if two sounds try to occupy the exact same space, they'll interfere and both will suffer.

Mix engineers use three specific ways to place sounds in acoustic space.

- Volume

Obviously, louder sounds are closer. Just remember that only one sound can predominate at a time. Don't try to make *everything* close.

Don't try to make things very far, either. Video mixing is not a subtle medium. If a sound effect or music cue seems to work best when the track is barely open, try turning it off entirely. You might discover it's not needed. If you miss it, try to find some way—using effects or timing changes—to bring it forward slightly. Otherwise there's a chance most viewers won't get to hear it on their sets.

- Equalization

Music engineers frequently call the midrange equalizer a "presence" control. It makes a big difference in how close a sound appears.

Boosting the midrange, particularly between around 1,200 Hz to 2,500 Hz, tends to bring voices forward. If you turn a music track down in these frequencies, it'll leave more room for the dialog. Mid-low frequencies, between 100 Hz and 250 Hz, can add warmth and intimacy to a voice. Be careful about adding too many extreme low frequencies; they just add muddiness in most video tracks.

High frequencies get absorbed as sound travels through the air. It's not enough to be noticeable in interior spaces, but turning down the highs can add distance to exterior sounds.

- Reverberation

This might seem counterintuitive, but reverberation makes things smaller by sending them farther away. Reverb is primarily an interior effect. When you go outside, the reflecting surfaces tend to be much farther away than the sound source, and unless you're in a situation where echoes could realistically be expected—in a courtyard, next to buildings, or shouting into a canyon—reverb can sound artificial.

Adding reverb to a voice-over, particularly to one who's selling us something, is a dated cliché. If someone really wants to sell us something, they'll come closer rather than stand far away and yell.

Stereo

Music and film mixers can also *pan*— adjust the relative left/right position—to help define physical space. You don't have much freedom for this in video. Even if viewers have a stereo receiver, chances are they are not sitting exactly centered between the speakers. Most people keep their TV sets off to one side of the room, where they might as well be mono. Some stereo sets have their channels reversed, or things get flipped at the broadcast station; some sets (and stations) even have one channel disconnected. And while many cable networks broadcast in stereo, you never know which local cable systems will carry the signal that way.

If you're mixing video for an environment where the playback system can be controlled, such as a corporate meeting, you can do more with stereo. But it's still not a good idea to pan dialog very far, since people on the left side of the auditorium will lose dialog that's directed solely to the right. On the other hand, you can put hard effects anywhere you want. Kiosk mixes can also be stereo—you know the viewer will be standing in front of the monitor, with a speaker on either side. It's still not a good idea to pan kiosk dialog all the way, since the speakers define a stereo field that's much wider than the video.

Television shows that advertise stereo in their opening credits are usually glorified mono. All the dialog, and any important sound effects, are strictly center stage. Only the music, background sounds, and audience reactions are mixed in stereo. This keeps the sound consistent and avoids the disconcerting situation of having characters cross the picture from the left to the right while their voices go in the other direction. Surround, in most cases, merely means that some ambiences and reverb from the music track are directed to the back of home theater systems.

The Time Dimension

A mix's acoustic space also uses the fourth dimension, and every element should have its own place in time. Music isn't the only audio element with rhythm, and you should stay aware of stress patterns in the dialog and effects as well. If two stresses happen at exactly the same time, they'll interfere with each other.

Even though you're nominally mixing, it's not too late to make minor edits. Try moving the music track half a frame or so. It might disturb some carefully planned hits against picture, but it often lets you mix the music a lot louder. If you have extra channels on your mixing console, patch in a delay line so the music appears in its original sync on one set of faders and slightly delayed on another. Or copy the music onto another track and slide it a half frame. Cross-fade between the two during sustained notes, and you get the best of both placements.

Hearing Two Things at Once

Humans have an amazing ability to follow multiple sound streams based on how close they are to the listener. While this function probably evolved so we could keep track of predators in the jungle, you can use it to separate individual sounds in a track. Since we're using basic presence cues, this trick works equally well in mono or stereo. A simple demonstration will help you understand the effect:

1. Start with two different, well-recorded narrations. Use two different narrators, but both should have similar deliveries. There shouldn't be any echo in the original recording.

2. Mix both at the same level and listen to the babel that results. You'll find it takes a lot of concentration to make sense out of either narration.

3. Now process the "B" narration to make it seem farther away. Using a shelving equalizer, turn down the frequencies below 300 Hz and above 9 kHz. Add a tiny amount of room reverberation to increase the apparent distance. You may also want to lower the overall level about 3 dB.

4. Mix the processed "B" with the original "A" narration and listen again. Chances are, you'll now find it easier to follow *both*. Not only is the up-front "A" voice easier to understand, but you can also make more sense out of the distant "B"!

Track 37 of this book's CD has some voice tracks you can use to try this experiment, along with a before-and-after demonstration.

You can use this presence phenomenon in documentaries to separate a narration from the interview without having to lose either. Or use it to push crowd walla further into the background, so it doesn't interfere with dialog. One handy trick is to patch a single track to two different faders in your mixer or workstation; apply the equalization and echo to only one of them, and then cross-fade between faders to move a sound closer or farther.

Mix Distortion

When two tracks are mixed together, the result is usually slightly louder than either one of them.[2] As you add more tracks to the mix, things get even louder. If you let them get out of hand, they'll be louder than the system can handle. If your studio hasn't been set up with proper gain-staging (Chapter 9), there'll be very little margin for error.

---

[2]How much louder depends on the individual waveforms and their relationship to each other.

When things get much too loud because you've combined a lot of loud tracks, you hear gross distortion and know to stop mixing. But the distortion can be subtle, occurring only on momentary peaks. Your eyes—and a calibrated digital level meter—are the best way to spot this. Don't rely on your ears alone because you can fool yourself into thinking that distortion has gone away by raising the monitor level. If you're mixing in a clip-based NLE, you might not even know there's distortion until you play back the final rendered mix and look for clipped waveforms.

The best way to avoid distortion during the mix is to remember that faders go down as well as up. Build your final track by lowering some sounds as you boost others. While the two mixers in Figure 2 have the same output level on their meters, the one on the left is probably seriously overloaded; the fact that its master faders are set very low should be an immediate giveaway. Besides, lowering some of the levels gives you a wider physical range in which you can set the faders, for a more subtle mix.

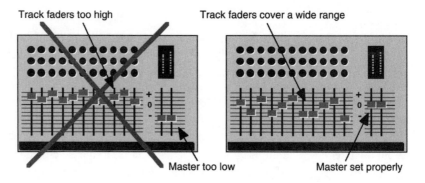

Track faders too high   Track faders cover a wide range

Master too low   Master set properly

Figure 2: Both mixes have the same overall level, but the one on the left won't sound as good.

This works for rubber-band mixing in an NLE as well. Check the settings in Figure 1. You'll see that most tracks there have been lowered; only the dialog is consistently raised.

Preparing for Someone Else to Mix

If you don't have good monitoring and mixing equipment, or the mix is particularly tricky and will require special skills, it makes sense to take your tracks elsewhere. This may be an outside studio that specializes in postproduction audio, a local general-purpose music studio, or your company's sound specialist down the hall. Most of the preparation will be the same.

Six Quick Rules for Better Mixes

These apply whether you're the producer, director, or hands-on mixer. Ignore them at your peril.

Saving time on the mix wastes time.

If you can't afford enough hours to do it right, take shortcuts while you're building individual tracks; a good mix will hide them. But don't take shortcuts while you're mixing, or else you'll have to remix it tomorrow.

Shh!

Working with the speakers on very loud may be exciting, but it has nothing to do with what your audience will hear. Pump *down* the volume.

All distortion hurts.

Listening at reasonable levels also helps you track down any fuzziness in the sound because the ear expects (and forgives) distortion in loud sounds. Turn down the volume, find the distortion, and fix it. Otherwise, subsequent broadcasting or duplicating will only make things worse.

It's never too soon to fix a problem.

As soon as you hear something you don't like, back up and remix it while you're still conscious of the overall flow. If you finish the mix and then go back, the new section may not blend in so well. You'll also run the risk of forgetting some of the places you wanted to touch up.

Don't be seduced by stereo.

It may sound impressive on the wall of speakers in your control room, but most of your listeners will never hear it that wide.

Watch TV with your eyes closed.

Listen to the finished mix at least once without picture. You may hear a lot of rough spots that were easy to ignore while the images were distracting you.

Ask the Expert

Many audio facilities try to standardize preproduction by assigning it to account executives or an operations manager, but this only works for standard situations. If your project is anything out of the ordinary (of course it is—who wants to do ordinary video?) you should talk to the engineer who'll actually do the work. Five minutes with the right person, a few days before the session, will save an hour of scrambling for equipment or experimenting with special setups.[3]

[3]Besides, we engineering types love to solve problems. Get us thinking about your project ahead of time, and we'll be more committed to doing it creatively

Start with the basics. How long does the video run? Is it dramatic, talking heads, vérité, or voice-over? Discuss how it will be shown, since mixing for a desktop VCR is very different from mixing for a theater or hotel ballroom. And don't forget subsequent uses, such as cutting the show into modules or a foreign-language version. These considerations affect what kind of equipment and procedures will work best.

Then talk about specific elements. If dialog or voice-over is simple, you've probably already cut them in your nonlinear editor. But fine-tuning sounds may be faster, more precise, and possibly cheaper on an audio workstation. Even damaged or noisy production audio may be fixable; a good sound editor will check alternate takes, lift specific syllables, and insert them on camera without disturbing sync.

Obviously, let the engineers know if you're planning to record a new voice-over or ADR. Warn them if you want to record narration while watching pictures, in case they need to set up monitors or a playback deck. You might have to arrive a few minutes earlier than the talent, so video can be transferred to a hard-disk playback system.

File and tape interchange

The one factor you absolutely can't forget to discuss is formats. Betacam SP is almost universally accepted for analog video and has very few interchange problems. But some facilities may require analog on 3/4-inch tape, VHS, or S-VHS—all of which have variability in how timecode and audio tracks are handled. Digital video comes in a variety of noninterchangeable formats, or a studio might prefer you to show up with reference video as a file on removable hard drive or CD-ROM.

Audio interchange has its own considerations. DAT—particularly timecode DAT—is a universal standard but can be inefficient if you have a lot of tracks to bring to the mix. Eight-track timecode DTRS (also known as DA-88) is standard in sophisticated postproduction studios, though music-based studios may prefer ADAT format instead. But any audio tape format will suffer if you can't get signals in and out of your editing system cleanly, and you need a digital connection between NLE and recorder to do this right.

Direct file transfers between NLE and audio mixing systems provide the best quality because they ignore your editing system's audio circuits completely. Avid's OMF may be the easiest way to transfer files. Although it isn't supported by every audio equipment manufacturer, translation software is available. Macintosh AIFF and Windows WAVE are universal and can result in the fewest problems. Broadcast WAVE (BWF), a variation on the Windows format supported by the European Broadcast Union, allows timestamping and may replace the proprietary OMF.

While you're verifying file formats, check that the studio will be able to handle the medium you bring them on. See if you should be using a removable hard drive or one of the CD variations, and if there is a preferred operating system. Also verify that the studio will transfer your audio directly as digital data; some facilities rely on analog wiring to move audio from computer to workstation. If this is the case, your track can be at the mercy of a computer's sound card.

Be aware of track assignment in your NLE's audio setup pages before you start transferring tracks to tape or rendering them to files. If you've routed two overlapping tracks to the same channel, their sounds will be mixed at full volume and there'll be no way to separate them.

Synchronization

If you're bringing timecoded tapes to an outside studio, sync shouldn't be an issue. Make sure you've done all your transfers digitally, or with recorder and NLE sharing a common video sync source. It's a good idea to tell the studio what timecode format you're using, in case they want to preformat a tape or preset their audio workstation.

But sync is never a sure thing. It's always a good idea to provide a sync reference. Most common is a one-frame beep on every track, matching a flash frame a few seconds before program start or the number 2 of a standard countdown leader. Drop them into your NLE before transferring files for the audio mix. If every audio track's "two pop" lines up against that visual frame, sync is verified . . . at least at the head. If you've got any reason to doubt that sync will be absolutely stable over the length of the program, it's wise to provide similar audio and video "post pops" at the tail.

What to Bring to a Mix

Obviously, you should bring your edited tracks and video when you're mixing at an outside studio, in the file formats you've all agreed on. It may even make sense to ship these before the mix session if the studio can preload them into their workstation.

But there are a few other things you should also pack. If there's any chance you'll need to rebuild dialog or grab effects, take the original shoot tapes and logs. If you're bringing master videotape for the sound studio to lay their final mix onto, make sure they'll be dubbing it to another medium before the session, or bring a working copy. Let them whip the copy around while they're mixing, so there's no chance of ruining the master.

You'll also need some paperwork. If your tracks are more complicated than just voice and music, go through them in your NLE and create a layout chart so the mixer can figure out where things are (Figure 3 shows a typical format). Bring contracts or a purchase order if necessary to keep the studio manager happy. And don't forget the phone and beeper numbers of anyone you might need to call during the session for changes or approvals.

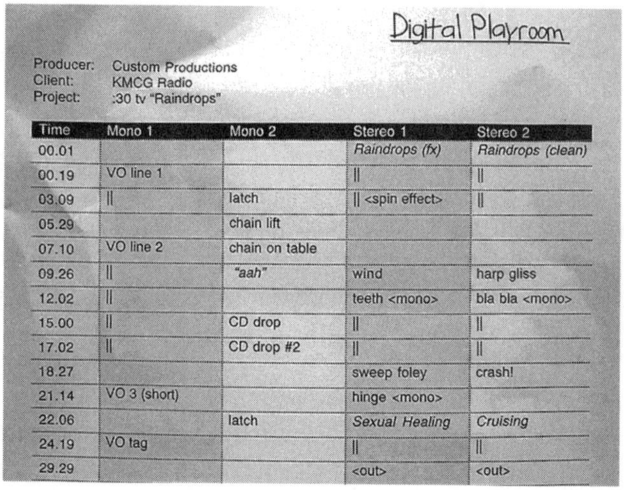

Digital Playroom

Producer:	Custom Productions		
Client:	KMCG Radio		
Project:	:30 tv "Raindrops"		

Time	Mono 1	Mono 2	Stereo 1	Stereo 2
00.01			*Raindrops (fx)*	*Raindrops (clean)*
00.19	VO line 1		||	||
03.09	||	latch	|| <spin effect>	||
05.29		chain lift		
07.10	VO line 2	chain on table		
09.26	||	"aah"	wind	harp gliss
12.02	||		teeth <mono>	bla bla <mono>
15.00	||	CD drop	||	||
17.02	||	CD drop #2	||	||
18.27			sweep foley	crash!
21.14	VO 3 (short)		hinge <mono>	
22.06		latch	*Sexual Healing*	*Cruising*
24.19	VO tag		||	||
29.29			<out>	<out>

Figure 3: A chart can save time by helping the mixer figure out what's on each track.

After the Mix

If you're mixing in an NLE, check the final rendered version carefully for sync and distortion. It may help to open the finished mix in a waveform viewer or clip window to verify there is sufficient level and no overloads. It should look similar to the properly digitized files in Chapter 10.

Mixing in a separate system, or at an outside studio, requires a couple of extra steps. If you haven't rendered a final NLE output, the best plan is to put the finished mix back into your editing system. Have the studio make a compatible file with the same sync pops you gave them in the edited tracks, load it into your editor, and line up the pops. Once you've done that, you can move the mix's in- and out-points so the beeps don't make it to the final rendering.

If you've brought a master videotape (and verified that the studio can handle it), they'll probably be able to dub your mix right onto the master. Be aware that the higher-quality FM audio tracks on analog BetaSP or S-VHS can't be dubbed without erasing the picture.

Most professional productions will also be copied to timecode DAT. Be sure the studio sets the DAT's sample rate to 48 kHz, and both timecode and sample rate are locked to the same video reference; otherwise it might not be possible to use the tape without an analog generation. Most video decks will reject digital audio signals that aren't synchronized this way.

M&E Mixes

Networks often request that a producer provides "M&E" mixes, or tracks of just music and effects. Common practice is to put all the on-camera audio and narration on separate mono tracks, all the sound effects on a stereo pair, and all the music on another pair. This is so they can create foreign-language versions easily. Since it's impossible to predict how much each line of a foreign narration will take, the music and effects should stay at a constant level and not be prefaded for the announcer. M&E mixes are usually provided on DAT or DTRS/DA-88 tapes, with the same digital audio and timecode specs as the master.

Backups

If you habitually copy NLE tracks to a data-archiving medium like streaming tape, and you haven't done much editing in an audio workstation, the only other backup you might want is a spare copy of the finished mix on DAT. If there's a lot of additional editing or effects in the audio workstation, back it up as well. The time it takes will not only protect you against catastrophic hard-drive failure, but also make life easier when the client requests changes.

If you've developed special sound effects or sequences, you might want to use in other projects, copy them as a separate audio DAT or separate files on a removable hard drive. It's a lot faster to find and reuse them this way than to reload a backup tape and look for them in the original tracks.

The Last Thing You Should Do

Put the tape on a shelf. Come back to it a month later, listen to it, and figure out what you'd do differently. Now start the process all over again.

Glossary

Every specialty creates its own jargon, verbal shortcuts to express precise situations quickly. Audio jargon can be confusing, particularly if you're coming from the more peaceful environment of desktop video.

Jargons are also sometimes used to create an aura of mystery that keeps outsiders from knowing what's going on. But that's not what this book is about, so here's a practical guide to what we audio engineers are talking about. If you don't find a term here, check the index.

ADAT: Alesis Digital Audio Tape, an eight-track format using S/VHS cassettes and named for the company that invented it. ADATs were the first practical low-cost digital multitracks and became a favorite of scoring composers. A similar but more robust eight-track format, Tascam's DTRS (also known as DA8 or DA88), uses Hi-8 cassettes. The DTRS format was adopted by Sony and is the standard in feature production. Both systems allow multiple decks to be linked for unlimited tracks. The two formats are not compatible.

ADR: Automatic (or Automated) Dialog Replacement, also sometimes known as "looping." Production audio can be noisy and, even if recorded on a quiet sound stage, can be inconsistent from shot to shot. ADR systems let actors go into a sound studio, hear short pieces of their own dialog repeated over and over in a constant rhythm, and then recreate the performance—line by line—in sync with picture. See Chapter 8.

AES/EBU: Literally, the Audio Engineering Society and European Broadcasting Union. But the combination of initials almost always refers to the standard for interconnecting digital audio devices. See Chapter 3.

AIFF: Audio Interchange File Format, the standard for Macintosh audio- and video-editing systems. Different from Microsoft's .wav format. Fortunately, most programs are smart enough to open either, and there are plenty of shareware converters for both platforms.

ATTC: Address Track Time Code. LTC recorded on a special track of an analog video tape or down the center of an analog audio tape.

Auto-conform: In the dark days of analog video editing, each generation would add noise to the soundtrack. Since a video master could be three or four generations removed from the original, the production audio was often treated just as reference. An automatic conforming system (or hapless audio engineer) would use the original field recordings and an edit list, and rebuild the sound. Modern nonlinear and online systems keep audio as 16-bit digital data, so this step usually isn't necessary.

BGs: Background sounds (the term is pronounced like the disco group). Usually a track or two of stock environments, such as crowds or traffic noises, edited to fit the length of a scene. Careful choice of BGs can eliminate the need for a lot of foley.

Bump: To adjust the timing between sound and picture in precise frame or subframe units, while both are running. Although this is most often used to fine-tune lip sync and sound effects placement, bumping a piece of music a frame or two can have amazing results.

Burn-in: A videotape with timecode numbers superimposed on the picture.

BWF: Broadcast Wave Format, an audio interchange format standardized by the European Broadcasting Union. It's similar to Microsoft .wav and can be read by standard audio programs, but software designed for this format also lets you embed sync and other information.

CD-quality: Properly speaking, a digital audio signal or device capable of 20 Hz–20 kHz bandwidth with very low distortion and a 96 dB dynamic range. Many manufacturers use the term improperly to imply a quality that isn't justified by a system's design. Unless you can verify specifications, the term is meaningless.

Click track: An electronic metronome played into headphones, or a track on a tape with that signal, so that musicians can perform to precise timing.

DA8, DA88, DTRS: See ADAT.

dBm: Decibels, referenced to 1 milliwatt across 600Ω.

dBv: Decibels, referenced to 0.775 volts.

dBV: Decibels, referenced to 1 volt.

Decibel: A precise, and often misunderstood, measurement of the ratio between two audio signals. See Chapter 1.

Distortion: Anything that changes the output of an audio system so it no longer reflects the input signal. Noise and changes in frequency response can be forms of distortion, though the term is usually reserved for unintentional, gross changes in the waveform.

Dither: Specially shaped random noise added to a digital signal to improve its quality at low levels.

Double-system: Recording production sound on a separate audio tape recorder while a video or film camera is running. This is almost always unnecessary with modern digital video camcorders.

Dropframe: A way of counting timecode so that frame numbers stay, on average, in sync with real-world time. No actual frames are dropped in the process. See Chapter 10.

Dynamic range: The range between the loudest signal a system can carry without distortion and its low-level noise that would obscure any softer signals, expressed in decibels. In a purely digital signal, each bit is worth 6 dB dynamic range. But when you start involving analog circuits, dynamic range gets harder to pin down. Low-level noise is contributed by the electronics itself, and high-level distortion sets in gradually as the volume increases.

Foley: Generating sound effects by duplicating the actors' on-screen movements in a sound studio. A team of good foley artists can watch a scene once, gather armloads of props, and then create everything from footsteps to fist fights in perfect sync. *Digital foley* refers to the process of matching those little sounds in an audio workstation (usually because good foley artists are expensive). The name honors Jack Foley, a Hollywood second-unit director and sound genius of the 1940s.

Hard effects: Also known as spot effects. Sounds that are impractical to foley (such as telephone bells, explosions, and 25th century laser guns) and usually important to the story. These are often drawn from large CD effects libraries, but may be created for the project. In feature film production, the term often refers to *any* sound effects that are in sync with picture.

High fidelity: An ambiguous term. It often refers to somewhere near a 20 Hz–20 kHz frequency range with less than 2 dB variation between sounds of different frequencies, and a dynamic range of at least 60 dB with less than 0.3% distortion. . . but the bar keeps getting raised as technology improves. Has nothing to do with whether a system is analog or digital.

Hitting a post: Audio people use this term to refer to the cues within a long sound effect or music track. It's not enough to make a sound begin and end in sync with the picture; you also have to make sure that internal elements match the on-screen actions. A good sound editor will make lots of tiny edits and use other tricks to hit as many posts as possible.

House sync: In large facilities, a single video signal (usually an all-black picture in color TV format) is distributed to just about every audio and video device. House sync is not the same as timecode. The former is a precise heartbeat, accurate to microseconds. It keeps signals compatible but can't tell one frame from another. Timecode identifies frames for editing but is only precise to a few dozen milliseconds. It's usually a mistake to control critical audio- or videotape speeds with it.

ISDN: Integrated Services Digital Network. A way of combining standard telephone wiring with special equipment to create 128 kilobit/second dial-up connections as needed. It's more reliable (as well as faster) than high-speed analog modems and more flexible than other systems like DSL or cable modems. In the world of audio, the term usually refers to real-time transfers and remote recording sessions using ISDN wiring along with audio data reduction equipment.

Layback: Copying a finished mix from an audio workstation or separate audiotape back to a videotape master.

Layup: Transferring production sound from edited videotape to an audio medium for further manipulation. Networked nonlinear editing systems can make both layback and layup unnecessary.

LTC: Longitudinal Time Code. SMPTE timecode data is actually a biphase digital stream in the audio range, sounding something like a fax machine signal. When it's recorded on an analog audio track it's called "longitudinal," since it runs parallel to the tape instead of slanting like a videotape track. LTC also refers to the biphase signal itself, so the wire that plugs into a timecode input is actually carrying LTC . . . even if the data came from a digital data track or VITC. See Chapter 10.

M&E: Music and Effects, a submix of a production's soundtrack with no dialog to make foreign translations easier.

Masking: A phenomenon where sounds at one frequency make it difficult or impossible to hear other simultaneous (or, in the case of *temporal* masking, closely occurring) sounds at a nearby frequency. The basis behind every system of perceptual encoding. See Chapter 2.

Mid-side (M-S): Stereo microphone technique with excellent control of width and mono compatibility. See Chapter 6.

MIDI: Musical Instrument Digital Interface, a common language and electrical standard for describing events such as the turning on or off of a note. See Chapter 12.

MOS: Scenes that are videotaped or filmed without any audio, usually because the camera setup or location makes sound impractical. The expectation is that a track will be created using foley and other effects. This is often a bad idea in video production, since any track—even one from a camera-mounted microphone far from the action—is better than nothing and may be usable for sound effects or a sync reference. Rumor has it, the term MOS originated when an early German-speaking film director wanted to work "mitout sound."

MP3: MPEG II Layer 3, the most common file format and data reduction scheme for delivering audio over the Internet.

Noise, pink: Electronic noise with an equal likelihood of a signal in each octave. Since any octave has twice as many frequencies as the octave below it, pink noise is created by filtering white noise so there's less energy as the frequency gets higher. It reflects how we hear better than white noise and is used for acoustic testing.

Noise, white: Random electronic noise with an equal likelihood of a signal at any frequency. This is the kind of noise commonly generated by analog circuits.

Octave: The musical interval of 12 semitones, or a frequency ratio of 2:1.

Offset: The difference in timecode between any two tapes. Video editors typically start their programs at 1:00:00:00 (one hour; no minutes, seconds, or frames) to allow for color bars and slates. If an audio operator decides to start that same program at 00:01:00:00, the sound would have a -59 minute offset. Some digital audio processors introduce delays to handle the sound more intelligently, so small offsets are sometimes necessary.

Production audio: Sounds recorded in the field while the picture is being shot, usually dialog. May be recorded directly on the videotape, or as *double-system*.

R-DAT: Exactly the same as a standard or timecode DAT tape. When it was first invented, some digital audio systems used stationary heads (like an analog audio tape deck) and others used rotating heads (like a helical-scan video deck). Our ubiquitous DAT was originally called "Rotating Digital Audio Tape."

SMPTE: Short for SMPTE timecode, the frame-accurate time data recorded on video and audio tapes to control editing and keep elements together. It stands for the Society of Motion Picture and Television Engineers, who invented the format.

s/pdif: A standard for interconnecting stereo digital audio devices, similar to AES/EBU but using a lower-cost wiring scheme and carrying information that's appropriate for consumer audio. See Chapter 2.

Timbre: A characteristic of a sound wave that has to do with the number and strength of a wave's harmonics (Chapter 1), often referred to as its *brightness* or *richness*. Timbre is different from volume or pitch, though an untrained ear can easily be tricked into confusing these characteristics.

VITC: Vertical Interval Time Code. Time data encoded as a series of dots at the top of each video field. Unlike LTC, it can be read when the tape is paused. This makes it easier to jog a tape to find a specific action and then match a sound to it. Unfortunately, VITC can't be read when the picture is distorted because of high-speed winding. Most professional analog video systems put identical VITC and LTC data on a tape and choose the most appropriate for the speed.

Wet/dry: Refers to echoes. Most foley, hard effects, and ADR are recorded dry, without any natural reverberation. Appropriate echoes are then added during the mix, to make the sounds appear to belong to the on-screen environment. But some effects are recorded wet—that is, with natural (or artificial) reverb. These have to be chosen carefully so the echo's quality matches the scene, and they can be harder to edit because you can't cut into the reverberations.

Wild: Recorded without synchronization. Sound effects are usually gathered this way and matched up in an editing system. But some things are wild by mistake and have to be carefully resynced. This can happen when a timecode generator or low-end audio workstation isn't locked to house sync, or when audio has been stored on an unstable medium such as audio cassette.

XLR: The standard connector for high-end analog and digital audio, originally known as Cannon's XLR product line. It was universally accepted and is now supported by most other connector manufacturers. It's rugged and has low contact resistance, but its primary advantage is that it can carry balanced wiring (Chapter 3). This makes cables more immune to noise and hum.

Zero level: Means two different things depending on whether you're working in analog or digital. Analog zero is a nominal volume near the top of the scale, and loud sounds are expected to go above it. Digital zero is an absolute limit, the loudest thing that can be recorded. Depending on the facility and style of audio mixing, analog zero is equivalent to somewhere between 12 dB and 20 dB below digital zero. See Chapter 10.

Resources

Many commercial and nonprofit organizations and individuals maintain Web sites where you can learn more about electronics, digital audio, and sound for video. Since the Web is an ever-changing thing, these sites may also contain links to other resources that evolved after I wrote this book. Of course, some of them may also have disappeared by the time you read this . . .

American Radio Relay League: www.arrl.org

This amateur radio organization publishes many books about electronics, including an excellent primer, *Understanding Basic Electronics*, for $20.

Cinema Audio Society: www.ideabuzz.com/cas

This organization of production sound mixers and boom operators has an informative journal, which is available online.

Digital Playroom: www.dplay.com

My Web site, which has a large tutorial section as well as some spoofs of our industry in streaming audio formats.

Digital Video Magazine: www.dv.com

This authoritative magazine posts information resources, equipment reviews, and the complete text of their back issues, including my monthly column on audio techniques.

Equipment Emporium: www.equipmentemporium.com

A commercial site for an equipment rental house, with lots of useful articles on aspects of soundtrack production.

Tomi Engdahl's Audio and Hifi page: www.hut.fi/Misc/Electronics/audio.html

Anybody interested in audio should know about this site, with indexed links to enough technical articles to write a few textbooks.

Quantel Digital Fact Book: www.quantel.com/dfb/index.html

Incredibly informative glossary—almost an encyclopedia—about every aspect of digital video and audio, from a leading manufacturer of high-end studio equipment.

Rane Corporation: www.rane.com/library.htm

Rane makes equipment for commercial sound installations and has posted a small library of easy-to-read booklets about topics such as reducing hum and interconnecting equipment.

Video University: www.videouniversity.com

This site has a few basic articles on audio, plus a lot of information about the technology and business of video.

Organizations

Audio Engineering Society (AES)

60 East 42nd Street
New York, NY 10165
212/661-8528
Fax 212/682-0477
www.aes.org

American Federation of Television and Radio Artists (AFTRA)

260 Madison Avenue
New York, NY 10016
212/532-0800
Fax 212/532-2242
www.aftra.org

International Television Association (ITVA)

9202 North Meridian Street
Indianapolis, IN 46260
317/816-6269
Fax 800/801-8926
www.itva.org

National Association of Broadcasters (NAB)

1771 N Street, NW
Washington, DC 20036
202/429-5300
Fax 202/429-4199
www.nab.org

Society of Motion Picture and Television Engineers (SMPTE)

595 West Hartsdale Avenue
White Plains, NY 10607
914/761-1100
Fax 914/761-3115
www.smpte.org

The CD

I decided to include a standard audio CD with this book, rather than a CD-ROM, for a couple of reasons. I wanted you to be able to play it on the best speakers you have, which are more likely to be part of your stereo system than connected to your computer. I also didn't want to limit the CD's usefulness to a particular platform or software generation—there's nothing colder than last year's shareware. Most of the examples on this disc will be valid as long as CDs are playable.

Of course, you should also use this CD as source material for the exercises and tutorials. I suggest you transfer it digitally—most NLEs have a way to strip audio tracks from their CD-ROM drive—to preserve sound quality and to keep the waveforms looking like the examples in this book.

Track 1.   Instrumental Waves with and without Harmonics   *2:16*
Most of what we hear as the characteristic sound of an instrument is its harmonics. Here are digitally generated waveforms for an oboe, violin, and trumpet along with a pure sine wave, all at concert A (440 Hz). When you can hear their full range, it's easy to identify the sources.

The second part of this track has the exact same waves, but played through a sharp filter at 600 Hz to eliminate all the harmonics. You may be surprised at how similar they sound.

Track 2.   High-Frequency Response Tests   *2:06*
The same short piece of music is played five times. Each time, it starts playing through a very sharp filter to eliminate everything above a specific frequency. The filter is switched off twice during each passage, to let the music's full range play through. If you don't hear a difference when the filter turns on or off, it's because sounds higher than the filter frequency aren't passing through your system anyway.

Don't be alarmed if you can't hear any difference at the higher frequencies; many speakers that are rated "full range" really aren't. Consider also that the system you're listening with includes your own ears, and high-frequency hearing deteriorates with age.

The filter frequencies are 18 kHz, 15 kHz, 12 kHz, 9 kHz, and 6 kHz. If you want to continue this experiment with other frequencies and source material, remember that the filter itself will influence the results. I used a DSP-driven one with a steep, 18 dB per octave cutoff; ordinary parametric or graphic equalizers will start affecting sounds considerably below their nominal frequency.

Track 3. **7.5 kHz Sine Wave on One Channel, for Acoustic Testing :28**

Track 4. **7.5 kHz and 400 Hz Sine Waves Equally Mixed**
on One Channel **:38**

Track 5. **The Effects of Low Bit-Depth Sampling** **2:06**

Music and narration, recorded at 44.1 kHz and 16 bits depth, then truncated to 12 bits, 8 bits, 7 bits, and 4 bits. The resulting audio was then resampled at 16 bits so it would be playable on a standard CD.

The 8-bit version probably sounds a lot better than you've heard in 8-bit multimedia files. That's because only the bit depth was limited; early computer sound equipment also suffered from analog noise and distortion.

Track 6. **Aliasing Distortion** **:22**

This is actually a simulation of what the distortion sounds like, but generated by other means. Aliasing is dependent on the sample rate and how much high frequency is in the original material, and I wanted something that would be immediately apparent on a wide variety of speaker systems.

Track 7. **Delta Encoding Demo** **:28**

Music and voice, processed through IMA 4:1 encoding and then decoded for the CD.

Track 8. **Perceptual Encoding (MP3) Demo** **3:23**

Music and voice, processed through MPEG Layer 3 at various degrees of compression and then decoded for the CD. The original file was 16-bit, 44.1 kHz stereo, with a file size of 4,147 kilobytes (KB).

Bitrate (kbps)	Coding Ratio	File Size (KB)
160	8.8:1 (11.3% of original)	471
64	22:1 (4.5%)	189
32	44:1 (2.3%)	94
16	86:1 (1.1%)	48
8	173:1 (0.6%)	24

Track 9.   **Various Mic Patterns, On and Off Axis**   **3:04**

The same voice, recorded in a quiet but somewhat reverberant studio, through omnidirectional, cardioid, and short shotgun microphones. Each mic is used head-on and then at a 90° angle to the voice.

Track 10.   **Boom Versus Lav, in Well-Treated**
                     Studio and on Location   **1:09**

These are recorded as split tracks, with the boom mic (a short shotgun) on the left channel and a collar-mounted lavaliere on the right.

Track 11.   **Restaurant Background from Two Mic Positions**   **:43**

The first recording uses stereo omnis mounted at table height; the second has the mics in the corner of a banquette. Notice how they're equally live-sounding, but there's much less clatter in the second version.

Track 12.   **1 kHz Sine @ -20 dBfs**   **:50**

This and the following track can be used for lineup tones at the head of a tape.

Track 13.   **1 kHz Sine @ -12 dBfs**   **:50**

Track 14.   **1 kHz Sine @ 0 dBfs**   **1:02**

For comparison, here's digital zero: the loudest tone that can be recorded without distortion. It's the loudest thing on this disk, so it would be a good idea to turn down your speakers before playing it.

Track 15.   **Searching Audio with Dynamic and Tapelike Scrubbing**   **:50**

Track 16.   **Sample Voice Track ("Speech is Made . . .")**   **:17**

Track 17.   **Bad Breath Edit**   **:17**

Track 18.   **Edit Tutorial I**   **:11**

Track 19.   **Edit Tutorial II**   **:10**

Track 20.   **Edit Tutorial III**   **:10**

Track 21.   **Edit Tutorial IV**   **:17**

Track 22.   **Mnemonic Speech**   **:12**

Track 23.   **Presidential Sound Bite**   **:11**

Track 24.   **Corporate Music**   **:37**

This music selection, and the two that follow, are © 1999 Franklin-Douglas, Inc., and used here by permission. They were contributed to the book by their composer, Doug Wood, who is also president of the Omnimusic library. You may copy them to your editing system and use them when trying the techniques in this book, but you can't incorporate them in a finished videotape without a specific license from Omnimusic.

For more information on the Omnimusic library, see track 40 of this disc.

Track 25.   **Jazz Music**   **:37**

Track 26.   **Orchestral Waltz**   **:34**

Track 27.   **Cricket Background**   **:30**

This track, and the sound effects that follow, are © 1991 The Hollywood Edge, Inc., and used here by permission. You may copy them to your editing system to try the techniques in this book.

If you'd like a CD with about a hundred equally good sound effects, along with license to use them in your production—free!—see track 41.

Track 28.   **Ocean Waves**   **:32**

Track 29.   **Car Crash, Original and Hyped**   **:13**

Track 30.   **Splash**   **:10**

rack 31.   **Acme Jet Voice-Over**   **:39**

Track 32.   **Limited Voice**   **:12**

Track 33.   **Compressed Voice**   **:12**

Track 34.   **How Compression Can Change a Sound Effect**   **:13**

The three sounds in this track are from one recording of a single .357 Magnum shot. The only processing done to them was compression; there was no editing, echo, or equalization.

Track 35.   **Reverberation Test Signal**   **:10**

Track 36.   **Preverberation**   **:22**

This eerie effect is easy to do in almost any editing system.

Track 37.   **Hearing Two Voices at Once**   **:33**

First the two separate voices, then the voices mixed without any processing, then the processing described in Chapter 14.

Track 38.   **Wes Harrison Sample (Funny!)**   **2:20**

Wes is the acknowledged master of mouth sounds. He created all of these effects using just a microphone and his mouth. For more about Wes and his techniques, see Chapter 8.

This is a brief excerpt from his full-length CD, *The One and Only*—a compilation of live recordings of the nightclub act he performs as "Mr. Sound Effects" around the world. (The recordings were done over a number of years, so quality may be uneven.) For a copy of the CD, send $10 to Wes Harrison, Post Office Box 901, Park Ridge, IL 60068.

Track 39.   Don Wescott Demo (Also Funny!)   2:53

Don is one of the busiest narrators in the Boston area and a regular voice on the PBS network. He contributed a lot of information about voice-over sessions in this book, along with voice tracks for the CD. He also wrote the two parodies he performs here. For booking information, contact him at 413/448-2888.

Track 40.   Omnimusic Demo   6:05

Omnimusic is one of the better midsized libraries (about 150 discs, as of this writing) and has supplied music for most of my recent productions along with virtually all of the music on this CD. For more information, contact them at 800/828-6664, 516/883-0121, or 52 Main St, Port Washington, NY 11050. www.omnimusic.com.

Track 41.   Hollywood Edge Sound Effects Demo   2:15

This is the first track from their demo CD, which also includes about a hundred clean sound effects, ready for you to use for free in your productions. Producers and editors can get a copy by contacting them at 800/292-3755, 323/603-3252, or 7080 Hollywood Blvd, Hollywood, CA 90028. www.hollywoodedge.com.

They figure that once you've heard and used the free sample, you'll purchase some of their commercial sound effects libraries. It worked for me.

Track 42.   Good-bye   :03

Credits and Caveats

The elegant voice in the editing tutorials is popular PBS announcer Don Wescott. For booking information, see the description of Track 39. The corporate-sounding female in the microphone demonstrations is my wife Carla Rose. For a funny story about her experiences voicing national commercials, see the beginning of Chapter 8; for booking information, contact momcat@pinkcat.com. The unpolished voice describing the CD's tracks is yours truly. I was cheap and handy.

The disc was edited and mastered on the Orban Audicy audio workstation in my studio, the Digital Playroom, with special effects processing using custom software on an Eventide DSP-4000. Multimedia files were manipulated in Bias' Peak software on a Macintosh. Additional recording was by Timm Keleher at Soundworks, Watertown, MA; and by Bill Wangerin at The Stable, Cambridge, MA.

Contact information, prices, and freebies were accurate when I wrote the book but subject to change.

Index